CONFEDERATES AND COMANCHEROS

CONFEDERATES AND COMANCHEROS

SKULLDUGGERY AND DOUBLE-DEALING IN THE TEXAS–NEW MEXICO BORDERLANDS

JAMES BAILEY BLACKSHEAR
AND
GLEN SAMPLE ELY

UNIVERSITY OF OKLAHOMA : NORMAN

Portions of the introduction and chapters 1 and 2 appeared in Glen Sample Ely, "Skullduggery at Spencer's Ranch: Civil War Intrigue in West Texas," *Journal of Big Bend Studies* 21 (2009): 9–29; and "What to Do about Texas? Texas and the Department of New Mexico in the Civil War," *New Mexico Historical Review* 85, no. 4 (Fall 2010): 375–408. Elements from both articles are used here with permission.

Library of Congress Cataloging-in-Publication Data

Names: Blackshear, James Bailey, 1954– author. | Ely, Glen Sample, author.
Title: Confederates and Comancheros : skullduggery and double-dealing in the Texas-New Mexico borderlands / James Bailey Blackshear and Glen Sample Ely.
Description: Norman : University of Oklahoma, [2021] | Includes bibliographical references and index. | Summary: "Exploration of American expansionism and Indigenous resistance in the southwest borderlands between the Comancheros, New Mexican merchant-traders, and the Texan Confederates during the Civil War"—Provided by publisher.
Identifiers: LCCN 2021010562 | ISBN 978-0-8061-7560-7 (hardcover)
Subjects: LCSH: Borderlands—Texas—History—19th century. | Borderlands—New Mexico—History—19th century. | Indian traders—Texas—History—19th century. | Indian traders—New Mexico—History—19th century. | Indians of North America—Texas—History—19th century. | Indians of North America—New Mexico—History—19th century. | Texas—History—Civil War, 1861–1865. | New Mexico—History—Civil War, 1861–1865.
Classification: LCC F391 .B59 2021 | DDC 976.4/05—dc23
LC record available at https://lccn.loc.gov/2021010562

The paper in this book meets the guidelines for permanence and durability of the Committee on Production Guidelines for Book Longevity of the Council on Library Resources, Inc. ∞

10 9 8 7 6 5 4 3 2 1

CONTENTS

ACKNOWLEDGMENTS

Glen Sample Ely has remained the driving force behind this publication since its inception. He first contacted me about collaborating on a book about the Texas–New Mexico borderlands in 2016. We met over a plate of steaming enchiladas and discussed Confederate spies and New Mexican Comancheros. Afterward, we cleared the table and rolled out some maps. The rest, as they say, is history.

Glen shared his voluminous research and numerous maps on nineteenth-century New Mexico. I have no doubt that the Comanchero component of this work could not have happened without his willingness to share this material. A kickoff of sorts to this collaboration included a visit to the ghost town of Loma Parda and drive to nearby Fort Union. Afterward, we took an hour-long hike in search of Ceran St. Vrain's tombstone. The local graveyard proved fruitless. We continued through an overgrown field, crawled over some tricky barbed-wire fences, and ventured into and over some deep arroyos. About the time I was ready to give up, there was Glen up ahead, pointing in the right direction. The same with this collaboration.

Many contributed to this research, including Doyle Daves and Marcus Gott-schalk, two of San Miguel County's most knowledgeable historians. The staffs at the Donnelly Library of New Mexico Highlands University and the Santa Fe Trail Interpretative Center also contributed to this work, as did the archivists at the New Mexico State Records Center and Archives. The same is true of the staffs at the county clerks' offices in both Mora and San Miguel Counties. Additionally, a great deal of debt is owed the two peer reviewers for their on-point criticisms and recommendations. They certainly made this work better. Carol Zuber-Mallison's vivid maps also play an instrumental role in recounting this history, as do the period photos Catie Carl, archivist at Santa Fe's Palace of Governors, procured. I also have to thank Durwood Ball and Gus Seligmann. Both of these historians gave me early support in my efforts to study this region of nineteenth-century New Mexico. I should also mention that much of the research concerning Comanchero passes and correspondences comes from the search engine Family Search (www.familysearch.org), which gives free access to a host of National Archives documents.

Additional thanks go to family: Mike, Lori, and Christian Kilmer; Jake, Karla, Lily, and Blake Blackshear; Joe and Cole Blackshear; and, of course, my wife Barb. Barb's unending patience with me is quite incredible. As Reggie Jackson once said, she is the "straw that stirs the drink."

James Bailey Blackshear

* * *

When I first envisioned this book, it was clear that the best person to tell the New Mexico side of the Comanchero story was James Bailey Blackshear. His University of Oklahoma Press publication on Fort Bascom (2016) demonstrated an excellent grasp of the subject material and considerable scholarship. His significant contributions to this collaboration exemplify those same qualities once again. My thanks to James for agreeing to do this book, and to him and his wife Barb for their gracious hospitality at their lovely, picturesque cabin in northern New Mexico.

I am also indebted to the late Harwood Perry Hinton Jr., my longtime mentor and noted scholar of the Southwest, who suggested a number of important leads for research. Additional thanks go to Col. Thomas "Ty" Smith; Rick Hendricks; Andy Cloud at the *Journal of Big Bend Studies* and the Center for Big Bend Studies; Durwood Ball at *New Mexico Historical Review*; Patrick Walsh at the Texas General Land Office Archives; Claudia Rivers at the Special Collections Library, University of Texas-El Paso; Suzanne Campbell and Shannon Sturm at the West Texas Collection, Angelo State University; Laura Saegert, Caitlin Burhans, Jelain Chubb, and Mark Smith at the Texas State Library and Archives Commission; New Mexico State Records Center and Archives; Christopher Geherin at the Center for Southwest Research at University of New Mexico-Albuquerque; Fort Concho National Historic Landmark Director Bob Bluthardt and Evelyn Lemons at the Fort Concho archives; Chief Interpretive Ranger John Heiner at Fort Davis National Historic Site and historian Mary Williams at the Fort Davis archives; Jim Bradshaw and Pat McDaniel at the Haley Memorial Library in Midland, Texas; Tai Kreidler, Monte Monroe, Lynn Whitfield, and Randy Vance at the Southwest Collection, Texas Tech University, Lubbock; Heather McClure at the Fray Angélico Chávez History Library, Palace of Governors, Santa Fe; Jim Ed Miller; Carlos and Luis Armendáriz; Cecil Lockhart Smith; Connie Krasinski;

Dottie Leonori; Dave Huber; Terrence Mattern; Carol Zuber-Mallison; Robert B. Elliott; Laurence W. Clark; Richard Schneiderman; Paul Cliff Salom; the staff at University of Oklahoma Press, specifically, J. Kent Calder, acquisitions editor; Leslie Tingle, copyeditor; and Stephanie Attia Evans, assistant managing editor. Finally, I dedicate this book to my wonderful wife and life partner of thirty years, Rev. Dr. Melinda Ann Veatch.

Glen Sample Ely

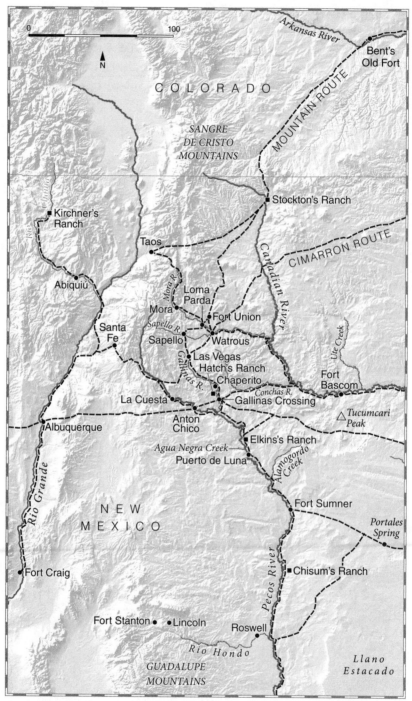

Southern Colorado and eastern New Mexico. Map by Carol Zuber-Mallison.

INTRODUCTION

The Texas–New Mexico borderlands, three hundred miles wide and six hundred miles in length, are bounded by the Canadian River on the north and the Rio Grande to the south. Cutting across the heart of this region is the Pecos River. The Pecos is born in the Sangre de Cristo Mountains in Mora County, New Mexico, then flows downstream in its serpentine, 926-mile course before finally emptying its briny waters into the Rio Grande near Comstock, Texas. Today large swaths of this region are desolate and empty. During the 1860s and 1870s, when much of this story takes place, the borderlands were even more so, making them a perfect venue for cloak-and-dagger intrigue and illegal dealings. In this forlorn and forbidding locale one could easily disappear into the landscape, avoiding prying eyes and evading inquisitive types.

In October 1862 Union soldiers from the Department of New Mexico established an outpost in the middle of these borderlands to keep a watchful presence on this no-man's-land. This small outpost, Camp Easton, was supplanted in August 1863 with the construction of the larger and more considerable Fort Bascom, located forty miles west of the New Mexico–Texas line. Fort Bascom was situated on the Canadian River and along the road from Fort Smith, Arkansas, to Santa Fe, a route long used by the military, merchants, Hispanics, and Plains Indians. Camp Easton's and Fort Bascom's wartime missions were identical: first, to guard the Canadian River, Fort Smith Road, and the Texas–New Mexico borderlands against a Confederate invasion from the Lone Star State; second, to prevent predatory Comanche and Kiowa incursions into eastern New Mexico from their strongholds in Texas's Staked Plains; and third, to interdict the tribes' long-established trade with New Mexico Comancheros, who exchanged guns, ammunition, whiskey, and other staples with the Indians for stolen horses, mules, and cattle from Texas.

This book examines the cat-and-mouse, rebel-Union skullduggery occurring in the shadowy Texas–New Mexico borderlands during the Civil War as well as the Comanchero-Comanche traffic in purloined Lone Star livestock throughout

1

the 1860s and 1870s that included double-dealing politicians, merchants, ranchers, and army officers. By the time the South seceded, this notorious commerce had already become well entrenched in both New Mexico's economy and its politics. Ironically, during the sectional conflict Comanches, Kiowas, and Comancheros were not the only ones driving beeves from Confederate Texas to New Mexico. Some Lone Star cattleman were also cashing in on an illegal and clandestine trade with federal beef contractors in New Mexico.

A consortium of Texas ranchers in Concho and Coleman Counties led by John Chisum provided the beeves, which were driven from Chisum's ranch to the Department of New Mexico by cowboys working for Union livestock dealers. These illicit, pioneering cattle drives during the latter part of the war blazed the trail for the tens of thousands of beeves that would subsequently follow in the late 1860s and 1870s during Texas's cattle-boom days. Erroneous popular mythology holds that Charles Goodnight and Oliver Loving made the first drives across West Texas and up the Pecos River to New Mexico markets in 1866 and 1867. In fact, this route was established prior to Goodnight and Loving and was known as the Chisum Trail decades before Goodnight's biographer branded it the Goodnight-Loving Trail.[1]

From August 1862 until June 1865 Department of New Mexico troops commanded by Brig. Gen. James Henry Carleton occupied New Mexico and the Texas Trans-Pecos under martial law. Among Carleton's pressing responsibilities was containing Confederate Texas and the Comanchero trade, both of which proved persistent problems throughout the Civil War. We turn first to the troubles with Texas: for two decades the Lone Star State had periodically vexed New Mexicans. Whether it was Texans invading New Mexico during the 1841 Santa Fe Expedition or the 1861–62 Baylor/Sibley campaigns, relations with Texas during the nineteenth century proved challenging.[2]

Regarding the incursions into New Mexico, in both cases Texas officials naively assumed that local populations shared their same beliefs and would enthusiastically welcome them as liberating heroes. During the 1841 Santa Fe Expedition, however, Texans "did not find nine-tenths of New Mexico's population ready to 'shake off the tiresome yoke of their [Mexican] task-masters,' . . . instead they discovered a fully mobilized Mexican citizenry, virulently anti-Texan." Mexican forces captured the expedition and imprisoned its participants.[3]

Over the next twenty years Texas apparently forgot this painful lesson, and in 1861 once again invaded New Mexico. After initial advances, first by Col. John Baylor and then by Gen. Henry Hopkins Sibley, the Confederate offensive fizzled out in the spring of 1862 when Union major John M. Chivington destroyed their supply train on March 28 at Johnson's Ranch (near Cañoncito, New Mexico). A postmortem on the military campaign by officers of the Fifth Regiment, Texas Mounted Volunteers, noted, "It had been erroneously supposed that the citizens of New Mexico would greet us as benefactors and flock to our standard upon our approach." The Texan officers instead discovered "that there was not a friend to our cause in the [New Mexico] territory, with a few honorable exceptions."[4]

Forced to abandon New Mexico and retreat to San Antonio, Texas, Lone Star troops in June and July 1862 encountered a local populace that was not only hostile to the Southern cause but also increasingly violent. Lacking adequate transportation and supplies for their long trek home, the Texans attempted to purchase the needed items from area Mexican Americans. Confederate colonel William Steele found that "the Mexican population, justly thinking our tenure [in the region] very frail and uncertain, showed great unwillingness to sell property of any sort for Confederate paper, which would of course be valueless to them" after the rebels departed. As a result, Steele "was obliged to seize upon such supplies as were required . . . [which] occasioned much ill-feeling on the part of the Mexicans," and as a result, "in many instances armed resistance was offered" by locals, who "became incensed by the acts of the Texans" while passing through their communities.[5]

From Mesilla, New Mexico, south to Socorro, Texas, a new and different kind of civil war erupted as depredating Confederate troops seized the belongings of Hispanic residents. Rebel soldiers were "committing outrages upon the inhabitants that they meet on the highway. They are almost on the point of starvation," one report noted, and "the Mexican population are much enraged against them on account of their rude treatment." Several bloody and intense clashes in the Mesilla area claimed up to fifty lives. At Socorro violent firefights between the retreating soldiers and two to three hundred Tejanos and Pueblo Indians left another twenty to fifty dead. A Houston newspaper lamented, "Instead of fighting the Yankees . . . we have to fight the Mexicans." When the last of Colonel Steele's raiding rebels finally straggled out of the Rio Grande valley towards San Antonio, many of the locals in El Paso County, Texas (90 percent Hispanic), were glad to see them gone.[6]

After the Confederacy abandoned New Mexico Territory and Texas west of the Pecos River in the summer of 1862, additional Union troops, notably the California Column, moved into the region the from the west. General Carleton assumed command of the Department of New Mexico on September 18, 1862.

Carleton was no stranger to New Mexico, having served there as a major in the First Dragoons from 1851 to 1857. The retreating rebels, in order to prevent the advancing bluecoats from utilizing area military installations in West Texas, vandalized Forts Bliss and Davis. In September 1862, as Union lieutenant Albert H. French and his men passed through the abandoned Fort Davis, they came under surveillance by rebel spies at the junction of the road to Presidio del Norte, Mexico. In his report, French noted that on the Presidio del Norte road, "I afterwards learned, were Mexican spies in the employ of one John Burgess [a local Confederate agent], who a few hours after we had passed down, came in and burned the Fort."[7]

General Carleton's Department of New Mexico also controlled the District of Arizona, an area bounded by Fort Thorn (near Hatch, New Mexico) on the north, the Rio Grande on the west and south, and Fort Quitman in El Paso County, Texas, on the east. Subordinate to Carleton, and commanding the District of Arizona at Mesilla, New Mexico, was Brig. Gen. Joseph Rodman West. West administered the district from September 1862 until February 1864, when Col. George Washington Bowie replaced him. In an ironic twist of history, troops from New Mexico had occupied part of the Lone Star State and were now issuing orders to Texans.[8]

Carleton referred to the Union-controlled portion of the state as "Northwestern Texas." While department guidelines delineated the District of Arizona's eastern boundary at Fort Quitman, Texas, on the Rio Grande, in reality, events forced the federals to maintain a military presence further east to the Pecos River and up into the Texas Panhandle. The Union's general-in-chief, Henry W. Halleck, granted Carleton much latitude regarding Department of New Mexico operations in the Lone Star State. "You will operate without regard to departmental lines," ordered Halleck, "and any portion of Texas which may be occupied by you will be considered as in your military department."[9]

Although the rebels had abandoned the Texas Trans-Pecos in July 1862, they fully expected to return someday and recapture the region. If and when the Confederacy attacked, it would be over one of three routes: first, along the Canadian River, via the road from Fort Smith to Santa Fe; second, up the Pecos River from Fort Lancaster and Horsehead Crossing; and third, via the Upper and Lower Roads from San Antonio to El Paso. In response, the Department of New Mexico garrisoned several outposts near the New Mexico–Texas line. Fort Bascom, located north of present-day, Tucumcari, New Mexico, guarded the Fort Smith Road and the Canadian River. In addition, Bascom provided flanking protection for Carleton's headquarters at Fort Marcy in Santa Fe and for Fort Union, the department's main supply depot in Mora County, New Mexico.[10]

Freighters hauling military supplies from Fort Leavenworth, Kansas, and St. Louis to Fort Union typically used either the Mountain or Cimarron routes of the Santa Fe Trail. Both of these trails entered New Mexico in the northeastern corner of the territory. Keeping these transportation arteries open was of primary concern to General Carleton. If raiding Texans or Indians severed these lifelines, the consequences would be devastating. As department quartermaster Maj. J. C. McFerran noted, the entire department depended on Fort Union, where supplies "are received and stored, and from thence distributed as required, by wagon transportation, to the various posts and commands."[11]

South of Forts Union and Bascom stood Forts Sumner and Stanton, which extended Carleton's defensive perimeter along the middle portion of New Mexico's boundary with Texas. Fort Sumner, situated on the Pecos River, guarded the approach to a long-used Comanchero road leading southeast from Anton Chico and Puerto de Luna to Comanche trading centers in Texas's Staked Plains. During the Civil War this Pecos River outpost included the Bosque Redondo Indian Reservation, established in 1863 for the Navajo and Apache tribes. In November 1862 General Carleton hired five Indians from the Tesuque Pueblo (north of Santa Fe) "to act as spies and guides at Fort Sumner." These men and their leader, Tesuque governor Carlos Vigil, knew "all the country around . . . and their services will be invaluable in watching out for . . . Texans." The Confederates also utilized Pueblo Indians as spies during the Baylor/Sibley campaigns in New Mexico from 1861 to 1862, including those from the Isleta Pueblo (near Albuquerque). Ironically, in an illustration of the layered loyalties that characterized many borderland relationships, a number of Tesuque and Isleta Indians were also Comancheros who had been trading with the Comanches for years. In one example from 1850, authorities issued trading passes to Governor Vigil and another Tesuque man, and in a second instance from the same year, they detained six residents of the Isleta Pueblo for operating without an official license.[12]

Fort Stanton, one hundred miles southwest of Fort Sumner, was situated on the Rio Bonito, a tributary of the Rio Hondo. Beginning in September 1862, General Carleton ordered Col. Kit Carson to send regular details from Stanton to several points on the Pecos River in Texas, including Pope's Crossing and Horsehead Crossing, "to guard against us being surprised by a [Texan] force coming up the Pecos from Fort Lancaster." Southwest of Fort Stanton, securing the department's southern flank along the Texas–New Mexico borderlands, were three garrisons

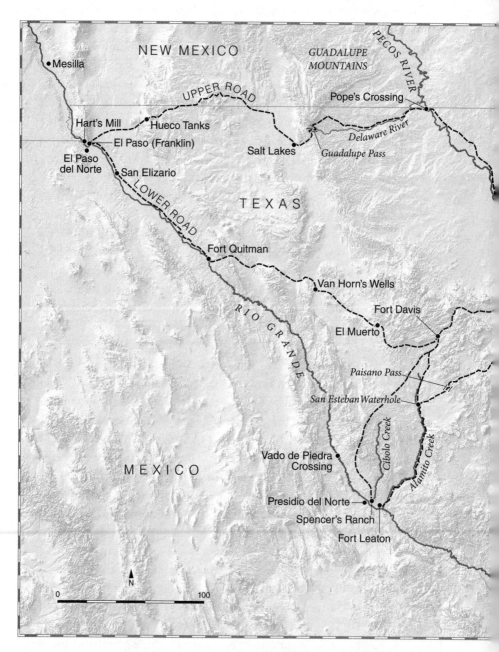

The Texas Trans-Pecos. Map by Carol Zuber-Mallison.

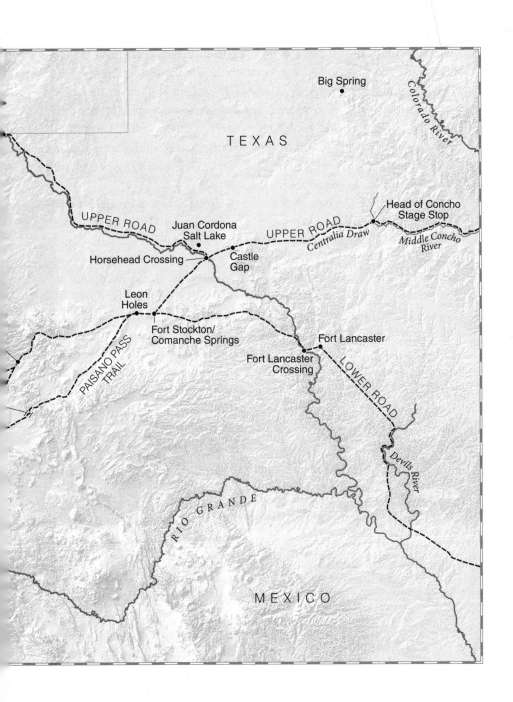

on the Rio Grande: one at Mesilla, New Mexico (near Las Cruces); and two in El Paso County, Texas—at Franklin (El Paso) and at San Elizario.[13]

The commanding general also posted satellite detachments from El Paso County to keep an eye on approaches from the interior of Texas: one at Fort Quitman, Texas, on the Lower Road, and a second at Hueco Tanks on the Upper Road. The department's southern boundary shared a common border with Mexico, which remained neutral throughout the sectional conflict. During this period Mexico and its president, Benito Juárez, were confronting their own civil war, battling serious internal divisions and invading French troops that had occupied much of the country.[14]

Confederate exiles and spies in Mexico, at El Paso del Norte (now Juárez) and at Presidio del Norte (now Ojinaga), proved vexing to General Carleton throughout the Civil War. A shadowy, elusive spy company led by former U.S. Army scout and stage driver Henry Skillman operated for several years throughout West Texas, the Big Bend, and the El Paso area, gathering operational intelligence on Union forces. In addition to establishing spy networks, Confederate officials in Texas continued to develop plans for several offensives against Carleton, including retaking the Southwest and disrupting Union supply lines.[15]

As previously mentioned, besides keeping an eye out for raiding rebels, commanding officers at Forts Bascom, Sumner, and Stanton were also charged with cracking down on the secretive and often illegal trade transpiring between New Mexico Comancheros and Comanches in Texas's Staked Plains. The traditional Comanche range encompassed the eastern face of the Sangre de Cristo Mountains in New Mexico, the Llano Estacado or Staked Plains, and much of Central Texas, extending as far south as the southern rim of the Edwards Plateau. The Comancheros, composed of both Pueblo Indians and local New Mexican mountain people, traded with the Comanches, sometimes legally and sometimes illegally. During its peak, from the 1850s to the 1870s, a thriving black market flourished, a transnational economy that funneled goods and weapons south and east in exchange for Texas horses and cattle. New Mexican ranchers, merchants, cattlemen, and politicians were interested in cheap livestock and were hardly concerned with where the Comancheros had acquired them, although they certainly knew.[16]

The Comanches moved south into the borderlands during the first decades of the eighteenth century. For most of the century the Comanches and Spanish settlers participated in an economy fueled by revenge wars, livestock raiding, kidnapped women and children, and slave labor. Such exchanges included every culture that populated the region. On the Spanish frontier all living things could be converted into commodities. These racial and cultural exchanges created an ethnic borderland free of predetermined loyalties based on treaties or geographic boundaries. Hundreds of Southwestern Indians and Hispanic women and children were "cross-cultured" through generations of trading, kidnapping, and slave trading. The Spanish and Comanches finally brokered a peace treaty in 1787, which led to a relatively nonviolent period in Hispanic–Plains Indians relations that lasted into the Mexican period. The Spanish government issued licenses to Pueblo Indians and Hispanos that granted them the legal right to barter with the Comanches, Kiowas, and other Southern Plains Indians.[17]

By the 1840s Hispano and Puebloan farmers and ranchers loaded with goods left their villages in August and September of each year and journeyed east with their pack mules toward the Llano Estacado. At the same time, the Comanches moved north with bison hides and stolen horses and cattle. The Indians met the Comancheros at predesignated locations to barter. The Comancheros, as cultural intermediaries, used their multiethnic heritage to their advantage. They traveled easily between the Euro-American and Indian worlds. Their ability to converse with a variety of nationalities allowed them to become significant players in the region as well as facilitators of a transnational black-market phenomenon. The Comancheros would ultimately link Mexican nationals, Comanches, Kiowas, Apaches, New Mexican businessmen, politicians, and federal soldiers into one trade network.[18]

Indian raids on livestock, especially in Texas, provided the Comanches and Kiowas the barter they needed to acquire weapons and manufactured goods from New Mexican entrepreneurs. Following the Mexican War (1846–48), this exchange helped the Southern Plains Indians reestablish, if only for a few years, much of their hold on traditional lands that they had previously and grudgingly abandoned. By the late 1850s Comanches and Kiowas who did not want to settle on reservations in Indian Territory had few places where they could continue traditional lifeways. The one exception was the Llano Estacado. Southern Plains Indians found refuge between the Red and Canadian Rivers, centrally located between their old trading partners in New Mexico and the Anglo settlements in Texas. As the Comanches and Kiowas began to increasingly rely on the Comanchero trade to remain independent, the U.S. Army was pressured to stop this exchange. If the Comanches did not have willing trading partners in New Mexico, the raids would diminish in Texas.[19]

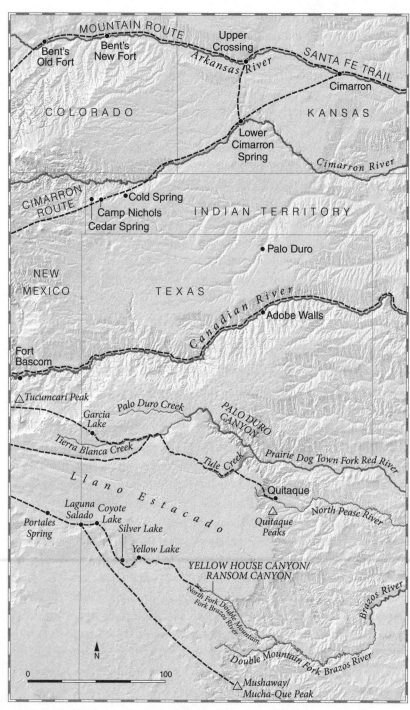

Southern Kansas, western Indian Territory, Texas Panhandle, and Texas south plains.
Map by Carol Zuber-Mallison.

New Mexico Comancheros typically made the trip to Texas over several established routes. Period maps describe one of the main Comanchero trails to the Lone Star State as a "Comanche Route said to be practicable for wagons" and as an "Overland route to the Texas settlements." This trail led southeast from Anton Chico and Puerto de Luna on the Pecos River to Las Cañaditas (northeast of Fort Sumner, in Gerhardt Valley along Truchas Creek), to Taiban Spring and Stinking Springs (near Taiban, New Mexico), to Little Tule Lake and Tule Lake (six miles south-southwest of Melrose, New Mexico), to Tierra Blanca Lake (four miles southeast of Floyd, New Mexico), and on to Los Portales (Portales Spring, six miles southeast of Portales, New Mexico). From Los Portales, the road went to Laguna Salada (the 2,300-acre salt lake in what is now the Grulla National Wildlife Refuge, New Mexico), located just west of the Texas state line. According to one Comanchero, Laguna Salada served as an intermediate meeting place "to which traders take goods and trade for cattle." From Laguna Salada the trail continued east to El Coyote (Coyote Lake, eleven miles southwest of Muleshoe, Texas), to the headwaters of Yellow House Draw (near Enochs, Texas), then along Yellow House Draw to Silver Lake (near Morton, Texas), past Yellow Lake (southwest of Littlefield, Texas), then southeast to one of the major rendezvous sites at Cañon del Rescate or Ransom Canyon (near present-day Lubbock, Texas), part of Yellow House Canyon.[20]

A second Comanchero route followed the road from the Pecos River to Laguna Salada, where it branched off and ran southeast to the 2,854-foot Mushaway or Mucha-Que Peak, an important trading site located in Borden County (southeast of Gail, Texas). A third trail led eastward from New Mexico along the Canadian River and the road to Fort Smith. The trail branched off from the Canadian River west of Fort Bascom, passing south of Tucumcari Mountain, and heading east/southeast to Arroyo Saladito, Arroyo Trujillo, and Arroyo del Puerto (all located southwest of Endee, New Mexico). From there the Comanchero trail led southeast along Arroyo del Puerto, passing by Round Mountain in the southeast corner of Quay County, New Mexico, to Garcia Lake (near Bootleg, Texas, in the southwest corner of Deaf Smith County), on to Tierra Blanca Creek, then east to its junction with Frio Draw (east of present-day Hereford, Texas), then southeast to Tule Creek, to another meeting spot at Quitaque (near present-day Quitaque, Texas), marked by the 2,838-foot Quitaque Peaks and Los Lingos and Quitaque Creeks, which form the headwaters of the North Pease River.[21]

Many of these routes had been used for generations. By the mid-eighteenth century the traditional barter system had been replaced by a profit-based commerce, one necessitated by survival. Cattle had become horned gold in New Mexico. Comanches understood that this new market offered them an opportunity to remain independent and worked with their old trading partners to ensure a steady supply of beef. The demand for beeves in the territory was almost insatiable. In exchange for livestock, Comanches requested hard-baked bread, blankets, shirts, and sugar. They also wanted pistols, powder, rifles, and whiskey. Only merchants could provide these products. While storekeepers rarely listed weapons in their ledgers, these items nonetheless found their way to Comanchería.[22]

The Comancheros began many of their journeys from the *placita*, or plaza, the hub of many communities. Typically, each plaza was surrounded by stores, saloons, hotels, meat markets, and a church. Several times a year Comancheros would position their wagons, mules, carts, and horses in the town center before sunrise. Sons, brothers, cousins, and neighbors would squint in the predawn darkness as they walked around inspecting the expertly packed goods strapped to mules and stacked in wagon beds. These products, along with the hard-baked black breads, came from prominent merchants such as Ilfeld, Delgado, and Rosenthal. Before heading out the men would check their perishables, water casks, and blankets one last time. As they rode away on the old roads toward Texas, some cast a final glance back toward their homes.[23]

The trails led to where the mountains ended and the plains began. During the trip the Comancheros camped along river bends and seeping springs and reacquainted themselves with old friends and distant relatives. The men talked about the lack of rain in Chama, the Mora corn crop, and their newborn babies. Most were farmers and small-time ranchers, employed by others to take these goods on the seven- to ten-day journey to Comanche trading centers. These clandestine trips often proved stressful and perilous. Only after the men had exchanged their goods and returned home with their cattle could they finally relax.[24]

To the casual viewer the Santa Fe Trail trade and the Comanchero trade appeared similar. In both, Hispano frontiersman drove caravans laden with supplies across desolate, wide-open spaces. These expeditions were often funded by the same people. While the history of the Santa Fe Trail mentions some of these New Mexicans, for the most part it details the experiences of intrepid Anglo entrepreneurs and hardy pioneers. The history of the Comancheros, in contrast, has been characterized as a tainted tale replete with Hispano thieves, double dealers, and ne'er-do-wells. Heretofore, much of this latter narrative has been left untold.

As with the Santa Fe Trail, the Comanchero trade attracted a diverse collection of people. Santa Fe merchants of German ancestry, such as Zadok Staab and Willie Rosenthal, Hispanos like Felipe Delgado and Manuel Chaves, and Americans James M. Giddings and John Sebrie Watts all participated in or funded Comanchero expeditions. Staab and Rosenthal were two of the most successful merchants in New Mexico. Delgado and Chaves were merchants, freighters, and government employees. Felipe Delgado had freighted along the Santa Fe Trail and served as the territory's superintendent of Indians Affairs. Manuel Chaves was a famed Indian fighter and Civil War hero who started a sheep and cattle ranch in the middle Pecos River valley. James Giddings was a Santa Fe merchant before becoming Chaves's Pecos River neighbor. Watts was a successful lawyer, congressional delegate, and chief justice of the New Mexico Supreme Court. Watts also leased the army the land that Fort Bascom was built on.[25]

On his way west in 1843, American trader Josiah Gregg met a Hispano caravan going in the opposite direction. Gregg remarked that these traders were made up of the "indigent and rude classes" of New Mexico. He noted in his journal that the Hispanos left their "frontier villages" twice a year to exchange goods with the Comanches. Later, U.S. Army personnel stationed in the west carried copies of Gregg's published account of his experiences, *Commerce of the Prairies* (1844), with them. When soldiers encountered similar trading parties, they too, described them as Comancheros. The term stuck. Gregg's crass and racially charged characterizations played into larger misconceptions associated with New Mexico's population. Americans came to believe that only the lower classes were involved in these illegal exchanges. In fact, every class and ethnicity in the territory was connected to the Comanchero trade. Complicating the murky ethics of this commerce, some of the trips these people made to Texas for cattle were perfectly legal.[26]

A number of Americans who came to New Mexico were immediately intrigued with the trade. Most were merchants who had followed the Santa Fe Trail westward. They quickly discerned that there was more to the business than trading hard bread and corn for buffalo hides. Too many wealthy Hispano merchants were involved. The commerce satisfied several different demands. Plains Indians wanted carbohydrates, metal tools, and guns. New Mexicans initially sought horses, bison products, and captives. The Hispanicized children of these captives later founded pioneer communities along the Mora, Canadian, and Pecos Rivers. The ties between Comanches and these pioneers created cultural and kinship bonds that facilitated this unique trade. The Comanchero trader served as the social middleman, someone with a foot in each world who spoke both languages. By the time the Americans arrived in the territory, the economic pipeline that funneled Texas horses and cattle to New Mexico was already well established.[27]

Following its acquisition of New Mexico, the U.S. government permitted the Comanchero trade to continue. As Mexican officials had previously done, the Americans required that traders acquire an approved pass before setting out for Texas. Over the ensuing years the approval process changed. In a land with few telegraph lines and evolving regulations, it was impossible to enforce uniform adherence. The superintendent of Indian Affairs in Santa Fe was largely responsible for approving the passes, yet at different times local Indian agents and military officers also held this authority. The lack of a constant, coherent policy left distant commissioners, suspicious cavalry officers, local merchants, Hispano ranchers, and Texas cattlemen in various states of confusion regarding what was a valid pass and what was not.[28]

The most complete record of the legal Comanchero trade is found within the records of the superintendent of Indian Affairs. As with the majority of government-directed operations, copies of the applications and the licenses were filed in Santa Fe. The application included the name of the person applying to trade in the "Comanche country" as well as the names and number of employees for the trip. The official form also stipulated how many months the expedition would take. Each pass required that a surety bond, generally at least a thousand dollars, be guaranteed. A trader forfeited his bond if he failed to honor the terms of his pass. Failure included selling the Indians unapproved products such as gunpowder, weapons, and whiskey. Taking more than the stipulated number of persons on an expedition was also a violation, as was not keeping to the approved timeframe. Many surety bond holders were merchants. Some were wealthy ranchers and politicians. The traders, bond holders, and government officials would all sign the form.

The documents detailing the Comanchero trade reveal the extent to which the power brokers of Santa Fe and Las Vegas were involved. The merchants who put up thousand-dollar bonds were not vouching for these frontier farmers and ranchers because they were charitable. These businessmen had a personal investment. It was the storekeepers that grubstaked the Comancheros with shirts, knives, vermillion, and other products that were then hauled to Texas.

After investigating these passes, it becomes clear that the oft-used phrase "legal Comanchero trade" is a misnomer. In actuality these permits allowed New Mexicans to go to "Comanche country" to trade for stolen cattle.[29]

Some Comancheros like Anastacio Sandoval were both traders and bond holders. Sandoval was a wealthy Santa Fe merchant, respected politician, and veteran of the Civil War. On February 27, 1865, he applied for and received a pass to trade with the Comanches. The superintendent of Indian Affairs in New Mexico at that time, Michael Steck, approved the application. While most passes were for two or three months, this one allowed Sandoval to send ten men up to "12 times during the year . . . with animals and packs to trade." The majority of passes noted that the Comancheros' destination was "Comanche country." The state of Texas was not mentioned. Sandoval remarked that since he would be making several trips, he would not always be taking the same people. The bondholders backing Sandoval's venture were Francisco Baca y Ortíz, former mayor of Santa Fe, and José L. Duran. Despite Steck's approval, William P. Dole, the commissioner of Indian Affairs in Washington, D.C., disallowed this pass because it lacked the required one-dollar Internal Revenue stamp for each permit. It is unknown whether any of Sandoval's trading expeditions to Texas had departed by the time the commissioner nullified his license.[30]

After the government replaced Steck in 1865, his successor Felipe Delgado approved another pass for Sandoval that September. The new permit allowed the traders to be gone for two months. Manuel Urioste and Manuel Sandoval of Santa Fe each provided the requisite thousand-dollar bond. In this instance the license noted that David Urioste, Manuel's brother, would lead the expedition, which included eleven employees. While Anastacio Sandoval secured this trading license, he did not accompany his caravan. During this same period, he was active in backing a number of other trading endeavors.[31]

Whether legal or illegal, the Comanchero passes provide much revealing information on this surreptitious trade that funneled vast numbers of stolen Texas livestock to New Mexico. Despite the significance of these permits, they have languished for more than a century in the files of the superintendent of Indian Affairs. These documents detail the host of merchants, politicians, and government officials who backed the expeditions. Such licenses provided a cloak of legitimacy to the practice, giving the well-to-do the legal cover they needed to participate in this commerce.

Another component of the trade's success was the familial web that tied Hispano farmers and ranchers to the Comanches. Acquiring a license from the authorities was only one aspect of this business. Gaining access to Comanchería required a different type of bond, one that was generations old and built on a mutual trust. It was this mutual trust that caught the attention of the U.S. Army as it endeavored to rescue Anglo captives from Southern Plains Indians. Comancheros were often called on to assist. Ultimately, then, the Comanchero trade concerned much more than cattle rustling. Understanding how the trade endured for so long opens a new window into our understanding the history of the nineteenth-century Southwest.

This is the story of American expansionism, indigenous resistance, cattle drives, and cattle thefts. In the midst of a cultural shatter zone, the Comanchero trade impacted government contracts, Indian reservation policy, military strategies, and settlement patterns. It turns out that a variety of bonds, not just those linking the Comancheros to the Comanches, weaves this history together: bonds that linked Prussian immigrants, Indian agents, Hispano ranchers, Anglo whiskey dealers, and Polish priests; bonds that involved Texas cattlemen and New Mexico politicians. By studying trading licenses, contemporary newspapers, arrest records, merchant journals, and court of claims depositions, a more multilayered and nuanced appreciation of this commerce comes into focus.[32]

After examining the New Mexico side of the Comanchero trade, the last two chapters of this work move eastward to the Lone Star State, presenting a different take on this story, this one from a Texan perspective. Thus, the narrative presented here is not always chronological. It moves back and forth across these borderlands. An event viewed one way by Texans might mean something completely different to the residents of New Mexico. This study endeavors to provide multiple perspectives, thus providing a richer, fuller, and more complete history of these borderlands during this period.

The peak of the Comanche-Comanchero activity in Texas occurred from the late 1850s to the mid 1870s. Incessant Comanche and Kiowa raids devastated Lone Star communities and cattlemen, who were increasingly frustrated by a mixed and uneven response from state and federal officials. Although it took several decades, eventually the combined pressure of the U.S. Army, Texas Rangers, and state officials proved effective against the tribes. By 1880 the Comanchero trade was finished. This, then, is the background for our story, which starts in the fall of 1862, as General Carleton and the Department of New Mexico consolidated Union control over New Mexico Territory and the Texas Trans-Pecos.

CHAPTER 1

When Brig. Gen. James Henry Carleton assumed command of the Department of New Mexico in September 1862, he established his office at Fort Marcy in Santa Fe. His subordinate, Brig. Gen. Joseph Rodman West, who administered the southern portion of the department (the District of Arizona), set up operations at Mesilla, New Mexico. Maintaining an outpost in Mesilla, however, proved problematic. In February 1863 West ordered his chief medical officer, Dr. O. M. Bryan, to assess which town—Mesilla or Franklin (El Paso), Texas—offered the healthier locale for district headquarters. Bryan determined that from a sanitary and hygienic point of view, Franklin was the superior location.[1]

Periodic flooding from the Rio Grande occasionally left Mesilla surrounded by pools of stagnant water and clouds of mosquitoes, resulting in a high rate of malarial fever among residents. Franklin, forty miles southeast, offered better drainage and possessed no similar problems. Rates of scurvy in Franklin were also far lower than in Mesilla. The doctor found that locals in Mesilla paid "but little attention to the raising of vegetables," resulting in high prices for produce, whereas in Franklin "fruits and vegetables [were] generally in abundance and prices reasonable."[2]

Surgeon Bryan's most serious health complaint about Mesilla concerned the numerous "grog shops" and prostitutes plaguing the town. "The most visible means of support among the male inhabitants is the retail of whisky," he lamented, and many of the women "have no other means of obtaining a living than the retail of venereal disease in its various forms; the market is *glutted* and *prices reduced*." The doctor concluded that with so many temptations at hand, it was "very difficult to prevent (by way of discipline) . . . disease and demoralization" among the troops. Franklin, in comparison, had few prostitutes and little whiskey available; as a result "it is seldom you see a case of syphilis or debauch."[3]

After receiving Bryan's report, General West recommended that General Carleton move the district's garrison, depot, and headquarters to Hart's Mill,

Texas, two miles above Franklin. Carleton approved the request. The following year, in 1864, the District of Arizona shifted its operational center once again, from Hart's Mill to Franklin. As the commanding officers soon discovered, moving the garrison and headquarters did not prevent corrupting influences from also relocating. A military inspection of Franklin in early 1864 found that "lewd women" were living in public quarters on post and recommended action to "correct this demoralizing practice."[4]

In addition to cracking down on military vices, General West's responsibilities included enforcing martial law in Union-occupied Texas. In April 1863 the general selected Miguel Sáenz to serve as the *alcalde*, or chief executive, of Franklin. As part of his duties Sáenz appointed constables and acted as majordomo of the *acequias*, or irrigation canals. West also gave the alcalde the power to arrest and imprison and to levy fines. Along with those duties, Sáenz was to serve as prosecutor at all military tribunals charged with hearing crimes and rendering verdicts in El Paso County. In his capacity as alcalde, Sáenz governed according to established Texas civil code. General West put all appointed officials on notice that they "shall hold office at the pleasure of the said commanding officer or his successor, during good behavior and until such time as the civil shall replace the military authorities in said county of El Paso, Texas."[5]

As late as January 1865 the commanding officer at Franklin was still appointing civil officials under martial law. All appointees were to ensure "that justice is done to every person under your control." The post commander also named Martin Lujan as alcalde and justice of the peace for Socorro, Texas. In addition, he tapped Gregorio García to serve as justice of the peace in neighboring San Elizario, Texas, empowering him to arrest and confine those who refused to work on public work projects such as the acequias. Under traditional Spanish and Mexican law, those who took water from the irrigation canals were required to help repair and maintain the water system. Apparently, some citizens of San Elizario were shirking mandatory public service, and García was ordered to jail any malingerers. In addition to his duties as justice of the peace, García occasionally served as a Union scout and spy for a dollar a day.[6]

Martial law also extended to travelers. During the last two years of the war, a wave of Texan refugees had flooded the Trans-Pecos. Many of these immigrants were tired of conflict and the Confederacy and were heading west for a fresh start. Some, however, were rebel agents. Union intelligence indicated that the Confederates might place spies among the exiles to reconnoiter federal troop strength and deployment in West Texas and New Mexico. This warning proved correct. In March 1864 the commander of Confederate North Texas, Brig. Gen. Henry E. McCulloch, recommended that Col. J. E. McCord, the head of the Texas Rangers, plant undercover operatives among the refugees.[7]

Union troops carefully interrogated all travelers. Department regulations required Texans to state their reasons for leaving the Lone Star State and directed that those over the age of eighteen take an oath of allegiance to the United States. All suspicious persons were to be confined pending examination by a military tribunal. In addition, military orders stipulated that anyone traveling in the Department of New Mexico carry a signed passport with an attached certificate attesting that the bearer had taken the oath of loyalty. The only exceptions to the passport requirements were "Mexicans passing from one town or place to another."[8]

Martial law in occupied Texas provided economic benefits to the Department of New Mexico, allowing the army to minimize real estate expenditures. At Mesilla the army paid rent for buildings that it used. At Franklin many of the town's finest buildings were vacant, abandoned by Confederate sympathizers in the summer of 1862. Federal authorities confiscated choice secessionist properties in El Paso County, and General West and his troops moved into several of these. The District of Arizona commander noted, "The free occupancy of all these premises is not likely to be disturbed until the Federal courts shall be reorganized in Texas."[9]

This issue of confiscating rebel real estate sparked considerable controversy. In the fall of 1862 U.S. Marshal Abraham Cutler, with approval from the District Court for the Territory of New Mexico, began seizing lands belonging to "treasonous" residents of El Paso County, Texas. Some of the secessionists' abandoned properties were highly prized. Those that the military did not use were rented out. One notable lease was with Nathan Webb and Henry Cuniffe, who rented Hart's Mill, ranked among the county's most valuable parcels.[10]

While General Carleton sanctioned the temporary seizure of secessionists' lands, he objected when the U.S. Marshal subsequently sold them. The general believed such sales were illegal and argued that New Mexico's district court had no jurisdiction in Texas. Subsequent developments proved Carleton correct. In March 1868 the U.S. Supreme Court nullified Abraham Cutler's sales of confiscated rebel property in Texas.[11]

Despite General West's optimistic expectations of enjoying free occupancy at Franklin, the Union army eventually ended up paying rent on a number of buildings in El Paso County. For example, in December 1864 the Department of New Mexico leased ten dwellings at Franklin for nine officers, a priest, the quartermaster, commissary storehouses, and the adjutant general's office. Of these ten homes, local resident W. W. Mills collected rent on six of them. Mills fully grasped the potential impact of government expenditures upon the local wartime economy. A steadfast Unionist originally from Indiana, Mills in 1862 secured an appointment from President Lincoln as customs collector for El Paso County. A short time later, following the federal occupation of western Texas, he positioned himself to maximize his financial opportunities by currying favor with newly arrived Union officers.[12]

After the Confederates' failed incursion into New Mexico and their subsequent retreat to San Antonio, the Department of New Mexico temporarily quarantined all travel into Texas, except that by *"loyal citizens . . . only on legitimate business."* Because of his position as federal customs collector, Mills was one of the first people allowed into Union-occupied El Paso County. Before traveling south to Franklin, Mills ingratiated himself with department officials as *the* person to consult regarding regional matters. Stopping at Fort Craig, New Mexico, in early August 1862, Mills visited with Union colonel Marshall Saxe Howe. Howe solicited Mills's assessment of "the state of affairs in Las Cruces, Mesilla, and Franklin," since the customs collector "had [formerly] resided a long time below" and was "well acquainted with all the people."[13]

As the result of his efforts at influence, Mills secured a number of lucrative federal contracts and leases throughout the remainder of the war. In early 1863 he started renting properties to the Department of New Mexico. Besides his real estate investments, Mills also bid on military supply contracts. In the spring of 1863 he made a tidy profit on an agreement to supply vinegar to the Union post at Franklin. In September of that year, Mills joined forces with Nathan Webb, the post sutler at Franklin, for a considerably larger deal (totaling $9,350), to supply the army 5,500 gallons of vinegar. Mills bragged to his father that the profits from this new arrangement "will set me on my pegs."[14]

Other El Paso County residents capitalizing on the department's wartime economy were Price Cooper, Eugene von Patten, and A. B. Rohman, all of whom supplied corn to the post at Franklin. Mills's vinegar associate, Nathan Webb, was in partnership with Henry J. Cuniffe to supply flour and bran to the military. Webb and Cuniffe ground their grain at Hart's Mill, the gristmill formerly operated by Simeon Hart, a rabid secessionist who had once been the richest man in El Paso County. Like Mills and Webb, Cuniffe maximized his revenues from the federal government by holding several jobs at once. Besides supplying grain to the army, Cuniffe also served as the U.S. consul in El Paso del Norte (now Juárez), Mexico.[15]

The competition for these military contracts in the Department of New Mexico occasionally turned nasty and assumed a personal nature. Some rivals attempted to gain an advantage by besmirching the reputations of their competitors and questioning their patriotism. Under General Orders No. 4, 1863, "All persons who desire to furnish supplies to the troops in [the Department of] New Mexico shall give unequivocal evidence of their loyalty to the U.S. government." Anyone suspected being a secessionist or providing aid to the rebels could not do business with the army.[16]

In November 1863 Ernest Angerstein of El Paso del Norte signed a contract to supply 6,000 *fanegas* (9,600 bushels) of corn to the Department of New Mexico for $6.75 per fanega (1.6 bushels), or $40,500. The agreement infuriated a number of competing merchants, who immediately informed General Carleton that the army had paid too much for the corn. Next, these competitors began sullying Angerstein's reputation, calling him a foreigner, a traitor, and a rebel collaborator. Upon receiving these reports, the army annulled the contract and solicited new proposals. The new corn bids were even higher, ranging from $7 to $8 per fanega. Ultimately, the department rejected these as well.[17]

A military investigation of the Angerstein contract found that "self-interest, prejudice, envy and jealousy appear to be the source of many reports, exaggerations and accusations." Quartermaster officers discovered that a number of merchants were speculating on local commodity markets, purchasing crops months in advance from farmers and creating deliberate shortages in order to drive up prices. By April 1865 corn deliveries to the post at Franklin had skyrocketed to $15 per fanega. The poorer Tejanos in neighboring San Elizario and Ysleta, Texas, could not afford the high grain costs and resorted to scouring the surrounding hillsides for wild potatoes to survive. Nathan Webb, the miller at Hart's Mill, donated a supply of cornmeal to Ysleta to help keep residents there "from actual starvation." In summation, the Angerstein report found that "patriotism and loyalty to a great extent . . . seem to be measured very much in this district, by the bestowal of Govt. patronage, favors and indulgences."[18]

Patronage aside, it was the federal government's economic engine that sustained El Paso County during the turbulent sectional crisis. Union military contracts provided jobs and business opportunities for many locals. Regarding the region's wartime population, a February 1863 survey estimated that there were 2,360 area residents: 100 people living in Franklin, 500 in Socorro, 560 in Ysleta, and 1,200 in San Elizario. Three years earlier, in 1860, El Paso County's census recorded 4,000 residents, almost double this figure. In 1863, as in 1860, more than 90 percent of the inhabitants were Hispanic.[19]

The Civil War sparked a series of intriguing population shifts among residents of the Trans-Pecos. When Texas joined the Confederacy in 1861, a number of secession opponents, including Henry Cuniffe, Vincent St. Vrain, and W. W. Mills, sought refuge in neutral Mexico. Living across the Rio Grande, however, was no guarantee of safety. On several occasions during the war both North and South violated Mexican sovereignty. On July 16, 1861, prominent secessionist Simeon Hart paid five rebel soldiers $200 to kidnap Mills. The troops seized him in the plaza at El Paso del Norte and carried him across the river to Fort Bliss, Texas, where they imprisoned him in the guardhouse. Mills stated, "The only reason the Confederates gave for my arrest was loyalty to the United States Government."[20]

By August 1862 the Stars and Stripes fluttered over the Rio Grande valley once more, and a number of El Paso County's wartime émigrés began returning. While the Union presence enabled some residents to come home, it forced others to leave. Twenty secessionists, among them John Gillett, Benjamin Dowell, Henry Dexter, and Hugh Stephenson, led a new Texan exodus across the river into Chihuahua. In October 1862 the refugees were living in El Paso del Norte and Zaragoza, Mexico. A Union officer reported that the group was "an outpost of the enemy," endeavoring "to learn the strength, position, and movements of our troops, and to communicate the same to the rebel commanders in Texas." In December 1862 the number of exiles south of the river was variously reported as between forty and eighty.[21]

The secessionists in Mexico, like their brethren in the Confederate South, fervently believed that their troops would recapture the Southwest and that one day the Confederacy would stretch to the Pacific Ocean. To help plan for this anticipated invasion, rebel military authorities needed a professional intelligence network west of the Pecos River, an operation far beyond the exiles' capabilities. In addition, the mission required a shrewd spymaster to run the regional network. The person best suited to command such a spy company was Henry Skillman.

A New Jersey native born in 1814, Skillman settled in El Paso County after the Mexican War. From 1847 to 1849 the U.S. Army employed him as a scout. Beginning in 1851 and up through the end of 1861, he worked as an overseer and stage driver for a number of mail contractors in the Southwest. In January 1862 Texas governor Francis Lubbock appointed Skillman to raise a regiment of frontier troops for El Paso and Presidio Counties. During the first two months of 1862 he served as an army hay contractor for the Confederate invasion of New Mexico, supplying 150 tons of hay to Fort Bliss, Texas, and Fort Fillmore, New Mexico. In May of the same year Brig. Gen. Henry Hopkins Sibley employed Skillman on a number of occasions to carry the Confederate army's mail from Fort Bliss to Fort Thorn, New Mexico, and Alamosa, New Mexico.[22]

Three months after Sibley's July 1862 retreat to San Antonio, Brig. Gen. Hamilton Prioleau Bee dispatched Skillman and twelve men to El Paso del Norte, Mexico, "to observe the condition and movements of the enemy in that section." Bee, the Confederate commander of Texas's Lower Rio Grande District, selected Skillman to lead the expedition because he considered him "one [of], if not the best, frontiersman now in Western Texas, and is reliable in every way." On October 18, 1862, Skillman's spy company left San Antonio.[23]

After crossing the Pecos River, Skillman left the main road to El Paso and turned south onto the Puerto del Paisano Road, a secondary trail leading from Leon Holes to the Rio Grande and Presidio del Norte (now Ojinaga), Mexico. This route, via Paisano Pass, San Esteban Waterhole, Alamito Creek, and Fort Leaton, was originally scouted by Capt. William Helmsley Emory in 1852. If Union troops from the Department of New Mexico patrolled the Trans-Pecos, the rebel spymaster knew they would likely stick to the primary roads, being unfamiliar with the region's more obscure trails. He had learned these secondary routes firsthand while scouting for the U.S. Army in the late 1840s and while working as a chain carrier on a number of Presidio County land surveys in the 1850s. After striking the Rio Grande, Skillman's group crossed over to Presidio del Norte rather than traveling on the Texas side of the river and risking detection by Union scouts.[24]

Passing through Presidio del Norte, the spy party proceeded up the Rio Grande. Arriving at the village of Aguas Calientes, most of the men went into camp to wait while Skillman and Joe Leaton continued upstream. Leaton was a man of some notoriety in the region. In October 1861 he inflamed regional tensions when he and five Confederate soldiers from Fort Davis, Texas, kidnapped Frederick Wulff, a Union sympathizer and alleged spy, in Presidio del Norte. The rebels got into a firefight with local residents and exchanged fifty shots, during which two Confederate soldiers and one Mexican died. Leaton subsequently escaped back to Texas and his home at Fort Leaton, Texas. Such violent confrontations were becoming all too common in the wartime Trans-Pecos.[25]

By December 2, 1862, Leaton and Skillman arrived in El Paso del Norte, Mexico, where they rendezvoused with secessionist exiles. During his three-day stay in El Paso del Norte, Skillman consulted six individuals about military operations in the Department of New Mexico. Two of these men, Guadalupe Miranda and James H. Lucas, had been prosperous merchants in Mesilla, New Mexico, when the war started. Other informants included John Gillett, a previous resident of Franklin, and two of Skillman's former neighbors at Concordia, Texas: José Flores and Hugh Stephenson. Stephenson, one of the wealthiest men in El Paso County, owned the land upon which Fort Fillmore, New Mexico, was situated, as well as a lucrative mine in the Organ Mountains near Las Cruces, New Mexico. He reportedly used some of his personal fortune to bankroll exile operations in El Paso del Norte.[26]

In a report to his superiors, Skillman vouched for his sources' reliability, "all of whom I had known before, and believe to be men of high intelligence, good information and truthfulness." The spymaster's informants, however, provided intelligence of mixed quality. On one hand, they were correct in their estimate that General Carleton's forces in the Department of New Mexico did not exceed three thousand men. On the other hand, their opinion that Carleton would soon evacuate El Paso County, Texas, and Mesilla, New Mexico, and retreat westward was erroneous.[27]

While gathering intelligence during his visit to El Paso del Norte, Skillman was also spreading misinformation. The crafty agent planted several stories, including one that a Confederate expedition of four to six thousand troops would soon be leaving San Antonio in a bid to recapture the Southwest. Lt. Albert H. French of the Union army, who returned to El Paso County in early December 1862 from a three-month-long trip transporting rebel prisoners of war to Fort Clark, Texas, questioned the reliability of these rumors. French remarked that although John Baylor was "reported as being ordered to raise six regiments for a certain expedition [to the Trans-Pecos and beyond], I know he has not anything to feed them on or money to buy supplies." French said that besides Native Americans, the country between Fort Quitman and Fort Clark was completely deserted. The first settlement he encountered was at Pedro Pinto, Texas, seven miles west of Fort Clark.[28]

A second rumor circulating around this time warned that "the gang of secessionists at El Paso [del Norte]" planned to attack the Union supply depot at

Franklin. The rebel invasion stories alarmed not only the diminutive Union force in the Trans-Pecos but also local Tejanos, who vividly recalled the violent clashes with Confederate soldiers only five months earlier. Shortly after Skillman's tale began making the rounds, Mexican Americans in Socorro, Ysleta, and San Elizario panicked and a general stampede ensued, with many families fleeing across the Rio Grande to safety in Mexico.[29]

In response to the rumor, General West ordered Maj. William McMullen, First Infantry, California Volunteers, and his men to reinforce the federal depot and calm Hispanic residents. "Let the people keep cool; try and instill in them some sort of confidence," West remarked. "It is really amusing that one man, Skillman, has frightened them." McMullen's efforts produced the desired effect. "The appearance of our troops has quieted the fears of the people to a great extent," the major observed, but "few [Tejanos] are now willing to acknowledge that any alarm was felt although a heavy stampede has taken place."[30]

When not busy soothing Mexican American anxieties, McMullen was keeping Henry Skillman under surveillance. By December 5, 1862, Skillman had concluded his interviews in El Paso del Norte, and, "having learned all [he] could hope for," the spymaster and his men departed for San Antonio. During their return trip Skillman's group stopped at Presidio del Norte, Mexico, where they attempted "to capture and convey into Texas certain American citizens temporarily sojourning in that town." The attempted kidnap victims in Presidio del Norte were either Union sympathizers or persons involved in a local feud between Confederate agent John Burgess and Edward Hall.[31]

A Scotsman born in 1821, Edward Hall and his wife Juana lived at Fort Leaton, Texas, across the Rio Grande from Presidio del Norte. The Halls employed tenant farmers to work the fields next to their fort. Juana, born in 1812, and her first husband, Ben Leaton, had established Fort Leaton in 1848, near the mouth of Alamito Creek. Skillman associate Joe Leaton was a son from Juana's marriage with Ben.[32]

In the summer of 1861 Ed and Juana Hall borrowed $1,707.46 from Burgess. John Burgess, born in 1824, originally hailed from Virginia. Burgess was a freighter, farmer, army contractor, and local Confederate agent. As collateral for their loan, the Halls offered their real estate in Texas, which included Fort Leaton and three thousand adjacent acres of rich farmland. When Burgess's loan came due at the end of 1862, Ed and Juana Hall defaulted. They refused to vacate Fort Leaton, and "the situation was left to simmer unhappily for years."[33]

As conditions in the war-torn region grew increasingly unsettled, a number of secessionists and Union men in Texas's Big Bend country moved across the river to Presidio del Norte and safe haven in Mexico, which tolerated the volatile mix because its merchants were making money from both sides. Notable rebels in Presidio del Norte were John Spencer and John Burgess, the latter known locally as "a violent and overbearing man." Northern sympathizers included William F. Hagelsieb and Milton Faver, who was known as "a quiet, prudent and silent man, faithful in his sentiments." Faver, a Missourian, was a freighter on the Chihuahua and Santa Fe Trails and became the first large-scale cattleman in the Big Bend.[34]

Back upstream in El Paso del Norte, Confederate exiles were welcoming a new member, a Union deserter named Phelps. Major McMullen immediately ordered Phelps's arrest. When Capt. E. B. Willis's troops crossed the river and seized the deserter, a crowd of secessionist refugees quickly confronted them. Mexican officials, intimidated by the armed exiles, refused to surrender Phelps, and the federal troops withdrew. General Carleton was discovering that he had little control over rebel Texans threatening his department from neutral Mexico.[35]

The Department of New Mexico repeatedly requested that Mexican authorities take some action regarding the injurious activities of Skillman and the Texan refugees in El Paso del Norte. Although the Mexican replies offered understanding and assistance, ultimately little changed. Fed up, McMullen took matters into his own hands. In late December he ordered his men into Mexico to apprehend several secessionists. The rebel agents, however, eluded capture, and the major's actions came close to sparking an international incident.[36]

In defending his actions, the major noted that Mexico was "permitting the *armed* enemies of the United States Government to establish an outpost in the town of El Paso [del Norte]"—enemies such as Skillman—"who [were] endeavoring to overthrow the Government." McMullen pointed out that the Confederates were also conducting cross-border kidnappings. He mentioned the W. W. Mills incident in 1861, when Mexican officials in El Paso del Norte had stood idle as rebel soldiers grabbed Mills and hauled him across the river to a prison in Texas.[37]

In his reply to McMullen, El Paso del Norte prefect José Uranga denied that Mexican authorities had sanctioned Mills's kidnapping. The prefect reminded McMullen that all Texan exiles had a right to asylum in Mexico—the same asylum "to which every citizen of the world is entitled to . . . whatever may be the party they belong to." Uranga concluded by restating official Mexican policy towards the American Civil War: "In my judgment we must remain neutral in your present difficulties." Neutrality aside, from 1862 to 1867 Mexico had its hands full dealing with an invasion by Emperor Napoleon III of France. By early 1865 Napoleon's forces had occupied much of the country. Dealing with rebel spies and exiles was the least of Uranga's worries. For General Carleton, the message was clear. Despite his best efforts, the question of what to do about Confederate Texans operating south of the border remained unresolved.[38]

CHAPTER 2

By early January 1863 the commander of the Department of New Mexico had calibrated a new, multifaceted strategy to deal with the rebel presence in Mexico. General Carleton's first approach was to cultivate stronger regional ties with the governor of Chihuahua, Luis Terrazas. Carleton's subordinate, General West, commanding the District of Arizona, advised Carleton to send an emissary to Chihuahua to try and reach an understanding with Terrazas. West told Carleton that "the impunity with which the rebels continue to plot and practice against us in El Paso [del Norte]" was unacceptable. Something had to be done immediately. After initial discussions with Union emissary Maj. David Fergusson of the First Cavalry, California Volunteers, Governor Terrazas pledged to curtail Confederate abuse of Mexican neutrality.[1]

The second part of Carleton's plan was to strengthen Union intelligence operations in Mexico. While in Chihuahua, Fergusson enlisted local businessman and Kentucky native Reuben Creel as a confidential agent for the Department of New Mexico. Creel was to report on developments in Mexico and Texas. In return for agreeing to become a Union asset in Chihuahua, Creel eventually received an appointment as the U.S. consul for that city, which included a regular stipend.[2]

Soon, a much-improved Union intelligence network began taking shape. M. M. Kimmey, Reuben Creel, and Henry Cuniffe, the U.S. consuls in Monterrey, Chihuahua, and El Paso del Norte, respectively, began working in concert and sharing information. One area Unionist assisting the consul at El Paso del Norte was David R. Diffendorfer. Downstream at Presidio del Norte, Union sources included Milton Faver, William F. Hagelsieb, and a band of friendly Apaches. Hagelsieb, a German, was Creel's primary point of contact in the region. In addition to the above measures, Carleton instigated the use of a secret cipher code that was used in the department's more sensitive, top-secret letters.[3]

Carleton acted none too soon implementing his new strategy. In March 1863 Henry Skillman returned to West Texas for several weeks. Reuben Creel informed the general that the friendly Apaches had spotted the rebel spymaster and twenty-five men on Cibolo Creek in the Big Bend, north of Presidio del Norte, Mexico. Another report said that this group numbered sixteen and included Tigua Indian scouts Bernardo and Simón Olguín. The Olguín brothers, formerly residents of Ysleta, Texas, had joined other secessionist exiles in Mexico when the Union army occupied the Trans-Pecos. While keeping an eye on Union operations, Skillman continued spreading rumors of an imminent Confederate invasion.[4]

Skillman's spy company also boasted a new intelligence asset; a close friend and former stage-coaching associate named Tom Rife. In January 1863 Confederate military authorities placed Rife on temporary detached service from his cavalry unit as part of Skillman's group. The following year Rife received a permanent assignment to the spy company. In requesting Rife's transfer to his group, the spymaster noted that he needed "not only good men, but good frontiersmen," adding that Rife's "perfect knowledge of the upper country [West Texas]" made his service invaluable to the Southern war effort. Indeed, the combination of Skillman's and Rife's considerable surveillance abilities posed an increased threat to Union operations in the region.[5]

General Carleton well understood the harm that Skillman's group was causing the Department of New Mexico. In the spring of 1863 the general again requested that the governor of Chihuahua prevent Confederates from using Mexico as a safe haven from which to spy on the United States. In his reply Governor Terrazas promised Carleton that he would take prompt action to prevent a reoccurrence. Despite such assurances, rebel agents continued to enjoy free access through Mexico. Terrazas penned a similar letter to General West in May 1863 that amounted to "nothing." West told Carleton, "These Mexican diplomatists are as velvety as cats," talking much, but saying nothing. West said that his patience was exhausted, pledging that if he caught a rebel in Mexican territory spying on Union operations, he would hang him high "and apologize for it afterwards."[6]

While Carleton took the Confederate spying seriously, he considered Skillman's recurring invasion rumors akin to the boy who cried wolf too many times. The Union general wrote, "At this moment I consider such probabilities so remote as to justify me in employing the troops under my command in chastising hostile tribes of Indians." Certainly, the Native American threat was of immediate concern, but Carleton was too nonchalant in his assessment of Texan intentions. In fact, the rebels were actively formulating plans to recapture the Southwest.[7]

In January 1863 the Confederate commander of Texas, Maj. Gen. John Bankhead Magruder, endorsed a two-pronged invasion of the Department of New Mexico. One force would travel along the Canadian River through the Texas

Panhandle and sever the Union supply lines to Fort Union, New Mexico. The second group would move through the Trans-Pecos, capturing Fort Bliss and Franklin. The major general discussed this plan with Gen. Douglas H. Cooper, former Choctaw Indian agent and commander of the Confederate Indian Brigade. Magruder appointed Col. Spruce M. Baird to command the expedition, which was to proceed through Texas and New Mexico to Arizona and "make a lodgment in that country." Although Baird, a prominent secessionist from New Mexico, was "an officer and a gentleman of much merit," as of January 1863 he still had not raised the necessary troops for such a movement.[8]

Another plan put forth by Confederate captain John Pulliam, Company B of Hardeman's Regiment, proposed disrupting vital supply lines to the Department of New Mexico. Pulliam wrote to Brig. Gen. Samuel Bell Maxey from Camp Garland in Indian Territory offering to take sixty men and launch guerilla raids on wagon trains traveling the Santa Fe Trail from Fort Leavenworth, Kansas, to Fort Union, New Mexico. Pulliam suggested that his group concentrate their attacks in the vicinity of the Arkansas River and its junction with the Cimarron Cutoff (near Cimarron, Kansas), where the trail left the river heading southwest to Fort Union.[9]

Ultimately, General Magruder put all of these proposals on hold until the Union campaign for control of the Mississippi River was resolved. "The operations of the enemy have, for the present," he wrote, "put a stop to any movements in that direction [the Southwest]." Magruder's superior, Gen. Edmund Kirby Smith, who commanded the Confederacy west of the Mississippi, vetoed any immediate invasion of the Trans-Pecos, New Mexico, and Arizona. Although Kirby Smith appreciated such patriotic efforts, he urgently needed all available rebel troops at "points more exposed to the advance of the enemy," such as the Mississippi River. When Vicksburg and the Mississippi fell to the Union in the summer of 1863, the invasion of the Southwest quickly dropped to a low priority. The federal campaigns at Galveston, Sabine Pass, Brownsville, and the Red River over the next year ensured that it stayed there.[10]

Union offensives in the eastern half of Texas during 1863 and 1864 heightened Confederate concerns that the Department of New Mexico might also launch an attack east of the Pecos River, threatening the state's western flank. In fact, such a prospect did arise in November 1863, when Union forces led by Gen. Nathanial P. Banks captured Brownsville, Texas. Banks wrote to Carleton through U.S. consuls Kimmey and Creel, suggesting a coordinated movement into the interior of Texas.[11]

Although Carleton endorsed Banks's plan in principle, he lacked the men and the resources to participate. Throughout the Civil War, federal troop levels in Arizona, New Mexico, and West Texas rarely exceeded three thousand men. With his forces stretched thin, the Department of New Mexico commander was already unable to address all of the challenges that confronted him, let alone mount an invasion into Texas. Given his limited means, Carleton focused on securing his department and maintaining a defensive posture against the Confederates on his eastern flank.[12]

Carleton stationed guards at Hueco Tanks, east of Franklin, to watch the Upper Road to the Pecos River and San Antonio, and at Fort Quitman on the Rio Grande, to keep an eye on the Lower Road to San Antonio. He also sent a detail of infantry and cavalry under Capt. Nathaniel Pishon, First Cavalry, California Volunteers, from El Paso County to scout the Upper Road to the Guadalupe Mountains and the Pecos River during November and December 1862. Rebel spies, led by Tigua Indian scouts Bernardo and Simón Olguín, shadowed Pishon's movements during part of his trip. Pishon's superior, Maj. William McMullen of the First Infantry, California Volunteers, reported that ongoing activities by the Olguíns and other Confederate agents in the region left "no doubt that all our movements were [being] communicated to the enemy."[13]

Carleton also ordered pickets posted at various points along the Pecos River to watch for rebel forces marching up the watershed. Troops subsequently established several intermittent scouting camps on the Pecos, including one at Horsehead Crossing, located near present-day McCamey, Texas. At this fabled ford, long steeped in western history and legend, several roads converged, including the Comanche War Trail, the Butterfield Overland Mail Road, and the Upper Road from San Antonio.[14]

In late November 1862 General West dispatched the chief of his spy company, Bradford Daily, on a secret mission to Horsehead Crossing. West ordered Daily, Capt. Washington L. Parvin, and ten men from the First Infantry, California Volunteers, to ascertain any recent rebel activity in the area. West directed that while the group was outfitting for their trip at Hart's Mill, Texas, they were to remain "out of sight as much as possible," and he cautioned that "no one . . . must know their business." For his services as Union spymaster, Daily was to receive $6 per day. West told Daily that if he was successful "in obtaining information of the enemy's movements," it would "be of great value to the government," and West would recommend that he receive a pay raise.[15]

The thirty-three-year-old Daily was an Illinois native who had previously worked as a merchant and freighter in Arizona and New Mexico. Daily, like Henry Skillman, had been a stage driver for the Butterfield Overland Mail before the war and was a seasoned frontiersman with an intimate knowledge of the region's geography. In mid-December his spy party arrived at Horsehead and found evidence that a group of fifty mounted Confederates with a wagon had been camping there earlier in the month. This party had subsequently crossed the Pecos River and taken the Overland Mail Road to Fort Stockton, Texas.[16]

To avoid detection, Daily's company set up camp on the east side of the Pecos, a mile and a half below Horsehead. Despite these evasive measures, Daily soon discovered that the rebels had returned to the area and were now following him. Fearing for his party's safety, he immediately crossed to the river's western side where he managed to evade his pursuers. When the spymaster returned to Mesilla just after Christmas, he told General West, "From the fact that the Texans had been in that vicinity the length of time that their signs indicated," they were likely "a scout of the enemy watching our movements" and nothing more. To prevent the Confederates from establishing a permanent outpost at Horsehead, West ordered Col. Kit Carson at Fort Stanton to immediately capture the Confederate company. If the Texans "offer resistance you need no reminder how to act."[17]

On January 15, 1863, Carson sent Lt. William Brady, Lt. L. A. Bargie, and forty-five men to Horsehead Crossing, each supplied with thirty-five days rations and sixty rounds of ammunition, to overhaul the Confederate encampment there. In his report of the scout, Brady claimed to have marched twenty-one miles from the junction of Delaware Creek and the Pecos River (near the Texas–New Mexico line) to Horsehead Crossing in one day. In fact, the actual distance is closer to 140 miles. After reading this report, General West chastised Brady, stating, "I am forced to believe that Lt. Brady never was at Horsehead Crossing, nor that he knows where it is."[18]

In the spring of 1863 Maj. McMullen sent a party of ten citizens from El Paso County to reconnoiter the crossing. The rebels had departed. But Horsehead was only one of two primary Pecos River fords used by the Confederates. The other, fifty miles to the southeast at Fort Lancaster Crossing, on the Lower Road to San Antonio, was also used by the rebels during the war. General West understood the strategic importance of this lower Pecos passage. In November 1862 he had advised General Carleton that "a scout near Fort Lancaster seems to me essential." The scouts did not happen. Because the Union army failed to keep an eye on Lancaster Crossing, it missed a number of rebel forays to and from West Texas and

Mexico, including those by Henry Skillman and his spy company. In March 1863 Skillman's party crossed the Pecos at Lancaster Crossing and proceeded west along the Lower Road to Leon Holes. Here they turned south onto the Puerto del Paisano Road. Upon reaching the Rio Grande, the party crossed into Mexico at Presidio del Norte.[19]

At Presidio del Norte, Skillman conferred with Confederate agent Jarvis Hubbell. Before the war, Hubbell had served as postmaster at El Paso, Texas, and as the surveyor for El Paso County. Skillman told Hubbell that he was making a reconnaissance of the Trans-Pecos for a pending expedition from San Antonio to recapture the Southwest. Hubbell informed Skillman that should Texas officials require any provisions for the expedition, John Burgess, the primary rebel contact in Presidio del Norte, was willing to assist. During his March visit to the Big Bend, Skillman had also established a temporary customs house at Spencer's Ranch (now Presidio), Texas, at the Rio Grande crossing to Presidio del Norte. His men collected taxes from wagon trains hauling salt to Mexico from Juan Cordona Lake near Horsehead Crossing.[20]

As part of his ongoing efforts to keep current on Skillman's movements in the Trans-Pecos and Mexico, in the spring of 1863 General West dispatched spies over the Lower Road to Forts Davis and Stockton. The Union agents reported the route was "overgrown with weeds, and that no wagons or troops have passed over it" since a small Union detachment the previous December. West's men, however, failed to investigate the intersection of the Lower Road and the Puerto del Paisano Road at Leon Holes (nine miles west of Fort Stockton), thus missing Skillman's tracks.[21]

In March 1863 Union intelligence sources reported that beyond Skillman's occasional forays, there was scant Confederate presence in West Texas and the Trans-Pecos. Chihuahua consul Reuben Creel correctly observed that Fort Clark, Texas, on the Lower Road to San Antonio, now served as the rebels' western defensive perimeter. Creel wrote, "The whole line from El Paso down to Fort Clark is now a desert given up to Indian and the wolf."[22]

Despite the intermittent nature of Skillman's trips, General Carleton was rapidly tiring of his visits to the Department of New Mexico. Carleton instructed West to develop plans for a rapid-strike, mobile force that could intercept and capture rebel parties passing through Fort Davis and Presidio del Norte. West was to ascertain how many men and what supplies would be needed and which routes would be the best to follow. Carleton said a detailed report on the matter would provide him a clearer understanding of how to respond to future incidents.[23]

Regular Union scouts to Horsehead Crossing and the Pecos River from April through June 1863 revealed no signs of Skillman or Indians. Then, on July 19, 1863, two hundred Apaches came close to annihilating Lt. Juan Marques, First New Mexico Volunteers, and his scouting party who were returning to Fort Stanton following a reconnaissance of Horsehead Crossing. During a six-hour fight with the Apaches on the Hondo River, Marques and his men ran out of ammunition. Outnumbered thirteen to one, the soldiers made a frantic dash for the riverbank with the warriors in close pursuit. Hiding beneath the Hondo's tall bluffs, the troops slowly wound their way upstream, finally evading their pursuers. Although the men suffered one fatality and several were wounded, they had "fought well." Maj. Joseph Smith, the commander of Fort Stanton, called their escape "a miracle." When a subsequent patrol came upon the battle site, it found articles of clothing "saturated with blood" and "pools of blood . . . on the ground occupied by the Indians."[24]

During another July reconnaissance from Fort Stanton to the Pecos, the commanding officer, Second Lt. Elisha E. Latimer, First Cavalry, California Volunteers, kept a "sharp lookout for Indians," fearing them more than the Texans. He believed his "detachment [was] much too small for the [scouting] duty." Latimer's superior agreed, and at the end of July he cancelled the Union picket at Horsehead. Major Smith at Fort Stanton believed that the camp on the Pecos was not safe for fewer than a company of men, "on account of the Indians running off their stock."[25]

Smith claimed that he lacked sufficient men to keep a permanent detail downriver in Texas, but he vowed to keep scouting the Rio Hondo to its junction with the Pecos. "At such time as it will be safe"—that is, when the Apaches were less menacing—the major would resume the patrols south to Horsehead. One additional reconnaissance from Stanton during October 1863 went as far as the Pecos's junction with Delaware Creek near the Texas–New Mexico state line. Ultimately though, the fort, with its manpower stretched to the breaking point, could not protect its own patrols.[26]

By this time Henry Skillman frequently evaded Union pickets by using Lancaster Crossing on the Pecos. He made two more trips to West Texas in 1863, one in early August and another in mid-November. In August Skillman consulted with Confederate agents at Presidio del Norte about waylaying Milton Faver and William Hagelsieb, the Union's two primary informants in the Big Bend region. Area sources warned Hagelsieb to be on his guard and to take extra precautions. The November expedition was motivated by rebel concerns that General

Carleton's forces might make a move east to the Pecos River and beyond. Maj. Andrew G. Dickinson in San Antonio ordered his Confederate spies westward to gather the latest intelligence on Union operations in the Department of Mexico. One spy company, composed of Tom Rife and six men, scouted the Lower Road to Fort Stockton, while a second detachment under Skillman reconnoitered the Upper Road to Franklin, Texas, and El Paso del Norte, Mexico.[27]

While visiting San Ygnacio, Mexico, in 1863, Skillman disseminated the story that he and his men were going to burn Hart's Mill and kidnap General West, the commander of the District of Arizona. Another rumor planted by the wily spymaster claimed that troops from Confederate Texas were in the Trans-Pecos at Fort Davis. Area residents, however, had learned by now that Skillman's visits were for spying and did not portend an imminent rebel incursion. One local said that despite the numerous and spurious invasion rumors over the preceding year, some people still raised "a great hullabaloo" whenever Skillman appeared, "as in these times it don't take much stretching to make a frog bigger than a mastodon." After spending several weeks in the region collecting information on Carleton's forces, the spymaster returned to San Antonio.[28]

By January 1864 Skillman was in Houston, receiving a new assignment from General Magruder, whose intelligence operatives in West Texas had heard rumors of the aforementioned advance by Union generals Nathanial Banks and James Carleton on the interior of Texas. These reports soon landed on Magruder's desk. The Confederate commander's instinct told him that Carleton's California volunteers would not be ready to move in the near future, but he had "no doubt that they will come sooner or later, and some time probably this spring [1864]." When Department of New Mexico troops did move east of the Pecos, General Magruder wanted advance warning. The logical person to provide such notice was Henry Skillman.[29]

At his meeting in Houston with Skillman, Magruder directed his spymaster to complete several tasks in West Texas. Skillman's first order was to compile a map of the routes in the region best suited for moving large numbers of troops. If, at some point, forces became available for a rebel invasion of the Trans-Pecos and beyond, Magruder wanted a logistical plan for such a movement.[30]

After determining the most suitable troop arteries across West Texas, Skillman was to move onto El Paso del Norte and establish a Mexican base of operations from which "to keep an observation of the enemy." En route to El Paso, Skillman was to investigate the troublesome rumor that Union captain Albert H. French had recently "visited Fort Lancaster [on the Pecos River] and made preparations for 3,000 men and that arrangements were being made for the advance" of Carleton's California troops.[31]

Financing Skillman's operation required special arrangements. In order to purchase information and supplies during his expedition, Skillman needed hard currency, as Confederate paper was not welcome in El Paso del Norte or in the Trans-Pecos. To raise the necessary funds, rebel authorities authorized the sale in Mexico of "a sufficient quantity of cotton to pay Captain Skillman and his company $500 in specie [gold or silver]."[32]

After meeting with Magruder, Skillman journeyed west to San Antonio to consult with Col. John Salmon "Rip" Ford, Confederate commander of western Texas. The spymaster spent February in the Alamo City, where he recruited a team of ten men and outfitted the expedition. The group included associates of Skillman from his time in San Antonio and El Paso County, most notably Tom Rife, "Clown" Garner, William Ford, and Jarvis Hubbell. The rebel spy party left San Antonio on March 6, 1864, en route for Presidio del Norte. As the reconnaissance party worked its way west, it collected information to support Magruder's projected movement of Confederate troops to West Texas. Skillman reached the Rio Grande on April 3 and went into camp at Spencer's Ranch, Texas, opposite Presidio del Norte.[33]

With Skillman embarked on his new mission, Magruder turned next to implementing defensive measures against a Union advance from the Trans-Pecos. The Confederate commander directed Colonel Ford to draft a plan to "occupy the Devils River with a considerable force to stop the further progress [of approaching Union forces] and defeat them." After carefully reviewing the topography of the Devils River, Ford ultimately selected Pecan Springs, above Camp Hudson, and a second site upstream at Beaver Lake (near present-day Juno, Texas) as the best places to defend against Carleton's troops. In late January 1864 Ford ordered his subordinates to keep an eye on the Lower Road from San Antonio to El Paso for approaching federal troops. In early February Major Alexander and seventy-five men scouted westward from Fort Inge at Uvalde, Texas, to the Devils and Pecos Rivers. Alexander's expedition and subsequent scouts that month detected no signs of the enemy.[34]

During the same month Ford ordered Fort Inge's commander, Maj. Thomas Riordan, to move his defensive line west to Fort Clark, near present-day Brackettville, Texas. Upon arriving at Fort Clark, the major reported he had "no protection whatever" and only twelve effective men scattered over a fifteen-mile range. Indians and Mexican marauders were driving off all the stock in the region, and Riordan lacked sufficient forces to pursue them. Riordan's picket remained at the outpost for only a short time. By the fall of 1864 regional lawlessness and disorder forced Confederate postal authorities to curtail local mail service because "there are no troops at Fort Clark, and it is considered hazardous to go there with any kind of conveyance whatever." For the remainder of the war, Confederate mail went no further west than Uvalde.[35]

Colonel Ford's patrols found no traces of the enemy because as of late March 1864, Carleton's California Volunteers were still in the Trans-Pecos. Despite repeated requests from his superiors to make a coordinated movement deeper into Texas with General Banks, Carleton was unable to move east of the Pecos River. The lack of adequate manpower, supplies, and transportation in the Department of New Mexico for such an expedition was "sorely felt." Carleton estimated that it would cost $300,000 in specie (gold or silver) to fund such an invasion and requested that Henry Halleck, General-in-Chief of the U.S. Army, make said funds available "to meet these pressing necessities." To save time and distance on the journey east from El Paso County, Carleton recommended securing permission from the governor of Chihuahua to cross the Rio Grande and travel through Mexico to Presidio del Norte.[36]

Carleton's primary objective was to cut the San Antonio–Presidio del Norte Road, thereby blocking Confederate access to supplies and information from Chihuahua. The Union commander recommended making Fort Leaton, Texas, his base of operations. Fort Leaton was near Spencer's Ranch and the Rio Grande crossing to Presidio del Norte. After securing the crossing, the federal troops would continue east to Eagle Pass, Texas. If developments prevented Carleton's men from reaching Eagle Pass, at the very least they would have eliminated a vital rebel supply route to Chihuahua.[37]

While Carleton waited to hear back from Halleck, he sent out several scouting parties. One group under Capt. Peter W. L. Plympton traveled into Chihuahua to make inquiries about purchasing transportation, foodstuffs, and forage for an expeditionary force. In the event that the governor of Chihuahua denied Union forces access through Mexico, Carleton ordered a second detail, commanded by Captain French, to reconnoiter the Lower Road to Fort Davis, Texas, reporting on the availability of water and grazing. Before sending any sizeable force into the field, the Union general wanted advance information regarding conditions along the route. Upon reaching Fort Davis, the captain and his men were to scout southward to Presidio del Norte and the Rio Grande. Throughout his reconnaissance, French was to keep a sharp lookout for the "notorious rebel and spy" Henry Skillman.[38]

On April 3, 1864, French left his base at San Elizario, Texas, with twenty-five men and rations for twenty days. During their assessment of the region's natural resources with an eye toward supporting a military expedition, the scouting party found adequate forage for livestock but judged that some of the regional springs might pose a problem. While a number of waterholes could support up to two companies of troops, others had enough for only one company.[39]

At Fort Davis the scouting company left the San Antonio Road and took the trail leading south to Presidio del Norte. After traveling forty miles, they intersected the Puerto del Paisano Road from Leon Holes to del Norte. At this intersection, near San Esteban Waterhole, French discerned signs of recent activity, noting "some 18 or 20 horse and mule tracks." The Union troops proceeded south with great caution, deploying their spies to scout ahead. On April 14, 1864, they reached Alamo Spring on Alamito Creek, fifteen miles above the Rio Grande. At the spring French discovered an inscription on a cottonwood tree indicating that Henry Skillman and his spy party had passed through eleven days earlier.[40]

French's scouts continued south along Alamito Creek to the Rio Grande. They found Skillman's spy party encamped in a "monte," or brush thicket, at Spencer's Ranch, a quarter of a mile east of the Presidio del Norte crossing. After the scouts returned, French moved his men down Alamito Creek. On April 15, shortly after one in the morning, the Union captain attacked the slumbering Confederate camp. French's company killed Skillman and a man named McMullen outright, mortally wounded two, and captured four prisoners. William Ford and a wounded Tom Rife escaped across the river into Mexico.[41]

General Carleton ordered the four captured spies, John Dowling, Jarvis Hubbell, Peter Allen, and "Clown" Garner taken to Santa Fe, where Maj. John C. McFerran interrogated them on May 23, 1864. All of them lied in their interviews, and some provided false names, birthdates, and birthplaces. They claimed that they had accompanied Skillman westward not to spy but to attend to personal and "private" matters. None knew what Skillman's mission was. In truth, Jarvis Hubbell was a rebel agent collaborating with John Burgess of Presidio del Norte on the Confederate reinvasion of the Trans-Pecos. William Ford, who escaped to Mexico in the April 15 attack, had been Hubbell's friend, business partner, and next-door-neighbor in San Elizario, Texas. Several hours after the ambush, Ford appeared in his underwear at Burgess's home in Presidio del Norte seeking shelter.[42]

The rebel scouting party had planned to move upriver by April 19 to observe Union operations in El Paso County. Earlier on the evening of French's attack, Skillman had visited Presidio del Norte. The spymaster had been at Spencer's

Ranch for almost two weeks, waiting to meet someone coming from Chihuahua. Skillman told his men he had misgivings about this latest trip, that something was odd and did not feel right. On the night of the attack he had gone to bed fully clothed. During the two weeks they were in camp at the crossing, Skillman's company "levied taxes" on Mexican salt caravans crossing the river, pocketing all the funds they collected. Many of these wagon trains harvested their salt from Juan Cordona Lake, near Horsehead Crossing on the Pecos River.[43]

The prefect of Presidio del Norte subsequently complained to Captain French about the rebels' extortion. The situation was amusing, considering that the Confederacy's jurisdiction in the region was questionable at best. The captain assured Prefect José Merino that Union troops would not molest Mexican citizens or their salt caravans. Ironically, Albert French, the man responsible for Skillman's death, later "persuaded" the spymaster's widow, Rufina, to sell her and her late husband's property located in Survey 6 at Concordia Ranch near El Paso to him for one dollar. French subsequently sold the same parcel for four hundred dollars.[44]

With Skillman's death General Carleton had dealt a serious blow to Confederate spy operations in Mexico and the Trans-Pecos. General Magruder's Confederate intelligence network west of the Pecos River never fully recovered. Although others, such as James W. Magoffin, a fervent secessionist and former post sutler at Fort Bliss, offered their services as spies, no one could fill Skillman's shoes. Carleton had eliminated one of Texas's most potent threats to his department.[45]

* * *

As one menace faded, another quickly took form in Indian Territory and the Texas Panhandle. A month after Skillman's death "a band of guerillas" attacked several freighting trains on the plains east of New Mexico. The first raid took place on May 21, 1864, in the vicinity of Cedar Spring and Cold Spring, on the Cimarron branch of the Santa Fe Trail (in present-day Oklahoma). During this attack the bandits stole approximately seventy mules and $10,000 from a caravan belonging to Manuel Antonio Otero, a prominent New Mexico merchant, freighter, and government contractor. Otero was the fourth-wealthiest resident of New Mexico, and he and his family were very active in the Santa Fe trade. On May 25, some sixty miles to the south, these same "rogues," described as forty-eight Americans, waylaid fourteen ox wagons at Palo Duro, a campsite on Palo Duro Creek in the Texas Panhandle. The wagon train belonged to José Ygnacio Esquibel and Félix García.[46]

Félix García was a Comanchero who traded with the Comanches in Texas and had been dealing with Native Americans for a number of years. In March 1856 the Bureau of Indian Affairs approved García's license to trade with the Pueblo Indians. The site on Palo Duro Creek, also known as Skull Creek, was twenty miles from Adobe Walls, the old trading post established by William Bent and Ceran St. Vrain on the Canadian River in the 1840s. Bent and St. Vrain attempted to capitalize on Comanche trade in the region, but their efforts ultimately failed, and by 1850 they had abandoned the post and ceded the trade in Texas to Comancheros from New Mexico such as García. Military reports noted that Comanche and Kiowa Indians occasionally camped at a site named Palo Duro along Palo Duro Creek and that New Mexico Comancheros visited this camp to trade.[47]

After killing one of Esquibel and García's herders during their initial attack, the Anglo desperados robbed the freighters of their clothing, provisions, and livestock. In a report on the raids, New Mexico governor Henry Connelly speculated that the thieves were from Franklin, Texas. Connelly remarked, "I should not be surprised if some of the correspondents of Mr. Skillman about El Paso, had something to do with this robbery." Even in death, Henry Skillman cast a long shadow.[48]

In fact, this gang was not from El Paso del Norte but from northern Texas. The group, led by brothers James and John Reynolds, consisted of twenty-two men, not forty-eight as stated in the reports. James Reynolds, who fancied himself a guerilla leader in the mold of William Quantrill, had escaped from a Denver jail early in the war and made his way down to Texas. The impetus for Reynolds's expedition in the spring of 1864 is disputed. Some participants claimed that the trip's purpose was "to recruit for the Confederate army, by order of (or permission of) General [D. H.] Cooper."[49]

However, another member of the group, Thomas Holliman, said that they had a far different mission. According to Holliman, the men comprising Reynolds's outfit were not Confederate soldiers or Texas state troops but were "brush men": draft dodgers who had been hiding out in the woods and thickets of North Texas for several months to avoid being conscripted into military service. James Reynolds persuaded these fellows to accompany him on a trip north to Colorado because "it was out of the war; times were good there and we could make money and not be molested by the draft." Holliman said they "took rations for a few days only," as they "feared the Confederate authorities would suspect [they] were going out of the country" and confine them. His fear of being detained infers that this excursion was not officially sanctioned. If it had been, there would have been no concern about rebel authorities. Whatever the truth of the matter, it is clear that the group spent considerably more time robbing than they did recruiting.[50]

During the second week of April 1864, Reynolds's band left Fort Belknap, Texas, for their first sortie. After attacking Otero's, Esquibel's, and García's wagon trains in May, the group apparently decided not to press its luck and returned to Texas, reaching Young County in June 1864. Later that same month, nine of the twenty-two men, including the Reynolds brothers, set out for Colorado for more mischief and mayhem. The other thirteen declined to accompany them. After plundering ranches, travelers, and a stagecoach, the nine were finally cornered by Union troops in August near Cañon City, Colorado.[51]

Five prisoners, including leader James Reynolds, were escorted to Fort Lyon, Colorado, to stand trial. Acting on orders from Col. John M. Chivington, the prisoners were "butchered" by troops of the Third Colorado Cavalry, "and their bodies, with shackles on their legs, were left unburied on the plains, and yet remain there unless devoured by the beasts of prey that don't wear shoulder straps [i.e., soldiers]." U.S. Attorney S. E. Browne reported that "when the news was first brought to Chivington of the death of these persons and the manner of their death, he sneeringly remarked, . . . 'I told the guard when they left that if they did not kill those fellows, I would play thunder with them.'" Lt. Joseph Cramer, who was part of the escort to Fort Lyon, said that the colonel "had issued an order that he would hang any 'son of a bitch' who would bury their bodies or bones." Chivington subsequently destroyed many of the official records relating to the Reynolds Gang. In November 1864, a few months after ordering the murder of these prisoners, Chivington led the infamous Sand Creek Massacre in eastern Colorado, during which his troops slaughtered more than 150 Cheyenne and Arapaho Indians, many of them women, children, and the elderly.[52]

For the remainder of the war, the greatest menace facing the Department of New Mexico in the northern borderlands came not from rebel robbers but from Kiowa and Comanche Indians attacking wagon trains on the Santa Fe Trail between Fort Leavenworth, Kansas, and Fort Union, New Mexico. During 1864 Native Americans from the Texas Panhandle were committing depredations along the supply routes and then returning to their camps along Palo Duro Creek and the Canadian River. In the summer of that year, the tribes went on the warpath, decimating the freighting business to and from New Mexico. In July and August, Kiowa and Comanche warriors killed twenty-three teamsters and made off with hundreds of mules and oxen. The two tribes were jealous that U.S. Indian agents had appeased raiding Cheyenne and Arapahos with a generous allocation of goods while they had received nothing.[53]

During one incident in early August, seventy Kiowa and Comanche warriors peacefully approached a wagon camp and after visiting a short while, suddenly attacked their hosts. The raiders killed five Americans but let the Mexican freighters go free, even providing them with a yoke of oxen with which to get home. The Indians told the Mexicans "to go back to New Mexico as they did not wish to kill them, but that they would kill every white man that came on the road." After learning of this attack, General Carleton angrily observed, "The discrimination which the Comanches have frequently made in favor of the [Mexican] people, and against Anglo-Americans cannot be regarded in any other light than as an insult to the Government."[54]

In mid-October officers from Forts Sumner and Bascom learned that three thousand Comanches and Kiowas were encamped east of Bascom, at Palo Duro, in Texas. Comancheros returning from a trading expedition at Palo Duro reported seeing large herds of American horses and mules at the Indian camp, many them branded "U.S." General Carleton ordered Col. Kit Carson to mount a retaliatory expedition to teach the depredating tribes a lesson. On November 6, 1864, Carson's force of 410 men, composed of soldiers, Apaches, and Ute Indians, left Fort Bascom and marched east into Texas, along the north side of the Canadian River.[55]

On November 25 a vast force of Comanche and Kiowa warriors attacked Carson's command at Bent's old trading post at Adobe Walls, south of modern Spearman, Texas. (Estimates range between one thousand and three thousand warriors involved.) In a series of running engagements lasting from morning until evening, the two sides fought fiercely. Despite the Comanches' and Kiowas' overwhelming numerical superiority, they were unable to overrun the Union force. Three important factors saved Carson's command: the wise advice of his Apache and Ute scouts, the protective walls of the old adobe fort, and two mountain howitzers ably manned by Lt. George Pettis's crew. They otherwise might have met the same fate as Lt. Col. George Armstrong Custer's expedition twelve years later. Although the battle at Adobe Walls sent a strong message to raiding Native Americans, the persistent Indian threat compelled General Carleton to commit considerable resources and manpower to protecting his supply lines for the remainder of the war. Even as late as May 1865, one-third of the Department of New Mexico's troops were on the plains providing escort to wagon trains and teamsters.[56]

While Comanches, Kiowas, and Apaches remained the greatest menace to department operations, Confederate spies in West Texas and Mexico monitoring Union activities continued to prove troublesome. Rebel agents en route to and from Texas, Chihuahua, Sonora, and California regularly crossed the Rio Grande at Presidio del Norte. Throughout the remainder of the war, the Big Bend region in the southern borderlands remained volatile and unsettled. In late May 1864 the U.S. consul in Chihuahua, Reuben Creel, alerted General Carleton: "Constant correspondence goes on from Paso [El Paso del Norte] to Texas, through this place [Chihuahua]. They are watching you and all your movements are reported. As this is neutral ground, this cannot be prevented."[57]

The following month a "grave disorder" occurred at Presidio del Norte when forty Texas desperados rode into town. The party, "well armed and mounted but moneyless," refused to reveal who they were, who commanded them, and what their purpose was. The group, a "very bad class of men," received aid from del Norte resident and Confederate agent John Burgess.[58]

Soon after, a violent firefight involving the newly arrived Texans erupted in the streets, "wherein a Mr. [John] Burgess and a Mr. [Edward] Hall were prominent parties." Creel noted that "the people of the Presidio were entertained with one of those scenes so common in Texas, but so little relished in Mexico." Three years after Burgess loaned Hall more than $1,700, the debt remained unpaid, and Burgess was still unable to take possession of Fort Leaton, Texas, and its adjacent farmland. Fed up with waiting, Burgess attempted to flush Hall out into the open and kill him. Moving door to door, Burgess and his rebel brigands attacked the homes of Mexican citizens in Presidio del Norte. Hall barely escaped death by taking "refuge in the house of the highest authority in the place; the result of all this was the wounding of the wife of Aguilirio Rodriguez with a ball [bullet]."[59]

Although no one perished in the spirited exchange of gunfire, petrified locals nonetheless demanded that Mexican authorities strengthen local law enforcement to prevent Lone Star ruffians from bullying their community in the future. Despite such pleas, Burgess and his associates persisted in their lawless actions. Secret agents continued their regular traffic through the Big Bend. In September 1864 Reuben Creel alerted General Carleton that "straggling [Confederate] Texans are constantly coming and going [through Chihuahua and Presidio del Norte]," and their "object appears to be, to obtain and carry information concerning your department."[60]

Just before Christmas another group, this one comprised of thirty Confederates traveling to Texas via Chihuahua, reached Presidio del Norte. Capt. Henry

Kennedy commanded the men, who upon their arrival on December 20, 1864, "were assisted from the house of John Broches [Burgess] with necessary provisions and powder and arms, as other [rebel] parties have been aided before." The food, guns, and ammunition cached at the Burgess residence came from "Espencer [John Spencer] and other residents [Southern sympathizers] of this place."[61]

Captain Kennedy was returning to Texas from a botched recruiting trip to California and Nevada. In April 1864 Maj. Sherod Hunter, commanding Confederate forces at Fort Duncan in Eagle Pass, Texas, had ordered Kennedy west to enlist men for an expedition to seize Arizona from the federals. Hunter's plan had Kennedy and his recruits attacking Arizona from the west, while the major and his force would mount an offensive from Texas. At Virginia City, Nevada, however, Union agents betrayed the rebel captain's designs, forcing Kennedy to flee back to San Antonio. For his part, Hunter also ran into trouble and aborted his expedition after a wagon broke down and Indians badly mauled his force in an engagement at Fort Lancaster on the Pecos. Upon the major's return home, General Magruder ordered him to rejoin his command "at once." Magruder expressed his sympathies to Hunter, noting, "I appreciate your zeal and patriotism and regret that your views and wishes could not be carried out by you."[62]

After Captain Kennedy received supplies from John Burgess at Presidio del Norte, he and his men crossed the Rio Grande into Texas, and on December 20, 1864, set up camp a few miles downstream of Spencer's Ranch near Fort Leaton. Next, they hoisted a red banner, the pirate flag, notifying local residents of their intention to pillage and warning them to expect no mercy. A number of those living in the Fort Leaton vicinity were tenant farmers from Chihuahua working for Edward Hall, Burgess's nemesis. Once again, as in the fracas six months earlier, Burgess enlisted the aid of Confederates passing through the Big Bend to help terrorize and/or kill Hall and gain control of the Fort Leaton property.[63]

After announcing their malevolent intentions, Captain Kennedy and his men forced their way into farmers' homes, holding the occupants prisoner while ransacking their possessions. The pillaging rebels stole guns, blankets, shirts, pants, coats, valises, pans, saddles, and books from their hapless victims before heading back to their camp. Since there was no federal force at Spencer's Ranch or at Fort Leaton, victimized residents instead turned to Mexican authorities in Presidio del Norte for help.[64]

City officials there quickly responded to their pleas on humanitarian grounds. After all, many of those robbed at gunpoint were Mexican citizens from Chihuahua. Lacking an interpreter to assist in communicating with the bandits, authorities in del Norte asked Confederate exile John Spencer for assistance. Spencer refused, but another resident, John Bihl, agreed to interpret. On December 21, 1864, eighty-six armed horsemen from del Norte crossed the river into Texas, where they joined forces with another forty-five men from area ranches and farms.[65]

The combined force moved on the pirate camp and a firefight erupted. Outnumbered four to one, Kennedy and his men abandoned much of their ill-gotten booty and quickly departed. When last seen the rebel party was fleeing east towards Alamito Creek and Alamo Spring. Official reports of the engagement noted, "The road over which they fled was marked in blood." Mexican authorities buried two dead looters, and after making a careful inventory of the stolen items, returned them to their rightful owners.[66]

By the third week of February 1865, Captain Kennedy was back in San Antonio, where he sanitized his official report concerning events in the Big Bend. He likely was embarrassed by the drubbing administered to his command and did not want the truth known. In any event, Kennedy claimed that on January 21, 1865, "the enemy, about 130 strong, attacked me in camp on the Cibolo." The captain stated that although his force of thirty men suffered in the engagement, "the enemy's loss was much greater in killed and wounded than ours."[67]

In fact, there were no Union troops in the Big Bend. Carleton first learned of this skirmish from the governor of Chihuahua. Kennedy provided his Confederate superiors no specifics concerning his adversaries. Official Mexican reports of the encounter have the same figures as Kennedy, stating that 131 local residents attacked thirty American renegades in camp on the Texas side of the river. The three Mexican reports, however, put the date at December 21, not January 21 as claimed by Kennedy. The captain also said that the fight took place on Cibolo Creek, when in fact it took place near Fort Leaton. In addition, during the engagement the rebel force, not the attackers, sustained the greater loss. Most importantly, Kennedy omits all mention of Burgess and the unseemly acts that he and his men committed in the Big Bend before fleeing eastward. Despite such omissions, a separate report from March 1865 written by Confederate major general John G. Walker, references Kennedy conversing with "Mr. Burgess" of Presidio del Norte.[68]

Regarding the Mexican perspective of events, Benigno Contreras, Municipal President of Presidio del Norte, voiced anger and frustration over the chronic lawlessness in the region related to the American Civil War. In a letter to the governor of Chihuahua, Contreras noted numerous incidents of rebel violence and brigandry, beginning with Joe Leaton's October 1861 kidnapping and near murder of Frederick Wulff in del Norte and continuing through Captain Kennedy's recent raid:

> Since war has been declared in the United States this point [Presidio del Norte], although far removed from the belligerent states, has suffered some wrongs from the numerous gangs of adventurers, or filibusters; . . . the numerous strangers who live in this town, who properly described [i.e., John Burgess], will be found to be no other than protectors of this class of bandits, for whatever may be the mission of the latter, it is certain that, upon leaving this frontier they never fail to commit some wrong, robbing or provoking a conflict of arms either in town or in the vicinity.[69]

After reading the official reports sent to him by the governor of Chihuahua, General Carleton endorsed the Mexicans' actions and expressed his sympathies to area residents, joining in the condemnation of "despicable" men such as Burgess and Spencer, "who take asylum in your State to render aid and comfort to these parties of desperadoes." Carleton regretted that he lacked sufficient forces to post a picket at Spencer's Ranch, Texas, but assured the governor that in the future, if Mexican troops crossed the river in pursuit of such thugs, "the government of the United States will approve their course."[70]

With Captain Kennedy's California-Nevada recruiting expedition a failure and Major Hunter's march to Arizona aborted, the invasion schemes of rebel Texans continued to come up empty. By late 1864 time was running out, and the Confederacy was unraveling. A number of diehard Texas secessionists, including James Magoffin, Bethel Coopwood, John Baylor, and Henry Kennedy, submitted various plans for capturing the Southwest to James A. Seddon, the Confederate secretary of war, for approval. After studying these, Seddon in December 1864 replied, "Our resources are fully taxed and our attention so engrossed that I must forego enterprises of this distant and contingent character." While Seddon could offer no help from Richmond, he ultimately left the final decision on such excursions to local commanding officers.[71]

By the spring of 1865 rebels in Texas possessed few realistic options for retaking the Trans-Pecos, New Mexico, and Arizona. One long shot remained: a scheme first discussed several years earlier by Gen. J. B. Magruder, Gen. D. H. Cooper, and Col. Spruce Baird. Under this plan, half of Baird's brigade would march west from Texas along the Canadian River. Along the way they would seize federal wagon trains on the Santa Fe Trail, severing the major supply artery for General Carleton's depot at Fort Union. The rest of Baird's force would march to Franklin, Texas, and capture Fort Bliss. As mentioned above, Magruder had never implemented Baird's plan because Union offensives in the eastern half of the state during 1863 and 1864 had kept rebel forces fully occupied.[72]

In early May 1865 a Union picket at Hueco Tanks in El Paso County intercepted nineteen refugees from Johnson County in Central Texas. The group's leader, William Davis, said that as of April, Spruce Baird was actively raising "a marauding party" to leave from Fort Belknap for El Paso at the beginning of May. Davis added, "These companies were composed of all sorts of men, bushwakers [*sic*] some of Quantrels [*sic*], Anderson's bushwakers [*sic*], etc. The impression that prevailed among the men was that they were coming out here . . . to overrun if they can, this country."[73]

Baird's troops never made it to El Paso County to prey on the Trans-Pecos. From December 1864 to April 1865 they were busy elsewhere, roaming Central Texas, committing "great outrages upon the citizens of McClennan and Williamson counties." General Walker called the "lawless" brigands "a terror to our own people [Confederates]." Upon learning of their behavior, a disgusted General Magruder in early April issued orders to "arrest all of Baird's men[.] I shall break up this organization. . . . They are useless." Before Magruder could arrest them, however, Baird's marauding mob fled north to Cooke County, Texas. Gen. Hamilton Bee quickly marched to Gainesville with two regiments to finally corner the depredating rebel troops. El Paso County and the Trans-Pecos had escaped another rampaging raid by Confederate ruffians.[74]

It was not until June 2, 1865, that Texas finally surrendered and the Civil War ended in the Department of New Mexico. Although the rebels never mounted a reinvasion of the Southwest, their spies and exiles in Mexico forced the department's commander to devote much of his attention and resources to combating their machinations. After a two-year struggle, General Carleton struck a decisive blow against the Confederate intelligence network in West Texas with the elimination of Henry Skillman. Skillman's death effectively signaled the passing of a long-held rebel dream, that of a Southern empire stretching to the Pacific. Ultimately, while Carleton was effective in containing Confederate Texas, he proved unsuccessful in resolving another persistent problem: curtailing the entrenched clandestine trade between New Mexican traders and Plains Indians.

CHAPTER 3

From 1862 to 1864 Gen. James H. Carleton had focused considerable attention and manpower on preventing a second Confederate invasion of New Mexico Territory. But with Confederate spy Henry Skillman out of the picture and the war in its final phase, he began to reallocate his meager resources toward ending the Comanchero trade. His efforts failed for several reasons. The most important was that many of New Mexico's most successful mercantilists had a pecuniary interest in keeping the trade going. Second, government officials and military leaders, including Carleton, often sent mixed messages concerning who could approve passes for these traders. Third, these same officials sometimes relied on Comancheros to negotiate the release of captives held by the Comanches, and these negotiations included exchanging trade goods for stolen horses and cattle. Particularly cattle.

Mercantilists and Comancheros had much common. Both transacted business on the frontier, often in tandem. Manuel S. Delgado had been in the freighting business, hauling goods to Chihuahua and Missouri, before becoming a merchant. His sons Felipe, Pablo, and Simón followed his lead. The Delgado family participated in both the wholesale and retail trade. They sold goods from their own stores as well as supplying their competitors with the same products. Pablo Delgado ran José Chávez's store on the San Miguel del Vado grant. He also supervised Chávez's frontier operations in La Cuesta (Villanueva) and Anton Chico, which were home to many Comancheros. Hispano farmers and ranchers in these communities purchased store goods with crops and livestock. Sheep and cattle were traded for textiles, tools, sugar, and coffee. In a land without banks, barter was the mechanism that fueled the economy, connecting distant ranchers to urban merchants.[1]

After the Mexican War ended in 1848, mercantilists of all stripes began to establish satellite stores on the frontier. Isolated villages provided ready markets for American products. Just like Delgado and Chávez, the newcomers sought those markets. Some European Americans had a head start, having settled in the region before the war with Mexico. For example, on August 15, 1846, Levi Keithley, Alexander Hatch, Burton Reese, Henry Connelly, and Edward Mitchell welcomed Gen. Stephen Watts Kearney and his Army of the West into Las Vegas, New Mexico. By that time these men had lived in San Miguel County for several years. All were traders and merchants.[2]

Kearney and his troops were also greeted by Americans in the next town, Tecolote, where William Moore ran a frontier store. Such men soon expanded their reach, establishing a presence as far south as Anton Chico. In 1854 Keithley, a territorial delegate and future Indian agent, purchased land on the Gallinas River where he operated both a store and a ranch with partner William Shepard. In 1860 they sold some of their land to Reese and Moore. Keithley and Shepard also had a connection with Comanchero José Piedad Tafoya, who lived in nearby Chaperito. A close look at San Miguel County's 1860 and 1870 censuses reveals that the children who had lived in Keithley's and Shepard's homes in 1860 were living with Tafoya in 1870. Keithley was a seasoned merchant, and Tafoya knew a lot of merchants, some better than others.[3]

Another early immigrant to the region was New Yorker Alexander Hatch. After running a store in Tecolote, he purchased property south of Las Vegas on the Gallinas River from Henry Connelly, a future territorial governor. This new property was close to both Keithley's and Tafoya's land. Records show that Hatch did business with Tafoya, transacting deals on crops and land in June 1859. If Hatch funded any of Tafoya's illegal expeditions into Texas, he did not document them. The expatriate New Yorker also did business with the military, which had moved operations south to protect the newcomers. The army rented land from Hatch for a military base, and he also sold the soldiers food, hay, and grain. Hatch's Ranch became associated with a military camp, and a trading post was later established there.[4]

A day's ride east of Hatch's, merchant Anastacio Sandoval grazed sheep at the junction of the Conchas and Canadian Rivers. Like Tafoya, Sandoval participated in the Comanchero trade. In 1863 seven thousand head of his sheep were stolen by Indians. Shortly after, this civilian showed up at Fort Union with an order from General Carleton that he delivered to Capt. Erastus Wood. Carleton had directed Wood to go after the perpetrators and had named Sandoval as his guide. Carleton assured the captain that this Santa Fe merchant was at home in San Miguel County and would be an excellent pilot. For the department commander to send soldiers on such a specific errand shows just how strong was the connection between Sandoval, the Comancheros, and Carleton.[5]

The activities of the Hispano merchants show that newcomers Keithley, Hatch, Moore, and Mitchell were not the first entrepreneurs to see the area's possibilities. Many Hispano elites owned stores and ranches up and down sections of the Gallinas and Pecos River valleys. Sometimes they worked with the newcomers and sometimes they competed against them.[6]

Kentuckian James M. Giddings was another early settler. He worked as a trader, going back and forth from Santa Fe to the states for several years. In 1840 he made the capital his permanent home. Like Manuel Delgado, he became a merchant. In the 1850s he established a ranch between Agua Negra Creek and the Pecos River, about fifty miles southwest of Sandoval's ranch. In October 1865 superintendent of Indian Affairs Felipe Delgado issued Giddings a license to trade with the Comanches. One of his bond holders was Santa Fe merchant D. Bernard Koch. With Giddings, Koch put up an additional bond for Comanchero Florencio Aragón. Along with Anton Chico merchant Edward Hamburger, Koch supplied another bond for trader Fernando Lucero. He did the same for Edward Martinas. Koch's business operations covered the entirety of northeastern New Mexico. One of his partners was Preston Beck Jr, who also partnered with Giddings on his Pecos River enterprise. He and merchant James Conklin put up a $1,200 bond for ex-trapper Gervais Nolan to trade with Indians. Such bonds were obligatory but did not explain why so many successful merchants were involved in the Comanchero trade.[7]

To be clear, there was nothing illegal from a New Mexican standpoint regarding these activities. Licenses gave the recipient the right to go to the Comanche country (as the documents identified Texas), to trade for stolen cattle. The legal aspect of these exchanges has seldom been written about. Instead historians have focused on the traders who ignored the law and thus attracted the military's attention. Whether legal or illegal, the collateral damage associated with these transactions was seldom discussed in nineteenth-century New Mexico. Raids carried out to procure cattle and horses also swept up women and children. (Comanches and Kiowas had little use for adult Anglo males. They either escaped, were killed, or were left for dead.) These captives were either incorporated into Native American societies or traded for something of value. Within this context, the army called on the same people they often arrested for illegal trading to help recover the captives: the Comancheros knew the Comanches better than anybody.[8]

The dual nature of Comanchero activities, legal and illegal, combined with the traders' earnest efforts to rescue kidnapped women and children, led to

confusion and aggravation within military ranks. In 1861 Union troopers stationed in eastern New Mexico were looking for the advance elements of a feared
Confederate invasion when a cavalry patrol apprehended five Comancheros on
their way back from Texas. These traders were from La Cuesta and Chaperito.
The troopers took them to Fort Union for questioning, where Lt. Col. Manuel
Chaves acted as translator for Lt. Henry B. Bristol. Pedro Urioste explained that
they had gone to Texas to trade for buffalo robes and skins, making clear that
they had not traded rifles, pistols, or gunpowder for these items. Even though
each trader named a different supplier, the goods they took east were the same,
including, "*biscoche* [the dark hard bread the Comanches craved; it was the one
item the Comancheros produced in bulk on their own], corn, shirts, blue drilling,
vermillion, and knives." Pedro had received his trade goods from territorial
legislator Miguel Sena y Quintana. Pedro's brother Manuel explained that his
came from Lucian B. Maxwell of Cimarron, an old mountain man who was one
of the territory's largest landowners, ranchers, and government contractors.
Phillipe Madrid received his goods from another member of the legislature:
merchant, politician, and rancher Antonio José Gallegos. The fourth trader,
Juan de Dios Tapia, had struck a deal with Las Vegas merchant Lorenzo López,
also a prominent politician and sometime-sheriff of that town.[9]

This was not the first or last trip for Pedro, Manuel, and the others who were
interrogated at Fort Union. Three years later New Mexico's then superintendent
of Indian Affairs, Michael Steck, employed some of these same traders for a different type of expedition. Steck was aware that some Anglo captives were being
held at a specific campground in Texas. To facilitate their release, he signed a
pass that allowed Manuel Urioste and twelve of his Chaperito neighbors to travel
east and trade for them. Despite having this pass, they were stopped by a Fort
Bascom cavalry patrol. The officer in charge counted twenty-four Comancheros,
but Urioste's pass stipulated that he could take only twelve. He and his men were
turned around because of this violation.[10]

Fort Bascom, under the command of Capt. Edward Bergmann, was closer to
Texas than Fort Union or Santa Fe. Bergmann reported this incident to General
Carleton and recommended that Steck be notified. Given the nature of the
Comancheros' expedition, such scrupulous adherence to the law might not
seem appropriate, but the New Mexico traders were notorious for disregarding
stipulations such as limiting the number of traders in their caravans. This event
also highlights the government's dependence on Comancheros in the recovery
of Comanche captives.[11]

This dependent relationship explains why General Carleton waffled between approving passes and eliminating them. His position hardened in late 1864, however, after he ordered Col. Kit Carson and several hundred soldiers and Indians auxiliaries into the Texas panhandle to seek out and eliminate Comanches and Kiowas he believed were responsible for raids along the Santa Fe Trail and in Texas. Before sending Carson east, he told Steck to stop issuing passes, fearing the New Mexicans might warn their trading partners.[12]

Carson's expedition faced much stiffer resistance than anticipated. Deep into the mission, the soldiers encountered a heavily populated Kiowa and Comanche village north of present-day Amarillo. While official records do not reflect this, Carson and his men barely escaped with their lives. In the middle of the action, a U.S. Army patrol apprehended two Comancheros coming back from Texas and in possession of several hundred head of cattle. The leader showed the officer in charge his pass, signed by Steck. Once notified, Carleton was infuriated, agreeing with Carson that these traders had warned the Indians of the approaching column. The general asserted that Steck had ignored his order to stop issuing passes. The superintendent disagreed, claiming he had approved these passes before receiving Carleton's message. While Carleton was also known to issue passes, he still used this near-catastrophe to help get Steck replaced.[13]

This superintendent's removal had no impact on the trade. The same men taken to Fort Union in 1861 continued to haul goods to Texas for various employers in the years following. In 1865 Anastacio Sandoval hired Juan de Dios Tapia to head one expedition and the Urioste brothers for another. Numerous legal and illegal caravans used the same routes and traded at the same locations year after year.[14]

While a reconstituted postwar U.S. Army would eventually defeat the remaining Southern Plains Indians and thus end this trade, military success would not come soon enough for fourteen-year-old Rudolph Fischer and many other Texans. In 1865, while searching along Pedernales Creek for his father's cattle, he stumbled on a band of Comanches who refused to live on the reservation. In a letter to President Andrew Johnson, Gottlieb Fischer explained that his son disappeared on July 29, 1865. He was barefoot and wearing buckskin pants, a hickory shirt, and a straw hat. That summer the Comanches also abducted Cola Caroline McDonald and her daughters Mahala and Rebecca; Alice, Dorcus, and James Taylor; and Alice Todd.[15]

Recovering captured people was a complicated business. A botched military engagement often led to the result parents and relatives feared most—death.

Even when an exchange could be negotiated, Comanches often backed out of such deals at the last minute. Sometimes they feared being double-crossed. Sometimes familial bonds had grown so strong that Indian families could not bear to let the captives go. And sometimes the captives themselves adjusted to Comanche life and did not want to return to their families of origin. In such difficult circumstances, government officials looked to New Mexican merchants and their Comanchero partners for help.[16]

Not all Comancheros spoke Spanish or were born in New Mexico. Prussian-born Marcus Goldbaum was a New Mexican trader who received his passes from General Carleton, whose headquarters were at Fort Marcy. Goldbaum was also a butcher and held the government beef contract for this post. In Santa Fe and Las Vegas, Goldbaum was a known Indian trader. Like Urioste, he was a frequent visitor to the Comanche country. He bartered manufactured goods and other products for hides, horses, and when working for the army, cattle. He was very familiar with the Texas campgrounds where such transactions took place and often camped at Quitaque, Yellow House Canyon, or Mucha-Que Peak.[17]

After returning from Mucha-Que Peak in 1866, Goldbaum reported to Carleton that in April he had counted twenty Texan captives in one village, most of them children. While there he had sought their release, an action that almost got him killed. Only an intervention by Comanche chief Puertas, an old friend, saved his life. After Puertas vouched for Goldbaum's character, the other leaders relaxed. He reported to Carleton that at first the Comanches refused to speak about these captives but relented after a few days. About the time the chiefs' stance softened, Goldbaum saw the boy Rudolph Fischer, who by that time had been with the Comanches for almost a year. The chiefs admitted that his release would be considered once the trader supplied them with "soldier's coats, sugar, silver crosses, firearms and gun powder." Back in New Mexico Territory, Goldbaum explained to Carleton that he intended to go back with all of the goods they requested, except the weapons and gunpowder. His goal was to retrieve the Fischer boy and as many of the other children as possible. He informed the general that he had already ordered silver crosses from Byers and Andrews Jewelers and then asked if Carleton could provide him with transportation for the return trip.[18]

Carleton pondered this request, eventually deciding to send an escort of seven soldiers and recently promoted Maj. Edward Bergmann of Fort Bascom with him. Bergmann's soldiers had deep experience looking for Comancheros. The major knew many of the traders on a personal basis. Not long after the Union built and occupied Fort Bascom, he purchased cattle from some local

New Mexicans so he could provide beef to nearby Comanches and Kiowas that these "citizens" traded with. When he submitted a bill of remittance for one of these purchases, he claimed Indians often arrived at the post seeking food and that he spent his own money providing for them.[19]

Bergmann also kept a ranch just south of the fort. It is clear that he did more than purchase a few cattle from locals to feed hungry Indians. He was involved in the cattle trade, and at one point he had employed José Piedad Tafoya to acquire cattle in Texas (at least that is what Tafoya said years later). After mustering out of the service, Bergmann applied for a legal license to continue such trades. Carleton knew of the major's relationship with both the traders and Comanches, which is why he picked him to lead the rescue mission.[20]

Bergmann was one of many major figures in this part of New Mexico who were entangled in the trade. The year before, John Sebrie Watts, a well-respected lawyer and territorial delegate, put up the bond for his son (also named John Watts) to trade with the Comanches. The senior Watts obviously pulled some strings to get John Jr. a legal pass to trade at Fort Bascom and in Texas. James L. Collins, the former superintendent of Indian Affairs in New Mexico, supplied half the required thousand-dollar bond. The son swore he would only employ citizens of "good moral character." It probably helped that the army leased the land where Fort Bascom stood from Watts Sr.[21]

Bergmann later detailed his rescue attempt in an after-action report to Carleton. He noted that he took butcher and cattle dealer Marcus Goldbaum with him, as well as Diego Morales, whom Bergmann called his interpreter. It seems likely that Morales was an employee or partner of Goldbaum's, since according to Bergmann both men were familiar with the rendezvous site. First, they traveled down the Pecos to the Bosque Redondo Indian reservation. The reservation was built on an old Indian campground where mountain people had been trading with plains people for centuries. Fort Sumner, constructed next to it, housed the soldiers who oversaw these Indians. Beef was needed to feed them, which is why Goldbaum had been in Texas when he recognized Rudolph Fischer.

After leaving the Bosque Redondo, the small party turned east. About sixty miles later they struck a well-worn trail that ran southeast across the Llano Estacado, passing landmarks such as Canada de Tule and Los Portales before crossing the state line. While neither Bergmann nor Goldbaum specified the rendezvous site, according to the distances, time frame, and directions that Bergmann alluded to in his report, they would have eventually passed Cañon del Rescate, or Ransom Canyon, a large trading center. Bergmann's report indicated that they found the Indians near Mucha-Que Peak. The major noted several trail ruts radiating away from the campsite.[22]

At a camp near present-day Gail, Texas, Goldbaum made good on his pledge, presenting the Indians with most of the trade items they had demanded. Despite this, the chiefs were in no mood to release anyone. The more Bergmann turned the conversation toward the captives, the more agitated they became. He noted that Fischer was there, but the Comanches were not interested in making a trade. He considered trying to take the boy by force but acknowledged to Carleton that such an act, occurring in the midst of 160 lodges filled with well-armed and defiant Indians and their Hispanic allies, would have been suicidal. They returned to New Mexico with a few stolen horses and nothing more.[23]

Desperate spouses and parents of those captives forced to remain with the Comanches failed or refused to understand how complicated such missions were, and they continued to agitate for results. They contacted politicians, newspaper editors, and army officers. They wrote letters to the president and the secretary of war. Once more the U.S. government turned to New Mexicans. Lorenzo Labadie was serving as the Indian agent at Abiquiú when Superintendent of Indian Affairs A. B. Norton relieved him of that duty and gave him a new job. Norton informed the forty-year-old Labadie that William F. M. Arny would be taking his place as agent there, while Labadie was to "proceed without delay to the frontier, either at Fort Bascom or such a place as you deem advisable and best for carrying out the enclosed orders." Those orders involved putting together a crew of his choice. Norton made sure Labadie knew this meant selecting people who knew the country and could speak Comanche: in other words, Comancheros. What was not in Norton's orders were the details of Bergmann's recent attempt. It was possible Labadie already knew of this failure, something that would not have surprised him. At this point it is probably worth reviewing why the superintendent picked this long-time Indian agent to lead such a dangerous mission.[24]

Lababie's grandfather emigrated to New Mexico from France in 1765. A physician, Domingo (Dominique) settled in Santa Fe and started a family. Grandson Lorenzo was an imposing figure, dark-haired, blue-eyed, and taller than most. He was well-versed in several Indian languages, including Ute, Jicarilla, Mescalero, Navajo, and Comanche. This was his second stint at Abiquiú, having served as the agent for these same Indians in the mid 1850s. He lived in Valencia County in the village of Tomé with his wife Rayitos (Reyes). Rayitos had a significant, if controversial, family tree. She was Petra Gutiérrez's illegitimate daughter. Petra was merchant James Marsh Giddings's wife, but Rayitos had been raised by her great-aunt, not her mother. That aunt was doña María Gertrudis Barceló, also known as doña Tules. Tules owned a very popular gambling house in Santa Fe. When she died in 1852, she left a good deal of property to her favorite grand-niece and Petra. One month after her death, fourteen-year-old Rayitos married Lorenzo Labadie.[25]

Lorenzo's relatives, both through blood and marriage, help to explain why he is such an important part of this history. One of his sisters, Vicenta, married Manuel Antonio Chaves when she was fifteen. Chaves's exploits as an Indian fighter, trader, territorial leader, and Civil War hero are covered in meticulous detail in Marc Simmons's *Little Lion of the Southwest* (1973). Back in 1861 he had served as Lieutenant Bristol's interpreter when they brought Comanchero Pedro Urioste and his associates to Fort Union.

Labadie and Chaves were more than brothers-in-law. In the early 1850s they partnered in a ranching enterprise that included land north of the Bosque Redondo on the Pecos River. They raised sheep and cattle ten miles south of Santa Rosa on Agua Negra Creek, near what became Puerto de Luna. Their ranch was perfectly situated between the Bosque Redondo and Anton Chico.[26] Shortly after establishing their business, Chaves put up the bond for brother-in-law Lorenzo to trade with the Navajos for three months. It is probable that like other bondholders, he supplied at least some of the trade goods that Labadie carried with his caravan.[27] Their ranch was often raided by these same Indians. Documents note that they blamed their losses on Navajos and Jicarilla and Mescalero Apaches. Probably because of the danger, both kept their main homes elsewhere. Manuel's was in Santa Fe. Lorenzo's family remained in Tomé.[28]

Labadie's first stint as the Indian agent at Abiquiú occurred about the time he was getting the Agua Negra ranch started. In that capacity he issued passes to locals to trade with the Utes. In 1854 he gave a three-month pass to Pedro Leon. In 1855 he gave a six-month pass to Bernardo Sánchez that allowed him to transact business from the Rio de las Animas to the Rio San Juan.[29]

As noted, his father-in-law also moved to Agua Negra Creek. Giddings partnered with Preston Beck Jr. in this enterprise, but his move to the Middle Pecos River was connected to Labadie's. The familial ties that linked Giddings, Labadie, and Chaves to this region had historical ripple effects within the territory for several decades.

By 1853 Giddings had created a settlement, not a ranch. In the years to come, between eight and thirty-three families lived there, farming and raising sheep and cattle. In 1854 James H. Carleton, then a major, and Second Lt. Henry B.

Davidson had passed this portion of the Pecos River looking for a place to build a frontier outpost. Carleton explained that Giddings lived within a fortress, a substantial structure built from adobe bricks and wood beams taken from buildings his workers had dismantled in Ojo Bernal, about fifty miles away. Prior to this move he had been the probate clerk of Santa Fe. He had administered doña Tules's will, which left both Petra and Rayitos homes in the capital. It was shortly after this that Giddings and Labadie purchased land on Agua Negra Creek. While merchant Beck was Giddings's business partner, documents and maps detail that Beck's own ranch was a few miles to the east, along Los Tanos Creek. Cementing the bond between the Labadies and Giddings even further, Lorenzo and Rayitos's daughter Benigna later married Giddings's son George in a Puerto de Luna ceremony.[30]

In 1854 Chaves and Labadie borrowed $6,200 from another Santa Fe merchant, Miguel E. Pino, who owned a large ranch within the Chaperito, Anton Chico, and Puerto de Luna triangle. Pino's hacienda was located east of Anton Chico near the Gallinas River. Documents do not indicate what the loan was for. It could have been to shore up their sheep ranching business. It could have been to purchase trade goods. As collateral for the Pino loan they put up their family homes. Since neither was foreclosed on, they must have paid this money back. Again, in a land without banks, putting up property as collateral for short-term loans was commonplace and something of a habit for Lorenzo Labadie. He often secured such loans from successful merchants. Many of these loans came from one of Santa Fe's most prominent businessmen, Lehman Spiegelberg.[31]

Pino was also involved in the Comanchero trade. In September 1865 he and Anastacio Sandoval put up the thousand-dollar bond for Comanchero Juaquín Larriva's trip to Texas. Larriva's pass allowed him to trade with the Comanches for two months. The pass did not stipulate what he would be trading for. A loan to Labadie and Chaves for a similar venture makes perfect sense.[32]

As noted above, Manuel Chaves was a well-known New Mexican frontiersman. Without as much fanfare Labadie participated in many of the same events and conflicts that made his brother-in-law famous. This included actions that took place both before and during the Civil War. In 1861 Labadie was appointed Indian agent for the Mescalero Apaches. He was on his way to Tucson to meet with some of their chiefs when a crowd of rowdy Texans stopped him in Las Cruces. He was told to leave immediately from what they called the Confederate Territory of Arizona or face severe consequences. Labadie, a true Unionist, ignored this threat and rode to Fort Filmore to inform officers there of what was taking place in Las Cruces.[33]

He was with Chaves at several battles during the Civil War but also served as a scout for Col. Kit Carson along the Rio Bonito. Carson once remarked to General Canby that he often relied on Labadie because of his experience as an Indian trader. His ability to interact with Indians intrinsically linked him with Carson for the next several years. For part of 1862 he operated out of Anton Chico as the Mescarelos' agent. After Carson's successful campaign to reign in the Mescaleros along the Rio Bonito, Labadie led them to the new Bosque Redondo reservation. Carleton then ordered Carson to conduct a similar campaign against the Navajos, who were lodged in Canyon de Chelly. Carson's scorched-earth strategy eventually forced them out of their ancient stronghold. Like the Mescaleros, they were marched to the Bosque Redondo. Labadie was already there, trying to guide the Apaches' efforts to become farmers, putting into practice Carleton's grand experiment to convert such Indians into agriculturalists. It was doomed to fail. Misplaced idealism, bad water, poor land, and insect infestations led to disaster. Additionally, the Mescaleros and the Navajos were traditional enemies. Dealing with the misguided mismanagement of the government and the army was largely Labadie's responsibility. That his own ranch was not far away led to other problems.[34]

Labadie argued that the Navajos should not be put on the same reservation as the Mescaleros. His recalcitrance regarding this decision led many military officers to brand him a troublemaker. Carleton instructed Fort Sumner officers to keep an eye on him, and negative reports began to show up at department headquarters. But the agent did not take his orders from Carleton (or anyone else in the military) but from Superintendent Steck. Against military rules Labadie was grazing sheep on reservation land. According to some observers, he was also purchasing sheep directly from the Mescaleros. Carleton ordered Capt. Henry Bristol to stop this practice. Soldiers soon found much worse to be concerned about.[35]

It was Capt. Prince Morton's job to incorporate the influx of cattle herds onto the reservation. Part of this process included branding them. Whether it was due to previous suspicions concerning Agent Labadie or just good diligence, word was sent to Carleton that Captain Morton was cutting some of these animals out of the herd. Instead of branding them, he was sending them to Labadie. On one occasion he sent seventy-five unbranded cattle to the agent. In a related incident, Second Lt. Edwin J. Edgar discovered a variety of government farm tools and sacks of corn in one of Labadie's wagons. When asked about this, Labadie explained that he had purchased these goods from William Calloway, the reservation's farm superintendent. A veteran of the California Column, Calloway had recently mustered out of the army. His last duty of any length had been at Fort Sumner. By then he owned a ranch and retail establishment of some kind north of Labadie's property on the Pecos River.[36]

Court-martial proceedings against Captain Morton failed to provide a guilty verdict. This did nothing to allay Carleton's suspicions. He believed Labadie was stealing cattle. The Indian agent claimed that he was being falsely accused because of his complaints concerning the poor quality of beef the government was supplying to the Indians. Carleton wanted him fired. Steck refused to do it. Instead, he ordered him to report to Santa Fe as soon as possible for another assignment: soon he would be bargaining for the Comanche captives in West Texas. Capt. Lawrence G. Murphy, also of the California Column, would eventually become the new Indian agent at the Bosque Redondo. After mustering out, Murphy moved to the region that became Lincoln County. Despite his role in selling government goods to Labadie, Calloway remained the civilian farm superintendent for several more months.[37]

Carleton remained perturbed. In a report to Washington he wrote that Labadie "has without a doubt been engaged in buying cattle [for himself] which had been delivered at Fort Sumner" and that he was "not fit to hold office under the government." Testimony also implicated the chief herder on the reservation, P. R. Goodfellow, who admitted that he had delivered other cattle to Labadie's ranch on more than one occasion. Carleton ordered that Goodfellow be taken to Santa Fe for further questioning, but before this could happen, he had disappeared. The general sent a similar directive regarding the recently tried Captain Morton, who had left for the states after the court-martial hearing. The general wanted him stopped, by force if necessary, so he could be questioned. It was reported that after Morton passed through Las Vegas, a merchant named Kitchens, probably Richard Kitchens, left as well. Carleton believed Kitchens's disappearance was linked to Morton's activities at Fort Sumner. Despite the general's insistence that these men be stopped, nothing more came of his efforts to get to the bottom of what he called this "outfit's" schemes.

Successful warfare against the Navajos and Mescaleros had created the conditions conducive to such fraud. The army relied on civilians to provide the bulk of the dry goods, hardware, and livestock needed to sustain the reservations and outposts. This was why Carleton had given butcher Goldbaum a pass to venture into Texas. In a roundabout way it is also why the superintendent of Indian Affairs issued so many passes. The government needed Texas beef to help feed the Indians they had recently defeated, and it could not afford to be too inquisitive about its procurement.[38]

Once the superintendent signed a pass, a master copy was sent to Washington, D.C., for final approval, although the latter was something of a formality before and during the Civil War. But early in 1866 Commissioner of Indian Affairs Dennis N. Cooley refused to endorse a pass for one of Labadie's neighbors, Celso Baca. His reasoning was that such passes should originate from Texas, where the Comanches lived. It was up to these Indians' agents or other proper officials in that state to approve such documents. The wording on this denial illustrates that people in Washington were beginning to reevaluate the entire approval process. While the trade certainly continued, the legal records trace this shift in thinking. Fewer passes were issued from Santa Fe after 1865.[39]

But during the latter part of that year, Pablo Lucero's September 13, 1865, pass noted that he could trade in Texas for two months. Lucero's brother Fernando received a similar pass two weeks later. Fernando's pass (license) allowed him to trade with the Comanches for three months wherever the Comanches could be found.[40]

Cooley might have had other reasons for denying Celso Baca's request. Like Labadie and Chaves, Baca was a veteran of both the Navajo and Civil Wars. He fought at Valverde against the Confederates. He had freighted goods along the Santa Fe Trail. Baca moved to Agua Negra Creek in the mid 1860s and built a substantial hacienda on the east side of the Pecos River. He did business with the Bosque Redondo reservation. Numerous oblique references also tie Celso Baca to the Comanchero trade during this same period. In his study of the trade, Charles L. Kenner notes that Baca and someone named "Labadi" were rumored to be "cattle thieves." Such rumors might explain why Cooley got so technical with Baca's request.[41]

While Labadie and Baca did not always get along, they were neighbors and had many of the same business contacts. By 1896 they became the majority owners, along with Santa Fe merchant and cattle broker Willie Spiegelberg and lawyer R. H. Longwill, of what came to be called the Agua Negra Land Grant. All four were later known as founding fathers of Santa Rosa, New Mexico.[42]

After the Mescaleros took it upon themselves to vacate the Bosque Redondo in 1865, Steck ordered Labadie to Mora and Taos Counties to try and convince the Jicarilla Apaches to take the Mescaleros' place on the reservation. That would never come about, yet this agent's continuing role within the superintendency illustrates that despite the controversy at Fort Sumner, Steck always held Labadie in high regard. He officially remained the Mescaleros' agent even after Carleton had him removed from the Bosque Redondo. Succeeding superintendents Felipe Delgado and A. B. Norton must have had similar confidence, for he was still an agent in 1867. He was serving in that capacity at Abiquiú when Norton tapped him for the new mission.[43]

He was to go to Texas, and demand that the Comanches give up Rudolph Fischer and any other captives—with no preconditions. Labadie was to warn the Comanches of the severe consequences that would befall them if they did not comply, as Norton put it. Labadie was to make clear that he was not there to give them gifts. Much is unspoken within this directive: that Norton had confidence that Labadie would not be harmed; that only New Mexican civilians would accompany him—people who knew the Comanches. Comancheros.[44]

Juan Labadie was one of them. He was not the agent's son; Juan was an Apache who had been in his employ for some time. Others included Valdez Carrero, José de la Cruz Padilla, Francisco Seguar, José Carrió, and Juan Hinojos. These men left before Labadie, fanning out in different directions to try and make contact with the Indians. They carried the message that Labadie was coming to Quitaque and needed to talk to the Comanche leaders. Approximately two thousand Comanches ranged from the Red to Concho Rivers during this period. By the time Labadie met up with the Indians in a secluded canyon, several hundred were waiting. According to Labadie, the closest Texas settlement was about ninety miles away.[45]

Describing this location, the agent noted that the region was full of bison and wild mustangs. He recorded that thousands of horses and mules were grazing in the canyon along with just as many cattle. He made a point of informing Norton that more cattle were herded into the valley every day. Labadie was enamored with this setting, describing the numerous shade trees that lined the stream and the abundance of wild grapes, plums, and nuts.[46]

Despite a warm welcome, once Labadie explained why he was there, the Comanches grew cold. He noted that at least two-thirds of the warriors were not present, and those who were there were confused about why they had to stop raiding the Texans. It had not been that long ago that Union officers urged them to take whatever they wanted from the Texans. When had the rules changed?[47]

Labadie saw Fischer and guessed his age to be about eighteen. Chiefs Quahip and Mowway were on a visit to Durango, and a third, Paruaquahip was on a mission to steal horses from the Navajos at the Bosque Redondo. In a common ploy to delay action, the remaining Comanche leaders explained that while these chiefs were absent, such an important decision could not be made. They implored Labadie to come back during October's full moon. If he did, they felt certain some kind of deal could be struck.

Labadie returned to New Mexico and in August wrote his report from his Agua Negra ranch. He related to Norton that the Indians seemed ready for peace but that they had no idea who their Texas agent was. They had never seen him. (It was Jesse H. Leavenworth.) Labadie told Norton that he had agreed to return in the fall and closed by letting the superintendent know that his expenses totaled about one thousand dollars.[48]

Norton sent his response the following month. It was hand-delivered by another Indian agent, Labadie's longtime friend Jesús María Sena y Baca. Both men were former sheriffs in Santa Fe County. Sena y Baca was also a politician, having served as the territorial clerk of New Mexico. Norton agreed that a second trip was warranted but let Labadie know that Puertas, the chief who had saved trader Goldbaum's life, was dead, killed by some Utes. It was possible the Comanches might think that the army had killed him. Norton informed Labadie that after the attack, one of Puertas's wives had gone to Chaperito seeking protection. As noted above, many part-time Comancheros lived in this Gallinas River village. Comanches often stopped there to trade. Given the uncertainties, Norton offered Labadie a military escort back to Texas.[49]

Only five years earlier soldiers posted to nearby Hatch's Ranch had stumbled on at least one hundred Comanches camping in Chaperito. Capt. Edmunds Holloway of the Eighth Cavalry noted they had been there for a while. A firefight followed, and the Indians eventually fled. Holloway commented that Comanches were frequent visitors to this town, where they traded with the locals for guns and powder.[50]

Chaperito was on the Gallinas River about fifty miles to the north of Agua Negra Creek. Labadie sent one of his men to see if Puertas's widow would go with them to Texas. He hoped that she could explain that neither New Mexicans nor the army had had anything to do with her husband's death. Once contacted, she agreed to go with them. Her decision indicates that she must have felt comfortable going back to Texas with Labadie.[51]

Shortly after the Comanche widow arrived at the Agua Negra ranch, the group left for Fort Sumner. Sena y Baca accompanied them. Under these more dangerous circumstances, Labadie sought the military escort that had been offered, but the post's commander explained he could not spare any troops. The few he had were off chasing down a band of escaped Navajos. If Labadie could wait, he would allocate some men when they returned. Not wanting to do so, Labadie left for Texas on October 12, 1867.[52]

Trying to recreate Labadie's route back to Texas is difficult due to the way he worded his second report on the rescue mission. He noted that during the first six days and nights of their journey, they did not follow a trail of any kind. At that point, he wrote, they arrived at Quitaque or Cañon del Rescate, but he mysteriously did not say which. These locations are not close to one another. His first mission had taken him to a camp at Quitaque. According to his first report he had agreed that the second meeting would take place at Cañon del Rescate. In his description of this second journey, though, he intimated that they headed northeast, which would have put them closer to Quitaque. The first campground they came across was empty. After discussing the situation with both Sena y Baca and Puertas's widow, they rode north. Labadie's second report implied here that he did not know the region they were traveling through, perhaps trying to get ahead of any future suspicions. Regardless of why he wrote the report the way he did, this early search proved fruitless.[53]

The next few weeks were just as frustrating. Nine days later they reached the Canadian River. By then they had lost two horses to exhaustion and decided to turn around. From the Canadian they rode south until they reached Palo Duro Canyon, where they rested for three days. Afterward, they continued southeast, eventually passing through Cañon Blanco. This trajectory pointed them toward Cañon del Rescate, the rendezvous site Labadie had originally agreed to in August. When they arrived at this prominent trading ground, no one was there, so they continued southeast. They finally found the Comanches on November 8, yet their journey was not over. A cholera epidemic had descended on the village: one of their chiefs, Parauquahip, had died the day they arrived.[54]

As was their custom, upon the chief's death the Comanches moved the entire village and reestablished the camp six miles downriver. Labadie and Sena y Baca did likewise. On November 11 they met with Chief Tainadita. The agent explained that they were to deliver a message from their leaders in Santa Fe. Tainadita arranged for a larger tepee so more people could hear what Labadie had to say. A group of about seventy community leaders assembled in the larger structure.[55]

Once Labadie delivered Norton's demands, the assembled Comanches became angry and talked about killing both men on the spot. Labadie and Sena y Baca acted as if they could not understand them, continuing to smile and nod their heads. This ploy seemed to work. After much agitation and many harsh words, the tepee grew silent and tempers cooled. The Indians must have realized that killing two messengers from Santa Fe would not make their situation any better. Seemingly looking for an excuse to delay, Tainadita explained that the absence of several chiefs, as well as the recent deaths of Puertas and Paruaquahip, left them in no position to make such a decision. Yet as had happened during Goldbaum's visit, after some time passed the Indians relaxed and agreed to trade their captives for tobacco, yellow paint, coffee, flour, shirts, several saddles, butcher knives, and pistols and powder—the same items that were typically freighted east by the Comancheros.[56]

Labadie explained that while he did not have the authority to approve such gifts, he would carry their demands back to his leaders. Once they realized he had not brought gifts, the Comanches again grew angry. They did not like meetings that ended without presents. At that point the Indians informed them that they only held one black and five white Texans and were no longer interested in continuing the discussion.[57]

In his report Labadie related to the superintendent that he knew they were lying. A Hispanic herder, long ago captured by this same band, had communicated to the New Mexicans that there were at least fourteen captives that he knew of in the village. At some point during their stay Sena y Baca had a quick conversation with two of them. One, Hubbard Wayne, was practically a Comanche, having lived most of his life with them. He thought he was about fourteen years old. Ten-year-old Richard Freeman had been captured only thirty days earlier. Sena y Baca related that both boys, crying in his presence, begged him to make some type of deal for their release. That did not happen. Labadie and Sena y Baca returned to New Mexico empty-handed. The agent reported that this second trip encompassed about 1,185 miles [58]

Norton had sent Labadie on this mission because of his knowledge of the Comanchero trade. Within one twenty-four-hour period in 1865, Superintendent Felipe Delgado had approved separate passes for José Piedad Tafoya and José Costillo. Labadie was the bondholder on both. The goods these men took to trade for cattle in 1865 were the same goods Tainadita demanded for captives in 1867.[59]

When Labadie had signed his name to these licenses, the trade was booming. After becoming superintendent following Steck's tenure, Delgado approved applications at an accelerated rate. By then Comancheros were making hundreds of trips to Texas each year. Often hidden under the approved goods in their pack trains were pistols, rifles, gunpowder and whiskey: high-demand items that could be exchanged for a lot of cattle. If Carleton thought replacing Steck with Delgado was the antidote needed to stop the illegal barter, he was horribly mistaken.[60]

It was also Delgado who approved the pass associated with Labadie's father-in-law, James Giddings, as well as those supported by merchants Edward Hamburger and D. Bernard Koch; Albuquerque businessman W. H. Henrie; Francisco Baca y Ortíz; ex-soldier, politician, and land magnate Miguel E. Pino; Indian agent Jesús M. Baca y Salazar; former Indian agent John Ward; Santa Fe denizen Anastacio Sandoval; chief justice John Sebrie Watts; former superintendent of Indian Affairs James L. Collins; and surveyor William White. All types of contracts were validated with bonds, yet these particular documents illustrate that in the mid 1860s, New Mexico's upper classes were not ashamed of the Comanchero trade. In fact, they openly supported it. They vouched for the traders and signed their names to numerous licenses. It is noteworthy, however, that these documents never mentioned Texas cattle.[61]

Individuals other than New Mexican businessmen and political elites were enticed by the trade, and Major Bergmann was not the only officer to get involved. Doing the math in his head, Capt. Patrick Henry Healy came to the conclusion that the thousands of heads of cattle that flowed into New Mexico were one of the key reasons so many territorial merchants lived like feudal lords. Healy had served in the First New Mexico Infantry during the Civil War and afterward. While patrolling between the Canadian and Pecos Rivers, he became well-versed in the cattle business. In 1866, the year he mustered out, he made a proposal to Commissioner of Indian Affairs Dennis N. Cooley. Pointing out the benefits of a new and improved (and legal) Comanchero trade, Healy claimed that this could only happen if the arms-and-whiskey-smuggling Hispanos could be eliminated from the trade. Healy suggested that Cooley restrict passes to a few honest, industrious men like himself.[62]

Only a few months earlier Cooley had recommended to Superintendent Norton that an Indian agent be placed at Fort Bascom to help solve problems associated with cattle theft. He knew that many of Texas's problems were associated with the Comanches' ready access to whiskey, gunpowder, and rifles. Without addressing the role stolen cattle played in this pipeline, Healy argued that an honest American might be able to provide the Indians with proper sustenance and manufactured goods that would help to wean them away from the more violent aspects of the trade. His proposal must have been music to Norton's ears. Here was a way to rectify Delgado's rampant abuse of the system.[63]

Healy promised to trade only legal goods, products found on the shelves of mercantile establishments in Santa Fe and Las Vegas. As it turns out, the Comanches' own agent, Jesse Leavenworth, approved of Healy's idea and recommended the recently retired captain and three other veterans be allowed to establish a trading post on the New Mexican frontier.[64] Soon after, Healy and the others were awarded their licenses. He immediately informed Carleton that Santa Fe officials could no longer issue passes to just anyone, and therefore the illegal trade was about to stop. This change, he alerted the general, came from Washington, D.C. Just to be clear, Healy shot off a separate letter to Acting Assistant Adjutant Cyrus De Forrest informing him that his (Healy's) group now constituted the government's officially sanctioned traders for New Mexico Territory, and the army should stop anyone else from going to Texas. By early 1867 Healy felt pretty confident that he had just cornered the Texas cattle market.[65]

The ex-captain's partners were all veterans of the California Column. Lt. Charles T. Jennings (who did a short stint as the Navajo agent at the Bosque Redondo before Lawrence Murphy took over), Capt. Rufus C. Vose, and Capt. Erastus Wood had all served together on numerous New Mexico posts. This included Fort Bascom and Fort Sumner. As newly minted Comanche traders they established their base of operations in the heart of Comanchero country, Alexander Hatch's old ranch on the Gallinas River, near Chaperito.[66]

Carleton responded directly to Healy's letter and also got in touch with Commissioner Cooley. The general told Cooley he did not think his department had the authority to stop New Mexican citizens from trading with the Comanches. He added that he had passed this information on to his superiors but was hesitant to curtail locals' ability to make a living. In essence, Carleton was not on board with his ex-subordinates' plans. Patrols were eventually stepped up, but increased military efforts really started after Carleton was replaced in July 1867.[67]

Hatch's Ranch was five miles north of the Gallinas Crossing, close to Miguel Pino's original hacienda. This crossing was a part of an old Indian trail that began in Albuquerque and ran all the way to Texas. Isleta Indians and other Puebloan-speaking peoples used it to venture east on their own trading expeditions. Near the Gallinas River this road split in two; one branch led to Quitaque, the other to Mucha-Que Peak. Labadie identified the branch that broke southeast, toward the Tucumcari Peak and beyond, as "the road of the Cibuleros [*sic*] and Comancheros." The other branch veered northeast, passed the new trading post, and eventually connected with the Canadian River.[68]

The Gallinas Crossing was situated a day's ride east of Anton Chico and the Pecos River. The entire region was a desolate, broken land of mesas, arroyos, and scrub brush. About fifteen miles east of this village another valley came into view, its slim greenbelt oddly out of place amid the arid environment. Down below, cottonwoods followed the Gallinas River as it snaked its way south. It was here that Pino had built his hacienda. Rancher and merchant James Elias Whitmore lived there when Healy brought his plan to fruition.[69]

Pino, Hatch, Healy, Tafoya, and Whitmore did not locate to this region just to ranch and farm. They established trading posts and stores along some of the most significant trading routes of the nineteenth-century Southwest, roads that started in Bernal, Tecolote, and Albuquerque. One branched off to the south, running along the Pecos River to the Bosque Redondo. All connected near Anton Chico, and all could be used to get to some part of Texas.

William Pelham, New Mexico's first surveyor general, was very interested in this region. When trying to substantiate land grant claims along the Gallinas and Pecos Rivers, he interviewed a number of locals. Three had been there for decades: Francisco Montoya, Louis Griego, and Francisco Salazar. Montoya described how this eastern route split into two more roads, both of which he declared were very old. One crossed the Gallinas River at Chaperito. It continued on to Conchas Springs before connecting with another that followed the Canadian River into Texas. Griego explained that Comanches provided mules to the traders who used this route to go east. Like Labadie, he called the lower route the Comancheros' Road. It had originally run by Pino's ranch. After crossing the Gallinas, it veered southeast before reaching Tucumcari Peak. It crossed another east-west route near this landmark. The U.S. Army later renamed a large portion of this route the Fort Smith Road. After crossing this trail, the lower road continued its southeastern trek toward the Double Mountain Fork of the Brazos River.[70]

Ironically, just like the businesspeople of Santa Fe and Las Vegas, Healy, Jennings, Vose, and Woods eventually turned to the very people they planned to shut out of the trade to help save their own. Although not dated, a document entitled "Office of Superintendent of Indian Affairs" reveals that Healy hired Julián Baca, Nabor Aragón, Pedro Marques, and Jesús Sandoval to haul the trading post's goods to the Comanches. Vose did this as well, seeking out Labadie's brother-in-law and business partner Manuel Chaves to hire people willing to take his goods to Texas. While Cooley's decision to deny traders like Chaves licenses might have hindered them for a while, Healy's and Vose's inability to get goods to Texas without help ended up providing for their own demise. After acquiring his license from Vose, Chaves turned around and sold it to Refugio Lucero and Manuel Sánchez. These two then hired their own crews to go into Comanche country. Charles Jennings did the same. He hired José Piedad Tafoya. He also employed Julián Padilla and Román and Blas Martinas. These individuals then took Jennings's pass and recruited their own employees. Erastus Wood either did not supply a similar list to the superintendent or was not involved in the trade to the same extent as the others. Some old Comancheros testified in 1893 that they had purchased their supplies on credit from Hatch's Ranch. They then took these items to Texas and traded for cattle. Once back in New Mexico, using the herd as money, they paid off their debts to the merchants. If the cattle were worth more than what they owed, the ranchers in Chaperito, La Cuesta, and Anton Chico kept the balance of the herd as their profits, sold them elsewhere, or traded them for other goods. Instead of the government gaining more control of over the trade, the opposite began to happen.[71]

When new superintendent of Indian Affairs A. B. Norton made his report to Commissioner Nathaniel G. Taylor in 1867 (Taylor had succeeded Cooley), he explained that the current chaotic state of the trade with the Comanches was not his fault. He pointed the finger at his predecessor, Delgado, and also pushed some of the blame toward Carleton. Things had not gone well since Norton had approved the idea of restricting the trade. He reported that it was out of control, explaining that hundreds of traders without licenses were doing business with the Comanches. He explained: "When no cattle or horses are found in the Comanche camp by the Mexican traders, they lend Indians their pistols and horses and remain at the camp until the Comanches have time to go to Texas and return, and get the stock they desire."[72]

In 1893 Tafoya testified in Charles Goodnight's depredation case. He was asked about the trade that Norton so explicitly described. What he had to say is worth repeating. Charles Jennings supplied him with a variety of dry goods, textiles, beads, and paints. When asked how he paid for these items, Tafoya practically gave the same answer as Norton had to Taylor: he paid Healy for the goods he had taken east with the cattle he returned with. Any surplus became Tafoya's to do with what he wanted. Sometimes he traded them in for store goods. Sometimes he sold these cattle elsewhere.[73]

Forts Union and Bascom soldiers also noticed the uptick in Comanchero activity that Norton described. This included the subtraders' dealings, but they also described the unanticipated consequences of subverting the old system from operating the way it had for decades. The new restrictions meant Comancheros quit applying for licenses but kept going to Texas. Depredations increased. Surprisingly, it was Labadie who informed Superintendent Norton that Healy, Jennings, Vose, and Wood had subcontracted their licenses to others. He informed Norton that these third-party traders were exchanging hoop-iron (used for arrow points), ammunition, and whiskey for Texas cattle. He did this even though his brother-in-law was one of the subtraders. In hindsight, this might not have been as underhanded as it sounds. Chaves and Labadie could have leaked this information still knowing they could benefit in the short term while setting the wheels in motion to get rid of the Hatch's Ranch operation. The explosion in thefts was real, and while Healy and his partners were certainly to blame for helping to ignite the activity, they were not the only Anglos interested in trading with Indians.[74]

Col. Oscar M. Brown also came to New Mexico as a part of the California Column. In the early 1860s he had served as post commander at Fort Sumner, and in 1864 he purchased a license to sell liquor and operate a mail-carrying business at the fort. He was still commander at the time. As odd as such an action sounds, it was not that uncommon. Lt. Col. Francisco P. Abreu held a similar license at Chaperito while serving as temporary post commander at Fort Bascom. Many of the officers who were scattered across New Mexico moonlighted for additional money. Colonel Brown was aware of the profits that could be made as the civilian sutler or post trader, dealing with soldiers and nearby reservation Indians. After mustering out, he lobbied the secretary of war to make him the new sutler at Fort Sumner and was awarded the franchise. Yet Brown's plans for a seamless transition were undermined by the current sutler, Joseph A. Larue. Larue was also a cattle broker. Once notified that he was about to be replaced, he argued that his store was stocked with several months' worth of goods. He would go bankrupt if forced to immediately hand over his business to Brown. Many officers, including Carleton, stood up for Larue. His removal was delayed so he could sell his products. This forced Brown to put his own supplies in temporary storage outside of the fort. Already angry, Brown then learned that the Navajos' agent had given Larue a license to sell his goods at the reservation. This was another goal of Brown's, so he complained to Commissioner Cooley, who was unaware that the Navajo agent was handing out passes. After much back-and-forth between the commissioner, Superintendent Norton, and the army, Brown eventually settled in as post sutler at Sumner. He did a lot of business with Las Vegas merchants like Charles Ilfeld, procuring goods that he could sell on the base. After a time, Brown also received a license to trade with the same Navajo Indians that he had once overseen as commander.[75]

Brown became sutler and Indian trader at about the same time the Hatch's Ranch enterprise started. While no documents tie Healy's old commander to the Comanchero trade, in the summer of 1869 Brown did purchase land along the Pecos River from Rufus C. Vose, a member of Healy's operation. One of Brown's new neighbors was Manuel Chaves. Brown called his new four-hundred-acre property the California Ranch. The implications from naming his property this are obvious, yet further records concerning any trade originating from that location have not been found. The California Ranch was located just north of James Giddings's and Lorenzo Labadie's properties. Puerto de Luna was right up the road.[76]

More confusion was created by ex-soldier John D. Henderson, the agent for the Pueblo Indians, who handed out passes to his charges so they could trade in Texas. In January 1867 Henderson wrote a pass for José M. Valdez of Canoncito that allowed Valdez to trade with the Comanches and Kiowas for a year, far longer than the average pass, which usually lasted for two or three months. Anastacio Sandoval and Faustin Valdez (José's brother) put up the $5,000 bond. This unusual arrangement allowed José to make several trips to Texas on one pass. He employed Realmico Valdez, Teodo Valdez, Rafael Valdez, and Thomas Laings—sons, brothers, and neighbors—to go with him. It was not long before Commissioner Taylor caught wind of what Henderson was doing.[77]

Just in case Superintendent Norton was unaware of Henderson's actions, Taylor brought him up to speed. He told him to explain to the agent that he did not have the authority to issue his own passes. Only Texas's Indian agent could issue passes to trade in Texas. Yet issues with Henderson did not end there.[78]

In September 1867 Capt. George W. Letterman of Fort Bascom came upon José Valdez and his employees on their way back from Texas with a large number of cattle. Letterman reported that this Puebloan possessed a pass signed by Henderson. Other ex-military personnel were also getting involved in the sale of Texas cattle.[79]

As noted, one of Capt. Lawrence G. Murphy's last stints before mustering out was as Indian agent at the Bosque Redondo. Murphy had begun his service in New Mexico in 1861, helping to reoccupy Fort Stanton after the Confederates abandoned it. Near the end of the war he was stationed at Fort Sumner when the government decided to use military officers as Indian agents to cut down on fraud, a decision fraught with irony. By then Charles Jennings was busy opening a trading post on the Gallinas River. Murphy and Emil Fritz remembered their time along the Rio Bonito. After mustering out in 1866, they opened a brewery and store on the edge of Fort Stanton's property line. They eventually moved these businesses nine miles down the river to Placita (which changed its name to Lincoln in 1869). Operations soon expanded to include the trading post, a hotel, a saloon, and a mercantile establishment. Murphy offered a variety of goods, including whiskey, to soldiers, civilians, and nearby Indians. His goal was to monopolize both the cattle trade and trade with the Indians. Part of this plan included trying to get the Bureau of Indian Affairs to appoint one of his subordinates to the position of Mescalero agent. By then the government had reverted back to employing civilian agents, but Murphy was not happy with any of them. When Lorenzo Labadie returned as agent in 1869, Murphy led a successful campaign to get him removed. A series of ineffective agents followed.

Through intimidation and economic coercion, Murphy enforced his will over each branch of trade. Agents had to sign off on the bills Murphy and Company submitted to the government. These invoices supposedly detailed what they were selling to the Indians. Oftentimes they represented phantom purchases for phantom Indians. At the same time, new post trader Paul Dowlin rented space in Murphy's store and sold the Mescaleros liquor that his former captain supplied. As to what he thought of the government trying to hamper these activities, Murphy once retorted: "It don't make any difference who the government sends here as agent. We control these Indians." This practice continued unabated through 1873.[80]

A large portion of Murphy and Company's profits derived from selling cattle to Fort Stanton. They acquired beef from both Hispanic and Anglo cattlemen, asking few questions as to where the animals came from. John Simpson Chisum began to compete for federal dollars against the House, as Murphy and Company was known. This set up a short-lived alliance of sorts between local Hispanos and Irishman Murphy against the hated Texans. It was not long before some of Chisum's cattle went missing. His cowhands reported that beeves with some mysterious brands were showing up at the Fort Stanton slaughter pens. Chisum believed Murphy and his partners were stealing his cattle, altering the brands, and selling them to the post. Such beliefs eventually led to violence. Lincoln was not the only region where the insertion of Texans into New Mexico led to conflict.[81]

In late 1868 the *Santa Fe Weekly New Mexican* reported that William P. Calloway of Pecos Bend and Emil Fritz of Fort Stanton were in town. Both were veterans of the California Column. The same paper noted that on December 1,

1868, Gen. Charles McClure had accepted proposals for contracts to supply beef and corn. Calloway, Fritz, and F. M. (Frank) Wilburn submitted bids to supply five hundred beeves to the military. As noted, Calloway ran a hotel, ranch, and store on the Pecos River north of Brown's California Ranch. Frank Wilburn and his brother Aaron did the same outside of Roswell.[82]

Emil Fritz's affiliation with Murphy eventually made him something of a sidebar within the annals of Southwestern history. Although competitors like Chisum were a thorn in its side, Murphy and Company still controlled most of the southeastern New Mexico cattle trade. Their partnership dissolved after Fritz died on a visit back to Germany. Jimmy Dolan took his place. By then Murphy was losing control of his operation due to the debilitating effects of long-term alcohol abuse. Dolan began to take on more of the everyday responsibilities, and Murphy ended up selling out to fellow Irishman John H. Riley. It was Dolan and Riley who ran the county when Englishman John Tunstall came to town and set off a violent chain of events that became known as the Lincoln County War—a war that involved cowboys, Hispano ranchers, lawyers, and politicians.

Many books and movies have been written about what happened on the streets of Lincoln in the late 1870s, yet the events that put many New Mexicans in early graves started long before Billy the Kid became a household name. As noted, daylight shootouts and vigilante justice were not unique to that part of the territory. Comancheros, merchants, and a couple of enterprising butchers played large roles in both the history of the cattle trade and the violence that followed these transactions to their bloody conclusions.

Commander of the Department of New Mexico during the Civil War years, Brig. Gen. James Henry Carleton (*front row right*) is pictured among fellow Masonic lodge members. Col. Kit Carson is seated front row center. Maj. Edward Bergmann is standing in the back row, far left. Beside him is fellow Prussian and former merchant Charles P. Clever. At the time of this photograph Clever was a territorial delegate, but he began his career in Santa Fe with the Seligman family, running a store on the plaza. Few people knew the Comancheros and their influence over New Mexico's economy as well as these men did.

Courtesy of the Palace of Governors Photo Archives (NMHM/DCA), no. 009826.

Photograph by Nicholas Brown, 1866.

Confederate spymaster Henry Skillman's signature on a land survey from
August 10, 1854, in San Elizario, Texas.

File 001208, p. 9, Presidio County Abstract No. 1683. Courtesy of Texas General Land Office Archives.

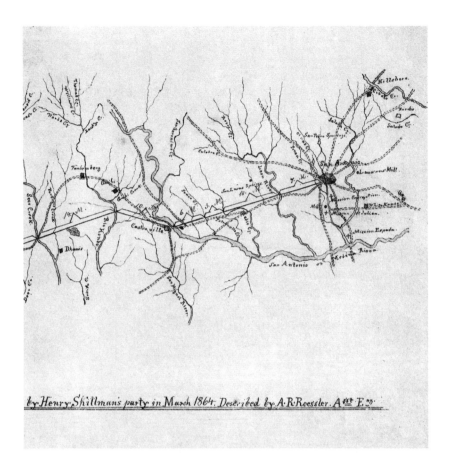

Detail from a series of maps compiled by Henry Skillman's Confederate spy company in March 1864. This map shows Skillman's suggested route to move rebel troops from San Antonio to West Texas.

Map 1004K, "Best Route for the Movements of Troops from San Antonio to El Paso."
Courtesy of Texas State Library and Archives Commission.

Know all Men by these presents, that we *Jose Costillo* ....
..................................as principal.... and *Jesus M.ª Baco - Lorenzo Labadi* as sureties
are held and firmly bound unto the United States of America, in the sum of *One thousand* dollars,
lawful money of the United States; for the payment of which, well and truly to be made, we bind ourselves,
and each of us, our heirs, executors, and administrators, jointly and severally, firmly by these presents; sealed
with our seals, and dated this *8* day of *October* 186*5*.

The condition of the above obligation is such, that, whereas, FELIPE DELGADO, Supt. Ind. Aff's. for New
Mexico, hath granted to the said *Jose Costillo* a license
dated *October 8.º* 186*5* to trade for *two* months with the
Camanche tribe of Indians, within the boundaries of the country occupied by said tribe.

Now if the said *Jose Costillo* so licensed, shall
faithfully conform to, and observe all the laws and regulations made, or which shall be made, "for the government of trade and intercourse with the Indian tribes, and in no respect violate the same," and shall trade
within the aforesaid boundaries and no other, and shall in all respects, act conformably with the license granted
to..............then this obligation to be void, else to remain in full force and virtue.

Signed and sealed in the presence of

Jose Castillo {L. S.}

Jesus M.ª Baca y Salazar {L. S.}

Lorenzo Labadi {L. S.}

A pass issued to Comanchero José Costillo to trade with the Comanches.
Bondholders are Lorenzo Labadi and Jesús María Sena y Baca.
Letters Received from the Commissioner of Indian Affairs, 1864–1865.
Courtesy of the National Archives, Washington D.C.

Know all Men by these Presents, That we F. M. Willburn & P. L. Stockton of Red River Station, Colfax County, Territory of New Mexico, and Charles Probst & August Kirchner, of Santa Fé, Santa Fé, County and Territory of New Mexico.

are held and firmly bound to the United States of America in the sum of Ten Thousand (10,000,) dollars, lawful money of the United States; for which payment well and truly to be made, we bind ourselves, and each of us, our and each of our heirs, executors and administrators, for and in the whole, jointly and severally, firmly by these presents.

Sealed with our seals, dated the Eleventh day of October in the year of our Lord eighteen hundred and sixty nine,

The nature of this Obligation is such, that if the above bounden F. M. Willburn & P. L. Stockton, Charles Probst or August Kirchner, their heirs, executors, and administrators, or any of them, shall and do in all things well and truly observe, perform, fulfill, accomplish, and keep, all and singular the covenants, conditions, and agreements whatsoever, which on the part of the said F. M. Willburn & P. L. Stockton, their heirs, executors, and administrators, are or ought to be observed, performed, fulfilled, accomplished, and kept, comprised or mentioned in certain articles of agreement or contract bearing date the Eighth day of October 1869 between the said Willburn & Stockton and Major Clinton, U. S. A. Supt of Indian Affairs Assistant Quartermaster concerning the delivery of the rations required to feed the Ute & Apaches at Cimarron, N. M., to the U. S. Quartermaster Department, Indian agent at Cimarron, N. M.

then the above obligation to be void; otherwise to remain in full force and virtue.

WITNESSES

(sgd.) A. Napier,
" David V. Catanach

(Signed) F. M. Willburn (SEAL)
" P. L. Stockton (SEAL)
" Charles Probst (SEAL)
August Kirchner

A True Copy –
W. Clinton
Major U. S. Army –
Supt. of Indian Affairs,
for New Mexico.

Cattle suppliers Wilburn and Stockton's contract with
butchers Charles Probst and August Kirchner.
Letters Received from Headquarters, District of New Mexico (U.S. Army), 1869.
Image 541, roll 10. Courtesy of the National Archives, Washington D.C.

"Freighters on the Santa Fe Trail, Bernard Seligman, Zadoc Staab, Lehman Spiegelberg, and Kiowa Indian scouts." These traders, dressed here as frontiersmen, belonged to three of the most powerful merchant families in New Mexico: the Seligmans, the Staabs, and the Spiegelbergs. Bernard's brother Adolph was one of butcher August Kirchner's staunchest defenders. Zadoc [Zadok] Staab often worked with Probst and Kirchner, as well as with Comanchero Félix García. The butchers also did business with the Spiegelbergs.

Courtesy of the Palace of Governors Photo Archives (NMHM/DCA), no. 007890.
Photographer unknown, date unknown.

"Hon. Stephen B. Elkins of W. Va." Elkins used his power as district attorney in New Mexico to become a leading political figure in the territory before moving to West Virginia and successfully running for the U.S. Senate. Along with brothers Samuel and John, he also owned a ranch on the Pecos River. 1865.

Courtesy of the Library of Congress Prints and Photographs Division, LC-BH832-114.

"Thomas Benton Catron. Delegate from New Mexico, 1885–1897; Senator 1912–1917. Walking." About the time this photo was taken (c. 1915), Thomas B. Catron testified in the Court of Claims on behalf of Probst and Kirchner, vouching for their honesty and integrity. The senator explained to the court that everyone who could participate in the Comanchero trade did, and no one thought it was illegal. Thirty years prior to this testimony, he and law partner Stephen Elkins had represented Texas cattleman John Hittson in his effort to reclaim stolen cattle in New Mexico.

Courtesy of the Library of Congress Prints and Photographs Division, LC-H261-2350.

Noted Texas cattleman and Confederate beef contractor John Simpson
Chisum started selling beeves to Union beef contractors from the
Department of New Mexico in the fall of 1864.
Photograph from James Cox, Historical and Biographical Record of the Cattle Industry
and Cattlemen of Texas and Adjacent Territory.

M. C. Smith worked as a cowhand for John Chisum in 1863 and 1864 before joining Union beef contractor James Patterson during 1864 and 1865.
Undated photograph from Sidney M. Smith, From the Cow Camp to the Pulpit: Being Twenty-Five Years Experience of a Texas Evangelist.

CHAPTER 4

Comanche and Kiowa Indians valued cattle as much as Anglo Americans, but for different reasons. By the late 1860s their raiding and trading was about survival, not empire-building. Exchanging stolen herds for weapons and other goods allowed them to remain on the plains and off the reservations. But by the 1890s, two decades after the army finally defeated the Southern Plains tribes, the victims of those cattle thefts looked to the government for reimbursement. They did this through a process deliberated in the U.S. Court of Claims. Anglo and Hispano New Mexicans and Texans detailed losses in amounts that ran into the tens of millions of dollars. The U.S. Court of Claims was set up to determine the validity of each application. Witnesses were brought forth who knew something about the thefts and the character of the people seeking redress. Lawyers usually accompanied the applicants. The U.S. government and whichever Indian nation was charged with the crimes were liable for substantiated claims. Any payments came out of reservation budgets. Thus, the government, in conjunction with the Indians' lawyers, produced witnesses to contradict the applicants' requests. In suits regarding Texas and New Mexico cattle, the claimants often tried to link the Comanchero trade to their losses.

In September 1896 Santa Fe butchers Charles Probst and August Kirchner made sworn statements to the Court of Claims regarding their losses. Beginning in 1859, Probst and Kirchner ran a butcher shop and livestock operation in the heart of Santa Fe. They maintained this business for two decades. After Probst left, Kirchner continued the business for another ten years. Both sat for depositions on September 30, filing four claims that totaled $160,000.[1]

August Kirchner and Charles Probst left the forest villages of Prussia in 1853 to seek new opportunities in the United States. It is unknown if they knew each other before leaving Europe, but they emigrated at the same time. After arriving in New York City, they joined the army in 1854. As a part of the Third U.S. Infantry, they served in the West. We do not know if they saw combat: on that point the record is silent. What is important for this study, however, is that the army brought them to New Mexico.[2]

After mustering out in 1859, twenty-four-year-old Probst and twenty-two-year-old Kirchner opened a butcher shop on San Francisco Street in downtown Santa Fe. They claimed to be coequal partners, but the 1860 census noted that only Charles owned personal property in the city. It was valued at $1,200. A decade later another Santa Fe census noted that each owned real estate valued at $1,500 and personal property worth $8,000.[3]

Their business was within walking distance of Fort Marcy, army headquarters for the territory. Anyone seeking to supply beef to the military wanted to be close to the people who awarded the contracts. Once the army's efforts to contain the Indians began to have the desired results, the U.S. government was left to deal with the consequences of the reservation system. This meant finding a way to feed the thousands of Navajo and Apache Indians who were relocated onto New Mexico reservations. This was partially accomplished through government beef contracts. Probst and Kirchner procured a lot of those contracts. So where did they get their beef?

Kie Oldham represented the Jicarilla and Ute Indians in many of the depredation cases, often working alongside assistant attorneys general in Court of Claims hearings. When the butchers came forward and testified about their losses, Oldman sought to portray Kirchner as a corrupt and inept old man—a cattle thief once-removed who was just as guilty as the Hispano traders who made the exchanges. Oldham argued that any cattle the two sought reimbursement for had been stolen from others; besides, it was inconceivable to think that they could ever have lost $160,000 worth of cattle to the Indians. If that was true, how could they account for the livestock that had not been stolen? Thus, the government basically charged that Probst and Kirchner were lying.[4]

Kirchner was a very old sixty-three when he testified. His answers were often disconnected and rambling. Judging from the transcript of his statements, it is clear that a lawyer of reasonable competence could easily shape his testimony into a solid case against any settlement. Indeed, this is what happened. Though they failed to support reimbursement, several depositions concerning Probst and Kirchner's four claims contain valuable information on the Comanchero trade.[5]

Kirchner testified in one deposition that in the summer of 1869 he was herding cattle down the Pecos River to Fort Sumner when he was attacked by Indians. This occurred on an early August morning and about seventy-five miles north of the post. The perpetrators were a band of Jicarilla Apaches. He recounted that they absconded with seven hundred cattle. The skeptical Oldman first argued that in 1869, the Jicarillas were not a threat in that part of New Mexico. (While the majority of these Indians lived further north by this point, less than a decade had passed since they had claimed this portion of the Pecos River valley as a part of their homeland.) Oldham quickly segued into trying to connect any cattle in Kirchner's possession to the Comanchero trade. When asked where the herd had come from, he replied that he had bought them from a Captain Rosenthal. When asked who Rosenthal had purchased the beeves from, Kirchner could not remember. Then, almost casually, he offered that he paid fifty thousand dollars for these cattle. He explained that Captain Rosenthal was a government agent, someone who procured beef for the army. The more Kirchner talked, the more muddled his answers became. At one point he recalled that some Texans and Rosenthal were helping him get the stock to Fort Sumner when the raid occurred. While this might seem a bit strange, many Texans were driving cattle to that post during the period in question. At another point Kirchner noted that Rosenthal was an agent for Texas cattleman Thomas L. Stockton. Any understanding of what happened to the Comanchero trade in the 1870s involves this man.[6]

In the same deposition Kirchner noted: "Rosenthal, he come and sold that beef, then [Stockton] asked him, Rosenthal[,] where did you get that beef [?], and he said not your damn business, and I says alright, he says pay me the money when you can, and the balance I'll wait; he was afraid the sheriff was coming after him or someone from Texas and trouble him, so he kept it secret, quiet." Kirchner's testimony links Stockton and Rosenthal to his business. While he often competed against both men for beef contracts, it is also true that they sometimes worked together. The old butcher's recounting of both Stockton's suspicions and Rosenthal's response is significant. Even if this conversation only took place within his jumbled memory, it summarized the tension that had existed between Texans and New Mexicans during this period. Kirchner's Captain Rosenthal could have been a representation of the many merchants, army officers, Comancheros, and Indians he had done business with. It is also possible that he was specifically talking about Rosenthal.[7]

By inserting a series of very leading questions and a couple of outright accusations into his interrogations, Oldham ensured that his inferences became a part of the public record. As far as the government was concerned, Kirchner had been herding stolen cattle when they were stolen again; therefore, he was not deserving of any reimbursement. Despite the lawyer's aggressive questioning, the butcher never admitted that he had ever knowingly purchased someone else's property.[8]

The Captain Rosenthal whom Kirchner named was William "Willie" Rosenthal, a member of the Rosenthal clan of Santa Fe, who were influential merchants with strong economic and political connections. Willie, among other things, was a government contractor who supplied beef to reservations like the Bosque Redondo and to several of the territory's military posts.[9] He was also a veteran, having once served in the quartermaster department. Such experience opened doors that civilians did not have access to. Rosenthal and Stockton submitted bids to supply beeves to posts all across the territory.[10]

Stockton's question to Rosenthal—"Where did you get that beef?"—hangs in the air like an accusation. Like many other Texans, he had driven thousands of cattle up the Pecos to Fort Sumner. In the late 1860s Stockton started a ranch south of Raton, New Mexico. Once there he developed a partnership with Frank Wilburn. Emil Fritz, Lawrence G. Murphy's partner, acted as Wilburn and Stockton's agent for many of their transactions. Wilburn and Stockton's main competition came from New Mexican merchants like Willie Rosenthal and butchers like Kirchner and Probst.[11]

Rosenthal was also a familiar face in Lincoln County. He was on a first-name basis with Murphy and Fritz. Anyone who sought to do business at Fort Stanton had to go through these two. As part of a mercantile dynasty, Willie and his family were prominent wholesalers and retailers in Santa Fe and Las Vegas. A large portion of their business involved supplying military posts and reservations. For decades, Willie, like Probst and Kirchner, was deeply involved in the territory's trade in cattle and with the Indians.[12]

Charles Probst also testified on September 30, 1896. The transcripts make clear that Kirchner was the talker. Probst often deferred to August's recollections. He admitted that it was his partner who usually traveled with the herds to their destination. Probst also offered that between 1859 and 1879, twenty thousand cattle passed through their businesses, undermining the government's claim that they were incapable of operating at such a scale. He noted that it was not unusual for his partner to bring back ten thousand dollars from his trail drives. To further substantiate their standing in Santa Fe, Probst testified that mercantilists like James L. Johnson (affiliated with both D. Bernard Koch and Preston Beck Jr.), Simón Delgado (Felipe's brother), and Gustave Elsberg had no problem extending them large lines of credit. As outlined in chapter 3, traders often purchased cattle from Texas Indians with merchandise acquired on credit.[13]

Once the government paid them for their cattle, the butchers could pay off these loans, either with cash or excess cattle. Thus, merchants were also heavily involved in the cattle trade. They also traded with one another. In 1868 Felipe Delgado purchased several hundred dollars in goods from the Staab brothers. One of the products was vermillion, a red-powder dye that was in great demand among the Comanches and Kiowas.[14]

Another government lawyer, R. J. Spearman, asked Probst where their cattle came from. Probst admitted that many were from Texas but made clear that his and Kirchner's transactions were always legal. Spearman was unimpressed. He claimed to know that the partners had funded Comanchero expeditions to that state. Who sold these animals to them? Probst remained vague, noting that a lot of people sold them cattle, including "Mexicans, Americans," and "Dutchmen."[15] (Germans were often described as Dutchmen in the United States during nineteenth century.)

William H. Robeson, Probst and Kirchner's lawyer, pushed back. He charged that the lawyers representing the government and the Indians were not interested in investigating the depredation cases. Instead, they only sought to impugn his clients' characters. Robeson staunchly defended them, declaring that no one had ever brought forward evidence that they had purchased stolen cattle.[16]

Both sides called witnesses to bolster their cases. In a rather odd attempt to verify one claim, the butchers produced Felipe Alarid, who testified that he recalled a raid at a place called Los Conejos. This was in southern Colorado, just north of a cattle ranch Kirchner maintained in New Mexico. The claim stated that Ute Indians had stolen five hundred head of Kirchner and Probst's cattle. Alarid explained at the time of the incident he and two friends were traveling to Colorado to prospect for gold when they ran into Kirchner, his former employer. More striking than this opportune meeting was who traveled with Alarid. Both of his fellow prospectors were residents of Chaperito: Rumaldo Apodaca and José Piedad Tafoya. Why Alarid would mention Tafoya, even if his story was true, is almost unfathomable. By the time he was deposed, everyone knew Tafoya's reputation. The butcher needed a witness, but this one might have given the government even more reason to refuse the claim. It is at least conceivable that Apodaca, Tafoya, and Alarid were all working for Kirchner at the time.

Oldham countered by bringing up the testimony of another ex-Kirchner employee, Felipe Vigil. Vigil had already confessed that his old boss had offered him a hundred dollars to lie about a similar claim. The government concluded by arguing that none of the butchers' witnesses could be trusted. Inserting Tafoya's name into this testimony probably hurt their case more than helped.[17]

Kirchner's ranch was north of Abiquiú. He called it La Porte Chiquito, perhaps a reference to the stream it was situated on, which ran through the Arroyo del Puerto Chiquito before joining the Chama River. While it may have been a coincidence, the street that ran behind their butchering enterprise in Santa Fe was once called Rio Chiquito. It later became Water Street.[18] Foreman Charles Dominick recalled that La Porte Chiquito was located eleven miles west of the spot where the town of Tierra Amarilla was established. Others called this location El Bado del Bado, Canada de Barbero, and Rincón de Tierra Amarilla. It was situated in a canyon cut ages ago by the Chama River. The path that crossed this stream was part of the Old Spanish Trail, which connected southern Colorado to California. Santa Fe was ninety miles to the south. Most of the beeves Probst and Kirchner kept at the ranch were herded to Santa Fe to slaughter, but they also took their herds straight to the forts that were scattered across the territory. Some were butchered on the banks of the Rio Chiquito.[19]

It is clear that Kirchner was often at his Rio Arriba ranch and made frequent trips back and forth to the capital. While employed by Adolph Letcher in Taos, young merchant Charles Ilfeld recalled that they often caught Kirchner as he passed through town on his way south, giving him cash to deliver to their supplier, Elsberg and Amberg. Kirchner had married a woman named Refugia Baca in 1860. A woman of the same name is listed in the Rio Arriba census for that year. The 1870 Santa Fe census notes that a Refugia Baca y "Kerchner" was living with August and Charles Probst in the capital. Refugia Baca y Kirchner kept her own account at the Second National Bank of Santa Fe. In 1873 she or her husband made three separate deposits that totaled six thousand dollars. Yet during the Court of Claims depositions of 1898, it was widow Nestora Lucero Perea Kirchner who sought a settlement. Without offering any specifics, Kie Oldham characterized the butcher's wife as being a member of a significant and wealthy "Spanish family" that had lived in New Mexico for generations.[20]

The Elsberg and Amberg mercantile establishment that young Ilfeld forwarded money to operated their main store out of Santa Fe. Like other New Mexico merchants, they often delivered goods to their competitors. They also sold the army cattle they acquired from middle-men like Kirchner. As noted, when Probst and Kirchner or Marcus Goldbaum, another Prussian, procured cattle from the Indians, they paid with the goods found in those merchants' stores. Merchants and the middlemen worked hand-in-glove. During the Civil War Albert Elsberg partnered with Probst and Kirchner to deliver 1,500 cattle to Fort Craig. This transaction was a perfect illustration of the Comanchero trade in action. The butchers exchanged merchandise acquired from Elsberg to the Comanches, who paid in stolen cattle. The merchants and traders then sold these cattle to the army. The latter two settled accounts after being paid.[21]

In a bit of an ironic twist, after leaving his command at Fort Bascom, Maj. Edward H. Bergmann was ordered to Rio Arriba County to establish a base camp, called Camp Plummer, near Kirchner's ranch. His new mission was to protect the people who lived in the county's numerous villages. The most significant of these was Las Nutritas, which later became Tierra Amarilla. Long before the arrival of American and Hispanic settlers, the Ute and Jicarilla Indians called this land home. They were not happy with their changing circumstances. One of Lorenzo Labadie's first stints as an Indian agent was at the nearby Abiquiú agency, where he served both the Jicarillas and the Utes. He moved around a bit in the 1850s, also operating out of Anton Chico, far to the south. Labadie returned to Abiquiú after falling into disfavor at Fort Sumner. He was there when Bergmann initiated Camp Plummer, just to the north.[22]

Bergmann found some of the same challenges along the Chama that he had faced on Canadian River. In May 1867 his troopers were involved in the separate arrests of don Felipe Madrill and Manuel Romero, who were on their way to Tierra Amarilla with 160 gallons of whiskey. In another incident, one Juaro Montaño was stopped with a keg of liquor. There was no mention as to the liquor's intended destination, but in a letter to headquarters Bergmann inferred that the availability of whiskey was behind many of the Indian raids on nearby communities. He seemed particularly upset with Indian agent Jesús María Sena y Baca. Labadie's old friend had failed to notify Bergmann of any troubles at his agency. While no paper trail ties these whiskey traders to Kirchner, their activities so close to his ranch are worth noting. After Madrill and Romero were arrested, they were turned over to civilian authorities.[23]

In a similar incident during the same year, Guadalupe Mars was arrested at Rayado for selling liquor to Indians. He was taken to Fort Union. Notifications of similar arrests were constantly being delivered to headquarters in Santa Fe. Stephen B. Elkins was the U.S. district attorney of New Mexico Territory at the time. After Assistant Adjutant General Cyrus De Forrest read the arresting officer's report about Mars, he wrote Elkins a letter. He informed the district attorney that Mars had previously been arrested for the same crime. Nothing had happened to him. Somewhat wryly, De Forrest wanted to know what he should do with this prisoner: "Complaints have been made before against this same man of which you were at the time informed." The inference, or accusation, was clear. Elkins was letting the whiskey traders go.[24]

De Forrest was not the only official complaining about the lack of prosecutions. Commissioner E. A. Rollins of the U.S. treasury department also wrote Elkins, noting that several people in his district had been arrested for selling alcohol, but no one ever served time for their crimes. Instead, they got off with a fine after pleading nolo contendere. Rollins wanted this practice stopped.[25]

An explanation as to what was going on can be found in the depredations claims of the 1890s and other documents. As noted, the government also called witnesses during these investigations. Robert B. Willison, a civil engineer and territorial surveyor in Santa Fe, had a lot to say about Probst and Kirchner. He believed them to be a disreputable duo who could not be trusted to tell the truth. He told the Court of Claims that they were heavily involved in the Comanchero trade. He also tied this trade to District Attorney Elkins. Willison claimed that 2,700 New Mexicans had been indicted for possessing stolen Texas cattle during Elkins time as district attorney. While that number seems high, even a third of that would be significant. As to Probst and Kirchner, he told Oldham that he had heard that the governor of New Mexico and the courts of Texas had filed charges against both butchers, but like most of the others, their case was nolle prossed—dismissed. Willison explained that the reason Probst's and Kirchner's cases were dropped was because they controlled the Democratic vote in Santa Fe County. He added that Elkins needed the men's support because he aspired to a seat in the territorial congress, inferring that the butchers convinced a lot of Comancheros to vote for him. As a result, Elkins became a territorial congressman, and Texans continued to lose their cattle.[26]

The meat-market business boomed. The proximity of Fort Marcy to Probst and Kirchner's shop was a major reason why. When new chief commissary officer Capt. Charles P. Eagan arrived in 1875, he reported that the two Prussians were practically running the entire commissary department. Willison noted that James L. Johnson, the merchant who often floated Kirchner and Probst loans, and cattle broker James Patterson also owned butcher shops in town. D. Bernard Koch, once Johnson's partner, funded several trading expeditions to Comanche country in the mid 1860s. It is not that much of a stretch to conclude where Johnson got his beef. Willison claimed that Johnson and Patterson were deeply involved in the Santa Fe butcher business.[27]

One of the main revelations extracted from Willison's testimony was related to the intersectional nature of the Comanchero trade and New Mexico politics.

August Kirchner was a powerful Santa Fe Democrat. Elkins was cognizant of this man's influence. Willison explained that they each possessed something the other desired. Elkins was able to use his power as district attorney to manipulate the electoral process. Kirchner played a role in this man's political rise. The politician had a role in the butcher's continued success.[28]

Elkins and Thomas B. Catron were old college buddies from back east who became law partners and much more in territorial New Mexico. Their careers ascended in the postwar years. They used their legal skills to represent a variety of people, including Hispano ranchers who were involved in land disputes. New Mexicans paid these lawyers with the only thing of value they owned, land. As a result, Catron and Elkins became two of the largest landowners in New Mexico. Both held interests in a number of land grants, including the Maxwell Land Grant and Railroad Company. Both were also involved in the cattle trade. Along with his brothers, Elkins ran a ranch on the old Preston Beck property southeast of Anton Chico in San Miguel County. Years later both became U.S. senators, Catron in New Mexico and Elkins in West Virginia. As their territorial powers crested, they continued to cross paths with the Prussian butchers.[29]

Willison was not the only person to present damaging testimony regarding Elkins. New Yorker Frank Warner Angel arrived in New Mexico in 1878 to conduct a multipronged investigation into political corruption and the murder of John H. Tunstall of Lincoln County. Two of his main targets at that time were territorial attorney general Thomas B. Catron and territorial governor Samuel Axtell. From May to August he interviewed a variety of people. One was John Taylor, a cattleman of substantial means who lived south of Las Vegas at Apache Springs. Of course, any investigation of Catron would involve Elkins, the focus of Taylor's ire. Speaking to Angel, he detailed a particular series of events that took place in 1873. His testimony was brief and to the point:[30]

I have been well-informed by various persons, well known to me, that during the first candidacy of Stephen B. Elkins for representation in the U.S. Congress, from this territory, many persons in San Miguel and Moro [Mora] Counties were arrested, charged with illegal trading with the Comanche tribe of Indians. Many of these persons were known to me. They were placed under bonds, and when they appeared for trial in Santa Fe they were released—as I am informed by them, and verily believe upon payment of fees to the prosecuting attorney and the agreement on their part to cast their ballots for the said Stephen B. Elkins.[31]

Taylor claimed that Elkins took advantage of the increased attention law officers were beginning to place on the Comancheros for his own political gain. They could avoid jail time and large fines if they worked with him. This relationship helps to explain why, after the war, the Texans became increasingly frustrated and angry with New Mexicans' inability or unwillingness to prosecute the persons involved in the trade for stolen cattle. Taylor probably had his own motives. His Apache Springs ranch was not far from Chaperito and Gallinas Springs. He admitted to Axtell that he was personally associated with many of the traders who told him about Elkins. Tax records note that this same Taylor, like many other New Mexicans who lived up and down the Gallinas and Pecos Rivers during this period, held a liquor license. He also owned some type of hotel and was involved in the mercantile business. The 1870 Apache Springs census lists him as a freighter.[32]

Merchant Adolph Seligman also testified during the Probst and Kirchner interrogatories, but he spoke on behalf of the claimants. Like the butchers, Seligman generally supported Democrats. He told the Court of Claims that by and large, he found August Kirchner to be "pretty straight." Like the Rosenthals, the Seligman brothers were New Mexican mercantilists with deep roots in the territory. They ran satellite stores in several frontier villages and also sold a variety of goods to Indian agents. Adolph was no stranger to the frontier and the multicultural mix of people who inhabited it. When Oldham informed him that Texas officials had once pressed charges against Probst and Kirchner for stealing cattle, Seligman was unimpressed. He explained that Texans often showed up in New Mexico with legal papers that they used as an excuse to steal New Mexican cattle. He argued that once seized, the cattle were taken north, not back to Texas. In essence, he did not see much difference between what the Comancheros were being charged with and what the cattlemen were doing. The Texans took cattle from local Hispano ranchers and sold them elsewhere. Seligman argued that Probst and Kirchner's purchases were always made through third parties that they had no reason to question. Such was the response of many defensive New Mexicans when asked about the trade.[33]

Oldman's follow-up questions dripped with incredulity. Surely he knew that Kirchner supplied the Comancheros with goods that were traded in Texas for stolen cattle. Seligman replied that like other New Mexicans in such businesses, they sometimes purchased Texas cattle, yet the merchant refused to accept the notion that there was anything illegal about these transactions. Thirty years after the fact, Adolph Seligman still defended the butchers.[34]

Affiant Thomas B. Catron also spoke on their behalf. By 1915 the original claimants were dead (the issue was still being pursued by their wives) and Catron was a U.S. senator. He recalled that he first got to know Probst and Kirchner shortly after he arrived in Santa Fe. In the coming years he was involved in a variety of legal proceedings that concerned them. While he did not get specific, his knowledge of their activities became more personal in 1869. These activities, he related, were of some note, offering that they were easily capable of taking out loans from between $100,000 and $150,000. He believed their business was strong enough to carry such a line of credit for twenty years. Catron explained that Probst and Kirchner ran tens of thousands of cattle through their operations, supplying beef to civilians and the government, contracting with both the Bureau of Indian Affairs and the army.[35]

August Kirchner and Charles Probst were dead by time Catron made these statements to the U.S. Court of Claims. By then it was their widows who sought some portion of their original claims. Catron vouched for Probst and Kirchner's honesty. Probst had married one of Kirchner's nieces. Completely contradicting Willison's characterization, the senator described them as truthful and trust-worthy Santa Fe businessmen. When asked if he had anything to gain from such testimony, the senator said no. That was not true. Beginning in 1910, Catron's law firm represented Nestora Kirchner and Augusta Probst in the depredations claim. Catron and Catron used Harry Peyton, a Washington, D.C., lawyer, to put the old claims before the government once again and continued to do so over the next several years. In return for Catron's efforts, the widows agreed to pay the firm a percentage of any settlement that ever came their way. When a settlement was finally reached in 1917, Augusta Probst received $175. Catron and Catron received $350.[36]

Such evidence taints Catron's statements, but the totality of what he had to say is still important. Kirchner's relevance to the history of both Santa Fe and the Southwest has never amounted to much, yet the senator provided a different perspective from what Oldham had presented to the Court of Claims. Testimony regarding Probst and Kirchner's large line of credit is significant, even if he exaggerated by half. While he might have had an ulterior motive, Catron's testimony about their involvement in the cattle trade was in line with what others said. Certainly, the documentary evidence suggests that they were more than small-time hustlers.

Catron also emphasized that by the time Oldham questioned Kirchner, he was not in his right mind; his ill-health meant he should not have been held responsible for some of the tales he told.[37] When questioned specifically about the Comanchero trade, Catron remained evasive. He refused to implicate the Prussians in any illegal activity and for context launched into a long-winded history of the New Mexico cattle business. Like Seligman, he was willing to acknowledge that Probst and Kirchner bought cattle from anybody willing to sell to them. He explained that everyone knew Comanche, Kiowa, and Cheyenne Indians stole cattle in Texas and traded them to the Comancheros, but these same traders carried on legitimate transactions as well. They provided a confusing array of bills of sale to show prospective buyers. Sometimes stolen cattle were mixed in with herds that had been purchased legally. Catron surmised that if Probst and Kirchner bought stolen cattle, they did so innocently.[38]

The senator also talked about the time a number of Texans came into the territory to take back their property. One 1872 scout led them to Rio Arriba County and Kirchner's La Porte Chiquito Ranch. Catron recalled that John Hittson's cowboys found six to seven thousand cattle there, many with Texas brands. Seligman also recounted how the Texans raided Kirchner's ranch and herded the cattle north. Kirchner immediately began legal proceedings to get them back. Catron admitted that he had represented the Texans in this matter, but what he advised them to do sounded like he represented Kirchner. He recommended that they give up their claims because of the receipts Probst and Kirchner possessed. He recalled that Kirchner's lawyers replevied (halted the removal of) the cattle, which meant the Texans could not take them out of the territory until the courts came to some kind of decision. This process dragged on until the Texans gave up. In other words, Kirchner got his cattle back. Catron gave similar advice to other Texans. The court system in New Mexico, the senator argued, looked on these bills of sale as legal documents and were hesitant to find for Hittson or anyone else, even though many Texas brands were identified among the herds. Catron argued that it was patently unfair for the Court of Claims to come to a different conclusion thirty-five years later.[39]

While Catron's thoughts on the Comanchero trade comport with those of other New Mexicans, they do not comport with Charles Goodnight's. Historians have scrutinized Goodnight's depredation claims for decades because his supporters' produced testimony that created a unique historiography of the trade.[40]

From the time Goodnight could ride a horse he was involved with cattle. As a young adult he partnered with brother-in-law John Sheek raising and selling beef. Once he moved his operations further west, he often came into contact and conflict with Plains Indians. During the Civil War he served as a scout for both the Texas Rangers and the U.S. Army. He is probably best known for his partnership with Oliver Loving. They drove tens of thousands of cattle into New Mexico and beyond. While historians have inaccurately argued that he was the first Texan to do this, there is no doubt of his impact on this era. Each trail drive was dangerous. In 1867 a Comanche attack left Oliver Loving with a wound that eventually festered and led to his death. Goodnight later filed several depredation claims associated with Indian raids on his and Loving's property.[41]

One attack occurred near Belknap at Cribbs (Krebs) Station, an old Butterfield stage stop. In the process of recollecting the particulars of this May 1867 raid, Goodnight detailed the cattle drive that followed. It was on this venture that his partner received the wound that eventually led to his death. Despite the raid, the substantial part of the herd did make it to Fort Sumner. What cattle that were not sold there were herded up the Pecos River to Colorado.[42]

About sixty miles up the Pecos, Goodnight and his trail hands turned north and followed the Gallinas River into San Miguel County. Soon they encountered several hundred cattle grazing in a large valley near Hatch's Ranch. While observing this herd, the Texans ran into Charles T. Jennings, one of the former California Column officers who had helped to set up the trading post. By the time Goodnight arrived, the Hatch partners' grand scheme was already falling apart.[43]

Goodnight counted six hundred cattle in the valley. Trail hand Bose Ikard identified several head that the Comanches had stolen from Cribbs Station. Jennings explained to a curious Goodnight that he had purchased them from Comancheros. One of the leaders was nearby Chaperito resident José Piedad Tafoya. As noted, Goodnight's lawyers brought Tafoya to Las Vegas to bolster the cattleman's case. After implicating others, the old Comanchero admitted that in 1867, when the grass began to grow, he traveled to Quitaque to trade. Once a deal was struck with the Comanches, he herded the stock up the Fort Smith Road into New Mexico. When Goodnight was asked why he did not use this shorter route, he explained that the Comanches would have killed him, his men, and taken the stock. Like all Texas cattlemen, he followed the more circuitous route west and north, around the heart of Comanchería and up the Pecos before arriving in the same general area. Rarely did anyone but Comancheros use the shorter route.[44]

When asked during the deposition who had given him the legal authority to transact such business in Texas, Tafoya named Jennings. As to where the cattle came from, he unsurprisingly answered that he did not know. Goodnight made no further comment regarding the outcome of his meeting with Jennings that summer day, but decades later he made sure the sixty-three-year-old Tafoya testified in the San Miguel County Court House regarding his claim.[45]

That summer in 1867, after passing through Chaperito, Goodnight continued up the Gallinas, keeping the eastern face of the Sangre de Cristo Mountains to his left. Not long after passing Las Vegas, he found the Santa Fe Trail and followed it north. After passing by the village of Sapello, they continued until they reached the junction of the Mora and Sapello Rivers. Instead of staying in Watrous (originally called La Junta), he remained a few miles to the southwest at William Kroenig's Phoenix Ranch.[46]

Kroenig, like Kirchner and Probst, had emigrated to the United States from Prussia. He came west in the late 1830s with Charles Bent and Ceran St. Vrain. For a while he farmed and ranched on St. Vrain's land grant in southern Colorado. He also ran a brewery in Costilla. His first visit to New Mexico was on business. After first trading a large crop of grains at Fort Laramie for cattle, he brought them south to his old friend, Englishman Alexander Barclay, who lived near the same river junction.[47]

Barclay also had a connection to Bent. In 1838 he was employed at Bent's Fort as his bookkeeper and store superintendent. In the late 1840s he moved to the confluence of the Mora and Sapello and built a trading post. Like Bent's fort, it protected travelers, and it also functioned as a frontier store. Barclay died in the mid-1850s, and Kroenig purchased the property from his family. Not long after moving there he expanded, building a flour mill on the Sapello and running cattle along this same river. Eventually he built the nearby two-story Phoenix Ranch and moved his store to that location. Along with father-in-law Samuel Watrous, he was perfectly located to provide whatever goods the Fort Union quartermaster, a few miles away, desired. This included both flour and beef.[48]

After spending the night at the Phoenix Ranch, Goodnight got up and took a look around. While admiring a herd of grazing cattle he noticed some with his brand. They were from the same group he had seen at Hatch's Ranch. Kroenig explained that he had purchased them from Comancheros. This was probably excess stock that remained after Tafoya settled with Jennings.[49]

Two roads led from this ranch to Fort Union. One ran due north, passing through Tiptonville before veering west to the post. The other ran due west a few miles before going through the village of Loma Parda, located on the Mora River, five miles south of the fort (see map 1 in the introduction). Like so many other New Mexican cattle brokers, the old Prussian did not appear to care where his beeves came from. What was important was getting a receipt for his purchases, even if they came from Tafoya.[50]

In his deposition for Goodnight, this Comanchero made clear that he was not ashamed of what he had been involved in. His answers were short, matter-of-fact, and nonchalant. Oddly enough, Goodnight's lawyers wanted to ensure that his integrity was not questioned. To substantiate his statements, they brought some of his Chaperito neighbors to Las Vegas to vouch for his honesty.

In addition to agreeing that Tafoya was a truthful and upright citizen, Manuel Gonzales offered additional information about the trade. He described himself as a cattle broker for "Jose S. Solabarri," (José Ulibarri) and admitted that during the period in question he purchased a lot of cattle from the Comancheros. He recalled that in July 1867, about the time Goodnight was passing through Chaperito, he was very busy buying incoming herds from all over San Miguel County. This substantiated both Goodnight's and Tafoya's testimony. He bought them from a lot of different merchants, who "furnished comanchieres [*sic*] with goods to trade the Indians and took their pay in stock." In another depredation claim Gonzales explained he had also spent a lot of his life in nearby La Cuesta, another known Comanchero village.[51]

Under cross-examination Gonzales explained that he never traveled to Texas to purchase cattle because he was afraid of what the Comanches might do to him. He preferred to make deals with the Comancheros, paying between fifteen and twenty dollars for four- and five-year-old cows and ten dollars for calves. Gonzales also offered that he purchased cattle from merchants as well, but he did not identify any.[52]

José Gertrude Medina was deposed the same day. While he was sixty-two years old by then, he seemed to enjoy recollecting his time with Tafoya in Texas. He usually took three or four mules or burros loaded with dry goods. He explained he preferred to take dry goods because they were lighter, which meant he could carry more. Somewhat enviously he explained that Tafoya used wagons. His friend could haul a lot more east and therefore bring back more cattle. When asked if he could remember any of the brands of these cattle, Medina identified several. He did exactly what Goodnight's lawyers wanted him to do, make clear that Tafoya had once been a Comanchero.[53]

Another deponent was former Lt. Col. Francisco Abreu of the First New Mexico Volunteer Infantry. Before and after the war he ran a freighting and mercantile business in Chaperito. His partner in this enterprise was Lorenzo Valdez. Like other merchants who lived along the Gallinas and Pecos Rivers, he maintained a liquor license. Business partner Valdez was a Comanchero. In October 1865 he used his legal license to trade in Texas for two months. Valdez employed many of his Chaperito neighbors for trips to both Quitaque and Mucha-Que Peak. Of course, there would have been no records of the unapproved trips. Abreu acknowledged that Tafoya was in the same business as his freighting partner.[54]

Merchants William B. Stapp and Eugenio Romero were also brought to the county courthouse to vouch for Tafoya's honesty. Stapp dabbled in the mercantile business and spent time on the frontier as the post trader at Fort Bascom. He partnered with Charles Hopkins selling dry goods, sundries, and liquor to the soldiers. Stapp also noted that they dealt in livestock, buying and selling to private individuals and the government. The partnership ended when Hopkins was killed in an Indian raid. Stapp did not doubt that Tafoya was an honest and truthful man, in a way implying that this Comanchero would not state that he had stolen Goodnight's cattle unless he had done so.[55]

While Stapp did business in Las Vegas, the Romero clan practically ran the town. As the leading Republicans in San Miguel County, Eugenio, Trinidad, Hilario, Benigno, and Margarito Romero had their fingers in everything, including the mercantile business and the cattle trade. Texan John Hittson found some of his cattle on the Romero ranch, located south of Las Vegas in the appropriately named Romeroville. Eugenio Romero also vouched for Tafoya's integrity.[56]

Neither Stapp nor Romero's affidavits explains why they were called to vouch for Tafoya's character or what their connection to him was during the period in question. Yet to be called by the Court of Claims to swear out affidavits attesting to the old Comanchero's integrity should raise a few eyebrows. Stapp reasoned that if Tafoya said he had purchased stolen cattle, you had to believe him. Eugenio Romero did the same, declaring that Tafoya would not lie.[57]

What Stapp and Romero were *not* asked was perhaps even more important. Despite being brought to Las Vegas to talk about Tafoya, neither Goodnight's lawyers nor the government's attorneys asked them about the Comancheros, whereas Catron and Seligman were deposed on the Comanchero trade. Kirchner and Probst were hammered with questions that practically charged them with theft. Goodnight's reputation probably protected these men from the types of probing the others endured, but make no mistake: both of these merchants were very familiar with the illegal trade and probably could have offered much more to historians had they been asked.

The record is clear that many elite New Mexicans functioned as the main suppliers of trade goods for the Comancheros. Along with a few entrepreneurial middlemen and some crooked politicians, they were able to short-circuit existing laws to keep this economy going long into the postwar years. As noted, by the late 1860s a second wave of newcomers, mostly from Texas, had inserted themselves into this economy. This insertion led to violence. From a distance such episodes appear isolated and disconnected. Yet a common thread—a seething animosity between Texans and New Mexicans—ties this history together. By the end of the decade the people who controlled the trade and the people who wanted to take it over were killing each other.

In early December 1868, just five days after William Calloway and Frank Wilburn put in their bids to supply beeves to the army, two cowboys, Albert Nance and George Fowler, employees of Frank and Aaron Wilburn, were ambushed just south of Apache Springs, which lay about eight miles south of Las Vegas, on the road to Fort Sumner. John Taylor, the stockman who had excoriated District Attorney Elkins in his deposition to Frank Warner Angel, lived in Apache Springs. Newspaper reports noted that these cowboys were sleeping when they were killed. The murder weapon was a hatchet. The perpetrators took their clothes, jewelry, and horses. Rancher Robert James Hamilton lived nearby on the Conchas River. He wrote a letter about the murders from Hatch's Ranch and sent it to the *Santa Fe Daily New Mexican*. In it he described one of the horses that had been stolen, hoping this might lead to the capture of the killer or killers. Quickly bringing the murderers to justice, Hamilton warned, was the only way to prevent a vigilante committee from taking the law into its own hands. He wrote this warning on December 12, 1868. It was published twelve days later, yet by then it had become irrelevant, for he had already joined such a committee. Hamilton had applied for a legal Comanchero pass in 1865 but had been turned down.[58]

According to a January 5, 1869, newspaper account, fifteen Texans rode into the small settlement of Los Esteritos on December 17 looking for their own definition of justice. Los Esteritos was located a few miles downstream from Anton Chico. A later account reported that these men were led by William Calloway. They rounded up all the males in the village and carried them about fifteen miles away. At an undisclosed location, one was hung and one was shot. The *New Mexican* reported that their actions were in response to the murders of Albert Nance and George Fowler.[59]

A few days later a meeting of angry locals was held in Puerto de Luna. Lorenzo Labadie and Manuel Chaves led this affair, producing a denunciation letter that was sent to San Miguel County authorities and the Las Vegas newspapers. Several Los Esteritos citizens who had managed to escape were at the meeting and described their ordeal. When the killing started, people ran in all directions through a hail of bullets. Two of the escapees identified Calloway as the leader but also implicated Hamilton. Hamilton's ranch on the Conchas situated him on the Comanchero trail that led to the Canadian River. Frank Wilburn was also identified as one of the raiders. The deceased Albert Nance and George Fowler had been his employees. Dick Fowler, the brother of one of the victims, was also there, as was Sam Gholson, a former Texas Ranger. Labadie and Chaves's denunciation indicated that this same group had recently terrorized Anton Chico and other Pecos River villages.[60]

However frightening these visits might have been, they were not particularly unique. New Mexicans would not have been surprised by such a raid; in fact, the Texans' actions would have comported with what most people already thought about them. Several Texans had straggled into the same villages in 1841, refugees of the failed Santa Fe Expedition—an expedition most villagers believed was meant to take over their country. More recently, Texans had returned as a part of the Confederate invasion in 1861, pillaging and committing atrocities along the way. Labadie had run into them in Las Cruces. He later served with his brother-in-law against these same invaders at the Battle of Glorieta Pass. Like most of his Puerto de Luna neighbors, Labadie already had a poor opinion of most Texans before the Los Esteritos incident, just as many Texans already held poor opinions of most New Mexicans.[61]

In his biography of Charles Goodnight, J. Evetts Haley wrote about this revenge raid. While his description of what happened varies somewhat from the contemporary newspaper accounts, it captures the ferocity of the attack. First, he described the murder of Aaron and Frank Wilburn's cowboys and how Dick Fowler, brother to one of the victims, put together a posse at the Wilburn's ranch, located south of Fort Sumner. Haley characterized this as a posse made up of Texans. He also mentioned Sam Gholson's role. His narrative detailed how Calloway, not from Texas, and the others found the murderers at a dance, attacked, and in the process found Albert Nance's rifle hidden in a woodpile. Haley then described how the suspect, along with "one or two others," was taken outside where two ropes were tied around each of the victims' necks and the other ends tied around the saddle horns of two of the Texans' horses. The raiders rode in opposite directions, decapitating both men. Afterward the culprits escaped back into to Texas. At least that is how Haley put it. He closed this episode by noting that the New Mexicans gave chase but were unable to catch them. They did come into contact with Goodnight, riding up the trail from the opposite direction. A standoff of sorts ensued until both sides warily rode around each other. In typical Haley fashion he explained that while the Anglo cattlemen were outnumbered, the locals wanted no part of them and rode away. As to the Los Esteritos attack, Haley characterized it in an offhand, callous way: "Goodnight said the trail drivers killed several Mexicans, but was pleased to recall that, 'among them they got the murderer.'" Such would be the sentiment of many Texans in the years to come.[62]

Haley left out another part of this history, but the newspapers covered it. Both Hamilton and Wilburn were later arraigned before a justice of the peace in Anton Chico. Calloway disappeared and was never arrested. Frustration dripped off the reporter's words as he related how these men were able to post bond and go back to their ranches. During this process Wilburn told the judge that Calloway led the attack and took twelve of his employees with him into Los Esteritos. His ability to shift the blame to this group seems to have served him well, as he continued in the cattle business afterward.[63]

Shortly after the raid, the acting governor of New Mexico placed a proclamation in the *Daily New Mexican* that shifted most of the blame on the missing Calloway. He announced a two-hundred-dollar reward for his capture. No one ever served time for Nance's and Fowler's murders, nor did anyone go to jail for what happened at Los Esteritos. Instead, another sort of justice prevailed.[64]

As the 1860s turned into the 1870s, the animosity between Texans and New Mexicans only increased. Encroachment into the territory by the likes of Goodnight, Wilburn, and Simpson, as well as an acceleration of the Comanchero trade, exacerbated these bad feelings. This tension was about more than the unraveling of an old frontier economy. It is possible that Fowler and Nance were victims of a subtle resistance that occasionally boiled into violence. Stealing cattle from people who were taking away their ability to make a living seemed like a fair trade to some. Perhaps Superintendent Delgado, Probst, and Kirchner, and many of the merchants of Santa Fe and Las Vegas felt the same way.

CHAPTER 5

The construction of trading posts and military installations in northeastern New Mexico altered indigenous economies and changed trading relationships across the Southwest. In 1852 Fort Union became the western army's main supply distribution center. This was also the first place new recruits were stationed before being transferred to other territorial posts. It was situated on the Santa Fe Trail just north of Watrous (originally La Junta) in Mora County, New Mexico. The presence of Fort Union impacted every village in the region.[1]

The Mora and Sapello Rivers run east out of the Sangre de Cristo Mountains toward the plains, passing just to the south of the post. The Mora was closer, approximately fifteen miles north of the Sapello. Both meander around juniper-covered plateaus and broken canyons before tumbling into valleys covered with sunflowers, gramma grass, and wheat. The rivers intersect near Watrous, just west of the Canadian River. Together, they flow into this larger river, which runs in a more southerly direction toward the Eroded Plains.

Towns like Mora, nestled in a mountain valley forty miles northwest of the fort, and every hamlet in between took advantage of their proximity to the post. The military needed corn and wheat, lumber and livestock, as well as a variety of different types of laborers, from masons to teamsters. Dirt roads as wide and worn as the Santa Fe Trail connected Mora, La Cueva, Ocate, Loma Parda, Watrous, Tiptonville, Barclay's Fort, Sapello, Las Vegas, and Tecolote. By the end of the 1850s a series of gristmills, blacksmith and butcher shops, saloons, distilleries, and lumber yards populated these villages. Ceran St. Vrain and his son Vicente built the largest gristmill in Mora. They ground thousands of tons of wheat and corn for the army, as did the other mills in the area.

This was the country that Charles Goodnight traveled through in 1867. When he confronted Kroenig about finding his own cattle grazing there, the old Prussian gave a nonchalant response. He had bought his stock at a fair price, and he was not concerned about how they had come into the sellers' possession. This was true all across eastern New Mexico. Any kind of bill of sale was good enough for purchasers and territorial officials.

Superintendent Felipe Delgado numbered among those officials. He was eventually replaced, in part because of his liberal dispensation of passes. Such passes (licenses) facilitated the distribution of Texas cattle to men like Kroenig. Similar cavalier attitudes regarding the trade permeated all levels of society, including law enforcement. At the behest of Gen. William Tecumseh Sherman, then commander of the Military Division of the Missouri, a more concerted effort to end the exchanges began in the latter part of 1868. The southern Plains Indians could be more easily defeated once the Comancheros were eliminated.[2]

The government's insatiable need for cattle made the elimination of the Comancheros incredibly difficult. New Mexican villagers looked forward to the seasonal expeditions as a way to supplement their way of life. The merchant class meant to maintain economic dominance by supporting them. The railroad's penetration of the West during this period complicated matters. With the construction of railheads in Kansas, the eastern market for beef grew stronger. In addition to feeding frontier armies and incarcerated Indians, Texas cattle could now be funneled east by railroads to feed millions of newly arrived immigrants from Europe.[3]

Despite renewed efforts to protect the herds, tens of thousands of cattle still ended up in the wrong hands. In the latter part of the 1860s and early 1870s, trail drivers Thomas and Slater, John Chisum, and Marion Meddling cumulatively lost over three thousand beeves to Comanche and Kiowa raids. According to the *Santa Fe Daily New Mexican*, a rogue group of Indians numbering around seventy-five were the main culprits. The accelerating demand was something of a godsend for the Comanches, who often hit the herds when they crossed into the open country that separated Texas from New Mexico.[4]

In the midst of increased tensions, Charles Probst and August Kirchner's butcher business thrived. They dominated a large segment of the growing market. No one knew this better than two of their competitors, Thomas Stockton and Frank Wilburn. It had only been a year since Wilburn participated in the vigilante raid at Los Esteritos. After that bloody episode, he parted ways with brother Aaron and headed north to partner with Stockton.

On October 8, 1869, Wilburn and Stockton signed a contract to provide cattle to the Cimarron agency and then turned around and signed another, that same day, with Probst and Kirchner. The latter agreement designated the butchers as subcontractors who would supply the beef to the Cimarron agency. Wilburn and Stockton signed a similar agreement to provide cattle to Fort Defiance and were awarded the job. Again they subcontracted with Probst and Kirchner. Each of these contracts called for the delivery of 2,500 beeves. Having to work with the butchers to make good on their bids illustrates why A. B. Eaton, Chief Commissary of Subsistence, later told his superiors that these two Prussian immigrants were practically running the commissary department. As partners with Probst and Kirchner, Wilburn and Stockton would have known that the livestock sold under these contracts came from Kirchner's Rio Arriba ranch.[5]

Additional documents related to the Fort Defiance agreement provide more evidence of Kirchner's ties to the Comancheros. Probst and Kirchner, along with Vicente García and Joseph A. Larue, backed up this contract with a $75,000 bond, essentially guaranteeing that the cattle would be delivered to Stockton's Ranch, also known as Red River Station. Within the chain of documents that went with this bond was another, whereby Félix García, Vicente's father, and Zadok Staab would supply the same number of cattle to Probst and Kirchner. This was how the Comanchero trade worked.[6]

Félix García was an old Hispano trader. As far back as 1854 he had been exchanging manufactured goods to Comanches for cattle. Why would the founding member of one of New Mexico's most successful merchant families cosign a document with this Comanchero? The obvious answer is that García represented the Comanchero pipeline into Texas. Staab represented the merchants who helped create the demand for this pipeline. Wilburn and Stockton represented the people who would have preferred to cut out such middlemen, but for the time being they were forced to continue this odd relationship with the butchers and their downstream suppliers.[7]

Probst and Kirchner also put up a bond for the Cimarron contract. This guarantee was much less, but it cemented the deal for their competitors/partners. If Wilburn and Stockton wanted to do business with the army, they were forced to use the butchers. Thus, any effort to eliminate the Comancheros would impact the Prussians' ability to maintain such dominance in the market.[8]

While Comanches were the main distributors of stolen livestock, Kiowas and Cheyennes also raided Texas and were reimbursed with the same types of goods. Anglo-Americans like Kansas hay contractor Samuel Parker purchased stolen horses with whiskey. Licensed trader W. A. Rankin traded gunpowder, lead, and percussion caps for livestock. Western guides and interpreters often found the opportunity to participate too enticing to resist. Historian Robert C.

Carriker observes that illegal "whiskey ranches" were common throughout the plains. These were nothing more than rendezvous camps where Anglos exchanged liquor and weapons for stolen cattle and horses. When the Tenth and Sixth U.S. Cavalries began to have success shutting down these illegal camps, Comancheros quickly filled the void. One Tenth Cavalry patrol from Camp Supply arrested a group of New Mexicans with several wagonloads of whiskey along the Canadian River in the Texas panhandle. Another patrol apprehended several Comancheros hauling four hundred gallons across the plains and destroyed it all.[9]

Other Plains Indians were also involved. In the 1840s and '50s Mescalero Apaches were extracting people, cattle, and horses out of Chihuahua and Texas and driving them north up the Pecos, where they were traded to the Jicarilla Apaches. The Jicarillas dominated the middle Pecos River valley until the latter part of the 1850s. They in turn made transactions with frontier New Mexicans. Territorial governor David Meriwether reported that the Mescaleros and the Jicarillas of that era worked "in tandem . . . participating in a brisk trade in stolen property."[10]

Indian Territory was not immune to similar corruption. In 1868 a Comanche and Kiowa peace treaty convinced several thousand Comanches to relocate near Cache Creek in the Eureka valley. Jesse Leavenworth located his agency there. Many Quahadis and their more defiant Kiowa cohorts refused to comply with this agreement and would not do so until the military forced them to in 1875. Those who came early created a new demand for cattle. Often these cattle were stolen in Texas.[11]

In 1869 new agent A. B. Boone was tasked with looking into the illegal trade that quickly developed after the creation of the Kiowa-Comanche reservation. His subsequent report detailed how Caddo and Wichita Indians delivered Texas cattle to nearby Indian traders who then sold them to the agency or, somewhat ironically, to other Texas cattlemen. Prussian immigrant William Griffenstein, known as "Dutch Bill," was one of those traders. That same year General Sherman accused Griffenstein of selling guns to these Indians and banned him from the region. Griffenstein later became one of the founding members of the town of Wichita, Kansas. Interpreter Philip McCusker implicated one of Leavenworth's employees, a trader named William Mathieson, who went by the nickname "Buffalo Bill" (not to be confused with Bill Cody). McCusker did not have evidence that Leavenworth was involved, but he noted there was some type of shady agreement between the agent and Mathieson that he could never put his finger on. The agent's clerk, a man named Wakely, was put in charge for a large part of

1868 while Leavenworth was absent; he purchased cattle with Texas brands from Griffenstein and Mathieson as well as from a Dr. Holmes and Irishman John Shirley, who along with his brother ran a trading post on the Wichita River. They all traded ammunition, pistols, and whiskey for cattle, horses, and mules. Most of these animals ended up at the reservation, but some were sold to the military at Camp Supply in Indian Territory. Clerk Wakely pleaded ignorance, believing that the Caddos were rounding up wild cattle from the Wichita Mountains. Thus, civilians and government officials all across the Southwest often turned a blind eye to what was really going on, using third-party intermediaries to insulate themselves from accusations of corruption.[12]

In the summer of 1870 the publishers of the *Santa Fe Weekly*, William Manderfield and Thomas Tucker, ran a column entitled "Indian Traders": "The goods of the traders are disposed to the Indians, usually at extravagant rates, and the property taken in exchange estimated at low prices. The stock is driven up into the settlements in New Mexico and commands ready sale at fair prices. . . . The trader has an exciting life, authorities seldom prosecute, the opportunity for profit is great, thus the temptation is great." The paper argued that such romantic notions ill-served the community. The editorial detailed that the trade incentivized Comanches to rape, murder, and destroy the lives of the territory's southeastern neighbors. Victim Dorothy Field of San Saba County, Texas, was used as an example, having been kidnapped and murdered in one such raid. Thus, the *New Mexican*'s publishers, in conjunction with Sherman's renewed efforts to defeat the Comanches, sought to reveal a facet of the trade that few in New Mexico wanted to think about.[13]

Over the next two years Tucker and Manderfield increased their criticism of the trade, beginning with a reprint of Gov. William H. Pile's denunciation of illicit activities. The governor noted that along with sheriffs and justices of the peace, probate judges would now be given the authority to arrest people involved in such traffic, expanding on the notion that it was not a victimless crime. He blamed Indian raids in Texas on elite Santa Fe citizens who funded the expeditions. In a caustic characterization, Pile charged that while such crimes continued, these citizens were "lying about fashionable hotels, smoking cigars and enjoying all the comforts of security, [and they] smile in gloated satisfaction at the murder and theft and Indian horrors . . . [that are the result] of their illicit business."[14]

As noted earlier, John Hittson was one of many Texas ranchers who suffered losses as a result of the trade. A contemporary and competitor of Goodnight, he was all too familiar with late-night raids and Comanche war cries. With each passing year such ranchers became angrier and more frustrated with the government's inability to stop the thefts. He knew many of the cavalrymen and officers responsible for going after the raiders, particularly those who operated out of Fort Concho, near San Angelo, Texas. Hittson occasionally joined in such pursuits. In the early part of the 1870s both he and old friend Thomas Stockton began to have conversations with Col. Ranald Mackenzie of Fort Concho about taking matters into their own hands. By then Stockton was living on his New Mexico ranch, which he had begun to call Clifton House (also known as Red River Station), six miles southwest of Raton.[15]

Their conversations revolved around the dangers Texas cattlemen were put through trying to get their beeves to market. On one such trail drive in May 1871, Hittson and his men came upon the charred ruins of a wagon train in North Texas. This was the route Goodnight said was too dangerous to use. Among the debris Hittson and his men found several dead teamsters. This was the Henry Warren wagon train, recently hit by a group of Comanches and Kiowas. Just a day earlier these same Indians, led by Satank and Santanta, had allowed General Sherman and a few officers to pass along the route because they were waiting on a larger prize. Sherman was in Texas to determine if its citizens' cries for more protection were valid or just a ruse. He was skeptical, believing most depredation claims were based on ex-Confederates' attempts to get the Union army out of the more settled parts of the state. The rumor was that they wanted the army out of southeast and Central Texas because that was where the freedmen lived. The raid of Warren's wagon train convinced Mackenzie and Sherman that the Texans were telling the truth. This realization led to significant ramifications for the Comanches and their trading partners.[16]

Sherman starting allocating more men and resources into Texas and New Mexico that spring. Cavalry were ordered to return to the recently closed Fort Bascom, where they began to patrol the borderlands. This move paid immediate dividends. On separate patrols Lt. Andrew Caraher and Capt. James A. Randlett of the Eighth Cavalry apprehended several Comancheros coming back from Texas with cattle. To the south another patrol arrested twenty-one Isleta Pueblo Indians with approximately two hundred cattle, a herd of burros, and several horses. These invigorated efforts caught the Comanches' attention. A newspaper reported that one band feared the increased patrols so much that it fortified the village of Portales and sheltered there, awaiting the attack that never came. Closer to Fort Bascom, an Indian woman and several New Mexicans were arrested for trading with the Comanches. This band's fate rested in the hands of a local grand jury.

Such grand juries, often made up of people who lived in the area, almost always found for the defendants or dismissed the case. While awaiting a decision, the suspects were ordered to take care of the cattle. Lorenzo Labadie often led these grand juries. In this particular case a small fine was paid and the charges were dismissed. The cattle never left the possession of the Comancheros.[17]

In an effort to allocate his few cavalry troops to the right locations, the new commanding general of New Mexico Territory, John I. Gregg, ordered an old army guide into the field to spy on local villagers, hoping to gather information as to how the traders were so adept at avoiding his patrols. Decades earlier sixty-year-old French Canadian Frank de Lisle had served with Kit Carson. During the Civil War he was Major Bergmann's scout at Fort Bascom. Why Gregg thought de Lisle could infiltrate the local river communities without garnering the Comancheros' suspicions leaves much unsaid. Frank de Lisle and many others who served at Fort Bascom had good relationships with these New Mexicans—in this case, so much so that Gregg used him as a spy to gather intelligence.[18]

The Fourth Cavalry also stepped up its efforts. After the Warren wagon train attack Sherman used Mackenzie in much the same way that Lincoln used Grant: to engage in a nonstop, relentless pursuit of the enemy that led him into the homeland of his foe. In the coming year Mackenzie and Sgt. William Wilson led several patrols across Comanchería in search of the traders and raiders. In the process they became familiar with the land and the routes across West Texas into New Mexico. On one of these patrols Sargent Wilson captured Comanchero Apolonio Ortíz, who gave up a wealth of information about his fellow traders. Ortíz was from La Cuesta (present-day Villanueva) on the Pecos River south of San Miguel del Vado.[19]

Before long, cavalrymen were searching for Comancheros and Comanches from Mucha-Que Peak to Quitaque, about 130 miles across some of the Southwest's most desolate country. They inspected old campgrounds and followed rutted trails north and northwest. Ortíz explained that a good horse could get you from Muchaque (Mucha-Que Peak) to Puerto de Luna in five days. He also informed them that northern Comancheros usually traveled through San Miguel and Bernal before following the Pecos south to Alamo Gordo, which was a staging area where traders from all over New Mexico congregated before heading into Texas. Both Alamo Gordo and Puerto de Luna were just south of Lorenzo Labadie's ranch.[20]

Building on this information, troopers stationed at Fort Concho followed a series of cattle trails into the valley of Double Mountain Fork of the Brazos River. Texas cattlemen turned around at this point. Mackenzie and his troopers did not. Using details extracted from young Ortíz and Sergeant Wilson's patrols, the officer the Indians called "Bad Hand" followed the well-trod path up and out of the valley and onto the Llano Estacado. The tens of thousands of cattle that crossed this way had worn a swale of broken earth across the plains. For several days soldiers rode through this arid, open country of no settlements and few waterholes. Eventually they crossed into the Pecos River valley. Soon after, they arrived at old Fort Sumner, which had been converted into Pete Maxwell's ranch. After conversing for a day or two with Lucien Maxwell's son, they moved north up the Pecos, following the same trail Goodnight, Chisum, and other Texans were so familiar with. They investigated many of the Pecos River villages Ortíz told them about. When they came to the Gallinas, like the drovers before them, they followed this weaker stream until it crossed the old Comanchero road that Louis Griego and Labadie had aluded to. When Mackenzie arrived it was being used by the military, stagecoach lines, and the U.S. mail connecting Fort Bascom to Albuquerque. A northern spur also tied it to both Las Vegas and Santa Fe. The troopers turned east at this crossing and followed it all the way to Fort Bascom. Here they rested and resupplied before making the long trip back to Texas.[21]

While Mackenzie did not score a major victory on this sojourn, he did collect valuable information: he located the rendezvous sites and found out where a majority of the traders lived; and his men charted the trails, streams, springs, and sinkholes. On this route they passed the sun-bleached bones of hundreds of army horses, a brutal reminder of all the lost patrols and failed expeditions that had preceded them. For decades the army had been thwarted in their efforts to bring this trade to an end, in part because they did not know the borderlands. Through the work of the Fourth and Eighth Cavalry, this was no longer true, which meant troopers began to make progress in the early 1870s.

Stumbling on the ruins of the Warren wagon train might have given John Hittson pause, but he pushed on with his herds, eventually ending up in Denver, Colorado. Once there he sold his cattle to James Patterson. Surely the cattlemen had a lot to talk about. Despite Mackenzie's efforts, neither expected the army or the territorial legal system to retrieve the cattle they had lost or to compensate them for that loss. In January 1872 Hittson returned to Denver with another herd, driving them right through the middle of town. By then he was well known in

Denver, having sold beeves there since 1868. Afterward he purchased a large swath of land from Patterson. It was located about sixty miles east of town. Other Texans were already in the region. Goodnight was ranching in Apisha Canyon, about forty miles northeast of Trinidad. Stockton's ranch was just south of Raton in northern New Mexico. While Hittson knew Goodnight, it was his connection to Patterson and Stockton that ties this history together. When these three began to talk in earnest about going after the Comancheros, they approached Goodnight, but he chose not to participate. Many Texans did.[22]

On the same Colorado trip that Hittson purchased land from Patterson, he began to make contact with other cattlemen in the area. He wanted to know if they were interested in participating in some kind of rogue action against the Comancheros and the men who backed them. Once he returned to Palo Pinto County, Texas, he did the same, telling local ranchers that he meant to go back to New Mexico and get his stolen cattle. He believed that going after the suppliers would lead him to the herds. Many Texans gave him the power of attorney to make the best deal he could for the cattle he retrieved. He notified law enforcement officials, politicians, and the military of his intentions. He also consulted with lawyers. There is evidence that some military officers and a few prominent New Mexicans were willing to give him free rein and perhaps some help in this operation. In retrospect it is clear that a select few had very clear reasons for doing so.[23]

While there is no exact consensus as to how many men Hittson recruited for these efforts, three separate bands participated. One worked out of northern New Mexico, including within the Chama, Mora, and upper Canadian River valleys. The second worked the Gallinas River area around and just south of Las Vegas. The third band searched across ranches in the Middle and Lower Pecos River valleys, which included the town of Puerto de Luna. The *Republican Review* of Albuquerque noted that each party included eighty men, 120 horses, and camp equipage that resembled a military expedition. This article, entitled "Stealing Along the Border," suggested that U.S. Army troopers participated in at least one of these operations. No military documents substantiate this claim, but some do indicate most officers who knew about it approved of the Texans' actions.[24]

The year 1872 was pivotal for New Mexico's cattle trade. Thousands of beeves were butchered in Probst and Kirchner's Santa Fe slaughter pens. The volume of refuse was so high that it often got them into trouble. Citations regarding the odors that emanated from these pens were already on the books when new ones were delivered that year. The shop and its corrals were located between

San Francisco and Rio Chiquito Streets. Rio Chiquito got its name from the spring that once ran along this road. As noted, it later became Water Street. The citations, which began in 1867, were still being filed five years later. Some included graphic descriptions of butchered animals, going into detail regarding the extraction of entrails and other viscera and how this resulted in large quantities of offal being left in piles that contributed to overwhelming odors, both "solid and liquid," that, according to the citations, pervaded half the city. Despite court appearances and continuances, Probst and Kirchner remained in business. Charges were eventually resolved with small fines and dismissals. The butchers' ability to maintain such a presence reveals that not everyone in Santa Fe objected to their operations. They were men of some note in New Mexico, and Stephen B. Elkins knew it. So did Thomas B. Catron.[25]

Elkins had convinced his old college friend (Catron) to join him in New Mexico after the Civil War. Once there Catron followed a similar career path. Just like his mentor, he first worked in Mesilla before moving to Santa Fe. Like Elkins, he began a law practice in the capital before becoming the territory's attorney general. In 1872 he was again following in his friend's footsteps, having just been appointed U.S. Attorney for the District of New Mexico. This occurred at the same time the new U.S. Congress was deliberating a big move regarding the territory's district judges.[26]

Many people in Santa Fe wanted to move Chief Justice Joseph G. Palen from the First Judicial District to the Third Judicial District, far from the capital. Only Congress could make such a move. Palen was a Republican, and that party controlled much of the city. Its leaders believed the removal of Palen would make them more vulnerable to legal challenges that they did not want to contemplate. Some of those challenges involved Elkins and Catron. After being prompted by his law partner, Catron set up a meeting with Kirchner.[27]

In January 1872 Catron talked to Kirchner about the Palen situation. Kirchner certainly knew that Elkins had put his friend up to this. When this meeting took place, Texas cowboys were entering the territory and making trouble—trouble that could directly impact the butchers' bottom line. The pressures Kirchner was already under, coupled with past experiences associated with Elkins, surely influenced his next move.

After the meeting ended and Catron left, Kirchner put it all down in writing and submitted it to the Santa Fe probate court. In February he walked over to the *Daily New Mexican* and told the publishers what he had testified to in front of Probate Judge Felipe Delgado. Catron had offered him a $500 bribe to convince

Democratic congressmen to change their votes on the Palen issue. This statement made the next day's papers. The butcher's intent seems clear. He meant to destroy Catron's reputation. In the process, Elkins would also be tarred with scandal.[28]

Decades later, during the U.S. Court of Claims process, Kie Oldham characterized August Kirchner as a lowlife nobody who was simply trying to take advantage of the system in his old age. While he was no angel, in 1872 Kirchner was a major political force in New Mexico. He led a coalition of Hispano cattlemen, traders, politicians, and Jewish merchants who supported Democrats' goals. Everyone within this particular alliance had ties to the Comanchero trade. That is not to say only Democrats participated in that economy. Elites on both sides of the political spectrum did, including staunch Republicans like the Romeros of Las Vegas. Yet historical references to these alliances are muddled because by the late 1870s many of these former Democrats had switched parties. By then political and social dynamics had changed, and Republicans were solidly in control of the territory. This explains why in 1878 Lincoln County's Jimmy Dolan called Willie Rosenthal a "paid up member of the Santa Fe Ring," when only six years earlier he had been a staunch supporter of the Democratic Party. Something happened.[29]

It was Kirchner's economic success that prompted the meeting with Catron, and both Catron and Elkins were keenly aware of the butcher's influence. Oldham conveniently ignored or refused to consider this when questioning the applicant in 1896. What happened after the butcher's attempt to ruin Catron's career helps illustrate the political transition that began to occur in New Mexico during this period.[30]

Catron and Elkins were used to people complaining about their tactics, but this was different. If the claim of political bribery stuck, Catron's political career was finished. In response, Catron, the territory's incoming U.S. attorney, sued Kirchner for libel. He demanded the butcher refute his claim. Supporters of each man lined up according to political affiliation. Within the newspaper article "Good Workers," Santa Fe residents James L. Johnson, Charles M. Conklin, David A. Catanach, and Sheriff Nicolás Quintana expressed their support for Kirchner. They vouched for his honesty and integrity. As a sidebar, all four had indirect ties to the Comanchero trade. Despite the support of Kirchner's allegations by many powerful New Mexicans, this event did not destroy Catron's career.[31]

The Santa Fe Ring was an unofficial alliance of successful New Mexican businessmen, politicians, and legal authorities who used their combined talents to try and monopolize control of the territory. After the Civil War both political appointments and U.S. government purse strings were controlled by Republicans. That is why Democrat Catron switched parties once he came to New Mexico. While the exact nature of the group's power is not fully understood, there is no doubt that this cabal could either help or hurt one's economic fortunes. The butcher had a decision to make. What could Elkins and Catron's combined power do to him? Would the citations start again? There were other butchers in Santa Fe who would be happy to see him hampered by more courtroom distractions and fines. What about the increasing interest newspapers were giving the trade? Only recently had anyone begun to care about how Texas cattle were getting to New Mexico. Despite strong support from many of the city's leaders, the butcher finally succumbed to Catron's demand and printed a humiliating retraction in the *New Mexican*. While surely embarrassing, it proved to be the the the right thing to do. Probst and Kirchner continued to thrive, albeit under changing circumstances. Many of the Comancheros and suppliers who supported him were not so fortunate. Documents indicate Elkins had something to do with that. With this success came more code violations.[32]

The butchers received another citation in April 1872. Charles Probst asked the judge for a change in venue, arguing that powerful Republicans like Tomas C. De Baca had too much influence over any jury pool that would originate from Santa Fe County. The new charge was similar to the others, involving detailed descriptions of rotting entrails and the stink that was associated with them. Probst argued that the new charges were not related to stink—they were related to politics. While it was Probst who complained, he intimated that Kirchner was the target. This was because his partner was a major contributor to Democratic Party.[33]

Republican Stephen B. Elkins once again entered the picture, offering Kirchner a way out of his dilemma. In a conversation that was reminiscent of John Taylor's testimony to Frank Warner Angel, the district attorney told the butcher that if he could get his followers to vote for him in the next congressional election, his problems with the city would end. As storm clouds concerning the illegal cattle trade gathered, Kirchner was forced to work with Elkins, using his influence to shift votes to the Republican party. Once New Mexican Democrats began to vote for the man many called "Smooth Steve," the citations stopped.[34]

Violence between Texans and Comancheros came to a head about the time Catron first visited Kirchner in 1872. As early as January three New Mexicans were killed during a shootout with some Texans near Alamosa, which was located along the Canadian River. The report from La Junta (Watrous) noted that several ranchers from the Lone Star State had come across Juan Taez, Patricio Griego, and Juan Cristóbal trying to escape with some stolen cattle. The ensuing shootout left E. M. Rossel wounded and Taez, Griego, and Cristóbal dead. A month later the *New Mexican* noted another shootout tied to cattle theft, this one occurring in La Pardita, located just across the Mora River from Loma Parda. In this case one person was wounded and another's horse was killed. In this second event the paper referred to both of the men under attack as cattle thieves.[35]

A week later an article entitled "Row in Trinidad" reported how sixty Texans had essentially taken over the town. Camping about sixteen miles away, they had been filling up the local saloons and causing general mayhem for some time when a mid-February fight over a card game led to a shootout that killed the sheriff. Surely these were some of Hittson's recruits.[36]

In the spring of 1872 the *Daily New Mexican* reported that fifteen Los Lunas traders who ventured off to Texas never made it back home. The rumor was that Pete Maxwell had caught them with some of his stock on the Pecos River and "sent them to kingdom come." Manderfield and Tucker continued to hammer the point that the profits derived from the Comanchero trade were too enticing to resist. One report noted that Indians from the Isleta Pueblo were still at it, continuing their expeditions to Texas to trade for stolen cattle. The publishers predicted that if local law enforcement did not take control, Maxwell's cowboys would. This certainly was a predictor of what was to come. Hittson and his men had established several bases of operations by then and were already looking for Texas brands amongst the thousands of grazing cattle that were scattered across New Mexico and southern Colorado.[37]

As the summer grasses began to grow, Texas cowboys, Comanches, Comancheros, U.S. cavalrymen, and New Mexican merchants and butchers made preparations for the upcoming drives that would bring more cattle into the territory. While drovers assembled their herds in Palo Pinto and Coleman Counties in Texas, New Mexican merchants like "Hughes and Church" supplied Comancheros from Puerto de Luna and elsewhere with the supplies they needed to strike bargains in Texas. Eighth Cavalry troopers rode out of Fort Bascom on extended patrols that took them as far east as the Texas border and as far south as Maxwell's Ranch.[38]

Despite these patrols, stolen cattle still made their way into the Comancheros' hands. In reference to this trade, Senator Catron later explained that everybody in New Mexico who could participate in this trade did so. Why he might have said this in 1915 was illustrated by an event that occurred in 1866 between young lawyer Thomas Catron and Marcus Goldbaum. Goldbaum owed Catron money; the previous year he had opened a meat market in Santa Fe. It is likely that these two facts were connected. With General Carleton's approval, Goldbaum, who was a government beef contractor, had gone to Quitaque to trade with the Comanches. As noted, while there he saw Rudolph Fischer within the Indians' encampment. In a case before the U.S. Court of Claims, Goldbaum's wife Sara testified that on one of his return trips to New Mexico, Goldbaum's cattle were stolen. She acknowledged that as a result, he was unable to fulfill a contract to supply beef to Fort Bayard. When Goldbaum's loan to Catron came due, he paid the lawyer back with cattle from his existing herds. Thus, four decades later, when Catron declared to the Court of Claims that everybody was involved this trade, he could have easily been including himself.[39]

There was no letup in the violence as spring became summer. Fort Bascom merchant and cattleman Charles S. Hopkins was killed during a summer raid on his Canadian River ranch. One of his employees was also killed, and his wife was wounded. By then reports of murders and thefts associated with cattle thieves had become a weekly occurrences. One *New Mexican* editorial detailing the violence tied it to the increased number of Texas cattle within the territory. Where were they coming from? Another blurb in the same edition provided the answer, noting that Probst and Kirchner had just driven a herd of Texas steers right through the heart of Santa Fe and that they would soon be available to the general public in the form of table steaks.[40]

Whether anyone picked up on this coincidence or not, the *New Mexican* continued to run editorials deriding the trade and the merchants who kept it going. While avoiding specific names, the implications were clear enough. The town's leading merchants included Zadok Staab, the Seligmans, and the Spiegelbergs, all strong supporters of the Democratic Party. The paper, the Republicans' mouthpiece, was blaming them without getting too specific. It is also true that everyone knew that even if the Comancheros were eliminated, the demand for Texas cattle would remain strong. The question became: Who would stand to profit from these traders eradication?[41]

By then Colonel Mackenzie and the Fourth Cavalry were applying the knowledge gained from previous patrols to close in on the Comanches. At the same time, Eighth Cavalry troopers operating along the Canadian River continued to have success, apprehending numerous Comancheros and taking possession of thousands of stolen cattle. At one point their success was so great that they did not know what to do with all the cattle they were collecting. The army's actions were certainly making the papers, but nothing came close to inflaming New Mexican passions like Hittson's raids. The Texans seemed to be everywhere.

By August 1872 Charles Probst and Taos merchant Julius Friedman asked probate judge Felipe Delgado for help. They complained of unknown riders terrorizing their communities and stealing their livestock. They told Delgado that they had done everything they could to protect their property, but the problem was much bigger than anything they could face on their own. Friedman, besides selling merchandise on the Red Willow Indian Reservation, also participated in the cattle trade. Kirchner's ranch was not far west of Taos. By then the Texans had removed cattle out of mountain villages from Puerto de Luna to Tierra Amarilla.[42]

As noted, three different camps of raiders were operating in New Mexico. One group remained south of Trinidad. While it is hard to pin down who participated in the raids that occurred in northeastern New Mexico, some historians link cowboys working for Charles and Albert Reynolds as well as "One-Armed Bill" Wilson (not to be confused with Sgt. William Wilson who rode with Mackenzie). Wilson and his brother George had recently settled in Colorado after working for Goodnight and Loving in Texas and New Mexico. Others note that Clay Allison and John "Chunk" Colbert were involved. These two often stopped by Stockton's Red River Station, which was more than a ranch. In 1866 he built a three-story hotel and stage stop where the Santa Fe Trail crossed the Canadian River. The Barlow and Sanderson stage line leased a part of the hotel, which he called Clifton House. Allison and Colbert were known to visit the hotel's bar. On a visit in 1874, these two hard-edged cowboys got into an argument that led to a shootout.Colbert was killed. While Frank Wilburn's name does not appear in any of the newspaper accounts of the 1872 raids, he was certainly no stranger to vigilante violence. In addition to his participation in the Los Esteritos raid in 1868, he and brother Aaron were a part of a posse that chased down and killed Lincoln County cattle thief Zack Crumpton. The Wilburn brothers were also aligned with John Chisum when he came into conflict with the Horrell brothers. It is almost inconceivable that Frank was not with his new partner Thomas Stockton when the 1872 raids began.[43]

While the Clifton House vigilantes focused on northeastern New Mexico, the group led by Hittson remained just east of Las Vegas. On one raid they visited Eugenio Romero's ranch. As noted earlier, Eugenio and his brothers were wealthy Las Vegas merchants and successful politicians. With something of a deft touch, Hittson negotiated the purchase of Romero's Texas-branded cattle. After the

Texans were gone Romero kept quiet about the sale. His Las Vegas neighbors assumed the worst. If this powerful family could fall prey to the hated Texans, what could an isolated rancher do against such devils?[44]

Most Hispanic ranchers were offered ultimatums, not money. Cattle were forcibly taken. At one point citizens of Las Vegas pressured don Miguel Otero to ride out to Hittson's camp and talk to him. Ten-year-old Miguel Otero Jr. recollected that his father met with Hittson just east of Las Vegas. In no uncertain terms don Miguel was told not to interfere. Hittson declared that he meant take all the cattle and horses he found with Texas brands, and if they [New Mexicans] had any sense they would just stay out of his way.[45]

Hittson, James Patterson, and Stockton often met in Santa Fe during this period. When they did, it made the papers. In late July Patterson was there with former Indian agent John Dalton, both registered at the Exchange Hotel. Dalton was another American who had sought a New Mexican license to trade with the Comanches but was turned down by Commissioner of Indian Affairs Dennis N. Cooley. Cooley had told him that the Comanches must do business with Texas traders. During this visit Dalton accompanied cattle broker Patterson to his San Francisco Street meat market. A subsequent issue of the *New Mexican* reported that Patterson, after having been "engaged for some time hunting up Texas cattle throughout the Territory[,]" left yesterday for the Pecos." Four days later the *Revista Republicana* reported that a group of Texans had stolen seven hundred of Alexander Grzelachowski's cattle. Grzelachowski was a prominent merchant who raised stock on the Pecos River outside of Puerto de Luna. After being captured by Sargent Wilson in 1871, Apolonio Ortíz had informed the Fourth Cavalry trooper that many Comancheros lived in this Pecos River village.[46]

Indictments and lawsuits followed in the vigilantes' wake. Such records help to identify both the leaders of the raids and their targets. Hittson was instrumental as well, not shy about talking with newspapermen or letting them reprint his correspondence. During the August term of the San Miguel County District Court, charges were filed against him as well as Stockton and Joseph (Martin) Childers for stealing four cows. The pitiable number of livestock they were accused of confiscating is irrelevant to this history, but the paper trail such documents leave sheds light on their activities.[47]

Several cases reveal the activities of the Texans involved. Desidero Romero, a politician and onetime San Miguel County sheriff, was a victim of the raids. In what became a common legal ploy, Romero filed an order of replevin against Hittson to prevent him from taking the cattle in question out of the territory.

While the *New Mexican* reported that Patterson had left for the Pecos River just before Grzelachowski reported that his cattle had been stolen, it was Hittson, not Patterson, who was charged with trespassing on this merchant's property. Grzelachowski had recently opened a new store in Puerto de Luna. Catron defended Hittson in this case. That Grzelachowski only filed trespassing charges is significant, for, as noted, the *Revista Republicana* reported that the Texans had taken several hundred of his cattle.[48]

Grzelachowski had come to New Mexico in the early 1850s as an ordained priest. He served in several communities before being defrocked because of an ongoing relationship with a woman. Afterward he got into the freighting business and traded along the Santa Fe Trail. He later became a mercantilist and owned a store in Sapello with Richard Dunn before establishing a larger footprint on the Las Vegas plaza. There he did business with Charles Ilfeld, acquiring government contracts to supply merchandise to military posts. By 1872 he was on the Pecos River doing the same. Like everyone in the area, he also raised cattle. While it was reported that his stock was taken by the Texans, no charges were filed regarding these thefts. Absent a bill of sale, it would have been difficult to file an order of replevin.[49]

Manuel Romero of San Miguel County did file such an order against Patterson. Again, this meant the cattle could not be taken out of New Mexico while the case was being deliberated. José María Montoya charged Joseph Martin Childers, an employee and triggerman for Stockton and Patterson, with trespassing on his property. In another action, wealthy Las Vegas lawyer and landowner Louis Sulzbacher filed a case of assumpsit against Hittson; in essence the suit accused him of an unlawful act involving an unwritten contract. Henry Birnbaum sought "an attachment in property" against Hittson, meaning this Mora merchant was in some sort of contractual dispute for a service rendered, possibly supplies. May Hays, another major merchant in Las Vegas, filed an additional assumpsit action against Hittson. All of these cases link some of the most prominent men in the region to the Comanchero trade and the Texans' raids. To repeat, at some point the question is not who was involved in this trade but who was not.[50]

The most written-about raid occurred at Loma Parda, situated in an obscure valley about five miles south of Fort Union. As noted above, a well-traveled road connected the fort to this town. Several other roads radiated out from the village. One ran east along the Mora River to Tiptonville, just a few miles away. Tiptonville was founded by William B. Tipton, who was, like William Kroenig, one of Samuel Watrous's sons-in-law. A nearby tavern was run by George Gregg.

Like the merchants in Loma Parda, both Tipton and Gregg (as well as Watrous and Kroenig) made money off of Fort Union soldiers. Tipton also sought beef contracts with Fort Union.

Another road led south out of Loma Parda, then split; one branch headed east and the other west. The eastern route led to William Kroenig's trading post, by then located at the Phoenix Ranch. Along the western branch several villages were strung out along the Mora River. These included La Pardita, La Cueva, and Mora. The western road split again just before it reached La Cueva and angled off to the south, to Sapello. (The town of Sapello and the Sapello stage station were not in the same location. While both were situated on the Sapello River, the town was much closer to the mountains. The stage stop was farther east.) Both roads led travelers to Las Vegas and Santa Fe. Northeastern New Mexican farmers, U.S. soldiers, and territorial merchants all had easy access to Loma Parda.[51]

Ready access meant plenty of opportunity for trade. In 1862 freighter Charles Raber hauled some of his Westport, Missouri, goods to Kroenig's before taking supplies that included whiskey, soap, bacon, tobacco, and candles to Loma Parda. Sam Watrous admitted that he had seen Comancheros trading with Comanches within his own settlement. Charles Goodnight had seen his own brands wandering around Kroenig's property. Illegal barter was not restricted to Quitaque and Mucha-Que Peak. It should come as no surprise that the Texans were interested in this part of New Mexico.[52]

Like other villages in the area, Loma Parda was situated within a bend of the Mora River. Limestone cliffs and high plateaus overlooked it on all sides. Junipers and cottonwood trees shadowed the river as it wound around the town before turning north and east. Translated, Loma Parda means "grey hill," alluding to the color of the broken limestone ledges that surrounded the town. It consisted of over ninety-four homes and businesses. Pasturelands, corn, and wheat fields spread out away from the town's buildings. Goodnight recalled that the rendezvous site known as Quitaque was located within a similar horseshoe configuration, with valley walls sheltering it from inquisitive eyes. Like Quitaque, Loma Parda's topography made it a natural holding pen for livestock. Even though the community was quite large, it was also very hidden. Travelers were practically within the town before they saw any of its buildings.[53]

Loma Parda's founding is unclear, but the 1870 census shows that 420 people lived there, and it supported a Catholic Church, at least two grocers, a mercantile establishment, a post office, a gristmill, a blacksmith shop, and, of course, saloons and dancehalls. Most buildings were single-story adobe structures with stone corrals running behind each. Some of the more elaborate buildings were faced with stones cut from the hills to the north. Adam and Sam McMartin's store was the most substantial structure in town, a two-story building that also served as the post office. It is likely that freighter Charles Raber sold his bacon, soap, and whiskey to the McMartins.[54]

Yet brothers Adam and Sam were more than mercantilists. They were also cattle brokers. Their most obvious customer would have been the Fort Union quartermaster. Like the merchants who lived at Kroenig's ranch, Tiptonville, and Watrous, their best chance to make a profit was linked to this post. They also owned a taxi-wagon that charged soldiers a dollar for a round-trip ticket between the town and the fort. Loma Parda's appeal involved more than the goods for purchase. Several prostitutes and card dealers hung out around McMartin's and other establishments. Prostitution was a well-known part of the town's economy. The sex workers moved there after the military forced them to evacuate the caves and ramshackle huts that had been situated closer to the fort. The back rooms that were attached to Julián Baca's saloon also served as places for assignations. So many soldiers spent their monthly pay in Loma Parda that Gen. James H. Carleton pushed the army to lease the land it sat on and then tear down all the buildings. That never happened.[55]

It did not happen because there were too many legitimate businesses and honest people who would have been displaced. Prussian Charles Deutschman was an experienced miller who located at Loma Parda because of its economic possibilities. Employing several other Prussians, he built a house and large gristmill southwest of the village along the river. During the late 1860s and 1870s farmers ground over a hundred thousand bushels of wheat and several thousand bushels of corn at this one mill. Much of this grain was sold to the quartermaster at Fort Union.[56]

As crazy as General Carleton's idea of destroying the town might have sounded to most New Mexicans, in recollecting his time there one soldier explained that Loma Parda's proximity to the post was the key element in its popularity. Frank Olsmith, a private, noted that there were restaurants, wine rooms, and plenty of dancing to be had. Soldiers with too much to drink got into fights, tore up property, and ended up in jail. A few were shot. While a stranger to this region might find the town hard to locate, soldiers had no such problem. At one point, Matías and Julián Baca and Antonio Montoya were forced to put up thousand-dollar bonds to ensure that they would no longer sell liquor to the soldiers. One way or another, they got around this stricture, for the dancehall and saloon generally associated with Julián Baca remained in operation for years to come.[57]

David P. Keener argues that historians have been wrong in their characterization of Loma Parda. It was much more than a hell-on-wheels den of inequity filled with gamblers, prostitutes, and rowdies. Using local census records, he claims that most inhabitants were simple farmers trying to eke out a living as best they could. Keener is correct that these villagers were farmers, but census designations do not tell the entire story. The 1870 census for Loma Parda notes that Frank Clark was a farmer, but other records show that by then he had been charged with selling liquor without a license. The same census details that he lived with the McMartin brothers—merchants and cattle brokers. This census also notes that Samuel Seaman was a farmer. It says nothing about him being the postmaster and sheriff, which was also true. Additionally, Thomas B. Catron recorded that a Samuel *Simmons* of *Samuel L. Simmons, Loma Parda v. the United States,* was charged with operating a retail liquor distributorship without a license. Records seem to indicate that Simmons was actually Seaman. The evidence is clear that a substantial number of this town's citizens were involved in the liquor trade: a trade that was often tied to the Comancheros.[58]

On August 17, 1872, Albuquerque's *Revista Republicana* reported that five people who lived in Loma Parda had been killed in the last ten days. Two Hispanos were found lynched about five miles from the Gallinas River. One of Hittson's camps was on the Gallinas. Charles Blanchard reported that a man named Samora "had gone for a walk in the other world" after being caught trying to steal Mora merchant Frank Metzer's horse. Most notable of all, Blanchard wrote: "We have received the news of the murder of J. T. Webber and Frank Clark" for stealing Texas cattle—the same Frank Clark who sold liquor and lived with the McMartins. Surely Clark and Webber were caught up in one of Hittson's region-wide roundups. Their demise was just a precursor of what was yet to come in this out-of-the-way village.[59]

Early in the morning of September 3, 1872, a Tuesday, several Texans rode into town and began inspecting the cattle that were corralled there. Hittson and James Patterson denied being among the party. Thomas Stockton and Martin Childers did not. It was Stockton's men who identified seven cattle with Texas brands and pulled them out of the stone corralls. By then the people of Loma Parda were awake. There must not have been many Texans in town that morning because the gathering crowd stopped this operation. Stockton's cowboys abandoned the cattle and left the village.[60]

Samuel Seaman (or Simmons), the town sheriff, was not mentioned in this first episode. That might be because the Texans left without incident. They returned the next morning. Since they arrived very early, they could not have traveled far. While Hittson and Stockton had good relationships with the army, it is doubtful that Fort Union officers would have let these men conduct their operation from the fort. Tiptonville, Watrous, or even Kroenig's ranch were more likely campgrounds. Watrous and in his sons-in-law often competed against the people who lived in Loma Parda for government contracts. It is less likely that Stockton's crew would have been welcome in the Hispanic mountain communities to the west, such as La Cueva or Mora. Regardless, when twenty Texans arrived Wednesday morning they were met by local police, led by Seaman, an old mountain man who had once served the army as a scout with Kit Carson. The Texans demanded that the cattle with their brands be turned over. Seaman and his men demanded to see bills of sale to prove ownership. The Texans ignored this demand but could not ignore the angry townsfolk who seemed ready to fight. They again left town without any cattle.[61]

The people of Loma Parda must have taken some satisfaction in standing their ground. Up to this point the Texans had been terrifying ranchers all across the territory for months. If the newspaper reports were true, they were responsible for the recent deaths of some of Loma Parda's own citizens. This was layered on top of an existing, long-held animosity toward all Texans, a dislike and distrust that had deep roots in New Mexico. The Lone Star State's longtime contention that New Mexico was a part of Texas, the failed Santa Fe Expedition that was meant to annex the territory, and the Confederate invasion during the Civil War, largely led by Texans, were woven into the fabric of most New Mexicans' memories. The Texans were invaders. They had always been invaders. On the third and fourth day of September, the people of Loma Parda stood up to them—and turned them away. It is probably true that by Wednesday night, the villagers were sleeping with one eye open, but no one came on Thursday. Or Friday. Or that weekend. Perhaps at this point Seaman and his men took a deep breath, celebrated a little, then went back to their everyday lives believing the Texans had moved on.[62]

The most contemporaneous account that historians rely on concerning what happened on September 10, 1872, was written from La Junta (Watrous) on September 15. Three days later it was published in the *Daily New Mexican*. The author, afraid to publish under his name, simply signed as "A Friend of the Right." He wrote that about forty Texans secretly came together near Loma Parda on the previous Monday afternoon. That night another twenty gunmen arrived. Again, this gathering's exact location is unknown, but it had to have been pretty close because when they rode into Loma Parda Tuesday morning, September 10, it was reported that no one was there. Over four hundred people lived in this village at the time. The author must have meant that everyone was asleep.[63]

Northeastern New Mexico is cold in September. That morning it is quite likely that frost coated the ground and a fog hung over the valley when sixty or so armed horsemen splashed across the Mora River and rode into town. They acted quickly, slipping into the corrals and herding cattle into the street. It must have been quite a scene. Lines of bawling cattle trotting past Texans who sat their horses with revolvers drawn, inspecting doorways and windows. The main road, which ran through the middle of town, would have been very crowded. Gunmen Clay Allison and Chunk Colbert would have felt right at home. Some of these cowboys began to see men with rifles looking down on them from rooftops. As the last corral was emptied, the vigilantes' rearguard backed slowly down the road and out of the village, splashing back across the river as they exited the valley. Silence followed. They were gone. But not for long.[64]

The author of this first report noted that about an hour later, the Texans returned. They had come into New Mexico to take back their stolen cattle, and they had accomplished this goal in Loma Parda. Yet here they came, splashing back across the Mora and riding up to the front of Julián Baca's saloon and dancehall. Baca had a large corral behind his business. It was probably pretty empty by then, but after calling the saloon owner out, they informed him that they had seen two stolen horses out back of his buildings and they wanted them. Baca refused. He claimed they were his. An argument ensued. It grew heated. The saloon owner was told that if he did not get the horses on his own, they would break down the corral gate and take them by force.[65]

Writing from La Junta five days later, the "Friend" reported that at one point during this standoff Baca tried to run into his house. The Texans caught him and beat him over the head with their pistols. Isadora, his wife, began to scream hysterically. Her cries must have broken the spell that had frozen the townsfolk. Toribio García lived across the street from the Bacas. He bolted out of his house carrying his rifle. At some point he stopped before he got to Julián's front door, perhaps because of the immediate attention the Texans gave him. Toribio dropped his weapon and turned back toward his house. That was when he was shot in the back of the head. Whether drawn by Isadora's screams or the shot that hit Toribio, Sheriff Seaman pushed his way through the crowd to get to Baca. Hittson and Patterson later claimed that Seaman ordered the New Mexicans to attack the Texans. The first account claimed that as soon as the old mountain man approached the crowd, one of the cowboys hit him in the face with the butt of his rifle. Seaman fell to the ground with a gaping facial wound. Before he had a chance to get up, he was shot in the back of the head. The La Junta reporter did not name any of the Texans who were involved in this melee. A few days later, the *Daily New Mexican* and Patterson did. Both claimed that Martin Childers led the raid into the village. Writing from Stockton's ranch on September 25, Patterson explained that the Texans were tired of waiting for law enforcement officials to act and blamed what happened on García and Seaman. If they had not tried to start a riot, the cattle-broker reasoned, no one would have gotten hurt.[66]

The first newspaper report noted that the Texans were firing their guns into the air and "yelling like Indians" when they left for good. Childers was one of the last to leave. On the outskirts of town he spotted a priest standing in the middle of the road with a rifle in his hand. The cowboy raised his own rifle and shot him. The bullet went through both of the priest's legs. Julián Baca, pistol-whipped and beaten to a pulp, lay limp and bleeding by his front door. Samuel Seaman and Toribio García lay dead in the street, both shot in the back of the head. None of the reports mention what happened to the two horses the Texans came back for.[67]

What is known is that on Saturday, September 14, four days after the attack and four days before the first account hit the newspapers, John Hittson was in Santa Fe making a pitch to Superintendent of Indian Affairs Nathaniel Pope. He wanted more beef contracts with the government. Thus, while his men were searching the Pecos, Gallinas, and Mora River mountain communities for cattle, he was trying to seal a deal to sell more beef. According to Vernon R. Maddux, Hittson's biographer, another rancher, Paul T. Herlon, was also at this meeting and like Hittson was registered at the Exchange Hotel. While this historian can find no other reference to a Herlon, a prominent German-speaking Santa Fean by the name of Paul F. Herlow opened a butcher shop on San Francisco Street in October 1872. This is the same street that Patterson's butcher shop was on (not to mention Probst and Kirchner's). Could Patterson have had a partner? Regardless of the name discrepancy, the timing of Hittson's meeting with Pope illustrates that these raids were about more than bringing stolen cattle back to Texas.[68]

The Texans continued to scout for cattle. In October fifty head were stolen from Eugenio Romero in San Miguel County. According to one newspaper account, the perpetrators included three locals and a Texan. Hittson put a notice in the same edition informing New Mexico that he was about to leave the state for a while. In his absence Patterson and Stockton would act as his agents, with full authorization to continue to round up stolen stock. Already outraged, New Mexicans demanded that authorities do their jobs and arrest the persons responsible for Seaman's and García's murders. Martin Childers was still in the territory. Another interesting notice was published in the same edition that mentioned Romero's cattle had been stolen.[69]

Stockton, Patterson, and Hittson were all registered at the La Fonda Hotel in Santa Fe on October 22, 1872. Hittson was about to leave for Texas. They were probably planning how they would proceed during his absence. The paper also noted that a fourth person was registered at the La Fonda that day, Samuel H. Elkins, Stephen's brother.[70]

As discussed in the previous chaper, Stephen B. Elkins served the territory as a district attorney, a U.S. attorney, and a territorial congressman. He also practiced law with Thomas Catron and later became a U.S. senator for the state of West Virginia. Just a couple of months before Hittson's raiders splashed across the Mora River into Loma Parda, Elkins had been involved in pressuring butcher Kirchner to use his political power to influence the electoral process. Yet his interest in Kirchner ran deeper than that. Elkins was also a cattleman, or at least he was in the cattle business. Along with brothers John and Samuel he owned a ranch east of Santa Rosa on the Pecos River.

Little has been written about this ranch, but it shows up in a few historical references. In 1875 doctor J. H. Shout of Las Vegas received an urgent message to come to Pete Maxwell's ranch at old Fort Sumner. Lucian B. Maxwell, who was living on his son's ranch, was very sick. Shout made every effort to get there as fast as he could, changing horses several times along the way. William A. Keleher writes that after traveling about eighty miles, the doctor arrived at the Elkins Ranch on the Pecos, where he was informed that Maxwell had already died.[71]

It appears John and Samuel ran the ranch, established on land that would eventually become part of the town of Santa Rosa. One map identifies the Elkins Ranch as located on the old Preston Beck Land Grant, located just a few miles downriver from the store and ranch of former California Column officer William Calloway. Agua Negra Creek was also very close. The district attorney's only documented ties to the Comancheros were related to his willingness to drop charges against them in return for votes, but that was not the case for many of his Pecos River neighbors: Giddings, Labadie, and Celso Baca were all directly involved in the trade. If the Elkins brothers were not involved, they would have been one of the few significant New Mexican families who lived in the area who was not.[72]

Prior to the Civil War Samuel Elkins followed brother Stephen to Mesilla, where he clerked in a dry goods store. During the war Samuel served in the quartermaster department at Fort Union, not far from Loma Parda. After the war he became a government storekeeper in Mora. While in Mora he got to know the largest merchant in the region, Ceran St. Vrain. Sam also knew Ceran's son Vicente, who carried on the family business after the elder St. Vrain died. A letter from Sam to Stephen indicates there was some type of business relationship between the two families, as at one point he reminded Stephen of the brand Vicente had requested. The letter does not mention what kind of brand he was talking about, but both the St. Vrains and the Elkins were involved in the cattle business.[73]

Brother John T. Elkins was also involved in this ranch, yet he is mostly known for having surveyed the Maxwell Land Grant in Colfax County with Walter G. Marmon. The results of this survey expanded the grant's boundaries by over a million acres. One of its owners was Stephen Elkins. Another was Thomas Catron. In 1878 surveyors John Elkins and Robert Marmon (Walter's brother) were sent to the Middle Pecos River, where they resurveyed the Anton Chico Grant. This survey also benefitted his brother's law partner, Catron, whose legal maneuverings usurped the land rights of many *nuevomexicanos* in the latter part of the nineteenth century. In this second survey John Elkins was evaluating land adjacent to the Elkins' ranch.[74]

In a brief biography of Samuel Elkins' life, William F. Switzer claims that Sam rode with Hittson in the 1872 cattle raids. This information makes it easier to connect the dots concerning his rather timely visit to the La Fonda Hotel on October 22, 1872. Sam was a merchant who had worked in Mora and served at Fort Union. He was probably selling more than dry goods. At least there is a hint of what else he might have been selling within the 1870 census of Mora County. By then he was clearly a merchant, yet it lists him as a laborer. What is most interesting is that it also notes that he was living with John May, a whiskey distiller from Bavaria. Such information illustrates at least two points: first, most nineteenth-century census records only tell a part of the story, as noted above; second, Samuel Elkins knew something about the liquor business, a key trade item amongst the Comancheros. Living in Mora, it is at least possible, if not probable, that he knew that Loma Parda sheriff Samuel Seaman was also a retail liquor distributor. The same would be true of anyone from that town who sold alcohol.[75]

Back in February, about the time Texas wranglers began to cause trouble in and around Trinidad, an interesting blurb appeared in the *Daily New Mexican*: "John Elkins, Esquire, left yesterday for his ranch on the Pecos." Ten months later this same paper reported that Martin Childers and several other Texans were arrested near Tanos Creek, which was a tributary of the Pecos River. Tanos Creek ran through the Elkins Ranch, about sixty miles southeast of Las Vegas. After his arrest Childers was brought to Las Vegas and locked up in the county jail. Why were the Texans at Elkins Ranch? Switzer might have given historians the answer in 1882. If Sam was a participant in the raids, the answer as to where Hittson's third base of operations was becomes evident; the Elkins Ranch. Hittson had already admitted that he received "valuable aid and assistance from the better and more influential citizens of New Mexico," but he never talked about who those people were.[76]

The three Elkins brothers were all connected to and familiar with some facet of the Comanchero trade. In 1871 John made a particularly interesting purchase from Las Vegas merchant Charles Ilfeld. The latter recorded that John T. Elkins and Company bought two dozen knives, some calico, a considerable amount of vermillion, and a dozen brass charms. Regarding the Indian trade, vermillion was the canary in the coal mine. Anyone who purchased this red-powder dye, not to mention brass charms, was involved in some type of Indian trade. Both Comancheros and Comanches collected brass charms to adorn their horses. Perhaps, like the ex-soldiers of the California Column, the Elkins brothers sought a shortcut to acquiring the type of wealth the cattle trade made possible in New Mexico. They and everyone else knew that would be easier to accomplish if the Comancheros were eliminated.[77]

Once the residents of Mora County, where Loma Parda was situated, knew Martin Childers was locked up in Las Vegas, they demanded that he be extradited to their county to stand trial for the murders. By then an investigation into the shooting was taking place, but the *Weekly New Mexican* reported that there was no information concerning its findings. Local citizens were worried.[78]

The paper reported on Childers's arrest twice, once on December 27 and again two days later. By then he had escaped the jail and was probably out of the territory, never to return. Most locals believed the jailor, who was arrested after the escape, was bribed. Back in June 1871 the *Santa Fe Weekly Post*, in a critical editorial about the Comancheros, posited that these traders deserved to be "shot down like so many dangerous dogs." This is what most Hispanos in Mora and

San Miguel Counties believed had happened on September 10, in Loma Parda, and now one of the main culprits had disappeared. Some surely remembered Calloway's bloody 1868 raid on Los Esteritos and how he also vanished, rumor had it, into the Lone Star State.[79]

While a devil in New Mexico, John Hittson became something of a national hero to the rest of the country. His written account of why he was doing what he was doing and how he was accomplishing it appeared in the *New York Evening Post*, the *Colorado Chieftain*, and the *Rocky Mountain News*. The narrative that the Texans rode into a foreign land and reclaimed what was "rightfully theirs" contained the mythic elements that captured the imaginations of Americans from New York to Texas. These national stories did not detail how Toribio García and Samuel Seaman had been shot in the back of the head, essentially making good on the recommendation of one New Mexico newspaper. They had been executed like "dangerous dogs."[80]

Regardless of what New Mexicans thought of Hittson, no one could say he lacked courage. When the district court met in the spring of 1873, he was back in the territory to defend his actions. He later claimed that in the only case against him that ever came to trial, he was found not guilty; the other cases filed against him had eventually been dropped.[81]

While his reputation as the quintessential western hero grew, there is little evidence to substantiate that he made the types of profits he envisioned during his meeting with Commissioner of Indian Affairs Nathaniel Pope, at least not from these raids. He told William Veale, Chairman of the Committee on Indian Affairs in Texas, that they had recovered between five and six thousand cattle, which were then herded to Colorado to be sold. The cattleman believed the future sale of this stock could amount to sixty thousand dollars. Yet this is just what he *anticipated*. His confident estimate of future profits circulated in a lot of newspapers whose accounts form the basis of much of the history of these raids. But such profits were never realized from these cattle.[82]

In 1915 Senator Catron estimated that Hittson did take that many cattle from Kirchner's La Porte Chiquito Ranch in Rio Arriba County. The senator recalled that the Texans did herd them into southern Colorado, but shortly thereafter the cattlemen returned them to New Mexico under court order. As his legal advisor, Catron told Hittson that he doubted if he would ever gain possession of them. The butcher had "bills of sale," and such receipts would hold up in court. After being "replevied [recovered] from them [the Texans] by the courts . . . they finally abandoned the effort [to keep them]."[83]

As the above details show, while the military played the most significant role in destroying the Comanchero trade, others were involved in its demise. Texans like Stockton and Hittson, cattle broker James Patterson, political elites in Santa Fe, and the press played important roles in the trade's elimination. New Mexico in the 1870s was not that different from Chicago in the 1930s. In both cases gangs moved in on someone else's territory. Blood was spilled. While Probst and Kirchner were certainly targets, they were also survivors. Politicians and competitors might loath them, but they understood their usefulness.

By 1873 the battle to control the cattle trade shifted south. More Texans were settling along the Rio Bonito and in the Ruidoso valley. Old-guard alliances understood this migration as a threat and looked warily on the newcomers, who seemed intent on upsetting the traditional ways of doing business. Juan Patrón, who came to La Placita (Lincoln) in 1870, participated in and experienced the growing animosity between the two groups.

A graduate of St. Michaels in St. Louis, Missouri, he came to La Placita to teach, but his leadership skills thrust him into a more violent role when people began to kill each other. After one group of Texans associated with the recently arrived Horrell family got into a drunken melee in one of the town's saloons, Juan Martín, the constable, was killed trying to get them to leave town. A posse led by Juan Patrón tracked down and killed two of the perpetrators, including one of the Horrells. The Horrells in turn targeted several of the town's Hispanics for revenge, including Patrón. Part of this revenge included attacking a local wedding in December 1873. One of the four people killed in this assault was Isidro Patrón, Juan's father. Juan was not there. Thus, what became known as the Horrell War began, and Juan Patrón was right in the middle of it.[84]

Just like in Mora and San Miguel Counties, there were overlapping issues at play here. One involved Texans moving in and attempting to take over the cattle trade. Another factor made the first even worse: the racial contempt each side held for the other. Thus, it was not that surprising when someone shot Juan Patrón in the back in 1875. While most pointed the finger at John H. Riley, Jimmy Dolan's future business partner, the assailant was never caught. Patrón refused to leave. He was there when John H. Tunstall came town, and he remained so for most of the events that made Lincoln, both the village and the county, the most dangerous place in the United States. James Patterson was also there.[85]

Patterson, who coordinated the raids in northeastern New Mexico with Hittson and Stockton, was involved in similar events in Lincoln County, where he had been doing business since 1872. After Lincoln sheriff William Brady was murdered, Patterson became a part of the posse that went after his killer, William Antrim, a.k.a. William Bonney, a.k.a. Billy the Kid. These vigilantes were originally organized to stamp out the rampant theft of Lincoln County cattle, an activity they believed the Kid was heavily involved in. Thus, not long after leaving Red River Station, Patterson inserted himself into another cattle war. By 1878 Hispanos like Patrón were aligned against people like Patterson and the Texans he associated with. This group often found themselves siding with the young man known as the Kid and his associates, who called themselves the Regulators. Patterson was with the posse that tracked down and killed Regulator Frank MacNab at Emil Fritz's ranch on April, 29, 1878.[86]

Catron kept a keen eye on these events. Dolan and Riley had owed him a considerable sum of money for some time. Unable to pay it back, in January 1878 they mortgaged over most of their property to him. This included the cattle that precipitated these wars. Thus, Dolan and Riley's silent business partner used his political power to put the Regulators in the worst possible light. Such patronage and the benefits he derived from its use made him part owner of the Consolidated Land, Cattle Raising, and Wool Growing Company; the Boston and New Mexico Cattle Company; the New Mexico Land and Livestock Company; the American Valley Company; and the New Mexico and Kentucky Land and Stock Company. By the end of the nineteenth century he owned portions of eight different land grants. This power was always connected with the cattle trade.[87]

People continued to die in Lincoln County. Only after the murders of John Tunstall and his business partner Alexander McSween did Patrón decide to leave the county. The person who convinced him was one of his best friends, Tranquillo Labadie, who was Lorenzo Labadie's son. Tranquillo attended school with Patrón at St. Michaels. That is how Juan Patrón ended up at Lorenzo Labadie's Agua Negra Ranch. Once there, he renewed his acquaintance with Tranquillo's sister Beatriz. They were married in the fall of 1879 in Anton Chico. It is interesting to contemplate what Lorenzo thought of this. He knew a lot about La Placita, having been the Mescalero agent at Fort Stanton. No doubt he had a few choice words to say about Lawrence Murphy, who had lobbied to get him removed from that agency a decade earlier. Surely Juan Patrón and his father-in-law had a lot to talk about.[88]

Soon Juan and Beatriz moved to nearby Puerto de Luna. Patrón became friends with merchant Alexander Grzelachowski and rancher Pete Maxwell. The three remained connected to William H. Bonney, the Kid. Numerous accounts detail how this notorious outlaw often showed up in Puerto de Luna, either hanging out at Grzelachowski's store or squiring Pete Maxwell's daughter at old Fort Sumner. Not long after his marriage, Patrón opened his own store with William Giddings, James Gidding's son. The year after Juan and Beatriz were married in Anton Chico, Pat Garrett also got married there. One year later, in July 1881, Sheriff Garrett found Billy the Kid at Maxwell's ranch and shot and killed him. Three years after that, Juan Patrón was shot and killed by Texan Michael Maney. Most accounts put the blame on Patrón, who was drunk and threatening to kill Maney. Whether a coincidence or just an irony, Maney was a cowboy who worked cattle on the J. J. Cox ranch, south of old Fort Sumner.[89]

The same year the worst of the troubles started in Lincoln County, 1873, Probst and Kirchner were making changes to their business model. In March the *New Mexican Union* reported that they were no longer in the market for Texas cattle. Kirchner was tired of fielding questions about where his beef came from. He now preferred to buy cattle from Colorado. A slew of complimentary stories on the butchers began to show up in Tucker and Manderfield's paper. In one article they wrote that an "epidemic of improvement has overtaken Probst and Kirchner. . . . They have completely overhauled their old butcher shop, putting down new floors, plastering, whitewashing and repairing. . . . Their meat was always clean and first class in quality, but it seems to have a new and sweeter flavor."[90]

Cattle flowed into their slaughter pens but no longer came from the Comancheros. The Comanches were in the midst of their last great battles, and these they could not win. Probst and Kirchner's new suppliers were Texans who had moved to Colorado. In 1874 the Prussians branched out to open the City Brewery. According to Paul Weideman's study of historic Santa Fe breweries, this might have been the first such establishment in Santa Fe. The two butchers went their separate ways in 1879. Kirchner kept the meat market, while Probst kept the brewery, which he renamed the Pioneer Brewery. That same year Kirchner married again, this time to old money. His new wife, María Nestora Perea, was the widow of Juan Miguel Perea. Perea, one of the wealthiest men in the region, had been several decades older than his wife. Soon after the wedding, Kirchner refaced the front of his San Francisco Street business with brick. In 1890 the Kirchners employed noted architect Philip Hesch to design and oversee the construction of their new home, located at 1411 Paseo de Peralta. Best known as the residence of nineteenth-century sculptor Eugenie Shonnard, the house is now owned by the Historic Santa Fe Foundation. Most reports related to its construction describe original owner Kirchner as a merchant and druggist. Few seemed aware that the Shonnard House would never have existed without the Comanchero trade.[91]

Probst had other businesses. He had run a stage stop and hotel in nearby Agua Fría since 1861. That year he also organized a company of Union volunteers who fought in the Civil War against the encroaching Confederates. Even though census records note he lived in Santa Fe in 1870, he is also known as one of Agua Fría's founders. The quieter of the two men, Probst appears to have been every bit the leader but not quite the talker—unless he had something important to say. The historical record identifies at least one time when he did have something to say.[92]

As noted in the previous chapter, one year before Probst and Kirchner dissolved their partnership, the Justice Department sent Special Investigator Frank Warner Angel to New Mexico to look into the murder of Lincoln County's John H. Tunstall. While there, he was also ordered to perform a general inquiry into the possible malfeasance of territorial power brokers like Catron, Elkins, and Gov. Samuel Axtell. John Taylor of San Miguel County told Angel that Elkins had used his position as district attorney as a stepping stone to gain political office.[93]

A reporter for the Santa Fe *Rocky Mountain Sentinel* interviewed Angel about his investigations in August 1878. When asked if any charges would be filed against Catron, he said there would be if Charles Probst's damning comments about the serving district attorney's activities were true. According to Angel's own notes, he believed Probst to be an honest man. What the butcher told him involved Catron, Elkins, John Hittson, and August Kirchner.[94]

He began with a summary of Hittson's plans and described how the cattleman wanted the Texas governor to pressure New Mexican politicians to admit that Probst and Kirchner were cattle thieves. These politicians included Marsh Giddings, the territorial governor. Once the butchers were outed by their own officials, it would be easier to extradite them to Texas to face charges.[95]

At that point incoming U.S. attorney Stephen B. Elkins approached Probst with a solution. First, he informed him that he and Catron were representing the Texans. It was possible, he said, that the butchers would soon be arrested. Angel related that Elkins then said, "If he, Probst, would give him, Elkins, three-thousand five hundred dollars and five hundred head of cattle, he, Elkins, would arrange to have the matter settled; that Probst at first refused, but finally his partner, Mr. August Kirchner, and wife [Nestora Perea Kirchner] gave Elkins a joint note that at maturity was worth $3,500.00." Probst suggested that if Angel needed proof of this transaction, he could find it at the First National Bank of Santa Fe. A paper trail existed within the records, which showed that Kirchner endorsed a $1,750 note over to Thomas B. Catron and another to Elkins for the balance. Angel, in the process of checking out this charge, told the reporter that if true, he would recommend that Catron and Elkins be removed from office and criminal proceedings filed against both. After receiving the special investigator's permission to talk to Elkins, the reporter ended the interview and went looking for one of New Mexico's more prominent territorial congressmen.[96]

He found him in his apartment above the First National Bank. Such was one of the perks of a bank president. Elkins was reluctant to give an interview because he was packing for a return to West Virginia. A widower until 1875, Elkins had married a U.S. senator's daughter from that state and was now more involved in land deals there than in New Mexico. He had recently made his home there. Yet when he heard about Probst's accusations, Elkins dropped everything and sat down for an interview.[97]

He called Probst statements a pack of "malicious lies." He also alluded back to the Comanchero trade. He offered that when he was the district attorney of New Mexico, Gen. George W. Getty had asked him to come down hard on people involved in these transactions. He said he did, arresting a lot of New Mexicans in the process. Angel had already interviewed John Taylor by then, who had alleged that Elkins had dropped or reduced a lot of those charges in return for votes. Elkins then explained that Hittson, Stockton, and other cattlemen came to him and his longtime law partner Catron seeking advice. The Texans hired them, putting up a $2,500 retainer for their help. The lawyers advised them to "procure certificates of brands [in Texas]" and then return to New Mexico and take their cattle "whenever they found them and had proof." Elkins made sure the reporter knew he told the Texans to never use violence.[98]

He pointedly noted that *Stockton* had taken seven hundred of Probst and Kirchner's cattle and that the butchers had responded with a writ of replevin. Much of this recounting tracks along with what Catron had to say in 1915, the exception being the number of cattle taken. Elkins detailed how this led to indictments against the Texans and counter indictments against Probst and Kirchner. At some point Texas issued extradition papers for the butchers that were sent to Marsh Giddings. It was then, Elkins told the reporter, that Kirchner agreed to settle everything out of court by paying the state of Texas $3,500.[99]

As to why the checks were written to the lawyers and not the state of Texas, Elkins lamely blamed Probst and Kirchner. He adamantly denied that he had blackmailed the butchers with the threat of indictment or that the payment was hush money. Instead, he claimed that it was the butcher's idea to write the checks out to himself and Catron. The lawyers' lawyer, William Breeden, was also a part of this arrangement. While this makes no sense, the future West Virginia senator and secretary of war (in the administration of Benjamin Harrison) stuck by this story and made it worse. He explained that once he and Catron had the money, Hittson directed them to pay themselves first, then write a check for the balance to the Texans. Based on how Angel began the interview and his personal thoughts regarding Probst's honesty, it is doubtful he swallowed such an excuse. Yet we know neither Catron nor Elkins was prosecuted. Why not?[100]

An interesting facet of both Elkins's and Catron's recollections is how they went out of their way not to implicate each other in this episode. Elkins made crystal clear that his partner had little to do with advising the Texans or handling these payments. Catron was the U.S. district attorney of New Mexico at the time. Elkins was so convincing that the reporter did not feel the need to interview Catron. When Catron was deposed decades later on the depredation claim, his perspective had probably changed, for although he told the court he had nothing to gain, as noted, he was representing the butchers' widows and would acquire a portion of whatever settlement that came out of it. It is also true that over time Kirchner and Catron came to terms with each other. Like so many other Democrats in New Mexico, Kirchner became a Republican. When Catron recounted his dealings with Hittson, he left Elkins completely out of his recollection.[101]

Angel sent a copy of his completed report to Catron and requested that he respond to what he had written. A deft and talented man, Catron stalled. At first he made the excuse that he did not have time to give a proper response. Delays continued. At the same time, Catron contacted Elkins in Washington, D.C., and requested that he get in touch with U.S. Attorney General Charles Devens. Perhaps the territorial congressmen could convince Devens to scuttle the entire probe or at least get him to come to an understanding that the more slanderous portions of the report were nothing more than fables put together by their political enemies. Catron urged Elkins to meet with Devens before the attorney general read Angel's report. Elkins tried to set this up, but Devens ignored the attempt.[102]

The report Angel submitted to the attorney general of the United States was based on the numerous interviews and depositions that he had taken while in

New Mexico between May and July 1878. While the information used to produce it revolved around Tunstall's murder, land grant scandals, and political corruption, according to his August interview in the *Rocky Mountain Sentinel*, Probst's affidavit was also a part of his findings. Additionally, while the newspaper did not mention John Taylor's assessment of Elkins, it surely colored the special investigator's conclusions. Events in Lincoln County however, continued to spiral out of control. In the midst of Angel's investigation, a major shoot-out took place in Lincoln County. Among others, Alexander McSween was killed. This happened not long after the president, Rutherford B. Hayes, had ordered Angel back to New York. One result of his report was that Governor Axtell was replaced by Lew Wallace. Perhaps due to the increasing rate of violence and continually changing circumstances, some of the illegalities Angel uncovered never led to further prosecutions. In other words, Catron and Elkins once again escaped disaster.[103]

Even so, Catron continued to worry about Angel's report. This account that detailed damning information on two up-and-coming Santa Fe lawyers remained somewhere within the dusty bowels of the Justice Department. What if an unsuspecting do-gooder or nosey reporter got their hands on it? Fifteen years later Catron got in touch with his old friend, Secretary of War Elkins, and requested that he look for it—and destroy it, if found. This really answers any questions one might have concerning the validity of Probst's charges. At one point Elkins wrote back that he could not find the report. Even if he had, it is doubtful that such an astute man would have written down what he did with it. The original that Angel submitted to Attorney General Devens can no longer be found.[104]

Like Catron and Elkins, Charles Probst and August Kirchner were survivors. When they went their separate ways in 1879, the meat market was still thriving. In an 1882 breakdown of individuals and families who owned more than 25,000 square feet of commercial property in downtown Santa Fe, Kirchner was sixth on the list. That same year Probst was one of the top three landowners in town. It is clear that two of the territory's most street-smart businessmen did not need each other, or the Comancheros, to continue to prosper.[105]

Charles Goodnight also prospered. As noted above, like many other Texans he moved to southern Colorado. In 1869 he ran cattle on his Rock Canyon Ranch, located on the Arkansas River near Pueblo, yet his ties to Texas remained strong. Economic difficulties in Colorado and the U.S. Army's successful prosecution of the remaining Comanches in the Red River Wars of 1874 eventually brought him back to his home state. In 1871 Goodnight had helped Ranald Mackenzie track down Quanah and the Quahadi Comanches in Palo Duro Canyon. He must have seen the value of such a place, for he came back in 1876 to claim it as his own.

By then Comanchero Nicolás Martínez was one of Goodnight's employees. How long he had been working for him is unknown. It is possible that it was Martínez, not Goodnight, who led the Fourth Cavalry into the canyon that led to the Quahadis' demise. What is known is that when the fabled Texan brought his first cattle into the same canyon, it was Martínez who led the way. Bison ran ahead of Goodnight's cowboys and the cattle they herded into Palo Duro. Goodnight and Martínez located the night's cow camp and the future headquarters of the JA Ranch. The Texas cowman and the New Mexican Comanchero knew the value of a good place to keep cattle. Sometimes the truth is far more interesting than anything that could have been made up.[106]

CHAPTER 6

Having examined the New Mexico side of the Comanchero trade, our story moves eastward across the borderlands to the Lone Star State, to present a different take on this activity, this one from a Texan perspective. It was not until the late 1850s that federal and state officials began to discern distinct patterns in Texas's rampant livestock thefts. In January 1858 raiders drove off more than six hundred horses from the North Texas frontier. After investigating the depredations, in June 1858 Texas Ranger captain John Salmon "Rip" Ford reported that traders north of the Red River were involved in a "nefarious and unholy traffic" with white outlaws and Native American tribes, freely swapping guns, ammunition, and supplies to Indians in exchange for horses stolen from Texas residents. U.S. Indian agent Samuel Blain concurred with Ford's assessment. Blain said that lawless men living in Indian country were causing much of the trouble, encouraging and assisting depredating Native Americans in disposing of stolen livestock.[1]

More information gradually came to light—specifically, where the thieves were taking their pilfered animals. Between November 1857 and January 1858, Indians ran off 325 horses from Brown and Coleman Counties. After one of these raids, Capt. Earl Van Dorn, commanding the U.S. Army's Camp Colorado, in Coleman County, Texas, dispatched a patrol to pursue the marauders. The captain noted that Indians had departed following the same northwest direction they had taken on previous raids. In early 1858 Texas Ranger lieutenant Ed Burleson and his men tracked a party of raiding Comanches for thirty-six hours from Young County northwest to the Double Mountain Fork of the Brazos River before his horses finally gave out. In another instance, Capt. T. J. Johnson of the Rangers pursued a band of Comanches to within sight of the Double Mountains in Stonewall County. Johnson observed that their tracks led northwest. In a confidential report to Texas governor Sam Houston in May 1860, Col. M. T. Johnson summarized his Rangers' findings: "All the trails and evidence as to where the stolen horses have been carried . . . point to the northwest, and large numbers have been taken, make no mistake about it. The horses are sold in New Mexico and Kansas."[2]

As Colonel Johnson correctly discerned, one destination to the northwest for this stolen livestock was New Mexico. Another was Kansas, which included eastern Colorado until Kansas attained statehood in January 1861. Colorado became a territory the following month. Before the Civil War Euro-American merchants routinely congregated at Bent's New Fort on the Arkansas River, near present-day Lamar, Colorado, and traded with Native Americans and Anglo rustlers for purloined Texas horses. Bent's New Fort (1853–60), the successor to Bent's Old Fort (1833–49), was situated at Big Timbers, a well-known Native American camping ground on the north side of the Arkansas.

The proprietor of Bent's New Fort was William Bent of St. Louis, who had come west with his brother Charles during the late 1820s. In a May 1860 letter from Indian Territory to the U.S. commissioner of Indian affairs, federal Indian agent Matthew Leeper said that a number of army officers in the region believed that an organized network of thieves and robbers were responsible for the widespread livestock thefts. Leeper noted that troops had followed many of the rustlers' trails, "and they invariably lead in the direction of Bent's Fort on the Arkansas River. The valley of the Arkansas near that place for many years has been the general rendezvous of all the roving bands of Comanches." As confirmation of the agent's conclusions, Leeper's letter bore the endorsements of four army captains and three lieutenants stationed at Fort Cobb, Indian Territory (in present-day Caddo County, Oklahoma).[3]

Others concurred with Leeper's assessment. One was Lt. Col. Robert E. Lee, who commanded the Department of Texas for much of 1860. A second was Lt. William Warren Lowe of the Second Cavalry, stationed at Camp Cooper, Texas. Lowe had read a number of well-documented reports on the thefts. He said that it was the general belief in North Texas that the majority of animals stolen in the state were disposed of at Bent's Fort. A third person who agreed was Texas governor Sam Houston, who complained to Secretary of the Interior Jacob Thompson that there were trading houses on the Arkansas River "where a continual exchange is going on between these tribes and those who buy the property stolen from the citizens of Texas." Houston lamented that "no check exists upon these villainies and . . . the trade is profitable, both to the Indians and to the . . . traders."[4]

Although constrained by a slender budget for frontier defense, Governor Houston was determined to make a breakthrough in the state's rustling epidemic.

In May 1860 he hired P. D. Turner of Old Camp Colorado (near Trickham, Texas) to act as his secret agent in Indian and Kansas Territories. The governor instructed Turner to proceed to the Wichita Indian agency. From there he was to journey out onto the wild prairies to determine exactly where the stolen horses were being sold and who was buying them. Turner was to maintain strict secrecy and not discuss the nature of his mission with anyone. To help expedite his spy's departure, Houston loaned him several mules for the journey.[5]

Unfortunately, Turner proved to be rather timid and never ventured far from the safety of the Wichita agency and area army camps to fulfill his mission. Turner told Houston that he tried to hire Native American guides to take him to Bent's trading house on the Arkansas River but was unsuccessful because the Indians were afraid to go out onto the plains without a guard of fifty men. Over the ensuing weeks Turner wrote the governor several additional notes attempting to justify his lack of progress and to buy more time, but Houston was having none of it. In early August, he pulled the inept Turner off the mission and ordered him to return to Texas with the borrowed mules.[6]

Had Turner reached his destination, he would have learned that from 1833 to 1860, Bent's Old and New Forts on the Arkansas served as important trade centers for whites, Comancheros, and Plains Indians. At Bent's forts buffalo robes were a popular commodity. Horses were another. Besides their utilitarian uses, horses served as a universal currency that Indians and outlaws could exchange for anything of value. When U.S. Indian agent Robert Miller visited Bent's New Fort in the fall of 1857, he found a considerable number of Hispanic traders, likely Comancheros, "continually roving over the country, and to whom many of the difficulties with the Indians may be traced."[7]

Miller said the traders brought various provisions, including rotgut whiskey, to exchange with the Indians and were "using their influence, which is in many instances very great, to keep up the hostile feeling against the whites." Miller observed "several of these miscreants around Bent's Fort during [his] stay there, going in and out whenever they chose[;] they have been in the employ of Bent for some time." The Indian agent was powerless over the situation. Miller believed that the military could rid the region of these unsavory dealers by posting a permanent detail at the fort as a deterrent.[8]

Another visitor to Bent's New Fort was Marion Sloan Russell who, at the tender age of fifteen, came here with her family to exchange a wagonload of goods. She said that the trading post, which reminded her of a country auction, was a sanctuary for both Native Americans and whites. Russell observed some of the bartering. The Indians desired guns and gunpowder, and the more of them that were present at the fort, "the better the trading, and for that reason, there were always Indians lounging around Bent's."[9]

The owner, William Bent, was an adroit entrepreneur who exploited the frontier economy to his maximum benefit. In addition to operating the trading post and working as a government freighter, William Bent served as U.S. Indian agent for the Upper Arkansas River. Cheyennes, Arapahoes, Kiowas, Apaches, and Comanches were among the various tribes living in the region. Among the Comanches, the Yamparika band dominated trade on the Arkansas and Canadian Rivers. The Yamparikas "acted as gatekeepers not only for Anglo-American parties traveling" through the region, "but also for . . . Comancheros venturing out from the settlements, as well as for the various Comanche and Apache tribes who had . . . horses to trade."[10]

Bent was a savvy merchant and trader and was very familiar with Plains Indians customs. In 1837 he married a Cheyenne woman and over the ensuing years spent much time in Cheyenne villages. Bent ably used his various positions and considerable frontier experience to increase profits. He endeavored to create a regional trading monopoly and encouraged Native Americans to trade at his fort. His efforts ultimately proved successful.[11]

The increased attention from Texas and federal officials regarding illicit business activities at Bent's New Fort naturally concerned its proprietor, who correctly perceived this scrutiny as a potential threat to his bottom line. In March 1860 A. B. Greenwood, the U. S. commissioner of Indian Affairs, wrote to Bent informing him that he had received complaints that Indians within his Upper Arkansas agency, in particular Penateka Comanches under Chief Buffalo Hump, were making constant raids into Texas and attacking local residents. Buffalo Hump's antipathy toward Texans was well known. In the fall of 1858 at Bent's Fort the chief had openly bragged of his hatred for Texans to Indian agent Robert Miller. The Comanche chief told the agent that as soon as their business at Bent's was concluded, he would head south and lead a raid against the whites. He kept his promise and subsequently departed with a sizeable raiding party. However, in his response to Greenwood's letter, Bent insisted that any recent reports placing Buffalo Hump in Texas were in error, as he had just seen the chief and his people in February 1860, and the Comanches had been on the Upper Arkansas continuously since August 1859.[12]

To deescalate the dispute, Bent suggested that the government hold a council with the Comanches to discuss drafting a new treaty and creating a permanent reservation for the tribe. The most central point within their range to hold such a council would be at Bent's New Fort. Bent proposed allocating $100,000 for the parley, which would cover provisions and presents for the Indians. Bent also recommended establishing the reservation on the Upper Arkansas, perhaps subtly inferring that the best location for this was also at Bent's Fort. Always on the lookout for new business opportunities, Bent understood that holding a council and establishing an Indian reservation near his trading post would provide a significant boost to his economic fortunes.[13]

The U.S. Army proved receptive to the Texans' complaints, while the commissioner of Indian Affairs sided with William Bent. In a letter to his superior, U.S. Secretary of the Interior Jacob Thompson, Commissioner Greenwood said that a military campaign against the Comanches on the Upper Arkansas would disturb the peace currently existing between the government and the tribe. Greenwood told Thompson that he supported Bent's idea of a parley and a new reservation. The army's general-in-chief, Winfield Scott, did not share Greenwood's assessment and ordered an attack against hostile Comanches and Kiowas in the region as soon as the weather permitted. Scott felt that this was not an appropriate time to be negotiating with these tribes, as "their depredations have been of such an aggressive character as to demand severe chastisement." The general-in-chief believed that the Indians would not honor any treaty until they experienced the power of the federal government firsthand.[14]

During the next six months Bent realized that regional tensions and conflict would only worsen, threatening trade at Bent's New Fort. In September 1860 he leased the site to the U.S. Army, which had recently built Fort Wise (later Fort Lyon) a mile upstream. That same month he resigned his position as Indian agent. Bent moved his business operations to a less prominent locale upstream, near Boggsville and the junction of the Purgatory and Arkansas Rivers. Ultimately federal officials refused to recognize his title to Bent's New Fort, declared him a squatter, and declined to honor their agreement.[15]

Comanches from Bent's former Upper Arkansas agency resumed their raids southward into Texas and Mexico. In 1860 Buffalo Hump led a foray to Coahuila, Mexico, where he and his band looted a wagon train. In January 1861 Agent Matthew Leeper wrote Commissioner Greenwood that Buffalo Hump and his Comanches were responsible for recent depredations in Jack County, Texas. Two months later the Penateka chief took fifty Comanche and Kiowa warriors on another sortie into Texas, where he and his braves engaged a group of Texas Rangers on the Upper Colorado River before continuing onto Coahuila.[16]

Although Bent's Fort closed in 1860, Big Timbers and the Upper Arkansas continued as a trading center for Comanches and outlaws seeking to dispose of purloined Texas livestock. Famed Texas cattleman Oliver Loving visited the region in 1862 and wrote that "the general rendezvous of the Indians who depredate upon the frontier of Texas is upon the Arkansas River." Loving said that during his trip he encountered a large group of Comanches with four to five thousand horses that had been taken from Texas.[17]

As Texas Ranger colonel M. T. Johnson correctly warned Governor Houston, the illicit livestock trade on the Upper Arkansas was only part of the problem facing Texas. After reading a speech on the topic by Governor Houston in the *San Antonio Daily Ledger and Texan*, Samuel B. Watrous, a prominent landowner near La Junta, New Mexico, penned a response to the newspaper. La Junta (now Watrous), where Watrous had settled in 1849, was at the junction of the Mountain and Cimmaron routes of the Santa Fe Trail and of the Mora and Sapello Rivers. La Junta was a popular rendezvous for Comancheros and Plains Indians. During his time there Watrous witnessed numerous transactions of a dubious character.[18]

In his letter to the *Daily Ledger*, Watrous noted that while Houston had mentioned the nefarious activities on the Upper Arkansas, he had said nothing of New Mexico: "I infer that he is not aware that New Mexico furnishes Market No. 2. If the citizens of Texas are ignorant of this fact, let them remain so no longer." Watrous pointed out that much of the livestock stolen by Comanches in Texas was sold to New Mexico traders, "who penetrate nearly to the frontier settlements of Texas, to supply these Indians with everything they need. . . . In many cases, the sweat is not dry on animals thus procured before they change owners." Concluding his remarks, Watrous observed that "this trade is carried on openly and extensively. Instead of its being frowned [upon] . . . and the traders punished, it is fostered and encouraged. Comanches come into our settlements and boast of the outrages committed in Texas, but the authorities take no notice of it."[19]

Early in the Civil War, Texas Rangers uncovered evidence of the clandestine Comanchero trade during one of their patrols of the northwest frontier. On a scout in April 1861 Capt. David L. Sublett and his Rangers followed the trail of two hundred mules and horses to the head of the Prairie Dog Town Fork of the Red River in Randall County, Texas. There Sublett found a recently abandoned Indian village of almost ninety campfires and tepees. At the site were remnants of several trade goods boxes, likely brought there by traders from New Mexico. The Ranger captain also discovered wagon train tracks heading westward. Because of the abundance of Indian signs in the vicinity, Sublett surmised that the location was frequently used as an encampment.[20]

During the Civil War the Comanchero trade underwent a significant transition. This change was spurred in large part by the establishment in 1863 of Bosque Redondo, a reservation to contain Navajos and Mescalero Apaches at Fort Sumner, New Mexico. At its peak, more than nine thousand Indians lived on the bleak and barren Pecos River reservation. Department of New Mexico commander James H. Carleton understood that he now had many more mouths to feed in addition to the troops stationed at various forts within his department. The numerous military outposts in the Department of New Mexico spanned an immense geographic area, from Arizona to the west, east to Fort Union, New Mexico, and south to El Paso County, Texas. To supply all of the Indians and soldiers, Carleton knew that he would need larger and more frequent deliveries of flour, corn, and, above all, beef.

Government beef contractors in New Mexico quickly realized they could not raise enough cattle to meet the increased demand. The word filtered down to the Comancheros and their Comanche trading partners. Soon, in addition to the usual traffic in horses, hundreds of stolen Texas beeves began appearing in New Mexico. By 1863 Texans living in the state's frontier counties were reporting a marked increase in raiding and sizeable losses.

Lacking adequate men and resources, Confederate troops and the Texas Rangers proved unable to defend Texas's western frontier during the Civil War. In February 1863 Confederate brigadier general William Hudson reported that Indians had recently swept through Cooke and Montague Counties, killing five Texans and driving off large numbers of livestock. Locals were gripped by fear. Citizens in Montague County had "forted up" at the county seat. Two weeks later Hudson observed that the depredations had greatly increased, with the Indians riding unopposed through a tier of counties. In response to the increased attacks, residents abandoned Clay County, much of Montague County, and portions of Cooke County.[21]

In early March 1863 at Gainesville, the county seat of Cooke County, Capt. J. J. Diamond found the "country invaded by Indians, Jayhawkers, etc., and our people almost ready to flee their homes and sacrifice to the foe large possessions of cattle and horses, as well as promising fields of grain." Just before Christmas 1863 Col. James Bourland reported from Gainesville that the Indians had killed twelve people, wounded seven, burned eight to ten houses, and run off numerous animals. Bourland wrote that the homes in the county seat were overflowing with anxious residents from the north and west part of Cooke County. Those remaining in the western part of the county were in a state of panic and threatening to leave their farms and ranches.[22]

One of the largest and most devastating of Texas's wartime depredations was the Elm Creek Raid on October 13, 1864. Led by Comanche chief Little Buffalo, five hundred to a thousand Comanche and Kiowa warriors swept through Young County and North Texas, killing eleven people and carrying off hundreds of horses, five to ten thousand head of cattle, and close to a dozen captives. As one historian characterized it, "This was a raid for horses, wealth, and prestige in leadership." Texan defenders killed Little Buffalo during the attack.[23]

The Elm Creek Raid terrified settlers on Texas's western frontier. Many of them packed their belongings and moved east. Lt. Col. Buck Barry observed that after the attack many counties in the region, including Stephens, Palo Pinto, Jack, Wise, Young, Montague, and Clay, were largely deserted. Barry, the number two ranking officer in the Texas Rangers, said that only a few cowhands remained in the region and had "forted up" at several of the larger ranches.[24]

Rip Ford, now a colonel, commanded troops guarding the Rio Grande, Eagle Pass, the western Hill Country, and the Lower Road to El Paso. He recalled, "The Texas frontier suffered greatly from Indian depredations during the war. A tier of counties, at least three deep, was quite depopulated." In 1864 the head of the Texas Rangers, Col. J. E. McCord, reported that the line of settlement was now eighty to a hundred miles west of Austin and San Antonio, or roughly along a line from Fredericksburg south to Uvalde. In many places in Texas the frontier had receded as much as 150 miles eastward to its former position in 1849.[25]

Overwhelmed by the incessant raids, ranchers in frontier counties found themselves powerless to prevent sizeable livestock losses. The trade for stolen horses and cattle remained brisk throughout 1864 and 1865. In one example, in the fall of 1864 residents of San Miguel County, New Mexico, returned from a trading expedition with the Comanches. The Comancheros advised Michael Steck, Superintendent of Indian Affairs in New Mexico, that the Indians had mentioned making several recent raids into Texas which netted them a considerable number of beeves.[26]

Noted Comanchero José Piedad Tafoya recalled that in 1864 he was living in San Miguel County and trading with Comanche, Kiowa, and Apache Indians in Texas. Often Tafoya would rendezvous with the Comanches at Quitaque (near present-day Quitaque, Texas) to trade his goods. Tafoya said that Quitaque was located on the eastern edge of the Staked Plains, where the eroded caprock gave way to numerous deep canyons. The site, which served as one of the Comanches' main trading headquarters, possessed ample water, grass, and shelter. It was an ideal hideout. The Indians would drive their purloined animals into one of the valleys, and the Comancheros would gather around and begin their bartering. After concluding his business at Quitaque, Tafoya would travel northwest until he struck the Fort Smith–Santa Fe Road, and from there he journeyed west to New Mexico. The Comanches were not always trustworthy in their transactions. Tafoya said that on occasion the Indians would rob the Comancheros of livestock they had just purchased or would demand that they pay for them a second time.[27]

Comanches, Comancheros, army officers, merchants, and livestock brokers were not the only ones conducting an illicit trade in Texas beeves. Union beef contractors and Confederate ranchers also sensed a mutually lucrative opportunity. By the fall of 1864 federal cattle dealers and army officers from the Department of New Mexico were venturing south into Texas's frontier counties at the very moment when cattleman John Chisum was looking westward for new markets. Both sides were ready to deal. Chisum represented a consortium of Texas stock raisers who were willing to sell their herds to the enemy, and the Union army stood ready to purchase all the beeves that Texas ranchers could provide, albeit surreptitiously.

During the first years of the war Chisum had been a Confederate beef contractor, supplying more than four thousand beeves to the rebel war effort. Exactly when Chisum resolved to sell his herds to the enemy in New Mexico is unknown. Most likely the plan started forming during the summer of 1863, after the South's devastating defeats in July at Gettysburg and Vicksburg. Following the loss of Vicksburg, the rebels lost control of the Mississippi River, and Chisum's beef markets east of the Mississippi evaporated. To make matters worse, his remaining customers west of the Mississippi paid him with an increasingly worthless currency. By 1864 the value of Confederate money in Texas had depreciated to ten cents on the dollar.[28]

If Chisum refused to sell his beeves for rebel dollars, he risked having them impressed by Confederate authorities. In January 1863 the Confederate commander of Texas, Maj. Gen. John Bankhead Magruder, ordered that all cattle be seized from stock raisers refusing to accept Confederate currency. These factors led Chisum to turn his gaze west toward new horizons and new markets. The

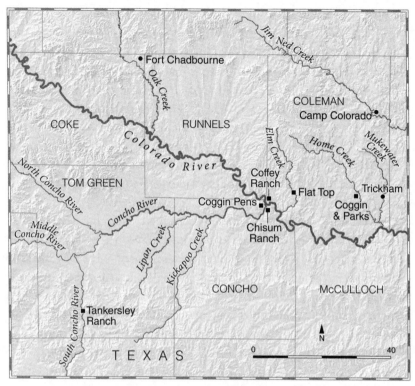

West Texas ranches in the vicinity of the Concho and Colorado Rivers,
including John Chisum's. Map by Carol Zuber-Mallison.

cattleman was a practical businessman. If the Confederacy would not buy his
beeves at a fair price, he would sell them to the Department of New Mexico. In
addition, Union contractors paid in a currency that actually had value.[29]

On October 15, 1863, Chisum began driving his herd west from Denton County
to Concho County. Arriving there on November 10 with 1,500 head, he situated
his new spread on the east bank of the Concho River, south of its junction with
the Colorado River. Chisum's Concho County ranch was located in the 337-acre
Abstract 746 originally granted to Theodor Sterzing and subsequently patented
by G. H. Sherwood in October 1858. As Sherwood was not in the area during
the war, Chisum, an unlawful tenant squatter, set up operations on his property.
During his time in Concho County, Chisum never purchased any acreage. His
herds roamed freely over an immense range.[30]

By the fall of 1864 the cattleman had moved more than 17,000 beeves to the Concho-Colorado confluence. Chisum cowboy M. C. Smith Sr. recalled that his boss "selected a place for his ranch building in a monte of large pecan trees and it proved to be a turkey roost. Here I saw more turkeys than I ever saw before . . . five hundred." The cattleman's Concho County home was a two-room wood structure that sat atop a limestone foundation. Nearby, his men constructed log huts for their living quarters. After they had completed the buildings, Chisum brought out an elderly African American woman from Denton County to cook their meals. The ranch's feisty foreman, Christopher C. Fitzgerald, was prone to cussing out his men.[31]

The Chisum site was a mile and a half from rancher Rich Coffey's place in Coleman County on the north bank of the Colorado, just east of the rivers' convergence. Coffey had moved to the area five weeks before Chisum, on October 1, 1863. To the southwest, forty-five miles from the Chisum and Coffey ranches, in November 1864 Richard Franklin Tankersley established his cattle operations at the headwaters of the South Concho River, near present-day Christoval, Texas. Prior to moving to the South Concho, Tankersley spent much of 1864 ranching at the mouth of the Concho River with Chisum, Fitzgerald, and Emory B. Peter (another long-standing Chisum associate and business partner). Tankersley and Chisum were close friends.[32]

The Concho and Colorado watersheds, while remote and vulnerable to Indian raids, offered the ranchers privacy from inquisitive state officials and Confederate cattle impressment agents. The closest Texas Ranger detachment to the Chisum and Coffey ranches was at Camp Colorado in Coleman County, thirty-four miles to the northeast on Jim Ned Creek. Another local Ranger outpost was at Camp Concho (near present-day Arden, Texas) sixty-two miles to the west on the Middle Concho River in Irion County (then part of Tom Green County).[33]

In addition to Chisum, Coffey, and Tankersley, a fourth ranching outfit in the region was Coggin and Parks. In 1861 Moses and Samuel Coggin moved three thousand head of cattle to Home Creek in Coleman County, thirty miles east of the Concho-Colorado confluence. During the war John Chisum had also established a presence on Home Creek, supplementing his Denton and Concho County operations with a third ranch, located south of present-day Santa Anna, Texas. Chisum made Home Creek his West Texas headquarters and supply base. To keep his cowboys and cattle drives well supplied, he purchased a general store and saloon nearby from William C. Franks. This location later became the town site of present-day Trickham, Texas.[34]

According to W. W. Hunter, who had moved to the area in 1860, Franks's log cabin trading post was on Mukewater Creek, a tributary of Home Creek. Hunter recalled, "Franks carried groceries and whiskey in stock and was a jovial fellow, always playing tricks on the settlers who came into his store"—hence its name Trick'em, later changed to Trickham. After Chisum purchased the store, he retained Franks to help run it with Emory Peter. Another early Mukewater pioneer, Dick Fiveash, said that Chisum "would send Franks to Austin after money to pay off his men and Franks would return with his saddlebags full of gold and silver; or he would be sent to Austin with the money received from the sale of a herd of cattle, to be placed in the bank."[35]

During this period regional stock raisers typically free-ranged their cattle over a wide area encompassing hundreds of miles. Chisum, Coffey, Coggin, and Tankersley cattle grazed an area bounded by Coke County on the north, the Llano and San Saba Rivers in Mason and Menard Counties to the south, Home and Brady Creeks to the east, and the South Concho River to the west. This range allegedly "was larger than the states of Massachusetts, Connecticut, and Rhode Island combined. Upon this great extent of uninhabited territory the cattle roamed without herders . . . and no man pretends to know from personal observation, how many cattle any owner possessed." One early cowboy, James Dofflemyer, joked that this free open range was so vast that their livestock "drank water out of the Rio Grande. We all used everybody's land." He recalled, "Of course we had open land. We didn't lease any land nor buy any land."[36]

Coleman County old-timer M. M. Callan remembered that during this time much of West Texas was a wild, open country with large herds of buffalo and plenty of game. During regional round ups ranchers would pool their hands and work the cattle together. Before heading out to gather the far-flung cattle, the men would take fifteen to twenty days' rations. All of the animals from area ranches grazed together. Since the beeves were branded, it was a straightforward task for the cowboys to cut out their cattle and turn the remaining ones back on the range. The cowhands could typically gather up to two thousand animals during a two-week period. Dofflemyer recalled that they collected "as much as they could get of them, but they had such a big country to gather over, they couldn't get all of them, not by a whole lot."[37]

Typically, these cooperative roundups took place each year during the spring and summer. In the spring the men would round up the beeves, brand them, and prepare them to drive to market. When collecting their spring herds, the cowboys typically started down by the San Saba River, at the southern end of the open range. When cold northers hit during the winter, the animals drifted south, sheltering in draws that provided a break from the frigid winds. Emory Peter, a partner in Chisum's cattle operations for many years, stated that the country around the head of the San Saba was "a mighty good place to protect them [the cattle]" during the winter as the terrain was "broken and brushy." During their spring and summer cow hunts to the San Saba in 1864 and 1865, Chisum cowhands collected 1,200 to 1,500 beeves. In 1866 they made five trips to the San Saba and Llano and drove 6,000 head back to the Concho County ranch.[38]

John Chisum also contacted other local stock raisers and offered to sell their beeves. To facilitate collection of area herds, he constructed a series of cattle pens stretching from Mason, San Saba, and McCulloch Counties north to Concho and Coleman Counties. Peter said that the cowhands conducted most of their annual branding at the Brady Creek pens. After gathering beeves at regional corrals, a group of cowboys would drive the herds to Chisum's Concho River ranch, which from 1864–68 served as the starting point for the New Mexico cattle drives. Fitzgerald, Chisum's Concho River ranch foreman, supervised assembling the herds for the trip west.[39]

Throughout 1864 Chisum supplemented his West Texas herd with large numbers of cattle from Denton and other area counties. Chisum cowboy David Waide recalled that the route for these cattle drives was from Bolivar in Denton County through Wise, Parker, and Palo Pinto Counties (crossing the Brazos, Pecan Bayou, and Jim Ned watersheds) and then onto the Concho. The cowhands pointed their herds toward Santa Anna Mountain, a prominent West Texas landmark situated twenty-six miles northeast of the Concho ranch and thirteen miles north of the Home Creek headquarters.[40]

As mentioned above, Emory Peter, a native of Kentucky, was Chisum's business partner in his Concho and Coleman County operations. Peter received a third of the proceeds from all stock cattle sales and 10 percent of all beef cattle sales. Peter started working for Chisum in 1860, and during the Civil War he helped Chisum move every herd from Denton County to the Concho County ranch. The last time they drove beeves to the Concho was in the fall of 1865, when they drew up their profit-sharing agreement. In exchange for his share of the proceeds, Peter was to pay all the expenses of the cowhands and horses and take care of the cattle.[41]

Chisum's large-scale movements of livestock soon attracted the attention of Texas and Confederate authorities. In the spring of 1864 Brig. Gen. Henry E. McCulloch, the Confederate officer commanding North Texas, sent Gov.

Pendleton Murrah a warning. McCulloch reported that Chisum and several other prominent ranchers, including William Ottley, a Mr. Winn, and a man named Aldridge, were moving sizeable herds from North Texas to West Texas. The brigadier general suspected that these ranchers were up to no good and in league with a group of military deserters with whom "they doubtless have an understanding and from whom they expect aid." McCulloch's intuitions proved correct.[42]

In early October 1864 Brig. Gen. J. S. McAdoo, a Texas Ranger commanding the Third Frontier District, reported that a party of thirty to sixty men driving 1,000 to 1,500 beeves had passed through the Hill Country en route to the San Saba or Concho Rivers. McAdoo believed that the group's ultimate destination might be a rendezvous point on the Pecos River (the final leg of the cattlemen's trail to the Bosque Redondo Indian reservation at Fort Sumner, New Mexico). Two months later, in December 1864, General McAdoo said that he had it on good authority that white men, likely agents or officers in the Union army, were deliberately inciting Comanches and Kiowas to raid the Texas frontier.[43]

Texas Ranger major George B. Erath penned a letter to Governor Murrah in March 1864 to inform him that men were driving large herds of cattle west. Six weeks later William Doss reported to the governor that a sizeable number of beeves had been driven off from the Hill Country. Doss said he believed that the region was slipping into anarchy and faced depopulation if action was not taken immediately. Texas Ranger brigadier general J. W. Throckmorton also wrote to Murrah informing him that the cattle drives were causing serious damage to the Confederate cause. In an effort to stem the westward movement of citizens and cattle, Governor Murrah issued a proclamation on March 26 "forbidding the immigration to, and settlement in, any unorganized counties of this state." (This included a number of frontier counties.) Murrah's proclamation was officially ratified by the Texas Legislature two months later on May 24.[44]

Despite popular legends, the first cattle drives west to the Pecos and beyond were not conducted by Charles Goodnight and Oliver Loving in 1866 and 1867. In 1864, contrary to explicit Confederate regulations prohibiting the exportation of Texas beef, nineteen-year-old William A. Peril drove a thousand head of cattle from Mason County to Presidio del Norte, Mexico. Peril's route passed R. F. Tankersley's ranch on the South Concho River and went on to Castle Gap and Horsehead Crossing on the Pecos before finally reaching the Rio Grande. Peril's wife, Mary Olive, recalled that Mexican buyers paid her husband in gold coins. In the fall of 1864 Maj. James M. Hunter of the Texas Rangers followed suit, trailing a herd of eight hundred beeves from the Texas Hill Country to Presidio del Norte. Confederate agent John Burgess maintained that Hunter sold only a portion of his cattle in Presidio and that a Union beef contractor in El Paso County, Texas, purchased the bulk of the herd.[45]

Regarding Texans' illicit cattle trade with the Department of New Mexico during the Civil War, it is unclear exactly who made the opening gambit in this arrangement: whether Union agents first contacted Chisum in Texas or if a Chisum emissary made the initial overture in New Mexico. The evidence suggests that William C. Franks, Chisum's storekeeper on the Mukewater, initiated the dialogue. During the summer of 1864 Franks traveled to Santa Fe. Arriving there in late July, he immediately linked up with beef contractor James Patterson, who was supplying cattle to the Union army in New Mexico. Ultimately, Franks brought together the key elements of the story. He knew John Chisum and other Texas ranchers who desired to sell their livestock, and he knew James Patterson in New Mexico, who wanted to buy cattle and could pay good prices for them.[46]

In the fall of 1864 Patterson and Franks added a third partner, Capt. Thomas L. Roberts, part of Gen. James Carleton's California Column and recently retired from military service in the Department of New Mexico. Within weeks the three men were in West Texas making surreptitious arrangements with John Chisum and other area ranchers for delivery of their herds to New Mexico. Throughout this process, Patterson, Franks, and Roberts kept the Department of New Mexico's commander well informed of their clandestine movements in the Lone Star State.[47]

Shortly after Patterson, Franks, and Roberts departed for the interior of Texas, a second group followed. In early December 1864 Sgt. James Conwell wrote to General Carleton requesting permission to go into Texas after cattle and drive a herd back to the Department of New Mexico for sale. Six months earlier Conwell had escorted fifty-three Texan emigrants from El Paso County, Texas, to Santa Fe. While visiting with these refugees en route to Santa Fe, Conwell likely heard about the abundant supply of cattle in West Texas, and perhaps about John Chisum.[48]

In his letter to Carleton, Conwell wrote that after three years of "faithful service" he would soon be mustering out of the army. He planned to enter the cattle business. He and eleven other men would soon travel to the interior of Confederate Texas and round up as many cattle as they could gather. Six of the men accompanying him were recent Texan exiles now living in the Department of New Mexico. The other five were, like Conwell, discharged Union soldiers.

Some of the cattle they would collect behind rebel lines belonged to these Texan refugees. The remaining beeves they would steal from Confederate residents.[49]

Lone Star authorities first learned of the two New Mexican intrusions into West Texas during January 1865, after arresting several members of the party that had ridden with Patterson, Franks, and Roberts. Writing to his Ranger superiors from Camp Colorado in Coleman County, Lt. Col. Buck Barry reported, "It might be well to inform you that we have five men here under arrest that say they were hired by one Patterson in New Mexico to drive beef from our frontier." Barry noted that Patterson and his men "had all the money to buy beef with and had gone to Fort Mason or San Saba or somewhere in that section to purchase beef."[50]

In his letter the lieutenant colonel also referenced a second group of Union men in the area, likely James Conwell's band. Barry wrote that Patterson's captured men "reported another party of jayhawkers that came to the frontier for the purpose of stealing cattle but did not know where they would strike." In fact, a group led by a man named Bonds made a raid at the junction of the Colorado and Concho Rivers sometime during the first part of 1865, stealing 530 beeves belonging to local ranchers. A posse pursued Bonds and his men west to Horsehead Crossing on the Pecos, where they killed two, captured one, and recovered the cattle. These rustlers may have been from Conwell's group, which included Texan refugees from the area. Reports indicated that while some of the herd had been stolen, a number of cattle did belong to those in the raiding party, which comports with what Conwell had told Carleton.[51]

Despite Barry raising the alarm, Patterson, Franks, and Roberts continued buying beeves to take back to the Department of New Mexico. Emory Peter recalled, "Patterson bought a herd in '65 and paid $8.00 [a head] for them [stock cattle], right there on the Concho." Before the men could leave, however, events delayed them. On January 8, 1865, the Battle of Dove Creek, involving Texas state troops and a group of Kickapoo Indians, occurred near R. F. Tankersley's ranch on the South Concho. A week after the fight, a group of wounded Texas Rangers straggled onto John Chisum's Concho County ranch to recuperate. The military presence forced Patterson and company to lay low for a few weeks. Some of the group tired of waiting and decided to head home to New Mexico, forcing the cattle buyers to hire local Texans to finish the job.[52]

Two of the new hires were M. C. Smith Sr. and Jim Spoon, former Chisum cowhands who helped build the Concho ranch in 1863. Chisum foreman C. C. Fitzgerald supervised assembly of Patterson's herd, which included a mix of cattle from Chisum's and area ranchers' herds. Finally, early in the spring of 1865,

Smith, Spoon, and the other cowboys began their clandestine cattle drive out of Confederate territory. The men followed the ruts of the old Butterfield Overland Mail Road, passing derelict stage stations along the Concho and Centralia watersheds on their way to the Pecos River. The cowhands forded the desolate and barren banks of the Pecos at Horsehead Crossing and pushed their beeves westward to Fort Davis, which despite being burned by retreating rebels in 1862 was still relatively intact and its corrals in good condition.[53]

As with many previous visitors, the scenery captivated M. C. Smith. He found Fort Davis a picturesque locale situated at the head of a rugged canyon and watered by a beautiful running stream. The cattle drive continued without incident until the men neared El Muerto, the old Butterfield stage stop thirty-five miles west of Fort Davis. After the party set up camp along the overland road, two cowboys named Gentry and Barefield got into an intense argument. Gentry shot Barefield, who subsequently died in transit the following day.[54]

The men buried Barefield at El Muerto, also known as Dead Man's Hole, an aptly named interment for the deceased wrangler. Most of the cowhands were incensed by Gentry's actions and wanted to lynch him. "I was but a beardless boy," Smith said, "but I think my pleading saved him." The men pushed on, passing through Van Horn's Wells, Eagle Spring, and Quitman Canyon before reaching Franklin (El Paso), Texas, at the end of May, where Patterson delivered the cattle to the Union army at Fort Bliss, making a sizeable profit in the transaction.[55]

Immediately upon delivering their herd, Patterson and his associates readied themselves for a return trip into rebel Texas for more cattle. On June 1, 1865 (the day before Texas surrendered), Patterson and Roberts wrote General Carleton a letter from Franklin, Texas, informing him of their intention to set out for Texas immediately. The two men requested permission to take a group of Texan refugees with them to help drive the cattle. Carleton approved their request, providing that all refugees had written proof of having taken an oath of allegiance to the United States.[56]

M. C. Smith was among the cowhands traveling back to the Chisum ranch in Concho County with Patterson. On the previous drive Smith had taken ill in Ysleta after his eyes became infected. He recovered quickly, however, and the group picked him up on their return trip. The men traveled the old Butterfield Mail route via the Upper Road, from Hueco Tanks in El Paso County east to the junction of the Delaware and Pecos Rivers.[57]

Upon arrival on the Concho River, Patterson met Robert K. Wylie, who, after loaning the cattle buyer $500, promptly signed on as a cowhand at the rate of $75 a month. Wylie, Smith, and the other cowboys collected a new drove of beeves, and the group struck out for New Mexico in what was to be their inaugural cattle drive from Texas to Fort Sumner. Interestingly, the men rode mules during the day, switching to horses for nighttime duty. Smith recalled the herd consisted of fifteen hundred beeves ranging in age from five to seven years. He stated that out all the drives he made, this bunch was the toughest to handle. "I would give $50," he said, "to see some of these modern-day cowboys have charge of such a herd."[58]

Traveling the old Butterfield Road once again, Patterson and his men found themselves barely able to contain this bunch of ornery beeves. During a stormy nighttime drive just west of Wild China Ponds, the cattle stampeded, and Smith discovered the entire herd barreling toward him like an avalanche. The nervous cowboy quickly started hollering and waving his saddle blanket in the air, which caused the animals to part, creating a small opening that he was able to slip through. The cattle were so close to him that he could have grabbed their horns as they passed by. Smith barely escaped a savage goring or stomping and passed through the rampaging herd unscathed. The cowhands managed to calm the bunch for a brief period, but the feisty livestock soon resumed their stampede. The herders were up all night and never got a chance to unpack their bedrolls. The next five days were much the same, with constant pandemonium and little sleep.[59]

Additional problems confronted Patterson and his men when they arrived at Castle Gap, twelve miles east of Horsehead Crossing on the Pecos. Passage through this canyon could be problematic, even with tame livestock, let alone a belligerent herd. Although the gap was some miles from the river, the cattle always smelled the water. Unless the cowboys were careful, the animals would stampede in a frenzied rush to the Pecos. There were a number of deadly alkali lakes near Horsehead Crossing, whose tainted water would quickly kill any thirsty, unsuspecting beeves. To help control the herd on their approach to the river, M. C. Smith rode on ahead to the crossing.[60]

Upon arrival at Horsehead, Smith saw a group of Mexican salt freighters on the west side of the river. The Mexicans were on their way home after gathering salt at Juan Cordona Lake, located five miles to the northeast. After "jabbering" to Smith in Spanish, a dozen of the freighters crossed over to the east side. "I knew very little of the Spanish language, but what few words I did catch did not sound good to me," the cowhand recalled, and then "one of them stuck out his hand and asked me to let him see my pistols." Smith was not about to oblige the Mexicans. "I drew one in each hand and aimed them," he said, "and they hit the water like bullfrogs." After the freighters had crossed back to the west side of the Pecos, Smith directed their attention to the dust cloud from the approaching herd, whereupon "they hitched up and left in a hurry."[61]

The cattle reached Horsehead Crossing safely, and the drive continued upriver to Fort Sumner without further incident. As per his army contract, Patterson delivered the beeves on time and in good condition. After resting a few days, the cowhands saddled up again and headed back to the Concho for more livestock, for what would be their third drive of 1865. After reaching Chisum's ranch, Patterson and company found the Concho ranchers eager to sell their stock. Within a short time, the cowboys had a herd of three thousand animals. The men drove the cattle in three groups of a thousand to Fort Sumner. Smith said this trip was much calmer as there were no problems with stampeding steers.[62]

By the summer of 1865 the Texas–New Mexico cattle trade was in full swing. William Franks recalled that during his partnership with Patterson from 1864 to 1866, he typically handled the Texas end of their business, while Patterson (and Roberts) managed matters in New Mexico. In August 1865 Patterson, Franks, and Roberts further strengthened their business relationship with John Chisum by hiring his brother Pitser to help move a herd from Texas to Fort Sumner. Upon arrival in New Mexico, Patterson retained Pitser Chisum's services full-time as a butcher. Up until this point, Patterson, Franks, and Roberts had worked as beef subcontractors, selling their livestock to C. S. Hinckley, the army's cattle supplier for Fort Sumner from September 1864 to September 1865. In 1865, however, Thomas Roberts won the beef contract, and in 1866 it went to James Patterson.[63]

In the fall of 1865 Patterson and his associates made two additional drives from Texas to Fort Sumner. In sum, in 1865 the partners undertook five trips from Chisum's Concho County ranch—one to Fort Bliss in El Paso County and four to Fort Sumner—delivering roughly 8,500 Texas beeves to the Department of New Mexico. The importance of this cattle trade to the department and its commander, General Carleton, is evident in the military correspondence.[64]

In July 1865 Carleton noted that the Department of New Mexico was still suffering after three years of irregular and scarce supplies of beef. He instructed Maj. William McCleave, commander at Fort Stanton, that "the introduction of cattle from Texas into New Mexico . . . is to be encouraged in every proper manner." Toward that end, he ordered McCleave to send eight to ten men as escort for a herd that Roberts was driving up the Pecos River from Texas. Carleton also suggested that the major send some reliable Apaches with the escort to serve as spies and guard against Comanche raids.[65]

The following month Roberts received another military escort for his herds, this time to Camp Nichols on the Cimarron Route of the Santa Fe Trail, where he also held the beef contract. A detachment of twenty mounted men from the First New Mexico Cavalry at Fort Bascom helped ensure that the contractor delivered his herd without incident to the Nichols garrison. In September Carleton reported that "Mr. James Patterson, . . . partner in business with Captain Thomas Roberts, . . . [who is] now contractor for furnishing fresh beef to troops at Forts Sumner and Stanton, N.M., . . . is now about to return to Texas to procure another lot of cattle." The general continued, "This enterprise of getting cattle across the plains from that state which has already been . . . accomplished by Mr. Patterson, is the beginning only, it is hoped, of a great and profitable trade." Since Patterson's group lacked sufficient arms for their trip through Indian country, Carleton authorized loaning them twelve to fifteen Sharps carbines from the military's armory.[66]

With Patterson, Roberts, and Franks handling the military's beef arrangements, Chisum's Texas operations flourished. Soon he was buying all the livestock that area ranchers could supply, selling them (along with his own livestock) to the New Mexico contractors. Patterson's outfit continued to dominate the Texas–New Mexico cattle trade until the summer of 1866, when Charles Goodnight and Oliver Loving made their first drive to Fort Sumner. By 1867 Patterson's business partnership with William Franks had dissolved, and Emory Peter and John Chisum began moving their own herds to New Mexico. Peter says that during the next six years, cowhands drove 80,000 Chisum cattle from the Concho and San Saba Rivers to New Mexico.[67]

Throughout this period Chisum typically offered area ranchers $10 a head for their stock cattle. This price included a herding and transportation surcharge of $2 to $2.50 per head. The cattle drives required experienced and seasoned cowboys who earned $40 a month and who had to be supplied with guns, ammunition, bridles, saddles, ropes, and food. Chisum estimated that the overhead for a typical drive from his Concho ranch to New Mexico averaged $3,000 in wages and expenses.[68]

It was not long before West Texas cowmen were calling this Texas–New Mexico cattle road the "Chisum Trail." Interestingly, Charles Goodnight later tried to take credit for pioneering this route, claiming that he and Oliver Loving were the first to drive a Texas herd to Fort Sumner. Goodnight biographer J. Evetts Haley writes, "And thus, upon the sixth day of June 1866, the most momentous day in young Goodnight's life, he left the frontier of Texas to blaze a new trail for longhorned cattle." In Haley's revisionist narrative of Goodnight and Loving, Patterson, Franks, Roberts, and Chisum all become background bit players.[69]

In his story of Goodnight and the road to Fort Sumner, Haley says, "The thousands of flinty hoofs that cut its grass to dust traced his name as well as his trail across the face of the Western World. Upon the dusts of that trail rose the tradition of the man, no longer a man of Texas, but now a man of the West." Despite such evocative and enduring popular myths, the historical record clearly shows that it was James Patterson and his associates, driving thousands of beeves belonging to Chisum and other Texas cattlemen, who blazed this legendary western cattle trail in 1865, more than a year before Goodnight and Loving made their first drive.[70]

CHAPTER 7

The end of the Civil War saw Lone Star cattle drives shift into high gear. From 1867 to 1873 John Chisum moved tens of thousands of beeves from Texas to his Bosque Grande headquarters on the Pecos River in New Mexico. Chisum said that during this period his herds often averaged from 30,000 to 50,000 head. Besides his own cattle, he continued to make large purchases of beeves from Coleman and Concho County ranchers on Home Creek and near the Concho-Colorado confluence, including Coggin and Parks, R. K. Wylie, Nat Guest, Rich Coffey, Dick Fiveash, the Dofflemyer family, Dick Robinson, Needham Harrison, Clay Mann, Sam Gholson, and John Elkins. By 1873 Chisum had shifted all of his operations west to New Mexico. Chisum's business partner Emory Peter sold the store at Trickham in the fall of 1873, closed up shop in Texas, and followed Chisum out to Bosque Grande.[1]

As previously mentioned, Charles Goodnight and Oliver Loving's first cattle drive to Fort Sumner was in 1866, followed by a second and a third drive in 1867 (the latter during which Loving was mortally wounded). Within a short time Goodnight was moving large herds of cattle from Throckmorton, Young, Jack, and Palo Pinto Counties in Texas into New Mexico. Throughout this period, Chisum and Goodnight dominated the Texas beef trade in New Mexico. During the late 1860s and the 1870s the two men frequently conducted business, with Goodnight purchasing tens of thousands of cattle from Chisum.[2]

It was not long before the westward wave of cattle drives piqued the interest of Indians, including Comanches, Kiowas, and Mescalero Apaches. Soon warriors were sweeping the open ranges of Texas and striking herds across the vast region. Several examples prove illustrative. In September 1865 Comanches took 2,000 head of cattle belonging to Charles Goodnight at the Neuhaus Pens in Throckmorton County, Texas. Goodnight cowboy Martin Scoggins and thirteen others followed the Indians' trail northwest for a hundred miles to the Double Mountain Fork of the Brazos, to within fifty miles of Quitaque, Texas. Comanchero José Piedad Tafoya was at Quitaque trading with the Comanches in September 1865 and saw many beeves there bearing Goodnight's CV mark. Tafoya waded out in the herd, made his selections, and then traded his goods to the Indians in exchange for the animals.[3]

The following year, in August 1866, Comanches made off with 1,500 beeves belonging to John Chisum and Emory Peter on the San Saba River in Menard County. Robert Wylie later saw some of these stolen steers in New Mexico between Anton Chico and Fort Sumner. The new owners of the animals said they had traded with the Comanches for them. Peter later filed a depredation claim with the government for his losses totaling $16,500. Of this amount, he eventually received $3,265.09.[4]

In May 1867 Comanches ran off another Goodnight herd totaling 2,500 head from Ben Krebs's old Butterfield stage stop in Young County, Texas. In the fall of that year, Goodnight was in New Mexico, where he saw some of his stolen cattle on a ranch belonging to an old German. Goodnight told the rancher that some of the livestock was his. The German said that "he guessed they were not [Goodnight's property;] that he had bought them from some Mexicans who had traded for them from the Indians down around Quitaque in Texas." Goodnight then showed the man the animals in question, all of which bore his CV brand on their horns. Upon further reflection, Goodnight said that since the German had purchased the beeves in good faith, he declined to press the issue.[5]

During his New Mexico trip Goodnight also paid a visit to Fort Bascom, situated on the Fort Smith–Santa Fe Road forty miles west of the Texas state line. While at Bascom Goodnight conversed with post trader William B. Stapp. Besides serving as Bascom's sutler, Stapp was also active in buying, selling, and trading cattle. Goodnight and Stapp walked around the fort's cattle pens, whereupon the Texas cattleman recognized a number of beeves bearing his brand. Stapp told Goodnight that the animals had been seized from Mexicans who had been trading with the Comanches. Stapp stated that these Comanches lived out on the frontier east of Fort Bascom in the Texas–New Mexico borderlands.[6]

José Piedad Tafoya recalled that in May 1867 the Comanches brought several large herds to Quitaque, many of them with Goodnight brands. The Comanchero said that he and other traders purchased almost 2,000 stolen beeves. Julián Baca was another Comanchero at Quitaque buying cattle with the Goodnight CV mark. Baca was unconcerned about trading for pilfered livestock. The Comanches and Kiowas had taken the animals and "it did not matter to us whether they were stolen or not, we were buying cattle."[7]

In 1866 and 1867 Goodnight cowboy William J. "One-Armed Bill" Wilson encountered large numbers of cattle being driven throughout New Mexico and Colorado. In nearly every herd he identified Goodnight brands. Wilson stated that during his travels, he saw between 3,000 and 4,000 stolen Goodnight beeves in the possession of Mexicans who had acquired them from the Comanches. A year after the Goodnight raid, in June 1868, Mescalero Apaches stole 1,100 beeves belonging to John Chisum on west side of the Pecos River near the Texas–New Mexico line. Chisum had purchased the cattle in Texas from various stockmen in the spring of 1868 to deliver to contractor James Patterson at Fort Sumner.[8]

In December 1869 Dennis Murphy, a prominent North Texas rancher and beef subcontractor at Fort Richardson, Texas, lost twenty-five work mules to the Comanches on the Brazos River near the Young–Palo Pinto county line. Several days after the raid, Murphy traveled to the Comanche-Kiowa reservation at Fill Sill, Indian Territory (in present-day Oklahoma). Upon arrival at Fort Sill, Murphy obtained the services of an interpreter. The rancher said: "[I then] shaved, dressed myself up and put on a stove pipe hat and told the Indians I had come to buy buffalo robes and mules. I bought some robes and then they brought me out my own mules and wanted to sell them to me." Murphy knew the animals were his because all of them bore his brand. Declining to purchase the mules, Murphy took the buffalo hides and robes that he had purchased and went to post headquarters at Fort Sill to file a report. After hearing Murphy's complaint, the post commander met with the Indians and informed them that they had until ten o'clock to bring Murphy his stolen mules. One of the Indians the officer was talking to glanced over at Murphy and upon recognizing him "dropped his eyes on the ground and drew his blanket around him and grunted and walked off." Murphy added, "I have never seen the mules since."[9]

Another large raid in Texas occurred in June 1871, when Comanches took a thousand head of cattle from Rich Coffey and William Beddo at Elm Pens in Coleman County. Beddo and his cowhands were preparing to drive the herd to New Mexico when between one and two hundred Indians struck, scalping and killing two men and wounding two others before driving off the livestock northwest toward the Staked Plains and New Mexico. According to One-Armed Bill Wilson, this northwesterly direction was a clear indication that Indians had taken the animals. The Comanches knew that no white men would follow them across the Staked Plains. "The Indians were so thick that [pursuers] would have been scalped and killed before they had gone 50 miles. . . . Nobody dared travel across that country without a strong military escort."[10]

After the raid Beddo received word that some of his cattle had been seen at Fort Bascom. Beddo went at once to Bascom, where found a number of his animals. Military officials informed him that the beeves had been seized from the Comanches. When the Texas cattleman demanded the return of his property, the commanding officer declined and told Beddo that he would have to file a claim. Thirty-three years after the Coleman County raid, in 1904, the government finally awarded Beddo $5,641 for his stolen livestock.[11]

In July, August, and December 1871, the Comanches also raided ranches in Concho, Throckmorton, and Tom Green Counties, driving off close to 14,000 cattle belonging to Coggin and Parks, R. F. Tankersley, and Dennis Murphy. After the July 1871 depredation, cowboys followed the Indians' trail 125 miles to the northwest, to the head of the Colorado River. The trace was immense, up to a quarter mile wide in some places. One of the cowhands in the party reported that the whole range had been stripped of cattle. Benjamin Jenkins, a sergeant in the Fourth Cavalry, also followed this same trail northwest with his men for sixty miles before abandoning the pursuit at Signal Peak. Jenkins said that the Indians had taken the beeves to New Mexico for delivery to Mexicans or white men. Dennis Murphy testified that after warriors made off with his animals in August 1871 at Elm Pens in Throckmorton County, they steered a northwest course toward New Mexico and Colorado. In a depredation claim for their July and December 1871 losses, Coggin and Parks claimed that "the character of the thefts, their magnitude, . . . the direction in which their booty was taken, the ponies, arrows, and saddles found, . . . lead irresistibly to the conclusion that the Comanches, whose habitat was the Staked Plains, and whose market was New Mexico, were the thieves."[12]

Indian depredation reports filed with the governor of Texas indicate that from June 1865, when Texas surrendered to the Union, to January 1880, 407 persons were killed, 76 were wounded, and 81 women and children were carried off into captivity. In addition, during this period Indians drove off 43,392 head of cattle and 20,521 horses. Maj. John B. Jones, commander of Texas's Frontier Battalion, believed that the actual number of losses was much larger. Jones said that he had seen "several hundred abandoned ranches on the frontier, on many of which people had been murdered or carried into captivity and the houses . . . burned by the Indians and of them very few were ever reported."[13]

Because of the increased depredations, the U.S. Army started providing armed protection for some cattle drives between Fort Concho (San Angelo, Texas) and the Pecos River, a section long notorious for Comanche raids. During the fall of 1867 Sgt. John DeLacy of the Fourth Cavalry and a detail of thirteen men escorted a herd from the old Butterfield stage station on the headwaters of the Middle Concho River (near Barnhart, Texas) to the Pecos. The passage was largely uneventful, save two of DeLacy's men deserting with four horses, sixty rounds of ammunition, and nearly all of the detail's rations.[14]

In July 1872 Sgt. Benjamin F. Jenkins of the Fourth Cavalry and ten men accompanied a cattle drive from Johnson's mail station on the Middle Concho River to Centralia mail station in Centralia Draw. That same month Indians attacked a large herd traveling without escort on the Pecos River. The July 6 raid occurred near the Great Falls of the Pecos, where three hundred warriors took Madison Tucker's entire herd of 1,500 beeves. Tucker, an Erath County rancher, had employed eight men to drive his cattle to New Mexico. The herders fought their attackers for more than two hours, killing the chief and another Indian. The cowhands recalled that the raiders "were painted and wore deer and buffalo horns on their heads, . . . wore no clothing, many of them wore feathers, and the chief . . . was covered with them. They were armed principally with bows and arrows."[15]

The drovers lost three of their party during the skirmish, two herders and a Dr. Bartlett. Bartlett was caught out in the open and his body mutilated and burned. The star-crossed doctor had recently been on another drive, in mid-June, when raiders took his entire herd of 850 head at Johnson's mail station. After burying Bartlett's body on the banks of the Pecos, some of the cowhands rode onto Fort Stockton, Texas, to report the attack to Maj. Zenas Randall Bliss, commander of the garrison. Bliss detailed Capt. Francis Safford Dodge with Troop D of the Ninth Cavalry to follow up on the raid and to provide escort up the Pecos for two additional herds totaling 2,650 beeves that were between Horsehead Crossing and the Great Falls of the Pecos.[16]

In October 1872 Second Lt. Frank L. Shoemaker and ten men left Fort Concho with several herds en route to the Pecos River. At Mustang Waterholes the leaders of the cattle drive told Shoemaker that since there were so many troops crossing the plains, they did not consider it necessary for the lieutenant to accompany them all the way to the Pecos. The herders were perfectly willing for Shoemaker to leave them and return to post. Shortly after the cowhands had resumed their westward journey from Mustang Waterholes, the lieutenant and his men started back to Fort Concho.[17]

In May 1873 First Lt. Gustave H. Radetzki of the Ninth Cavalry escorted 2,300 cattle to Horsehead Crossing on the Pecos. Upon reaching Horsehead, the herd's cowboys, nervous about their exposed and isolated position, requested that the lieutenant continue accompanying them upstream from Horsehead to New Mexico. Radetzki sent a note to the commander of Fort Stockton asking that a fresh detail be sent to escort the cowhands and their beeves. The commander of Fort Stockton, Captain Dodge, complied with the request and dispatched ten mounted men to accompany the herd as far as Blue River, New Mexico. Dodge did not consider the section of the route from Johnson's mail station to Seven Rivers, New Mexico, safe for travel.[18]

In a report to his superiors, the captain suggested that the cavalry could be put to good use providing protection for these drives, but pointed out that if the same number of beeves were "driven over the road this season as in previous years, it would take half a regiment to furnish the required details." Dodge believed that the cattlemen relied "altogether too much on the protection to be furnished by the troops." To illustrate this point, Dodge said the previous year he had seen a group of fifteen to twenty cowhands "in charge of about 1,000 cattle." The cowboys, "in addition to their pistols, had only two or three old worn out muskets in their party," hardly an adequate deterrent to raiding Indians. In comparison, period reports note that some Indian warriors were armed with Spencer rifles and Remington pistols.[19]

When not providing an armed guard, cavalrymen occasionally served as cowhands. In August 1873 First Lt. Patrick Cusack of the Ninth Cavalry and fourteen men traveled with a cattle drive from Fort Concho to Centralia mail station in Centralia Draw. Cusack said that from Centralia it took them six days to reach the old Butterfield stage station at Head of Concho, where, because of the herders' neglect, some of the herd had wandered during the night. The lieutenant's men recovered ninety of the strays. During his return trip to Fort Concho, Cusack met John Chisum at Johnson's mail station. Chisum had a letter from headquarters requesting that Cusack and his men turn around and escort Chisum and his herd across the Staked Plains. During his trip with Chisum, the lieutenant did not see any Indian signs, but he did observe that severe overgrazing by hundreds of cattle passing over the route that summer had decimated regional grasslands.[20]

Comanche and Kiowa warriors continued to devastate Texas cattle herds until the mid-1870s. Indian incursions into the Lone Star State did not diminish until the end of the Red River War in June 1875, when the U.S. Army finally defeated these tribes and permanently relocated them to a reservation in Indian Territory. The federal government and various tribal representatives had originally agreed to establish this Comanche-Kiowa reservation in October 1867. In 1868 various bands of these tribes began moving to their new three-million-acre reserve at Fort Sill, Indian Territory.[21]

But as William Hagan notes, "It took another seven years of military operations and delicate negotiations to persuade all of a basically nomadic people to give up their wandering ways." Hagan points out that it was an economic hardship for the Indians to suddenly stop stealing Texas livestock. In addition, some Kiowas and Comanches that settled on the reservation adopted a flexible perspective on their new situation. They accepted rations and annuities from the government while continuing to depredate in the Lone Star State. "During the seven years which it took the Kiowas and Comanches to locate on the reservation surrounding Fort Sill," Hagan writes, "they killed scores of Texans, made captives of hundreds more, and stole thousands of horses and mules. Their blows fell heaviest on the Texas cattlemen."[22]

Finding a successful strategy to disrupt Comanche raids and the Comanchero trade in Texas remained elusive until a major breakthrough came in late March 1872. On March 28 a scout under Sgt. William Wilson and a Fourth Cavalry detachment from Fort Concho attacked a Comanchero camp at the junction of Beals Creek and the Colorado River, south of present-day Colorado City, Texas, killing two, wounding three, and capturing one. The prisoner was a twenty-nine-year-old farm laborer from La Cuesta, San Miguel County, New Mexico, named Apolonio Ortíz. During subsequent military interrogations Ortíz yielded a treasure trove of intelligence on the illicit Comanchero traffic, including the trade routes from New Mexico to Texas and the location of clandestine Comanche rendezvous sites.[23]

Within weeks of questioning Ortíz, the U.S. Army ordered a scout under Capt. Napoleon Bonaparte McLaughlen and a Fourth Cavalry detachment to Mucha-Que Peak in Borden County, Texas, one of the major Comanchero-Comanche meeting sites. Ortíz served as the guide for the trip. He told army officers that during a visit to Mucha-Que in February and March 1872, he had seen a Comanche and Mescalero Apache encampment of 150 to 200 lodges. Upon arrival at Mucha-Que in early May, McLaughlen discovered the village recently abandoned and signs that the Indians had been holding more than a thousand animals at the site. Subsequent army campaigns from 1872 to 1874 disrupted the Comanchero traffic and forced hundreds of Comanches and Kiowas to leave their Staked Plains haunts for the Fort Sill Indian Reservation.[24]

The presence of Mescalero Apaches at Mucha-Que revealed that Comanches and Kiowas were not the only tribes stealing Texas livestock. Mescaleros seized numerous herds in West Texas during this period. As in the case of the Comanches and Kiowas, the federal government had established a reservation for the Mescaleros, but various bands of the tribe resisted resettlement. Located near present-day Ruidoso, New Mexico, the Mescalero reserve was officially established in May 1873. Some of those agreeing to settle at the New Mexico site adopted the same opportunistic mindset as Comanches and Kiowas at Fort Sill, accepting government rations and annuities while continuing to go off reservation and depredate.[25]

It should also be noted that white outlaws and some residents near these reservations harassed the Indians by trespassing, stealing livestock, ruining crops, and frequently resorting to violence and murder. Graft and corruption among federal employees and contractors proved a pervasive problem. Comanches, Kiowas, and Mescaleros did not receive rations in the quantity or quality promised. Periodic reports found the Indians in a starving condition. It is no wonder, then, that there was little incentive for these tribes to abandon their traditional lifeways and stay on the reservations.[26]

Cattleman John Chisum filed several claims against the federal government for Mescalero depredations in Texas and New Mexico during the 1870s. Chisum said that in June 1872, warriors made off with 120 horses and 30 large draft mules worth $16,500 near Horsehead Crossing on the Pecos River. In April 1873 raiders took 70 horses and 35 mules valued at $13,300 at sundown on the edge of the Staked Plains near Castle Gap, east of Horsehead Crossing. In July of that same year, Mescaleros stole 72 horses and 25 mules worth $9,510, near Emigrant Station, the old Butterfield stage stop on the Pecos. The following month, in August 1873, the Indians struck Chisum's cowboys at Bosque Grande on Pecos, taking 130 horses, 15 mules, and 88 beeves valued at $19,260. During two additional raids in July and November 1874, Chisum lost 262 horses, 72 mules, and 352 head of cattle. Ultimately, John Chisum filed depredation claims totaling almost $144,000 with the government for livestock losses to various Indian tribes. Chisum had been dead for almost twenty years when the government finally awarded his heirs $24,755 in 1903.[27]

In August 1874 Chisum wrote to E. P. Smith, U. S. Commissioner of Indian Affairs, stating that some mules and horses with his brand had been brought to the Mescalero reservation. Chisum told Smith, "I have been unable to recover [these animals] and have thought [if] you would give me permission to take with me 15–20 men and . . . an officer . . . [with] a few of the soldiers, I might be able to recover a good many of my horses peacefully." Mescalero Indian agent W. D. Crothers subsequently held a council with the head men and chiefs of the tribe, who admitted that they had taken horses, mules, and cattle from Chisum. The tribal leaders said, however, that the guilty Mescaleros who had done most of the stealing were currently away among the Comanches, to whom most of the stolen stock had been traded.[28]

Several reports noted that the Mescaleros drove their ill-gotten livestock east to clandestine Comanche meeting sites. Rancher James Reynolds stated that the connection was widely understood: "In the country at that time[,] . . . it was common talk among them who knew, . . . that the Mescalero Apaches stole horses in New Mexico and traded them to the Comanches." Reynolds said that the two tribes would meet in the Staked Plains near Little Tule Lake, Tule Lake, Tierra Blanca Lake, or Portales Spring in eastern New Mexico to trade, and if interrupted or pursued, they would head east into Texas, to Yellow House Canyon or to Quitaque. Reynolds said that on several occasions he had followed Mescaleros and their stolen stock from the Pecos River to Tierra Blanca Lake, forty-five miles east of Fort Sumner.[29]

Echoing Reynolds's observations, in July 1874 Second Lt. John William Wilkinson of the Eighth Cavalry followed up on a report from rancher-merchant Lucien B. Maxwell that Mescaleros were driving livestock stolen from his ranch and from John Chisum's east toward the Staked Plains Comanche trail. A party of six men had trailed the Indians from Fort Sumner to Tierra Blanca Lake before abandoning their pursuit. The following year, in May 1875, Lucien Maxwell hired a posse of twelve men to travel east to the Comanche-Kiowa agency at Fort Sill to recover his animals. The group returned two months later with forty of Maxwell's horses.[30]

Concurring with these statements, Capt. James Franklin Randlett reported that Mescaleros frequently left their reservation to commit depredations, trading their stolen livestock to Comanches they met out on the Staked Plains. In an 1874 letter to the post adjutant at Fort Stanton, the army outpost neighboring the Mescalero reservation, Randlett vented his frustration regarding the numerous raids. Randlett said that he and area settlers were firmly convinced that the reservation was "nothing more or less, than a rendezvous for a thieving and murderous band of Indians." The captain believed that the problem stemmed from the federal Indian department being too lenient with the Mescaleros. He complained that there was scant evidence of restraint or discipline and that until the Indians were compelled to remain at the reserve nothing more could be done. Randlett wanted the military to hunt down and kill any Indians found off the reservation.[31]

Randlett's complaints regarding the Mescalero reservation echoed those being voiced by the governor of Texas concerning the Comanche-Kiowa reserve at Fort Sill. Writing to E. P. Smith, U.S. Commissioner of Indian Affairs, in late 1873, Gov. Edmund Jackson Davis observed, "The Indian troubles on our northwestern frontier have not sensibly abated." Davis told Smith that if anything, the raids had markedly increased. "I am satisfied from information (and my own observation at Fort Sill)," Davis said, "that the two tribes, Kiowas and Comanches, have now in their possession not less than from 2,500 to 3,000 head of horses and mules stolen in Texas." The governor pointed out that per Texas's treaty with the Indians made at Fort Sill in 1868, the Indians were obligated to return all captives and livestock taken from the Lone Star State. Davis noted that no measurable action had been taken to give back the stolen animals, and there had been no arrests of Comanches depredating in Texas. In sum, Davis felt there was little to no supervision of the Indians at Fort Sill.[32]

The Comanchero trade continued, although greatly diminished after the Red River War and the surrender of the Quahadi Comanches in 1875. The Indians and their trading partners adapted. During a scout of the Pecos River in Texas during the spring of 1878, Capt. Alexander Scammel Brooks Keyes of the Tenth Cavalry paid a visit to a remote cluster of adobe buildings located at the Great Falls of the Pecos, near the Reeves-Pecos county line. Keyes reported, "I am inclined to believe that the Falls is a rendezvous for horse thieves and Indian traders. Horses known to have been stolen by the Quahadi Comanches from New Mexico in 1875 have been seen at this settlement." In a telling sign of the illicit trade's decline, the captain noted that the Indians had "virtually given up their old range on the plains between the head of the Brazos and the Pecos. The signs of them at all the watering places I visited were several years old."[33]

Some aspects of Keyes's assessment, however, proved premature. In early December 1878 a number of Indians left the Fort Sill reservation and headed for their traditional ranges in the Texas Panhandle and south plains. Some of these Indians had official passes to go hunting for buffalo, while others left without permission. Anxious citizens of Donley County, Texas, sent a petition to authorities in Austin asking for protection as "there are at the present time about two thousand Indians in this part of Texas." On December 29 the commander of

Fort Elliott (Mobeetie, Texas) dispatched Second Lt. Alexander McCarrell Patch and Company F of the Fourth Cavalry to investigate. Patch found sixty-four Comanches, sixty-seven Kiowas, seventeen Pawnees, and fifty Kiowa Apaches in the vicinity of Charles Goodnight's ranch in Palo Duro Canyon.[34]

Some of the Indians showed Patch their hunting passes. All of the permits had expired. Patch reported that the Indians were close to starving. If Goodnight had not given them cattle to stay alive, they would have been forced to slaughter some of his herd. The lieutenant urged the Indians to return to Fort Sill, but they objected. The Kiowas and Pawnees told Patch they did not receive sufficient rations at the reservation to survive. The Indians were hungry and wanted to hunt buffalo. But most of the buffalo were now gone, having been hunted into near extinction during the previous decade. The Indians told the lieutenant they meant no harm to settlers and were not depredating.[35]

According to Goodnight, however, when he first encountered the Indians, they were in the lower reaches of Palo Duro Canyon and were, without permission, slaughtering his beeves "at a fearful rate." Approaching the Kiowas, Goodnight found them "in an ugly mood, and it looked like trouble." Soon after, Quanah Parker and a number of Comanches rode up. Goodnight and Quanah agreed to have a parley the following morning to find some resolution to the standoff. At the meeting the Indians reproached Goodnight, telling him, "Don't you know this country is ours?" The Texas cattleman replied that he "had heard the great Captain [governor] of Texas also claimed it and was making me pay for it." Goodnight said that the controversy "was a matter between them [the Indians] and the State of Texas, and if they owned the land, I was quite willing to settle with them." Quanah replied that this was reasonable.[36]

Goodnight then told the assembled Indians that he had "plenty of guns and plenty of bullets, good men and good shots, but I don't want to fight unless you force me." Turning to Quanah, he said that he would give them two beeves every two days if they agreed not to harm his ranch or livestock. After holding a council, the Indians agreed to Goodnight's terms. The standoff was resolved and the Kiowas and Comanches kept their promise. Goodnight said that "he never knew an Indian who failed to keep his [word]."[37]

The Indians at Goodnight's ranch eventually returned to Fort Sill in the spring of 1879. Not all of those who had left Fort Sill, however, went back to Indian Territory. Some renegades remained off reservation, raiding area ranches. A Texas Ranger report estimated that between December 1879 and March 1880, marauding warriors took a total of 254 mules and horses from a number of Texas cattlemen, including Jesse Hittson, W. B., J. B., and C. C. Slaughter, and Coggin and Wiley's outfit. The majority of losses occurred near the Double Mountains and Double Mountain Fork of Brazos River, Catfish Creek/Blanco Canyon, Tobacco Creek on the headwaters of the Colorado River, the South Pease River, North Wichita River, and Yellow House Creek.[38]

In response to reports of Indians being off reservation and depredating, Maj. John B. Jones, commander of Texas's Frontier Battalion, dispatched Texas Ranger lieutenant George Washington Arrington and Company C from Throckmorton County to make a reconnaissance of the Wichita and Pease Rivers. Arrington was not the most diplomatic person for the mission. Some army officers and area residents considered him a hothead and a loose cannon. In February 1879 Capt. Sumner H. Lincoln of the Tenth Cavalry informed his superiors that during the previous month, Arrington and his men had conducted an exploration of the Pease River region. While there, the Rangers discovered a group of Indians who were hunting buffalo with an escort of troops from Fort Sill. Captain Lincoln said that the Texans killed and scalped a Kiowa Indian they found near the soldiers' camp. Lincoln remarked that the Kiowa's slaying might provoke a reprisal. The captain stated that other than the Rangers murdering innocent Indians, there was no reason to expect further trouble in the region.[39]

In his account of the incident, Lieutenant Arrington said that he and his men had found an Indian near the fork of the North and South Pease Rivers and killed him. The victim was White Cowbird, a prominent Kiowa. Soon after that killing, the Rangers located a Pease River encampment of fourteen Kiowa lodges, eighteen warriors, twenty women and children, and 150 ponies. Charging the camp, Arrington ran into the Tenth Cavalry soldiers who were chaperoning the Kiowas during their hunt. Forced to stand down, Arrington went to the sergeant leading the party and turned over a Springfield carbine he had taken from the dead Kiowa. The carbine belonged to a Tenth Cavalry corporal, who had loaned it to the murdered Indian to hunt with. According to the Kiowas, Arrington and his men shot White Cowbird "through the body and both arms, scalped him, and cut off a finger upon which was a ring." Upon their return to Fort Sill, the Kiowas requested that authorities arrest Arrington and his men. After no action was taken, the brother of White Cowbird led a revenge raid into Texas to even the score, killing and scalping a white man they met on the trail.[40]

In July 1879 the commissioners of Wheeler County, Texas, wrote to Gov. Oran Milo Roberts complaining about Arrington (recently promoted to captain) and his detachment, asking that they be withdrawn from the area. "Since their arrival here the report has been circulated that they are here for the purpose of killing any or all Indians that may be found within the limits of the Panhandle," the commissioners said, "and finding that should this body commit any such act they would only provoke the Indians to merciless and useless war." Arrington replied to his superiors that the commissioners misunderstood him. "They say I will bring on an Indian war as I intend to kill the first Indian I see. . . . I did not say that my orders were to kill the first Indian I saw," Arrington said, "but . . . that if I found Indians coming into the state with arms and in sections where they were depredating that I would certainly go for them." Arrington pledged that he would not be indiscreet and kill any Indians he found near the Texas–Indian Territory line, "as at present there is great danger of an Indian war, but should I find a raiding party [I] will attack them."[41]

Arrington also reported that the sutler at Fort Elliott had told him that the post commander, Lt. Col. John Wynn Davidson, would order his men to arrest or open fire on Arrington's company if they attacked any Indians in the Panhandle. During a subsequent meeting between the two at Fort Elliott, Arrington confronted Davidson with this report. In response the lieutenant colonel asked the Ranger captain if he intended to kill any Indians that he encountered. Arrington replied that he would attack them if they were armed. The self-assured and arrogant Arrington boasted that his presence in the area was having its desired effect, as "at present every bunch of Indians I hear of is making for the line, saying, 'Texas soldiers *no buenos.*' . . . The Indians have a dread of Texans." Arrington promised his superiors that he was keeping a low profile, minding his own business, and was not interfering with federal forces in the region. His only interest was preventing Indian depredations.[42]

Compounding these state and federal tensions were the continuing and "habitual" sales of arms and ammunition to Comanches and Kiowas by unscrupulous traders in the Texas–Indian Territory region. Col. P. B. Hunt, the federal Indian agent at Fort Sill, complained to post commander Lt. Col. John Porter Hatch about illegal gun transactions transpiring at Doan's Store, a trading post located near the Red River (north of Vernon, Texas) in Wilbarger County. Opened in 1878 by Jonathan Doan and his nephew Corwin Doan, Doan's Store supplied cowboys, cattle drovers, and travelers passing through on the Western Trail.[43]

The depredations continued. In May 1879 thirty warriors killed two men camped near the mouth of Yellow House Canyon and made off with fifty horses. A posse of local cowmen pursued the Indians to the Double Lakes (near Tahoka, Texas), capturing their camp, its equipment, and all of the horses. In late December 1879 another group of raiders struck the Slaughter brothers' ranch on Catfish Creek (now Crawfish Creek) in Blanco Canyon taking close to thirty mules and horses. The Slaughters followed their trail northeast to within twenty miles of the Fort Sill reservation. Fort Sill commander Colonel Hatch acknowledged that "the actors in these raids have been Apaches with a few Comanches who ran away from this reserve last spring."[44]

Following this December attack Captain Arrington left his base camp in Blanco Canyon with twenty men of Company C of the Texas Rangers on an extended scout for Indians on the Staked Plains. During this forty-day, 830-mile scout in January and February 1880, Arrington and his men visited Cedar Lake, Yellow House Draw, and Silver Lake in Texas, as well as Ranger Lake in Lea County, New Mexico. Heading west twelve miles from Ranger Lake, Arrington journeyed to a chain of four lakes near present-day Tatum and Caprock, New Mexico. The Texans found freshwater springs at three of these lakes and copious Indian signs. From numerous cattle carcasses at the site, it was evident that the lakes served as a frequent refuge for raiding Native Americans. Arrington noted, "Every cow head [found at the site] has a large hole cut in forehead to get the brains for dressing pelts, which proves that they camp here with their squaws." On January 22 a Ranger corporal spotted thirteen Indians near the lakes. Arrington did not pursue them on account of his jaded horses. In his report of the scout the Ranger captain expressed a desire to return to the Texas–New Mexico borderlands as soon as possible. He wanted to locate a site known as the Lost Lakes and other meeting places known to "renegade Indians from [the] Sill and Stanton reservations."[45]

Arrington was not aware that the chain of four lakes he had just visited was in fact the Lost Lakes. Colonel Hatch at Fort Sill read Arrington's report and discussed it with the Quahadi Comanches on the reservation, "who [had] formerly made the [four] lakes described by the Captain a place of refuge." Hatch said that the four lakes were in fact "what is known to rumor as the 'Lost Lake[s].'" The commander of Fort Sill said that prior to Arrington's scout, no white man had ever visited this site. The Lost Lakes seemed to hold a mystical aura for both the Texas Rangers and the U.S Army. Hatch said that the army had known of their existence for some time, but because of their considerable distance from Fort Sill, no scouts were sent to find them. The Comanches had not known of the lakes until 1872, when the Mescaleros revealed their location. The Indians apprised Hatch that the journey to Lost Lakes required an arduous two-day stretch without water.[46]

Summing up the significance of his 1880 scout forty years later, Arrington proudly observed that his men had "penetrated a region . . . that was at that time absolutely unknown to white men and discovered lakes of water in the heart of the great desert." The Rangers had also located "the hiding place of this band of hostile Indians, which had been raiding the frontier of Texas from time immemorable and broke up their rendezvous." Arrington said this "forc[ed] them to move further west, and they were never known to make another raid on that part of the frontier of Texas again."[47]

Following the discovery of the renegade Comanche and Apache hideouts in the Staked Plains, the number of Indian depredations dwindled. Comancheros found it increasingly difficult to conduct business. In one telling incident at Fort Elliott, Arrington's Rangers prevented a Comanchero trading party from rendezvousing with some Plains Indians near the federal outpost. A newspaper account of the incident mentioned that the bold Texans had confronted the Comancheros, who were forced to seek protection at Fort Elliott. In his report Arrington noted that a group of Pueblo Indians from New Mexico had arrived at the fort. He was told by locals that the New Mexicans frequently traded arms and ammunition to Comanches and Kiowas from the Fort Sill reservation. The Ranger captain said that he had repeatedly complained to Colonel Davidson at Fort Elliott about Indians depredating in the region but that the post commander had done nothing to force these Indians to return to their reservation. Davidson sheltered the traders for several days at the post before providing an armed escort "to take them beyond the scope of the Rangers." In the end, the Pueblo Indians, "heavily loaded with various commerce to trade, . . . had to return from whence they came."[48]

By 1880 the Comanchero trade was largely finished. In September of that year sixty-three Pueblo Indians journeyed east to Indian Territory to trade with the reservation Indians. The traders visited various camps and enjoyed a long visit. Ultimately, however, the trip was a disappointment as the Plains Indians had little of value to exchange. The 1880 expedition proved to be the last. In the fall of 1881 the noted Kiowa warrior Big Bow traveled to the Pueblos to pay the Comancheros a return visit. After 1881 contact between the groups waned.[49]

Abandoned by traders from New Mexico, the Comanchero trails between New Mexico and Texas were now used by outlaws and rustlers, including Billy the Kid. Noted Lincoln County lawman Pat Garrett recalled that Billy the Kid and his gang rode the Anton Chico–Yellow House Canyon road in late 1880 while moving stolen livestock. The Kid stopped at some of the same waterholes used by Comancheros and Indians, notably Las Cañaditas and Los Portales. Sheriff Garrett, who killed the Kid at Fort Sumner in July 1881, said that the outlaw frequently hid his purloined cattle at Los Portales (Portales Spring). The New Mexico lawman described Portales Spring as a small cave with two adjacent pools "of cool clear water, furnishing an ample supply for at least 1,000 head of cattle." When Garrett and his posse arrived there in October 1880, they discovered that the Kid recently held a herd of sixty beeves at the spring but had since moved east toward the Texas state line. A few months later Garrett and his men cornered the Kid at an abandoned ranch house at Stinking Springs, another waterhole on the old Comanchero trail near Taiban, New Mexico.[50]

In April 1881 Captain Arrington reported that he was headed with his Rangers to Yellow House Draw on the Comanchero Trail in search of rustlers from New Mexico operating in Texas. He said that while authorities had been successful breaking up Billy the Kid's gang the previous winter, there were still four hundred stolen beeves unaccounted for. The captain had information that the cattle were on the Comanchero Trail in Texas at Coyote Lake. In June 1881, three weeks before Garrett killed the Kid, rumors circulated that the outlaw was on the Pecos River. Ranger lieutenant Charles Lilborn Nevill of Company E said that he had received information that the Kid and twenty men had been stealing horses from federal troops stationed on the Pecos. Following the July 14 death of Billy the Kid, the clandestine Comanchero trail from New Mexico to Texas, long-steeped in illicit activity and notoriety, gradually faded into obscurity. The Comanchero trade and the outlaw heyday had yielded to a new order in the Old West.[51]

CONCLUSION

Today the Texas–New Mexico borderlands are no longer a no-man's-land, no longer a vast, wide-open expanse in which to disappear. Instead of being an empty land conducive to skullduggery and double-dealing, now interstates, highways, county roads, and powerlines crisscross the landscape, connecting ranches, farms, towns, and cities. With all of this interconnectivity, the world has gotten much smaller. Over the last 150 years, the prominent names and places of the nineteenth-century borderlands have receded into obscurity. Important sites like Fort Bascom, Coyote Lake, New Bent's Fort, Loma Parda, Horsehead Crossing, and Spencer's Ranch and significant persons such as Henry Skillman, James Carleton, José Tafoya, August Kirchner, and Chief Puertas of the Comanches command scant recognition today. Not all, however, has been lost. Digging beneath the sediment of time, one uncovers the vivid and vibrant history that unfolded at these locales and discovers the remarkable parade of people that visited them: Comanches, captives, Comancheros, ranchers, merchants, freighters, and soldiers, both Union and Confederate.

In 1841, and again in 1861–62, Texans earned the enmity of residents when they invaded New Mexico and attempted to seize control. In both instances they failed. Undeterred, the Texans redoubled their efforts to capture New Mexico and the Southwest throughout the remainder of the Civil War. Rebels such as Henry Skillman, John Bankhead Magruder, John Baylor, Spruce Baird, James Magoffin, Sherod Hunter, Henry Kennedy, and John Burgess worked actively to bring these plans to fruition. Union agents and military leaders dedicated to thwarting these Confederate reinvasion schemes included James Carlton, Joseph West, George Bowie, William McMullen, Bradford Daily, and Reuben Creel. For its part, the federal army in 1863 and 1864 considered a joint operation against Texas under the combined forces of General Banks and General Carleton, but a lack of funds, supplies, and manpower precluded the Department of New Mexico from participating, and the plan never came to fruition. Throughout the conflict, the Texas–New Mexico borderlands provided an atmospheric, picturesque setting as the two sides engaged in a cat-and-mouse game, gathering intelligence on their counterparts while constantly jockeying for a strategic edge. While both sides violated Mexican sovereignty during the war, the rebels were more complicit in this regard, engaging in repeated kidnappings, violence, and mayhem on both sides of the Rio Grande.

The aforementioned antipathy that New Mexicans felt towards Texans certainly influenced the Comanchero trade and helps explains its longevity. Many of those involved in these illicit transactions experienced few pangs of guilt while acquiring thousands of stolen cattle taken from Lone Star ranches. Some likely felt the Texans deserved it. From local courts up through New Mexico's state courts, Texas ranchers found it nearly impossible to effect the return of their livestock. Faced with such daunting odds, ranchers such as John Hittson took the law into their own hands and resorted to violence. Of course, the images of Texans attacking New Mexicans yet again only served to further aggravate the deep-seated animosity that Land of Enchantment residents harbored toward Lone Star interlopers.

Literally every level of society and every ethnicity in New Mexico participated in the Comanchero trade. Dusty store ledgers, surety bonds, trading passes, and period newspapers reveal the breadth and depth of the activity. Farmers, ranchers, merchants, butchers, cattle brokers, soldiers, politicians, Anglos, Hispanics, and Pueblo Indians were all involved. By the mid-nineteenth century, the traffic in stolen cattle had become too entrenched and too profitable to ignore. The returns on one's investment were significant; it would be foolish to miss out. Plains Indians participated in the exchange for different reasons. For Comanches, Kiowas, and Apaches, the guns, ammunition, and trade goods they received in exchange for Texas livestock helped maintain their independence and enabled them to avoid federal reservations in New Mexico and Indian Territory for as long as possible. Ultimately, the entrenched, systemic resistance among the participants toward curtailing this illicit business meant that it was left to the U.S. Army to end it. The military was delayed in this mission by the Civil War as well as by internal confusion over trading passes and federal policy. It took several decades for the army to coalesce around a unified strategy, but from the early 1870s onward, the focused military campaigns against the Plains Indians began to take their toll. By 1880 the Comanche and Kiowa raids into Texas had ceased, and the Comanchero trade was finished. The enduring surreptitious economy that had bound the borderlands together for over a century had finally come to a close.

APPENDIX

Comancheros, Their Employees, and Their Bond Holders

The superintendent of Indian Affairs in Santa Fe was largely responsible for overseeing the legal Comanchero trade in New Mexico. The following list of Comancheros, their employees, and their bond holders help to illustrate how this trade involved all strata of New Mexican society. A majority of the information found in the following tables comes from the Records of the New Mexico Superintendency of Indian Affairs in the National Archives. As noted in the bibliography, these records include Letters Received from the Commissioner of Indian Affairs. The passes and applications used to make the following tables can be found in Rolls 6 and 7. The respective images of these documents are also noted in the tables.

Duplications of passes and more than one listing of each person noted are unavoidable The duplications illustrate how some participants were involved in more than one aspect of the trade. This list also details just how many New Mexicans were involved. The majority of persons listed applied and received passes from Santa Fe officials, yet three are noted who applied but were turned down: Robert James Hamilton, J. A. Larue, and Oscar Brown. Similar activities that were conducted without official approval make up a large part of this history, but the superintendent of Indian Affairs did not keep records of this shadow economy. Many of the same people were involved in both.

Passes, Bonds, and Employees

E = Employee, T = Trader, BH = Bond Holder, S = Supplier, NL = Not Listed

Names		Date	Pass	Roll	Image	Bond	Description or source
Abeytia, Aniceto	BH	10/5/1865	2 months	6	1272	1,000	For the trader Agapito de Hererra and Julian Flores
Abeytia, Manuel	E	7/8/1865	1 month	6	1204	$1,500	For the trader Anastacio Sandoval
Ainifo (?), José L.	E	7/10/1865	3 months	6	207	1,000	For the trader Juan Padilla
Alarid, Encarnación	E	10/09/1865	2 months	6	1292		For the trader José P. Tafoya
Alercan, Antonio	E	10/14/1865	2 months	6	1295		For the trader Lorenzo Valdez
Anerrijo, Juan (Armijo)	E	9/13/1865	2 months	6	1235		For the trader Anastacio Sandoval
Anallee, Jesús (Anaya)	T	10/20/1864		6	588–89	NL	Letter from Steck about granting pass to Analee/Costillo
Apodaca, Francisco	E	9/13/1865		6	1243–44		For the trade Juaquín Larriva
Apodaca, José	E	9/27/1865	2 months	6	1259		For the trader Rafael Leyba
Apodaca, Placido	E	10/14/1865	2 months	6	1295		For the trader Lorenzo Valdez
Aragón, Florencio	T	10/30/1865	3 months	6	1310	1,000	
Aragón, Nabor	E	2/8/1905		7	432–33		For the trader Captain P. Healey
Aragón, Navar	E	8/23/1865	45 days	6	1224	500	For the trader Pedro Antonio Marques
Aragón, Pablo	E	10/09/1865		6	1292		For the trader for José P. Tafoya
Aragón, Pedro	E	10/14/1865	2 months	6	1295		for the trader Lorenzo Valdez
Aragón, Pedro	E	10/09/1865	2 months	6	1292		For the trader for José P. Tafoya
Aragón, Víctor	E	10/10/1865	2 months	6	1289		For the trader Julio García
Archeluta, Marian	E	9/13/1865	2 months	6	1243–44		For the trader Juaquín Larriva
Archuleta, Mariano	E	10/14/1865	2 months	6	1295		For the trader Lorenzo Valdez
Armijo, José M.	E	9/27/1865	2 months	6	1259		For the trader Rafael Leyba

Name		Date	Duration		Page	Bond	Notes
Baca, Celso	T	3/20/1866		7	22		Applied for pass but not granted
Baca, Eusebio	BH	11/19/1865		6	1138		For the trader Juan Chama (bond held with John Ward)
Baca, Julián	E	2/8/1905	NL	7	432–33		For the trader Captain P. Healey
Baca, Luciano	BH	10/5/1865	2 months	6	1272	1,000	For the traders Agapito Hererra and Julián Flores
Baca y Ortíz, Francisco	BH	2/28/1865	1 year	6	838–41	2,000	For the trader Anastacio Sandoval
Baca y Salazar, Jesús M.	BH	8/23/1865	45 days	6	1224	500	For the trader Pedro Antonio Marques
Baca y Salazar, Jesús M.	BH	10/8/1865	2 months	6	1281	1,000	For the trader José Costillo
Banos, José Mario	E	10/14/1865	2 months	6	1295		For the trader Lorenzo Valdez
Baros (?), Louis	E	8/23/1865	45 days	6	1224	500	For the trader Pedro Antonio Marques
Beck, Preston	BH	12/29/1855	12 months		670	1,200	For the trader Gervais Nolan
Blea, Nives	E	8/23/1865	45 days	6	1224	500	For the trader Pedro Antonio Marques
Brown, Oscar	T	9/28/1866	NL	7	480–81		Not granted
Chama, Juan	T	11/19/1865	2 months	6	1138	1,000	For the trader A. Sandoval (bond held with Antonio Ortíz y Salazar)
Chávez, J. M.	BH	7/8/1865	1 month	6	1204	1,500	
Chávez, Jesús M.	BH	11/18/1865	2 months	6	1330	1,000	For Manuel Urioste, with Anastacio Sandoval
Chávez, Jesús	E	11/4/1865	3 months	6	1183		For the trader Antonio Gutierrez
Chávez, Sixto	E	10/09/1865		6	1292		For the trader José P. Tafoya
Collins, J. L.	BH	10/28/1865	12 months	6	1304	1,000	For the trader John Watts, the son (bond held with J. Sebrie the elder)
Conklin, James	BH	12/29/1855	12 months		670	1,200	For the trader Gervais Nolan
Costillo, José	T	10/20/1864		6	588–89		Found in a Micheal Steck letter on granting pass
Costillo, Jose	T	10/8/1865	2 months	6	1281	1,000	For the trader Gervais Nolan (bond held with Preston Beck)

(continued)

Passes, Bonds, and Employees (*continued*)

E = Employee, T = Trader, BH = Bond Holder, S = Supplier, NL = Not Listed

Names		Date	Pass	Roll	Image	Bond	Description or source
Crespin, Marcelino	E	10/09/1865		6	1292		For the trader for José P. Tafoya
Crespin, Trinidad	E	10/14/1865	2 months	6	1295		For the trader Lorenzo Valdez
Dalton, John	T	3/25/1866		7	24	NL	Applied for pass but not granted
Durán, José L.	BH	2/28/1865	1 year	6	838–41	2,000	For the trader A. Sandoval (bond held with Francisco y Baca y Ortiz)
Durán, José María	E	11/18/1865	2 months	6	1330	1,000	For the trader Manuel Urioste
Durán, Pedro	E	10/14/1865	2 months	6	1295		For the trader Lorenzo Valdez
Durán, Polonio	E	10/14/1865	2 months	6	1295		For the trader Lorenzo Valdez
Farria (Tafia?), Pablo	E	9/13/1865	2 months	6	1235		For the trader Anastacio Sandoval
Florez, Esquipula	E	10/10/1865	2 months	6	1289		For the trader Julio García
Florencio, Miguel	E	9/13/1865	2 months	6	1235		For the trader Anastacio Sandoval
Flores, Gregorio	E	10/09/1865		6	1292		For the trader José P. Tafoya
Flores, Julián	E	7/10/1865	3 months	6	207		For the trader Juan Padilla
Flores, Melguiades	E	8/23/1865	45 days	6	1224		For the trader Pedro Antonio Marques
Flores, Rumaldo	E	8/23/1865	45 days	6			for the trader Pedro Antonio Marques
Gaiduno, Juan	E	8/23/1865	45 days	6	1224		For the trader Pedro Antonio Marques
Galis, Nabor	E	10/09/1865		6	1292		For the trader José P. Tafoya
Gallego, Esquifoula	E	10/09/1865	2 months	6	1292		For the trader José P. Tafoya (all employees from San Miguel Co.)
Gallego, Fernando	BH	11/4/1865	3 months	6	1185	1,000	For the trader Antonio Gutierrez (bond held with Anastacio Sandoval)
Gallego, Gregario	E	10/09/1865		6	1292		For the trader José P. Tafoya
Gallego, Ynacio	E	11/4/1865	3 months	6	1183		For the trader Antonio Gutierrez

Name	Type	Date	Term		Bond No.	Amount	Notes
Gallegos, Fernandis	E	8/30/1865			1227–28	NL	For the trader Robert James Hamilton, whose application was denied
Gallegos, Gerónimo	E	9/13/1865		6	1243–44		For the trader Juaquín Larriva
Gallegos, Gregario	E	10/14/1865	2 months	6	1295		For the trader Lorenzo Valdez (Valdez is in Chaperito)
Gallegos, Ignacius	E	7/10/1865	3 months	6	207		For the trader Juan Padilla
Gallegos, Antonio José	S						"Fort Union National Monument: Ethnographic Overview and Assessment"
Gallegos, José	E	10/10/1865	2 months	6	1289		For the trader Julio García
Gallegos, Juan	E	7/10/1865	3 months	6	207		For the trader Juan Padilla
Gallegos, Merced	E	9/13/1865	2 months	6	1243–44		For the trader Juaquín Larriva
Gallegos, Marelisa	E	8/23/1865	1.5 months	6	1224		For the trade Pedro Antonio Marques
García, Aniceto	E	10/19/1865	2 months	6	1289		For the trader Julio García
García, José	E	9/13/1865		6	1243–44		For the trader Juaquín Larriva
García, José de la Cruz	E	7/10/1865	3 months	6	207		For the trader Juan Padilla
García, Julio	BH	10/9/1865		6	1293	1,000	For the trader José Piedad Tafoya (bond held with Lorenzo Labadie)
García, Julio	T	10/10/1865	2 months	6	1291	1,000	Bond holders Jesús M. Baca y Salazar and Pablo Moya
García, Rafael	E	8/30/1865			1227–28	NL	For the trader Robert James Hamilton, whose application was denied
García, Rumaldo	E	11/4/1865	3 months	6	1183		For the trader Antonio Gutiérrez
Giddings, James M.	T	10/30/1865	3 months	6	1306		
Gilean, Jose	E	7/8/1865	1 month	6	1204	1,500	For the trader Anastacio Sandoval
Gonzales, (Illegible)	E	9/13/1865	2 months	6	1235		For the trader Anastacio Sandoval
Gonzales, Bonifacio	E	9/13/1865	2 months	6	1235		For the trader Anastacio Sandoval

(continued)

Passes, Bonds, and Employees (*continued*)

E = Employee, T = Trader, BH = Bond Holder, S = Supplier, NL = Not Listed

Names		Date	Pass	Roll	Image	Bond	Description or source
Gonzales, Francisco	E	10/14/1865	2 months	6	1295		For the trader Lorenzo Valdez
Gonzales, Francisco	E	8/30/1865			1227–28		For the trader Robert James Hamilton, whose application was denied
Gonzales, Francisco	E	10/19/1865	2 months		1296	1,000	For the trader Lorenzo Valdez
Gonzales, Guadalupe	T	8/30/1865			1227–28		For the trader Robert James Hamilton, whose application was denied
Gonzales, José Antonio	BH	9/22/1865	2 months	6	1253–54	1,000	For the trader Juan Antonio Leyba (bond held with Ascencio Pena)
Gonzales, José de la Cruz	E	8/23/1865	45 days	6	1224	500	For the trader Pedro Antonio Marques
Gonzales, Juan	E	10/10/1865	2 months	6			For the trader Julio García
Gonzales, Roger (Roque)	BH	11/4/1865	2 months	6	1323–24	1,000	For the trader José Manuel Pacheco (bond held with Rafael Ortiz)
Gonzales y Esquibel, Jose	E	9/13/1865	2 months	6	1235		For the trader Anastacio Sandoval
Gutierrez, Antonio	T	11/4/1865	3 months	6	1185	1,000	For the trader Julio García
Gutierrez, José	E	10/10/1865	2 months	6	1289		For the trader Anastacio Sandoval
Gutierrez, Ygnacio	E	7/8/1865	1 month	6	1204	1,500	For the trader Anastacio Sandoval
Hamburger, Edward	BH	10/2/1865	3 months	6	1267	1,000	For the trader Fernando Lucero (bond held with D. Bernard Koch)
Hamilton, Robert J.	T	8/30/1865			1227–28	NL	For the trader Robert James Hamilton, whose application was denied
Healey, Patrick	T	2/8/1865		7	432	NL	
Henrie, W. H.	BH	11/17/1865	6 months	6	1134	1,000	For the trader W. T. Strachan (bond held with Morris Miller)

(continued)

Name		Date	Term		No.	Bond	Description
Hererra, Agapito/ Julián Flores	T	10/5/1865	2 months	6	1272	1,000	For the trader Rafael Leyba
Hererra, Agapito	E	9/27/1865	2 months	6	1259		For the trader Pedro Antonio Marques
Hererra, Agapito	E	8/23/1865	45 days	6		500	For the trader Antonio Gutiérrez
Herrera, Pablo	E	11/4/1865	3 months	6	1183		For the trader Juaquín Larriva
Hurtado, Dolores	E	9/13/1865		6	1243–44		
Jaramillo, Benigno	E	7/8/1865	1 month	6	1204	1,500	For the trader Anastacio Sandoval
Jaramillo, Gregario	T						Mentioned by Apolonio Ortiz in Kavanagh's *The Comanches*
Jaramillo, Gregario	T	11/3/1865	2 months	6	1319	1,000	For the trader Gregario Jaramillo (bond held with Ramón Roblato)
Jaramillo, Luciano	BH	11/3/1865	2 months	6	1319	1,000	
Koch, D. Bernard	BH	10/30/1865	3 months	6	1306	1,000	For the trader James Giddings (bond held with José M. Romero)
Koch, D. Bernard	BH	10/30/1865	3 months	6	1310	1,000	For the trader Florencio Aragón (bond held with James Giddings)
Koch, D. Bernard	BH	10/2/1865	3 months	6	1267	1,000	For the trader Fernando (bond held with Edward Hamburger)
Koch, D. Bernard	BH	9/30/1865	2 months	6	1265	1,000	For the trader Edward Martinas
Koch, Keman D.	BH	9/30/1865	2 months	6	1265	1,000	For the trader Edward Martinas (bond held with D. Bernard Koch)
Labadie, Lorenzo	BH	10/9/1865		6	1293	1,000	For the trader José Piedad Tafoya (bond held with Julio García)
Labadie, Lorenzo	BH	10/8/1865	2 months	6	1281	1,000	For the José Costillo (bond held with Jesús M. Baca y Salazar)
Lacombe, Agustín	T	9/04/1854	6 months	2	285	1,000	Bond with M. Alverez and H. Mercure (trade w. Navajo)

Passes, Bonds, and Employees (*continued*)

E = Employee, T = Trader, BH = Bond Holder, S = Supplier, NL = Not Listed

Names		Date	Pass	Roll	Image	Bond	Description or source
Laings, Thomas	E	1/9/1867	1 year	7	940		For the trader José M. Valdez
Larriva, Juaquín	T	9/13/1865	2 months	6	1243–44	1,000	For the trader Juaquín Larriva
Larue, J. A.	T	9/18/1866					
Leon, Pedro	T	3/04/1854	3 months	2	672	1,000	
Leyba, Francisco	BH	9/27/1865	2 months	6	1258–60	1,000	For the trader Leyba (bond held with Antonio Sena)
Leyba, Juan Antonio	T	9/22/1865	2 months	6	1253–54	1,000	
Leyba, Rafael	T	9/27/1865	2 months	6	1258	1,000	
Lopes (López?), Juan José	T	11/20/1865	2 months	6	1315	1,000	
López, Lorenzo	S	8/–/1861					"Fort Union National Monument: Ethnographic Overview and Assessment"
Lopes (López?), Rafa	BH	11/20/1865	2 months	6	1315	1,000	For Juan J. Lopes (bond held with Anastacio Sandoval)
López, Ramón	E	9/18/1865	2 months	6	249–251	1,000	For the trade José Benito Mestas
Lucero, A.	T	3/04/1854	6 months	2	282–83	NL	Bond held by M. Alverez and H. Mercure (trade w. Navajo)
Lucero, Esquifaula	T	8/30/1865			1227–28		For the trader Robert James Hamilton, whose application was denied
Lucero, Fabriano	T	2/14/1872				NL	Account from Kavanagh, *The Comanches*, regarding Apolonio Ortiz
Lucero, Fernando	T	11/20/1865	3 months	6	1129	1,000	
Lucero, Fernando	T	10/2/1865	3 months	6	1265–67	1,000	
Lucero, Jesús M.	E	10/14/1865	2 months	6	1295	1,000	For the trader Lorenzo Valdez

Lucero, José María	E	10/09/1865		6	1292		For the trader José P. Tafoya
Lucero, Juan de Dios	E	10/09/1865		6	1292		For the trader José P. Tafoya
Lucero, Pablo	T	9/13/1865	2 months	6	1234		For the trader Anastacio Sandoval
Lucero, Refugio	E	2/8/1905		7	432–33		For the Manuel Chávez-Vose subcontract
Lujan, José Octoviano	BH	11/4/1865	3 months	6	1322	2,000	For the trader Jesús Ortíz y Roibal
Maca, Justo	E	9/13/1865		6	1243–44		For the trader Juaquín Larriva
Madrid, Franco	E	8/23/1865	45 days	6			For the trader Pedro Antonio Marques
Madrid, José	E	7/10/1865	3 months	6	207		For the trader Juan Padilla
Madrid, José María	E	9/13/1865	2 months	6	1235		For the trader Anastacio Sandoval
Madrid, José María	E	8/23/1865	45 days	6			For the trader Pedro Antonio Marques
Madril, José Felipe	E	10/14/1865	2 months	6	1295–96		For the trader Lorenzo Valdez
Madrid, José Felipe	E	8/23/1865	45 days	6	1224		For the trader Pedro Antonio Marques
Marcureno, Guadalupe	E	9/18/1865	2 months	6	249–251		For the trader José Benito Mestas
Marcureno, Juan Bautista	E	9/18/1865	2 months	6	249–251		For the trader José Benito Mestas
Marcureno, Santiago	E	9/18/1865	2 months	6	249–251		For the trader José Benito Mestas
Mares, Gabriel	E	11/4/1865	3 months	6	1183		For the trader Antonio Gutiérrez
Mares, José	E	9/13/1865		6	1243–44		For the trader Juaquín Larriva
Mares, Manuel	E	7/8/1865	1 month	6	1204		For the trader Anastacio Sandoval
Marques, Pedro	E	2/8/1905		7	432–33		For the trader Captain P. Healey at Hatch's Ranch
Marques, Pedro Antonio	T	8/23/1865	45 days	6	1224	500	
Marques, Pedro	E	11/18/1865	2 months	6	1330	1,000	For the trader Manuel Urioste
Martín, Antonio	E	7/10/1865	3 months	6	207	1,000	For the trader Juan Padilla
Martín, Antonio	E	10/10/1865	2 months	6	1289		For the trader Julio García
Martín, Antonio	E	11/18/1865	2 months	6	1330	1,000	For the trader Manuel Urioste
Martín, Guadalupe	E	9/18/1865	2 months	6	249–51	1,000	For the trader José Benito Mestas
Martín, Polinarious	E	7/8/1865	1 month	6	1204	1,500	For the trader Anastacio Sandoval

(*continued*)

Passes, Bonds, and Employees (*continued*)

E = Employee, T = Trader, BH = Bond Holder, S = Supplier, NL = Not Listed

Names		Date	Pass	Roll	Image	Bond	Description or source
Martin, Roque or Roger	BH	10/19/1865	2 months	6	1296	1,000	For the trader Lorenzo Valdez
Martin, Victorino	E	10/10/1865	2 months		1291		For the trader Julio García
Martinas, Eoward (Edward?)	T	9/30/1865	2 months	6	1264	1,000	
Martines, Antonico	E	9/13/1865	2 months	6	1235		For the trader Anastacio Sandoval
Martines, José	T	8/30/1865			1227–28	NL	For the trader Robert James Hamilton, whose application was denied
Martinez, Blaz	E	9/10/1867		7	423–432		For the trader Charles Jennings at Hatch's Ranch
Martinez, Román	E	9/10/1867		7	423–432		For the trader Charles Jennings at Hatch's Ranch
Medina, José Gertrudes	T	10/5/1865	2 months	6	1179	1,000	For the trader Antonio Gutiérrez
Medina, Rafael	E	11/4/1865	3 months	6	1183		
Mestas, José Benito	T	9/18/1865	2 months	6	251	1,000	
Miller, Morris	BH	11/17/1865	6 months	6	1134	1,000	For the trader W. T. Strachan (bond held with W. H. Henrie)
Montoya, Francisco	BH	8/23/1865	1.5 months	6		500	For the trader Pedro Antonio Marques
Montoya, José del la Ascensión	BH	11/20/1865		6	1129	1,000	For the trader Fernando Lucero
Moya, Pablo	BH	11/4/1865	3 months	6	1322	2,000	For the trader Jesús Ortiz y Roibal (bond held with José Octoviano Luna)
Moya, Pablo	BH	10/10/1865	2 months	6	1291	1,000	For the trader Julio García (bond held with Jesús María Baca y Salazar)

Name	Type	Date	Duration	No.	ID	Amount	Description
Munir, Benedicto	E	9/18/1865	2 months	6	249–51		For the trader José Benito Mestas
Munir, José María	E	9/18/1865	2 months	6	249–51		For the trader José Benito Mestas
Munir, José Miguel	E	9/18/1865	2 months	6	249–51		For the trader José Benito Mestas
Munir, Pedro	E	9/18/1865	2 months	6	249–51		For the trader José Benito Mestas
Munir, Ramon	E	9/18/1865	2 months	6	249–51		For the trader José Benito Mestas
Ortega, Albino	T	10/05/1865	2 months	6	1285	1,000	For the trader José P. Tafoya
Ortega, José M.	E	10/09/1865			1292		For the trader José P. Tafoya
Ortega, Narciso	E	10/09/1865	2 months		1292		For the trader José P. Tafoya
Ortega, Rafael	E	11/4/1865	3 months	6	1183		For the trader Antonio Gutiérrez
Ortiz, Dupy	E	9/27/1865	2 months	6	1259		For the trader Rafael Leyba
Ortiz, Felipe	E	11/4/1865	3 months	6	1183		For the trader Antonio Gutiérrez
Ortiz, Félix	E	9/27/1865	2 months	6	1259		For the trader Rafael Leyba
Ortiz, Francisco Baca	BH	2/28/1865	1 year	6	838	2,000	For the trader Anastacio Sandoval (bond held with José L. Dúran)
Ortiz, José Feliz	E	8/23/1865	45 days	6	1224		For the trader Pedro Antonio Marques
Ortiz, Juan de Mata	T	11/2/1865	2 months		1313	1,000	For the trader Antonio Gutiérrez
Ortiz, Porfiro	E	11/4/1865	3 months	6	1183		For the trader Antonio Gutiérrez
Ortiz, Rafael	BH	11/2/1865	2 months	6	1313	1,000	For the trader Juan de Mata Ortíz (bond held with Jesús M. Baca y Salazar)
Ortiz, Rafael	BH	11/4/1865	2 months	6	1323	1,000	For the trader José Manuel Pacheco
Pacheco, Domingo	E	8/23/1865	45 days	6	1224		For the trader Pedro Antonio Marques
Pacheco, José Manuel	T	11/4/1865	2 months	6	1323	1,000	For the trader José Manuel Pacheco
Padilla, Baltazar	E	10/10/1865	2 months	6	1289	1,000	For the trader Julio García
Padilla, Juan	T	7/10/1865	3 months	6	207		For the trader Julio García
Padilla, Julian	E			7	432–33	1,000	For the trader Charles Jennings at Hatch's Ranch

(continued)

Passes, Bonds, and Employees (*continued*)

E = Employee, T = Trader, BH = Bond Holder, S = Supplier, NL = Not Listed

Names		Date	Pass	Roll	Image	Bond	Description or source
Pena, Ansencio	BH	9/22/1865	2 months	6	1253–54	1,000	For the trader Juan Antonio Leyba (bond held with José A. Gonzales)
Pino, Miguel E.	BH	9/13/1865	2 months	6	1243–44	1,000	For the trader Juaquín Larriva, with Anastacio Sandoval
Quintana, Juan	BH	1/28/1905	3 months	2	672	1,200	For the trader Pedro Leon
Quintana, Rafael Rodrigues	BH	10/3/1865	2 months	6	1179	1,000	For the trader José G. Medina (bond held with Anastacio Sandoval)
Quirrino (?), Valencia	E	8/23/1865	1.5 months	6			For Pedro Antonio Marques
Rael, Luis	E	10/10/1865	2 months	6			For the trader Julio García
Roblato, Ramón	BH	11/3/1865	2 months	6	1319	1,000	For the trader Gregorio Jaramillo (bond with Luciano Jaramillo)
Rodríguez, Augustín	E	9/18/1865	2 months	6	249–51		For the trader José Benito Mestas
Rodríguez, Brigido	E	9/18/1865	2 months	6	249–51		For the trader José Benito Mestas
Rodríguez, Juna José	E	9/18/1865	2 months	6	249–51		For the trader José Benito Mestas
Rodríguez, Manuel	E	9/18/1865	2 months	6	249–51		For the trader José Benito Mestas
Rodríguez, Matías	E	9/18/1865	2 months	6	249–51		For the trader José Benito Mestas
Rodríguez, Pedro	E	9/18/1865	2 months	6	249–51		For the trader José Benito Mestas
Roibal, Jesús Ortiz y	T	11/5/1865	3 months	6	1322	2,000	For the trader Julio García
Roibal, Jesús Ortiz y	E	10/10/1865	2 months	6	1289		For the trader Julio García
Roival (Roybal?), Albino	BH	9/18/1865	2 months	6	251	1,000	For the trader José Benito Mestas
Romero, Donaciono	E	11/18/1865	2 months	6	1330		For the trader Manuel Urioste
Romero, José	E	11/18/1865	2 months	6	1330		For the trader Manuel Urioste
Romero, José M.	BH	10/30/1865	3 months	6	1306	1000	For the trader James Giddings (bond with D. Bernard Koch)

(*continued*)

Name		Date	Duration		Page	Amount	Description
Romero, Miguel	E	11/18/1865	2 months	6	1330		For the trader Manuel Urioste
Romero, (Illegible)	E	7/8/1865	1 month	6	1204		For the trader Anastacio Sandoval
Sais, José	E	8/23/1865	1 1/2 mths	6	1224		For the trader Pedro Antonio Marques
Sais, Simón	E	8/23/1865	1 1/2 mths	6	1224		For the trader Pedro Antonio Marques
Salas, Sebastián	E	7/10/1865	3 months	6	207		For the trader Juan Padilla
Salas, Tedorio	E	10/19/1865	2 months	6	1296		For the trader Lorenzo Valdez (see note at end of table)
Salas, Teodosio	T	8/30/1865			1227–28	NL	For the trader Robert James Hamilton, whose application was denied
Salas, Todorio	E	10/14/1865	2 months	6	1295		For the trader Lorenzo Valdez
Salazar, Antonio Ortiz y	BH	7/8/1865	1 month	6	1204	1,500	For the trader Anastacio Sandoval
Salazar, Jesús M. Baca	BH	11/02/1865	2 months	6	1313	1,000	For the trader Juan de M. Ortiz (bond with Rafael Ortiz)
Salazar, Jesús M. Baca	BH	10/08/1865		6	1281	100	For the trader José Costillo (bond with Lorenzo Labadie)
Salazar, Jesús M. Baca	BH	8/28/1865	45 days	6		500	For the trader Pedro Antonio Marques
Salazar, Jesús M. Baca	BH	10/10/1865	2 months	6	1291		For the trader Julio García (bond with Pablo Moya)
Sánchez, Isidoro	E			7	432–33		For the traders Manuel Chávez-Vose subcontract
Sánchez, Manuel	E			7	432–33		For the traders Manuel Chávez-Vose subcontract
Sánchez, Roger	E	9/13/1865		6	1243–44		For trader Juaquín Larriva
Sandoval, Anastacio	BH	4/3/1864		6	1163–64		For the trader Manuel Urioste
Sandoval, Anastacio	T	2/27/1865	1 year	6	1166		As often as 12 times per year
Sandoval, Anastacio	T	2/28/1865	1 year	6	838		
Sandoval, Anastacio	T	4/14/1865		6		2,000	Application denied because pass did not have govt. stamp

Passes, Bonds, and Employees (continued)

E = Employee, T = Trader, BH = Bond Holder, S = Supplier, NL = Not Listed

Names		Date	Pass	Roll	Image	Bond	Description or source
Sandoval, Anastacio	BH	1/9/1867	1 year	7	940	1,000	For the trader José M. Valdez
Sandoval, Anastacio	BH	7/10/1865	3 months	6	207	1,000	For the trader Juan Padilla
Sandoval, Anastacio	T	7/8/1865	1 month	6	1204	1,500	
Sandoval, Anastacio	BH	10/05/1865	2 months	6	1285	1,000	For the trader Albino Ortega (bond with William White)
Sandoval, Anastacio	BH	10/05/1865	2 months	6	1179	1,000	For the trader José G. Medina (bond with Rafael Rodrigues y Quintana)
Sandoval, Anastacio	BH	11/4/1865	3 months	6	1185	1,000	For the trader Antonio Gutiérrez (bond with Fernando Gonzales)
Sandoval, Anastacio	BH	11/20/1865	2 months	6	1315	1,000	For the trader Juan José López (bond held with Rafael López)
Sandoval, Anastacio	BH	11/18/1865	2 months	6	1330	1,000	For the trader Manuel Urioste (bond held with Jesús M. Chávez)
Sandoval, Anastacio	T	9/13/1865	2 months	6	1235–38	1,000	
Sandoval, Anastacio	BH	9/13/1865	2 months	6	1243–44	1,000	For the trader Juaquín Larriva (bond with Miguel E. Pino)
Sandoval, Jesús	E	2/8/1905		7	432–33		For the trader Capt. P. Healey at Hatch's Ranch
Sandoval, Manuel	BH	9/13/1865	2 months	6	1238	1,000	For Anastacio Sandoval (bond held with David Urioste)
Sena, Antonio	BH	9/27/1865	2 months	6	1258	1,000	For the trader Rafael Leyba
Sena, Juan	BH	7/10/1865	3 months	6	703	1,000	For the trader Juan Padilla
Sena, Antonio	BH	9/18/1865	2 months	6	251	1,000	For the trader José Benito Mestas
Sena, Polonio	E	11/18/1865	2 months	6	1330	1,000	For the trader Manuel Urioste

190

Name	Type	Date	Duration	No.	Ref.	Amount	Notes
Sisneros, José de la Cruz	E	10/09/1865		6	1292		For the trader José P. Tafoya
Solano, Miguel	E	9/13/1865	2 months	6	1235		For the trader Anastacio Sandoval
Solano, Miguel	E	11/18/1865	2 months	6	1330	1,000	For the trader Manuel Urioste
Strachan, W. T.	T	11/17/1865	6 months	6	1134	1,000	
Tafoya José Piedad	T	10/9/1865	2 months	6	1292–93	1,000	Bond holders Lorenzo Labadie and Julio Gacia
Tafoya, José Piedad	E	9/10/1867		7	423–432		For the trader Charles Jennings at Hatch's Ranch
Tapia, (Illegible)	E	10/14/1865	2 months	6	1295		For the trader Lorenzo Valdez
Tapia, Juan de Dios	E	7/8/1865	1 month	6	1204	1,500	For the trader Anastacio Sandoval
Trujillo, Florentine	T	8/30/1865			1227–28	NL	For the trader Robert James Hamilton, whose application was denied
Trujillo, Guadalupe	E	9/13/1865		6	1243–44		For the trader Juaquín Larriva
Trujillo, Joux Antonio	E	9/13/1865		6	1243–44		For the trader Juaquín Larriva
Trujillo, Pablo	T	8/30/1865			1227–28		For the trader Robert James Hamilton, whose application was denied
Ulibarri, Atanacio	E	9/13/1865	2 months	6	1235		For the trader Anastacio Sandoval
Ulibarri, Balentin	E	9/13/1865	2 months	6	1235		For the trader Anastacio Sandoval
Urioste, David	E	9/13/1865	2 months	6	1235–38		For the trader Anastacio Sandoval
Urioste, David	E	7/8/1865	1 month	6	1204		For the trader Anastacio Sandoval
Urioste, David	BH	9/13/1865	2 months	6	1238	1,000	For the trader Anastocio Sandoval (bond held with Manuel Sandoval)
Urioste, David	E	11/18/1865	2 months	6	1330	1,000	For the trader Manuel Urioste
Urioste, Manuel	T	2/27/1865	2 months	6	1163–64	NL	With 12 men to purchase captives
Urioste, Manuel	T	4/3/1864			1366		Bond held by Anastacio Sandoval
Valdez, (Illegible)	E	10/14/1865	2 months	6	1295		For trader Lorenzo Valdez
Valdez, Faustin	BH	1/9/1867	1 year	7	940	5,000	For the trader José M. Valdez (bond held with Anastacio Sandoval)

(continued)

Passes, Bonds, and Employees (*continued*)

E = Employee, T = Trader, BH = Bond Holder, S = Supplier, NL = Not Listed

Names		Date	Pass	Roll	Image	Bond	Description or source
Valdez, Forricu	E	9/13/1865	2 months	6	1243–44		For the trader Juaquín Larriva
Valdez, Teodo	E	1/9/1867	1 year	7	940		For the trader José M. Valdez
Varas, Manuel	E	9/27/1865	2 months	6	1259		For the trader Rafael Leyba
Varas, Mariona	E	9/27/1865	2 months	6	1259		For the trader Rafael Leyba
Varas, Merselino	E	9/27/1865	2 months	6	1259		For the trader Rafael Leyba
Vetado (Hurtado?), Manuel	BH	11/20/1865		6	1129	1,000	For the trader Fernando Lucero (bond held José de la Ascensión)
Vigile, Agapito	E	9/13/1865	2 months	6	1235		For the trader Anastacio Sandoval
Vose, R. C.	T	2/8/1905		7	432	NL	Sublet his license to Manuel Chávez
Vigil, Antonio	BH	1/28/1905	3 months	2	672	1,000	For Pedro Leon (Labadie issued pass in 1855)
Vigil, José Antonio	E	11/4/1865	3 months	6	1183		For the trader Antonio Gutiérrez
Ward, John	BH	11/19/1865	2 months	6	1138	1,000	For trader Juan Chama (bond with Esubio Baca)
Watts, John	T	10/28/1865	12 months	6	1304	1,000	Bond holders John Watts Sr. and J. L. Collins
Watts, John Sebrie	BH	10/28/1865	12 months	6	1304	1,000	For trader John Watts (bond held with J. L. Collins)
White, William	BH	10/05/1865	2 months	6	1285	1,000	For the trader Albino Ortega (bond with Anastacio Sandoval)
Ygnacio, Pedro	E	9/18/1865	2 months	6	249–51		For the trader José Benito Mestas

Fort Union National Monument: Ethnographic Overview and Assessment, Sánchez, Joseph P., et al.
All image numbers are from familysearch.org, using designated microfilm roll from National Archives (refer to bibliography).
Bond prices are only noted for traders and bond holders, not employees.

NOTES

Abbreviations

AGO   Adjutant General's Office

CGP   Office of the Commissary General of Prisoners, National Archives, Washington, D.C., Record Group 249

CIA   Commissioner of Indian Affairs

CSR   Center for Southwest Research, University of New Mexico Albuquerque

DA   District of Arizona

DNM   Department of New Mexico

FT   Frank Temple Microfilm R1, Records of the War Department, U.S. Army, Reports of Scouts, Fort Concho, Texas, 1872–81, and Fort Stockton, Texas, Reports and Maps of Explorations and Scouts, 1873–79, Fort Davis National Historic Site Archives

GLO   Texas General Land Office Archives

HTO   *Handbook of Texas Online*

IDC   Indian Depredation Cases, U.S. Court of Claims, National Archives, Washington, D.C., Record Group 123

LR   Letters Received

LS   Letters Sent

M   Microfilm, Microfilm Series

NA   National Archives, Washington, D.C.

NACP   National Archives, College Park, Maryland

NMRCA   New Mexico State Records Center and Archives, Santa Fe

OIA   Office of Indian Affairs

OR   *War of the Rebellion: A Compilation of the Official Records of the Union and Confederate Armies*

R   Roll

RFP   Rip Ford Papers, UDC Collection, Haley Memorial Library

RG   Record Group

RNMSIA   Records of the New Mexico Superintendency of Indian Affairs, National Archives

SIA   Superintendent of Indian Affairs

SMCA   San Miguel County Archives, Las Vegas, New Mexico

SMDC   San Miguel County District Court, Las Vegas, New Mexico

TNMA District of Texas, New Mexico, and Arizona
TSHA Texas State Historical Association
TSLAC Texas State Library and Archives Commission
WIA Wichita Indian Agency

Introduction

1. Glen Sample Ely, *Where the West Begins: Debating Texas Identity* (Lubbock: Texas Tech University Press, 2011), 61–74. On June 24, 1897, M. E. Ragsdale, a civil engineer in Brownwood, Texas, drew a map that provides much detail on area ranches in Coleman, Runnels, Concho, and Tom Green Counties during 1866–71, the peak period for Chisum's cattle operations in West Texas. Ragsdale certified that his drawing "was compiled . . . from maps of the state of Texas, United States Geological Survey maps, and other reliable information obtained and is correct to the best of my knowledge and belief." On this map Ragsdale labels the cattle route leading from the Concho River watershed to Horsehead Crossing on the Pecos River as "the Chisum Trail." See M. E. Ragsdale map, *Richard F. Tankersley v. The United States and the Kiowa and Comanche Indians*, Case No. 6501, NA, RG 123, U.S. Court of Claims, Indian Depredation Cases (endnote quotations; hereafter Indian depredation cases heard before the U.S. Court of Claims are identified by case number, IDC). J. Evetts Haley's biography on Charles Goodnight (1936) includes interviews regarding the Goodnight-Loving Trail that Haley did with Goodnight in the late 1920s, thirty years after Ragsdale drew his map. For more on Haley's and Goodnight's revisionist history of the first West Texas/Pecos River cattle drives, see J. Evetts Haley, *Charles Goodnight: Cowman and Plainsman* (Norman: University of Oklahoma Press, 1989), 127.

2. Portions of the introduction, chapter 1, and chapter 2 appeared in Glen Sample Ely, "Skulduggery at Spencer's Ranch: Civil War Intrigue in West Texas," *Journal of Big Bend Studies* 21 (2009), 9–29; and Glen Sample Ely, "What to Do About Texas? Texas and the Department of New Mexico in the Civil War," *New Mexico Historical Review* 85, no. 4 (Fall 2010), 375–408, and are used with permission. A number of Texas history books, in their discussion of the Civil War, neglect to mention that the enemy occupied part of the state, the Trans-Pecos, for almost three years. The story that unfolded in the Trans-Pecos during the war runs counter to the deeply ingrained Texan myth of exceptionalism. According to this inaccurate legend, Texas, unlike her sister states in the Confederacy, successfully repelled all Union attempts to invade and occupy her territory. For examples of this traditional narrative, see Seymour V. Connor, *Texas: A History* (Arlington Heights, Ill.: AHM Publishing Corp., 1971), 197; Rupert Norval Richardson, *Texas, The Lone Star State* (New York: Prentice-Hall, 1943), 252; Rupert Norval Richardson, *Texas: The Lone Star State*, 8th ed. (Upper Saddle River, N.J.: Prentice-Hall, 2001), 218; Stephen Harrigan, *Big Wonderful Thing: A History of Texas* (Austin: University of Texas Press, 2019), 305; Stephen A. Townsend, *The Yankee Invasion of Texas* (College Station: Texas A&M University Press, 2006), 148; Stephen A.

Dupree, *Planting the Union Flag in Texas: The Campaigns of Major General Nathanial P. Banks in the West* (College Station: Texas A&M University Press, 2008), 198.

3. Andrés Resendéz, *A Texas Patriot on Trial in Mexico: José Antonio Navarro and the Texan Santa Fe Expedition* (Dallas: William P. Clements Center for Southwest Studies, 2005), xix (quotation). While Texas exerted a questionable claim to New Mexico as part of its republic, residents there considered themselves citizens of Mexico, and viewed the Santa Fe Expedition of 1841 as an aggressive encroachment into Mexican territory.

4. Jerry D. Thompson, *New Mexico Territory during the Civil War: Wallen and Evans Inspection Reports, 1862–1863* (Albuquerque: University of New Mexico Press, 2008), 2–6; John P. Wilson, *When the Texans Came: Missing Records from the Civil War in the Southwest, 1861–1862* (Albuquerque: University of New Mexico Press, 2001), 305 (quotations). The Texan officers submitted their assessment in May 1862.

5. Wilson, *When the Texans Came*, 288–91, 311–14; Steele to Cleaver, June 26, 1862, and June 27, 1862, NA, RG 109, Letters Sent (LS), Confederate general William Steele's Command, Ch. II, Vol. 270, March 1862–May 1863; Steele to Cooper, July 12, 1862, *The War of the Rebellion: A Compilation of the Official Records of the Union and Confederate Armies* (*OR*) (Washington: United States Government Printing Office, 1880–1901), Series (Ser.) 1, Vol. 9, 722 (quotations one through three). Besides dealing with enraged locals, Steele also found himself confronting angry Texas soldiers, who "were on the point of open mutiny, and threatened to take matters into their own hands unless they were speedily marched back to San Antonio," ibid. (endnote quotation). See also, Eyres to Chivington, July 10, 1862, NA, RG 393, Headquarters, Dept. of New Mexico (DNM), Unregistered Letters Received, June–Sept. 1862 (quotation four). In May 1862 Confederate officials in Texas debated whether or not to try and keep possession of El Paso. Ultimately the decision was made to retreat back to San Antonio and to establish the Rebels' western defensive perimeter at Fort Clark, Texas. Brig. Gen. Hamilton P. Bee reported that Col. William Read Scurry of Sibley's Brigade wanted Confederate troops to hold El Paso, "as possession of that valley will enable the enemy to gradually take possession of Fort Davis and all the posts down to Fort Clark." Bee, however, felt that "it would be more advantageous to make the fight at Fort Clark, than at El Paso, . . . the intermediate country being utterly valueless except the valley of El Paso." See Brig. Gen. Hamilton P. Bee to Gen. Paul O. Hebert, San Antonio, Texas, May 19, 1862, NA, RG 109, Entry 106, Box 1, Folder 26, Letters Received (LR), Dept. of Texas, 1861–62 (endnote quotations).

6. Ely, *Where the West Begins*, 29; Wilson, *When the Texans Came*, 288–91, 311–14; *Houston Tri-Weekly Telegraph*, Aug. 18, 1862 (quotation three); *San Antonio Semi-Weekly News*, July 21, 1862; Howe to Chapin, July 15, 1862, NA, RG 393, Southern DNM, Entry 734, LS, Vol. 118/300. It is understandable that locals would not want to conduct business with the rebels. A July 1862 report from El Paso del Norte, Mexico, noted that "Confederate money is selling at 20 cents on the dollar and large amounts could be bought for less if there were any purchasers." See enclosure in Canby to Chivington, June 18,

1862, NA, RG 94, Adjutant General's Office (AGO), LR, Microfilm Series (M) 619, Roll (R) 122 (quotations one, two, and endnote quotation). The Houston newspaper account claimed that the engagement in Socorro, Texas, between retreating rebels, Pueblo Indians, and Tejanos left the town's church in ruins, but some El Paso County historians are unsure if the church was damaged.

7. Francis B. Heitman, *Historical Register and Dictionary of the United States Army, from Its Organization, September 29, 1789, to March 2, 1903* (Washington, D.C.: Government Printing Office, 1903), 1:282; Aurora Hunt, *Major James Henry Carleton, 1814–1873: Western Frontier Dragoon* (Glendale, Calif.: Arthur H. Clark, 1958), 26, 108, 113–67. Carleton was born in Maine in 1814 and died there in 1873. Heitman notes that Carleton was a captain in the First Dragoons during 1851–57; however, Hunt points out that Lieutenant Carleton was promoted to captain on February 16, 1847, and then to major on February 23, 1847. See also Capt. A. H. French Report on Scout and Skillman Attack, April 24, 1864, NA, RG 393, DNM, LR, M1120, R22 (hereafter cited as French Report); French to West, Dec. 3, 1862, NA, RG 94, AGO, LR, N446, 1862 (quotation). Confederate agent Jarvis Hubbell stated that one hundred Indians burned Fort Davis in August 1862. Hubbell, former El Paso County surveyor, along with Edward Hall of Fort Leaton, Texas, and several other men were at Fort Davis scavenging any military property "worth removing" just before and immediately after the conflagration. Hubbell's party found a group of sick rebel soldiers at the post and transported all but one of them for care to Presidio del Norte, Mexico. Before Hubbell and Hall could return for the remaining wounded man, Indian raiders killed him. See Hubbell to Teel, Oct. 13, 1862, Jarvis Hubbell Confederate Citizen File, NA, RG 109, M346 (endnote quotation). Union lieutenant Albert H. French, visiting Fort Davis a month after Hubbell and Hall, reported that the outpost was burned *after* his men passed through in early September 1862 by spies in the employ of another Confederate agent, John Burgess of Presidio del Norte, Mexico. See French to West, Dec. 3, 1862, NA, RG 94, AGO, LR, N446, 1862. See also Shirland to Cutler, Sept. 12, 1862, *OR*, Ser. 1, Vol. 9, 577–79; Zenas Bliss, *The Reminiscences of Major General Zenas R. Bliss: From the Texas Frontier to the Civil War and Back Again*, eds. Thomas T. Smith, Jerry D. Thompson, Robert Wooster, and Ben Pingenot (Austin: Texas State Historical Association, 2007), 233. Bliss was in command of Fort Quitman in April 1861 when the rebels took over. He also served at Fort Clark, Fort Stockton, Fort Davis, and Camp Hudson.

8. Operations on the Pacific Coast, Summary of Principal Events 1862–63, *OR*, Ser. 1, Vol. 50, Part I, 2–4; General Orders No. 82 and 83, Sept. 18, 1862, *OR*, Ser. 1, Vol. 9, 581–82. Arizona was part of New Mexico Territory until February 24, 1863, when Congress and President Lincoln approved the creation of Arizona Territory. During the Civil War the Department of New Mexico administered both the District of Western Arizona and the District of Arizona. Maj. David Fergusson, First California Cavalry, commanded Western Arizona until Sept. 5, 1862, when Major Theodore A. Coult, Fifth California Infantry, assumed command. For period maps of New Mexico Territory (including Arizona), see *Carte Generale des États-Unis et du Mexique Comprenant l'Amerique Centrale et les Antilles*, E. Andriveau-Goujon, Paris, 1865; *The New Naval and Mili-*

tary Map of the United States, by J. Calvin Smith, 1862, J. Baker & Co. Publishers; *The Washington Map of the United States by the Superintendent U.S. National Observatory,* Washington D.C., 1861, S. Taintor & Co. Publisher; and *Map of the Military Department of New Mexico: Drawn under the Direction of Brig. Gen. James H. Carleton,* 1864, all from David Rumsey Historical Map Collection, www.davidrumsey.com.

9. General Orders No. 82, Sept. 18, 1862, *OR,* Ser. 1, Vol. 9, 582 (quotation one); Halleck to Carleton, Feb. 6, 1864, *OR,* Ser. 1, Vol. 34, Pt. 2, 256 (quotations two and three).

10. Various period maps also show the Fort Smith–Santa Fe Road as the Fort Smith–Albuquerque Road. On October 5, 1841, most of the Texan invaders from the Santa Fe Expedition surrendered to Mexican authorities at Laguna Colorado, New Mexico, approximately twenty miles southwest of the later site of Fort Bascom. General Carleton hoped that Fort Bascom would help foster settlement in the Canadian River region. See Carleton to Thomas, Sept. 30, 1862, NA, RG 94, AGO, LR, M619, R123 (temporary outpost); Carleton to Drum, Sept. 15, 1865, *OR,* Ser. 1, Vol. 48, Pt. 2, 1231 (Bascom); Robert W. Frazer, *Forts of the West* (Norman: University of Oklahoma Press, 1988), 95. In April 1864 Fort Bascom reported an aggregate (i.e., those present for duty) troop strength of 166. See DNM Troop Returns, April 1864, *OR,* Ser. 1, Vol. 34, Pt. 3, 371–72 (TS64). In May 1865, the last month before Texas surrendered, the number of men present for duty at Bascom was 142. See Troop Strength Report, DNM, May 14, 1865, NA RG 94, AGO, LR, M619, R390 (TS65).

11. McFerran to Meigs, July 27, 1865, *OR,* Ser. 3, Vol. 5, 442–44; McFerran to Meigs, July 26, 1865, ibid., 444–45, 446 (quotation), 447. In one example of this distribution network, McFerran in June 1864 signed a contract with freighter Epifianio Aquirre to transport military stores and supplies from Fort Union, New Mexico, to other department posts at a rate of $2 to $2.25 per 100 pounds per 100 miles. See U.S. House, *Contracts Made by the Quartermaster's Department,* 38th Cong., 2nd Sess., 1865. House Exec. Doc. No. 84, Vol. 14, Serial 1230, 127.

12. J. H. Carleton to Capt. J. C. McFerran, Santa Fe, New Mexico, November 18, 1862, NA, M1072, DNM, LS, Vol. 13, 156 (quotations); Joseph P. Sánchez, Jerry L. Gurulé, and Larry D. Miller, *Fort Union National Monument: Ethnographic Overview and Assessment* (Washington, D.C.: National Park Service, 2006), 72; George Gwyther, "The Three Pueblo Spies, A Reminiscence of the Late Civil War," *Overland Monthly* 13, no. 4 (July 1874), 337–41. On May 19, 1850, Tesuque Pueblo governor Carlos Vigil received a pass to trade with the Comanches. The pass had no time limit. See Thomas W. Kavanagh, *The Comanches: A History, 1706–1875* (Lincoln: University of Nebraska Press, 1999), 340, 342, 368, 380. The history of the Bosque Redondo Reservation at Fort Sumner, New Mexico, falls outside the scope of this present work. For more information, please see Gerald Thompson, *The Army and the Navajo: The Bosque Redondo Reservation Experiment, 1863–1868* (Tucson: University of Arizona Press, 1975); Lynn Robison Bailey, *Bosque Redondo: The Navajo Internment at Fort Sumner, New Mexico, 1863–1868* (Tucson, Ariz.: Westernlore Press, 1998).

13. In May 1863 Fort Sumner and Fort Stanton had aggregate troop strengths of 112 and 100, respectively. See May 10, 1863, DNM Troop Returns, *OR,* Ser. 1, Vol. 15, 725 (TS63).

In April 1864 the troop numbers were 213 and 87 (TS64) and in May 1865, troops numbered 317 and 70 (TS65). See also Carleton to Thomas, Sept. 30, 1862, NA, RG 94, AGO, LR, M619, R123 (quotation). Kit Carson sent scouts down the Pecos through the end of 1862. Also, over the years there has been some confusion regarding El Paso, Texas, prior to the Civil War. During its formative period, El Paso had two names: El Paso and Franklin (after early pioneer Benjamin Franklin Coons). U.S. Postmaster General records for March 31, 1855, officially designate the name of the post office here as El Paso, Texas. There was no post office for Franklin in El Paso County. Additionally, in December 1851 letters to Texas governor Peter H. Bell and U.S. president Millard Fillmore, leading citizens of El Paso County addressed their correspondence as being from "El Paso, Texas." The first official plat of the community, drawn by Anson Mills and dated February 28, 1859, is titled "Town of El Paso." Lastly, the 1860 U.S. Census for El Paso County includes listings for both El Paso (encompassing 11 pages) and Franklin (2 pages). See U.S. Postmaster General, Record of Appointment of Post-masters, El Paso Co., Texas, NA, RG 28, M841, R123; Charles Hoppin and Simeon Hart to Peter Hansbrough Bell, Dec. 20, 1851, Peter Hansbrough Bell Papers, folder 3, box 301–18, TSLAC; Hugh Stephenson, Simeon Hart, et al., to Millard Fillmore, Dec. 20, 1851, ibid.; Anson Mills, *My Story* (Washington, D.C.: Byron Adams, 1918), 56–57; Anson Mills's Feb. 8, 1859, survey of Juan M. Ponce de Leon Survey 145 (El Paso County Abstract No. 52), El Paso County Surveyor Field Notes Book A, no. 1 (survey includes El Paso); 1860 U.S. Census, El Paso Co., Tex., RG 29, M653, R1293, 7–17 (El Paso), 18–19 (Franklin).

14. The Mexican civil war and the French intervention in Mexico are outside the scope of this present work. For more on this, see Thomas David Schoonover, *Dollars over Dominion: The Triumph of Liberalism in Mexican–United States Relations, 1861–1867* (Baton Rouge: Louisiana State University Press, 1978); Mark Wasserman, *Capitalists, Caciques, and Revolution: The Native Elite and Foreign Enterprise in Chihuahua, Mexico, 1854–1911* (Chapel Hill: University of North Carolina Press, 1984); Michael C. Meyer and William L. Sherman, *The Course of Mexican History* (New York: Oxford University Press, 1991); Matías Romero, *A Mexican View of America in the 1860s: A Foreign Diplomat Describes the Civil War and Reconstruction*, trans. and ed. by Thomas Schoonover (Cranbury, N.J.: Associated University Presses, 1991); Colin M. MacLachlan and William H. Beezley, *El Gran Pueblo: A History of Greater Mexico, Vol. 1, 1821–1911* (Englewood Cliffs, N.J.: Prentice-Hall, Inc., 1994).

15. Glen Sample Ely, "Gone from Texas and Trading with the Enemy: New Perspectives on Civil War West Texas," in *Lone Star Blue and Gray: Essays on Texas and the Civil War*, 2nd ed., eds. Ralph A. Wooster and Robert Wooster (Denton: Texas State Historical Association, 2015), 166.

16. James Bailey Blackshear, *Fort Bascom: Soldiers, Comancheros, and Indians in the Canadian River Valley* (Norman: University of Oklahoma Press, 2016), 9–11.

17. Ibid., 22–23, 33.

18. Ibid., 25.

19. Ibid., 33–34, 37, 42. During the 1850s the demand for stolen horses and cattle increased exponentially, tied to a reduction in bison and an increase in cattle ranching that was related to Anglo-American westward expansion. Comancheros could not remain viable trading partners without providing barter equal to the value of livestock flowing toward them from Texas.

20. Charles L. Kenner, *The Comanchero Frontier: A History of New Mexican–Plains Indian Relations* (Norman: University of Oklahoma Press, 1994), 191; Maj. John P. Hatch to Gen. Gordon Granger, Fort Concho, Tex., April 16, 1872, in Ernest Wallace, ed., *Ranald S. Mackenzie's Official Correspondence Relating to Texas, 1871–1873* (Lubbock: West Texas Museum Association, 1967), 50 (quotation three); Map #US-329, *1874 Map of Parts of Indian Territory Texas, and New Mexico, by Lt. L. H. Orleman*, RG 77, National Archives at College Park, MD (NACP); Map #575, *1864 Map of the Military Department of New Mexico, Drawn under the Direction of Brig. Gen. James H. Carleton by Capt. Allen Anderson*, W83–2, RG 77, NACP; Map #580, *1875 District of New Mexico Military Map by Lt. C. C. Morrison*, W197–1, RG 77, NACP; *1876 Map of the Country Scouted by Colonels McKenzie and Shafter, Capt. R. P. Wilson and Others in the Years 1874 & 1875 by Alex. L. Lucas*, RG 77, NACP, Southwest Collection, Texas Tech University; Map #1480a, *1878 Rand McNally Map of Texas*, TSLAC (quotations one and two); *1879 Rand McNally Map of New Mexico* and *1879 U.S. Department of the Interior General Land Office Map of the Territory of New Mexico*, both at David Rumsey Historical Map Collection, www.davidrumsey.com; My Topo Terrain Navigator Pro Software, Version 10.3, topographic maps and aerial photographs, Muleshoe, Tex.; Clovis, NM; and Santa Rosa, NM; Dolores Mosser, "Ancient Portal for Ancient People: The Portales River Valley Passageway to the South Plains"; Holle Humphries, "Yellow House Draw: Geographic Corridor"; and Austin Allison, "From Wagon Trails to Flight Paths: Drone Technology in Surveying Sites along the Yellow House Draw," all presentations made on April 7, 2017, at the West Texas Historical Association Conference in Lubbock. Southeast of Silver Lake, Yellow House Draw passes near modern Shallowater, Texas, in Lubbock County, before merging with Blackwater Draw at Mackenzie Park in present-day Lubbock. Yellow House and Blackwater Draws form the headwaters of the North Fork of the Double Mountain Fork of the Brazos River. Cañon del Rescate (Ransom Canyon) near Lubbock refers to the ransoming of Comanche captives. The prominent Comanche landmark, the 2,438-foot Double Mountains, is situated five miles east of the Kent-Stonewall county line. See *Texas Road and Recreation Atlas* (Santa Barbara, Calif.: Benchmark Maps, 2019), 48–49, 61–63; *DeLorme Atlas and Gazetteer of New Mexico* (Yarmouth, Maine: Delorme, 2016), 34–35, 43.

21. J. Evetts Haley, "The Comanchero Trade," *Southwestern Historical Quarterly* 38, no. 3 (January 1935), 161–62; Kenner, *Comanchero Frontier*, 181; *1875 Map of Portions of Texas, New Mexico & Indian Territory, including The Staked Plains (Llano Estacado) by Major G. L. Gillespie*, RG 77, NACP; *1890 Military Map of New Mexico, Texas, Indian Territory, Arkansas, Louisiana, and Mississippi*, Sheet 4, RG 77, NACP; Map #Q196, RG 77, NACP; *1875 District of New Mexico Military Map by Lt. C. C. Morrison*, W197–1, RG

77, NACP; *Map of the Country Scouted by Colonels McKenzie and Shafter, Capt. R. P. Wilson and Others in the Years 1874 & 1875 by Alex L. Lucas*, RG 77, NACP, Southwest Collection, Texas Tech University; Map #US-329, *1874 Map of Parts of Indian Territory Texas, and New Mexico, by Lt. L. H. Orleman*, RG 77, NACP; *DeLorme Atlas of New Mexico*, 35; *Texas Road Atlas*, 44–46, 50, 60–61, 71–72. Comanchero Apolonio Ortíz identified these New Mexico to Texas trade routes after being captured in March 1872 by Sgt. William Wilson and a detachment of Troop I, Fourth Cavalry, from Fort Concho, at the junction of Beals Creek and the Colorado River, south of present-day Colorado City, Texas. See Maj. John P. Hatch to AAG, Dept. of Texas, Fort Concho, Texas, March 30, 1872, Records of the War Department, U.S. Army, Reports of Scouts, Fort Concho, Texas, 1872–1881, Frank Temple Microfilm Roll No. 1, Fort Davis National Historic Site Archives; Thomas T. Smith, *The Old Army in Texas: A Research Guide to the U.S. Army in Nineteenth-Century Texas*, 2nd ed. (Austin: Texas State Historical Association, 2020), 172–73; Adjutant General's Office, *Chronological List of Actions, &c., With Indians, From January 1, 1866, to January, 1891* (Washington, D.C.: Adjutant General's Office, 1906), 26; Maj. John P. Hatch to AAG, Dept. of Texas, Fort Concho, Texas, June 16, 1872, in Wallace, *Mackenzie's Official Correspondence*, 47–51, 53, 69–71.

22. For more on these trails, see John Miller Morris, *El Llano Estacado: Exploration and Imagination on the High Plains of Texas and New Mexico, 1536–1860* (Austin: Texas State Historical Association, 1997), 84; Kenner, *Comanchero Frontier*, 96.

23. On plazas and placitas, see Richard L. Norstrand, *The Hispano Homeland* (Norman: University of Oklahoma Press, 1992), 35; Marc Simmons, *Spanish Government in New Mexico* (Albuquerque: University of New Mexico Press, 1968), 186n104. Charles Ilfeld was a Las Vegas merchant with business ties all over the Territory. See William J. Parish, *The Charles Ilfeld Company: A Study of the Rise and Decline of Mercantile Capitalism in New Mexico* (Cambridge, Mass: Harvard University Press, 1961), 55–60. The same was true of the Rosenthals. This history pays particular attention to Willie Rosenthal. Like all the merchants who will be mentioned, the Rosenthal brothers of Santa Fe were also cattle brokers. They sought and acquired several contracts to provide beef to the Indian reservations in New Mexico. See Henry J. Tobias, *A History of the Jews in New Mexico* (Albuquerque: University of New Mexico Press, 1990), 71. Felipe Delgado was from a family of merchants. He owned a store on the plaza in Santa Fe. He also served as the superintendent of Indian Affairs. See Susan Calafate Boyle, *Los Capitalistas: Hispano Merchants and the Santa Fe Trade* (Albuquerque: University of New Mexico Press, 2000), 97.

24. Kenner, *Comanchero Frontier*, 172.

25. Chaves sublet a license from Hatch's Ranch trader R. C. Vose in 1866. See "List of Traders," from Office of Superintendent of Indian Affairs, September 10, 1867, Records of the New Mexico Superintendency of Indian Affairs (RNMSIA), LR from the Commissioner of Indian Affairs (CIA), 1865–66, R7, NA; Watts held the bond for his son John Watts to trade with the Comanches in 1865. See pass for John Watts, Oct. 28,

1865, RNMSIA, LR 1864–65, R6. James M. Giddings applied for and received a pass to trade with the Comanches in the fall of 1865 for three months. See Giddings pass, Oct. 30, 1865, RNMSIA, LR 1864–65, R6.

26. Kenner, *Comanchero Frontier*, 78; Josiah Gregg, *Commerce of the Prairies* [1844], ed. Maurice Garland Fulton (Norman: University of Oklahoma Press, 1941), 257.

27. There is a robust historiography concerning the relationships that developed between the Plains Indians and New Mexicans during the Spanish and Mexican periods. Specific references to the use of carbohydrates in this trade include Pekka Hämäläinen, *The Comanche Empire* (New Haven, Conn.: Yale University Press, 2008), 38. Probably the best work on *genizaros* and the blending of these frontier cultures comes from James F. Brooks, *Captives and Cousins: Slavery, Kinship, and Community in the Southwest Borderland* (Chapel Hill: University of North Carolina Press, 2002), 33, 63–68, 288–89; Richard Norstrand *The Hispano Homeland* (Norman: University of Oklahoma Press, 1992), 62–64; Brian DeLay, *War of a Thousand Deserts: Indian Raids and the U.S.-Mexican War* (New Haven, Conn.: Yale University Press, 2008), 56–60; David J. Weber, *The Mexican Frontier, 1821–1846: The American Southwest Under Mexico* (Albuquerque: University of New Mexico Press, 1982), 214–15.

28. The bulk of documents are organized within the RNMSIA, 1849–80, in the National Archives. Within these records are fourteen rolls: Letters Received from the Commissioner of Indian Affairs, Letters Received from the Abiquiu and Cimarron Agencies, and Letters Received from Headquarters, District of New Mexico (U.S. Army). The documents found within these rolls detail the applications and licenses that make up the legal Comanchero trade from 1854 to 1871. The bulk of the passes are found in rolls 5, 6 and 7, but approvals to trade with a variety of Southern Plains Indians can be found in some of the first documents. Most of the material in these files involve correspondence between Indian agents, the superintendent, and the commissioner of Indian Affairs in Washington, D.C.

29. In an 1867 report to Washington, new superintendent Norton informed Commissioner N. G. Taylor that in his opinion General Carleton was as guilty of giving out too many Comanchero passes as anyone else. See A. B. Norton, Superintendent of Indian Affairs (SIA), New Mexico, to N. G. Taylor, Commissioner of Indian Affairs (CIA), Washington City, D.C. *Report of the Secretary of the Interior, 1867*, 194–95. Pueblo Indian agent John Henderson approved a Comanchero pass for José Valdez, Jan. 9, 1867, RNMSIA, LR 1865–66, R7.

30. Anastacio Sandoval was a man of some influence. See Phillip B. González, *Política: Nuevomexicanos and American Political Incorporation, 1821–1910* (Lincoln: University of Nebraska Press, 2016), 508, 614, 694; Jerry D. Thompson, *Civil War History of New Mexico Volunteers and Militia* (Albuquerque: University of New Mexico Press, 2017), 57, 196. On the actual passes, see RNMSIA, LR 1864–65, R6. Sandoval's license was signed by Steck on Feb. 27, 1865, ibid.; William P. Dole to Felipe Delgado, April 14, 1865, ibid.; Sandoval license signed by Felipe Delgado, Sept. 13, 1865, ibid.

31. Sandoval license signed by Delgado, Sept. 13, 1865, RNMSIA, LR 1864–65, R6.

32. The reference to a cultural shatter zone comes from Benjamin Nathans's excellent history on the Jews in Soviet Poland, *Beyond the Pale: The Jewish Encounter with Late Imperial Russia* (Berkeley: University of California Press, 2002), 380.

Chapter 1

1. Bryan to West, Feb. 26, 1863, NA, RG 393, Pt. 3, District of Arizona (DA), ULR, 1862–70, ARC Identifier 1715290, MLR A1-3, 20

2. Ibid. (quotations one and two).

3. Ibid. (quotations one through five). In May 1863 the post at Las Cruces, New Mexico (adjacent to Mesilla), reported an aggregate strength of 97 troops (TS63). In April 1864 the number increased to 195 (TS64), and in May 1865 the total was 106 (TS65). For the posts at Las Cruces and Mesilla, see 1864 Carleton Map.

4. West to Cutler, Feb. 27, 1863, *OR*, Ser. 1, Vol. 50, Pt. 2, 329–30; Inspection Report of Franklin, Tex., by Assistant Inspector General Col. N. H. Davis, Jan. 8 to Feb. 1, 1864, NA, RG 393, Pt. 1, NM, Entry 3215, LR, Staff Officers 1856–66, Box 1 (quotations one and two). Davis listed the garrison's aggregate strength for February 1864 at 286 men. In a January 13, 1865, follow up appended to Davis's report, General Carleton noted that the post's new commander "has been admonished with reference to the matter of lewd women being in and about the men's quarters."

5. Bennett to McMullen, Special Orders No. 20, April 7, 1863, NA, RG 393, Pt. 5, Fort Bliss, Texas, entry 18, General Orders 1863–64, Box 9 (quotation). For examples of Carleton's martial law decrees, see James H. Carleton Proclamation Assuming Control over Arizona as its Military Governor, June 8, 1862, and General Orders No. 15, Aug. 14, 1862, RG 393, Headquarters, NM, ULR, June–Sept. 1862.

6. Major Commanding Fort Bliss to Captain Stombs, Jan. 11, 1865, and Jan. 29, 1865 (quotation), NA, RG 393, Pt. 5, Fort Bliss and Franklin, Tex., Entry 2, LS 1865, Vol. 1; Report of Persons and Articles Employed and Hired, May 1865, NA, RG 393, Pt. 3, Fort Bliss and Franklin, Texas, Entry 510, Quartermaster Reports and Returns 1865; Maj. William McMullen to J. R. West, San Elizario, Texas, Dec. 21, 1862, NA, RG 393, Pt. 3, DA, ULR 1862–70.

7. See Texas refugee discussion in Carleton to Bowie, July 6, 1864, Carleton to Thomas, Aug. 6, 1864, Carleton to Fort Marcy, Aug. 7, 1864, all from NA, RG 393, LS, DNM, M1072, R3. Spy question raised in Kimmey to Carleton, Dec. 12, 1863, LR, DNM, Box K 28, 1864; McCulloch to Turner, March 15, 1864, *OR*, Ser. 1, Vol. 34, Pt. 2, 1045. For more on the westward wartime exodus from Texas, see Ely, *Where the West Begins*, 58–61.

8. Smith to Commanding Officer at Franklin, Texas, General Orders No. 9, June 21, 1864, NA, RG 393, Pt. 5, Fort Bliss, Texas, Entry 18, General Orders 1863–64, Box 9 (quotation). One such military tribunal occurred on October 22, 1864, in Santa Fe (see NA, RG 393, DNM, Pt. 1, Entry 3161, Misc. LR 1863–65).

9. West to Cutler, Feb. 27, 1863, *OR*, Ser. 1, Vol. 50, Pt. 2, 330 (quotation). In May 1863 aggregate troop strength at Hart's Mill, Texas, was 228 (TS63). By April 1864 the num-

ber of troops at Franklin, Texas (the new district headquarters, replacing Hart's Mill), increased to 372 (TS64), but by May 1865, had declined to 85 (TS65). Total Department of New Mexico (including District of Arizona) aggregate strength for May 1863 was 2,866 (TS63); in April 1864 it was 3,619 (TS64); and in May 1865 the number was 2,313 (TS65). This decline was the result of expired enlistments combined with a dearth of reenlistments and reinforcements. General Carleton's pleas to Union general-in-chief Henry Halleck for more troops in the second half of 1864 and again in early 1865 were largely unpersuasive.

10. W. W. Mills, *Forty Years at El Paso: 1858–1898*, ed. Rex Strickland (El Paso: Carl Hertzog, 1962), 83, 134, 179–81; Hunt, *James Henry Carleton*, 271–72. In another example of confiscation, in February 1865 the army collected $164 ($5,248 today) in rent on twenty-seven rooms formerly owned by Henry and John Gillett, Braxton Gillock, and Benjamin Dowell. See Statement of Rent Collected from Confiscated Property at Franklin, Texas, February 1865, NA, RG 393, Pt. 3, Fort Bliss and Franklin, Texas, Entry 510, Quartermaster Reports and Returns 1865. Other rebel properties seized included those belonging to J. F. Crosby, James Wiley Magoffin, Joseph Nangle, and A. B. O'Bannon. See Eugene O. Porter, ed., "Letters Home: W. W. Mills Writes to His Family," Pt. 3, *Password* 17, no. 3 (Fall 1972), 120. The Union Army also confiscated John McCarty's home in San Elizario, Texas, which Capt. A. H. French used for his cavalry unit. U.S. Marshal Abraham Cutler, of the Third Judicial District of New Mexico, offered McCarty's land for sale in December 1865. See El Paso County Deed Records, Dec. 19, 1865.

11. General Carleton expressed little sympathy for El Paso County secessionist Hugh Stephenson or his son-in-law Frederick A. Percy, "a Southern sympathizer" and "our enemy," over the confiscation of their property at Concordia, Texas. See Carleton to West, May 29, 1863, NA, RG 393, Pt. 3, DA, ULR 1862–70, ARC Identifier 1715290, MLR A1-3, 20 (endnote quotations one and two). District of Arizona commander Gen. Joseph R. West participated in land seizures and confiscations in the Rio Grande Valley, using his authority to expand powers granted under District General Orders No. 1. See West to Cutler, Jan. 4, 1863, NA, RG 393, Pt. 1, DNM, Entry 3161, Misc. LR 1863–66, Box 1. U.S. authorities subsequently indicted Marshal Cutler, who directed the confiscations, on embezzlement charges, but in October 1867 a jury voted not to convict him. Hunt, *James Henry Carleton*, 271–72.

12. Report of Persons and Articles Employed and Hired, Jan. 1865, NA, RG 393, Pt. 3, Fort Bliss and Franklin, Texas, Entry 510, Quartermaster Reports and Returns 1865; Mills, *Forty Years*, 83, 134–35; Porter, "Letters Home: Mills," Pt. 3, 120–27. For his duties as customs collector, Mills received $5 per day. Another El Paso County resident, A. B. Rohman, was also active in leasing buildings to the federal army during this period. Monthly fees for each building typically ranged from six to forty dollars ($192 to $1,280 in today's dollars). In February 1865 Mills collected $234.93 in rents ($7,517.76 today). See Abstract of Expenditures, Feb. 1865, NA, RG 393, Pt. 3, Fort Bliss and Franklin, Texas, entry 510, Quartermaster Reports and Returns 1865. For historical currency conversion, see Measuring Worth, "Purchasing Power of Money in the United

States from 1774 to 2007," http://www. measuringworth.com/ppowerus/# (accessed Nov. 29, 2020). The site computes $1 in 1860 as worth approximately $32 in 2020.

13. Special Orders No. 50, Sept. 25, 1862, NA, RG 393, Pt. 5, Fort Bliss, Texas, Entry 18, General Orders 1862–64, Box 9 (passports); Howe to Chapin, Aug. 7, 1862, NA, RG 393, Southern Dept. of New Mexico (SDNM), Entry 734, LS, Vol. 118/300 (quotation two); ibid., Howe to Carleton, Aug. 9, 1862 (quotations one, three, four, and endnote quotation); Mills, *Forty Years*, 83, 134–35. The departmental quarantine on travel was somewhat porous. On August 7 Colonel Howe reported that a large party "has passed down the Jornada [del Muerto] & professing at least to be attached to the beef contractor."

14. Eugene O. Porter, "Letters Home," Pt. 4, *Password* 17, no. 4 (Winter 1972): 182, 185–87. By March 1865 Mills had expanded into new ventures and was now supplying tallow to the federal post at Franklin. See Abstract of Purchases Paid at Franklin, Texas, March 1865, NA, RG 393, part 3, Fort Bliss and Franklin, Tex., entry 510, Quartermaster Reports and Returns 1865.

15. Abstract of Purchases Paid at Franklin, Texas, March 1865, NA, RG 393, part 3, Fort Bliss and Franklin, Tex., entry 510, Quartermaster Reports and Returns 1865. In March 1865 Eugene von Patten furnished 14,000 pounds of corn to the army at Franklin for $1,200 ($38,400). Webb and Cuniffe supplied 10,445 pounds of bran for $365.57 ($11,698.24). Price Cooper delivered 718 feet of tallow, 1,690 pounds of corn, and 22,400 pounds of hay for a total of $526.70 ($16,854.40). Three months earlier, Cooper signed a 600-ton hay contract for the post at Franklin, at $27.50 per ton, or $16,500 ($528,000). See U.S. House, *Contracts Made*, 124. Regarding Price Cooper's contracts, in December 1862 residents of Franklin voiced "much complaint" after Cooper neglected to pay his hay cutters, the effect of which "greatly injured the credit of the Government with the working class," as "they cannot distinguish the difference between the Govt. and a contractor." See McMullen to West, Dec. 6, 1862, NA, RG 393, Pt. 3, DA, ULR (endnote quotations). See also Porter, "Letters Home," Pt. 4, 188; Mills, *Forty Years*, 177. Early in the war Simeon Hart supplied Confederate troops at Fort Bliss. Later he became a major and quartermaster for the Confederate Army in Texas. See Simeon Hart Citizens File, NA, RG 109, M346.

16. Carleton to Thomas, Feb. 28, 1864, NA, RG 94, AGO, LR, M619, R283 (quotation).

17. Davis to Carleton, Jan. 29, 1864, ibid.

18. Ibid. (quotations one and three); Toole to McFerran, April 3, 1865, NA, RG 393, Pt. 3, Fort Bliss and Franklin, Texas, Entry 510, Quartermaster Reports and Returns 1865 (quotation two).

19. 1860 U.S. Census, El Paso County, Texas, NA, M653, R1293; "Itinerary," Fergusson to Bennett, Feb. 18, 1863, NA, RG 393, Pt. 1, DNM, Entry 3183, Misc. Records 1850–66, Box 1.

20. Porter, "Letters Home" Pt. 3, 121, 125; Anson Mills to James Speed, St. Louis, Mo., Sept. 6, 1865, Simeon Hart Pardon File, Case Files of Applications for Former Confederates for Presidential Pardons, 1865–67, NA, RG 94, M1003, R53; Mills to McMullen, Jan. 1, 1863, NA, RG 393, Pt. 3, DA, ULR (quotation). In 1870 a jury ordered Simeon Hart

to pay W. W. Mills $50,000 ($1.6 million today) for his wrongful kidnapping and imprisonment of Mills in July and August 1861. See El Paso County District Court Records, Nov. 9, 1870.

21. McMullen to West, Franklin, Texas, Dec. 1, 1862; McMullen to West, San Elizario, Texas, Dec. 6, 1862; McMullen to Bennett, Mesilla, New Mexico, Jan. 16, 1863 (quotations), NA, RG 393, Pt. 3, DA, ULR; Scott C. Comar, "The Tigua Indians of Ysleta Del Sur: A Borderlands Community" (PhD diss., University of Texas at El Paso, 2015), 220–21.

22. Ralph P. Bieber, ed., *Exploring Southwestern Trails, 1846–1854* (Glendale, Calif.: Arthur H. Clark, 1938), 311; 1860 U.S. Census, El Paso County, Texas, NA, M653, R1293, 3; Special Orders No. 1, Jan. 4, 1862, NA, RG 109, Misc. Special Orders, Adjutant General of Texas, 1862–65, Ch. 7, Vol. 277, 28; Henry Skillman Citizens File, NA, RG 109, M346, Confederate Papers Relating to Citizens or Business Firms, 1861–65. For delivering 148 tons of hay, Skillman received $3,520 in Confederate money. For his four trips as a military courier to New Mexico, Skillman collected $250. From 1851 to 1854, Skillman also worked as a mail contractor in Texas and New Mexico.

23. Henry Skillman, Report of Scout to El Paso, contained in Gray to Dickinson, Dec. 27, 1862, Henry Skillman Citizens File, NA, RG 109, M346 (cited hereafter as Skillman Report) (quotations).

24. Ibid. The secondary road Skillman that took from Leon Holes, Texas, to Presidio del Norte was part of the famous freighting trail that ran from Chihuahua, Mexico, to San Antonio and Indianola, Texas. Presidio County land surveys from the 1850s list Skillman as a chain carrier on a number of surveys ranging from Fort Davis to Spencer's Ranch.

25. Case of A. F. Wulff, *OR*, Ser. 2, Vol. 2, 1526–30; West to Fergusson, Jan. 3, 1863, *OR*, Ser. 1, Vol. 15, 635–36; Skillman Report; Porter, "Letters Home," Pt. 3, 128. In addition to Joe Leaton, Union major William McMullen identified a number of others in Skillman's spy company, including Thomas Miller, a Mr. McKee, Alfred Fry, Andrew and Ashford McClung, and a former stage driver named Ray (possibly Thomas Rife). See McMullen to West, Dec. 6, 1862, Rigg to West, Nov. 11, 1862, and McMullen to Bennett, Jan. 16, 1863, NA, RG 393, Pt. 3, DA, ULR. The District of Arizona reports cited in this endnote estimated the size of the rebel exile community in El Paso del Norte, Mexico, at between forty and eighty persons.

26. Skillman Report; Mills, *Forty Years*, 191; 1860 U.S. Census, El Paso County, Tex., NA, M653, R1293, 3, 9; 1860 U.S. Census, New Mexico Territory, M653, R712, 3, 61. Hugh Stephenson leased Fort Fillmore to the Confederate army and furnished supplies to General Sibley at Fort Bliss during the Confederate campaign in New Mexico. See Hugh Stephenson Citizens File, NA, RG 109, M346.

27. Skillman Report (quotation). Aggregate troop strength for the Department of New Mexico in May 1863 was 2,866 men. This included troops stationed in Arizona, New Mexico, and Texas (TS63). Generals Carleton and West developed contingency plans in case of a Confederate invasion by superior forces, which included destroying local food supplies and retreating westward. These fallback measures were to be utilized only as a last resort and were never implemented.

28. French to West, San Elizario, Tex., Dec. 3, 1862, NA, RG 393, Pt. 3, DA, ULR (quotation).

29. Porter, "Letters Home" Pt. 3, 128; Porter, "Letters Home," Pt. 4, 177; McMullen to West, Dec. 1, 1862, and McMullen to West, Dec. 6, 1862, NA, RG 393, Pt. 3, DA, ULR; West to Cutler, Nov. 9, 1862, NA, RG 393, Pt. 1, DNM, Entry 3161, Misc. LR 1863–66, Box 1 (quotation).

30. West to McMullen, Dec. 25, 1862 (quotations one and two), and McMullen to West, Dec. 6, 1862 (quotations three and four), NA, RG 393, Pt. 3, DA, ULR.

31. McMullen to West, Dec. 6, 1862, NA, RG 393, Pt. 3, DA, ULR (quotation one); Skillman Report, (quotation two); West to Fergusson, Jan. 3, 1863, *OR*, Ser. 1, Vol. 15, 635 (quotation three). Skillman omitted mention of this kidnapping attempt in his official report, noting that nothing of interest occurred during his return trip.

32. 1860 U.S. Census, El Paso County, Tex., NA, M653, R1293, 73; Jefferson Morgenthaler, *The River Has Never Divided Us: A Border History of La Junta de los Rios* (Austin: University of Texas Press, 2004), 115–17.

33. 1870 U.S. Census, Presidio County, Tex., NA, M593, R1601, 2; Morgenthaler, *The River Has Never Divided Us*, 115, 116 (quotation); Fergusson to West, Feb. 13, 1863, *OR*, Ser. 1, Vol. 15, 685 (farmland).

34. 1860 U.S. Census, El Paso County, Tex., NA, M653, R1293, 75; Creel to Carleton, Nov. 10, 1864, NA, RG 393, DNM, LR, M1120, R23 (quotations).

35. Willis to McMullen, Dec. 20, 1862 (quotation), McMullen to West, Dec. 25, 1862, NA, RG 393, Pt. 3, DA, ULR. McMullen identified these rebel agents as Simón and Bernardo Olguín, Joe Leaton, Ben Dowell, John Gillett, a Mr. Beckwith, Dr. Boyd, and a Mr. Rogers. Tigua Indian Simon Olguín served as a scout for the U.S. Army before the Civil War, for the rebels during the conflict, and once again, for the army following the Civil War. This noted Pueblo frontiersman was killed by Apaches on June 11, 1880, at Vieja Pass near present-day Valentine, Texas. See Smith, *Old Army in Texas*, 182.

36. McMullen to West, Dec. 21, 1862, Uranga to McMullen, Dec. 24, 1862, McMullen to West, Dec. 25, 1862, and McMullen to Bennett, Jan. 16, 1863 (endnote quotation), NA, RG 393, Pt. 3, DA, ULR; West to Cutler, Mesilla, NM, Nov. 9, 1862, RG 393, DNM, Misc. LR 1863–66. The rebel Texans were planning to travel along the river from El Paso to Guadalupe or San Ygnacio, Mexico, but became alarmed and instead took the road to Chihuahua. McMullen's only regret was that "I permitted the scoundrels to escape."

37. McMullen to Uranga, Dec. 25, 1862 (quotations one and two), McMullen to West, Dec. 25, 1862, and McMullen to Bennett, Jan. 16, 1863, NA, RG 393, Pt. 3, DA, ULR.

38. Uranga to McMullen, Dec. 29, 1862 (quotations), ibid.

Chapter 2

1. West to Cutler, Mesilla, NM, Dec. 9, 1862, *OR*, Ser. 1, Vol. 50, Pt. 2, 245 (quotation); "Memorandum of verbal instructions given to Maj. David Fergusson," and West to Fergusson, Jan. 3, 1863, *OR*, Ser. 1, Vol. 15, 635–36; Carleton to Thomas, Feb. 23, 1863,

ibid., 681–82; Fergusson to West, Feb. 13, 1863, ibid., 682–86; Fergusson to U.S. Consul, Jan. 27, 1863, ibid., 686; Carleton to Terrazas, Feb. 20, 1863, ibid., 687; Fergusson to West, Feb. 13, 1863, ibid., 687–88; "Trip Itinerary," Fergusson to Bennett, Feb. 18, 1863, NA, RG 393, Pt.1, NM, entry 3183, Misc. Records, 1850–66, Box 1. This last item cited is an unpublished journal chronicling Fergusson's trip, which accompanied his published report and is important as it contains many firsthand observations of everyday life in Mexico, Texas, and New Mexico during the Civil War.

2. Carleton to Thomas, Feb. 23, 1863, *OR*, Ser. 1, Vol. 15, 681–82; Fergusson to West, Feb. 13, 1863, ibid., 682–86; Fergusson to U.S. Consul, Jan. 27, 1863, ibid., 686; Carleton to Terrazas, Feb. 20, 1863, ibid., 687; Fergusson to West, Feb. 13, 1863, ibid., 687–88.

3. Fergusson to West, Feb. 13, 1863, *OR*, Ser. 1, Vol. 15, 682; Creel to Carleton, Nov. 10, 1864, NA, RG 393, NM, LR, M1120, R23; Creel to Carleton, May 4, 1863, *OR*, Ser. 1, Vol. 50, Pt.2, 426; Hagelsieb to Creel, Presidio del Norte, Mexico, Oct. 2, 1863, RG 393, DNM Headquarters, ULR, M1120, R29; *Handbook of Texas Online* (hereafter *HTO*), s.v. "Milton Faver," by Julia Cauble Smith, https://tshaonline.org/handbook/online/articles/ffa16 (accessed Nov. 13, 2020); Carleton to West, Santa Fe, Dec. 16, 1862, NA, RG 393, Pt. 3, DA, ULR, 1862–70 (endnote quotations). In this December 16 letter, Carleton instructed West to give Fergusson the cipher code to use when needed. Next Carleton, using this code, told West to be on his guard against "pme Sipubo" and against "Bucvsh."

4. Creel to Commanding Officer at Mesilla, March 31, 1863, *OR*, Ser. 1, Vol. 50, Pt. 2, 377; Creel to Carleton, May 3, 1863, ibid., 425–26; Creel to Carleton, May 4, 1863, ibid., 426; Jenkins to West, May 2, 1863, NA, RG 94, AGO, LR, M619, R195.

5. Jan. and Feb. 1864 Company Muster Roll, March 1865 Regimental Return (detached service records); and Skillman to Ford, Feb. 4, 1864 (quotations one and two); Tom Rife, Confederate Compiled Service Record, NA, RG 109, M331. For more on Tom Rife, see Glen Sample Ely, *The Texas Frontier and the Butterfield Overland Mail, 1858–1861* (Norman: University of Oklahoma Press, 2016), 311.

6. Terrazas to Carleton, April 11, 1863, NA, RG 94, AGO, LR, M619, R195; West to Cutler, Hart's Mill, Texas, May 12, 1863, NA, RG 393, Pt. 3, DA, LS, Sept. 1862–Aug. 1869 (quotations).

7. Carleton to Thomas, May 10, 1863 NA, RG 393, Pt. 3, DA, LS, Sept. 1862–Aug. 1869 (quotation).

8. Magruder to Cooper, Jan. 8, 1863, NA, RG 109, District of Texas, New Mexico, and Arizona (TNMA), LS, Ch. 2, Vol. 132 (quotations); Walter Earl Pittman, *Rebels in the Rockies: Confederate Irregulars in the Western Territories* (Jefferson, NC: McFarland & Company, 2014), 169–70.

9. Capt. John R. Pulliam, Company B, Hardeman's Regiment, to Brig. Gen. S. B. Maxey, Feb. 2, 1864, Camp Garland, Indian Territory, *OR*, Ser. 1, Vol. 34, Pt. 2, 960–61; Lt. E. H. Ruffner's *1877 Department of the Missouri Map*, Sheet 2, NACP; Pittman, *Rebels in the Rockies*, 175. Camp Garland was located on Choctaw Chief Samuel Garland's plantation in McCurtain County, in the southeast corner of Indian Territory (near present-day Tom, Oklahoma). Chief Garland, who was principal chief of the Choctaw Nation from

1862 to 1864, owned numerous slaves, grew cotton, and operated a trading post on his plantation, located on the Doaksville Road. See Find a Grave Online, s.v. "Chief Samuel Garland," https://www.findagrave.com/memorial/32236979/samuel-garland (accessed Oct. 30, 2019); Choctaw Nation Online, s.v. "Samuel Garland," https://www.choctawnation.com/chief/1862-samuel-garland (accessed Oct. 30, 2019).

10. Magruder to Cooper, Jan. 8, 1863, NA, RG 109, TNMA, LS, Ch. 2, Vol. 132 (quotations one and two); Kirby Smith to Magruder, April 5, 1863, NA, RG 109, Dept. of the Trans-Mississippi, LS, March 1863–Jan. 1864, Ch. 2, Vol. 70 (quotation three).

11. Banks to Carleton, Nov. 5, 1863, *OR*, Ser. 1, Vol. 26, Pt. 1, 788; Magruder to Ford, Jan. 24, 1864, NA, RG 109, TNMA, LS, Ch. 2, Vol. 126.

12. Halleck to Carleton, Feb. 6, 1864, *OR*, Ser. 1, Vol. 34, Pt. 2, 256; Carleton to Halleck, March 20, 1864, ibid., 671–72; Halleck to Carleton, April 11, 1864, ibid., Pt. 3, 137–39.

13. McMullen to West, San Elizario, Tex., Dec. 6, 1863; McMullen to Bennett, Mesilla, NM, Jan. 16, 1863 (quotation), NA, RG 393, Pt. 3, DA, ULR, 1862–70. McMullen endeavored to seize the Olguín brothers in Mexico and interrogate them, but the prefect of El Paso del Norte, Mexico, demanded proof of the Olguíns' guilt before delivering them up to McMullen.

14. Carleton to Thomas, Sept. 30, 1862, NA, RG 94, AGO, LR, M619, R123; Carleton to Thomas, Dec. 20, 1862, ibid.; West to McFerran, May 8, 1863, ibid., Box N131, 1863; Special Orders No. 26, May 8, 1863, ibid.; Pishon to Cutler, Mesilla, NM Jan. 5, 1863, "Journal of March from November 16, 1862, to December 31, 1862, Capt. Nathanial J. Pishon, 1st Cavalry, California Volunteers," NA, RG 393, DNM, Box 1, #3165, LR from Post Commanders 1860–63, DNM Misc. LR 1863–66. For more on Horsehead Crossing, see Ely, *The Texas Frontier*, 200–205, 216–18, 388–89.

15. West to Pishon, Mesilla, NM, Nov. 29, 1862; West to Willis, Mesilla, NM, Nov. 29, 1862 (quotation one); West to Daily, Mesilla, New Mexico, Nov. 29, 1862 (quotations two and three); West to McFerran, Mesilla, NM, Nov. 29, 1862, all in NA, RG 393, Pt. 3, DA, LS 1862–66. Daily's company also included "three Mexicans of Garcia's party." This may refer to Gregorio García or Miguel García, residents of San Elizario, Texas, who occasionally served as Union scouts. See Pishon to West, Camp Ojo del Martin, Tex., Dec. 22, 1862, RG 393, Pt. 3, DA, ULR 1862–70 (endnote quotation).

16. West to Cutler, Mesilla, NM, Nov. 30, 1862, *OR*, Ser. 1, Vol. 15, 605–6; West to Cutler, Mesilla, NM, Dec. 28, 1862, *OR*, Ser. 1, Vol. 50, Pt. 2, 266; West to Carson, Mesilla, NM, Jan. 6, 1863, ibid., 278; Richard H. Orton, *Records of the California Men in the War of the Rebellion, 1861 to 1867* (Sacramento, Calif.: J. D. Young, 1890), 331, 359. Col. Kit Carson at Fort Stanton kept Captains Abreu and Pfeiffer scouting down the Pecos through the end of December 1862. See Carson to Carleton, Dec. 14, 1862, NA RG 94, AGO, LR, N447 1862. Before the war Bradford Daily drove stagecoaches with Henry Skillman. Skillman did not mention this December 1862 Horsehead Crossing encounter to his superiors, but occasionally he omitted details from his official reports, and he was in the area at this time. Another possibility is that these rebels on the Pecos were secessionist exiles from El Paso County, led by Tigua Indian scouts Simón and Bernardo Olguín. "On one occasion Tigua scouts Simón and Bernardo

Olguín observed Union troop movements for [exile Ben] Dowell," Scott Comar says, "on another, two Tiguas guided Dowell and other Confederate sympathizers to San Antonio." See Comar, "Tigua Indians of Ysleta Del Sur," 221 (endnote quotations); Mills, *Forty Years at El Paso*, 177; Dan L. Thrapp, *Encyclopedia of Frontier Biography* (Lincoln: University of Nebraska Press, 1991), 1:368. Capt. W. L. Parvin participated in the expedition as a private citizen, having resigned from Company F on Nov. 26, 1862. Brad Daily and his party returned to Mesilla from their scout on December 26, 1862.

17. West to Cutler, Dec. 28, 1862, *OR*, Ser. 1, Vol. 50, Pt. 2, 266 (quotations one and two); West to Carson, Jan. 6, 1863, ibid. (quotation three).
18. Headquarters, Fort Stanton, NM, Special Orders No. 5, Jan. 15, 1863, NA, RG 393, Pt. 1, Unregistered Letters, DNM; Brady to Post Adjutant, Fort Stanton, NM, Feb. 19, 1863, NA, RG 393, Fort Stanton, LR; General J. R. West, Endorsement No. 32, March 4, 1863, NA, RG 393, Pt. 3, Entry 14, DA, Endorsements (quotation).
19. West to Cutler, Mesilla, NM, Nov. 23, 1862, NA, RG 393, DNM, Pt. 1, Entry 3161, Letters and Routine Reports Received and Misc. LR 1863–66 (quotation); William H. Emory, *Report on the United States and Mexican Boundary Survey*, Vol. 1 (Washington, D.C.: Cornelius Wendell, 1857), 88–89; *Charles W. Pressler's 1867 Traveller's Map of the State of Texas*, GLO.
20. Edmund P. Turner, San Antonio, Tex., April 30, 1863, *OR*, Ser. 1, Vol. 15, 1064; Hubbell to Baird, San Antonio, Tex., April 28, 1863, ibid., 1065; Burgess to Scurry, Presidio del Norte, March 17, 1863, ibid.
21. West to McFerran, Hart's Mill, Tex., May 2, 1863, NA, RG 393, Pt. 3, LS, DA, Sept. 1862–Aug. 1869; West to Creel, Hart's Mill, Tex., May 26, 1863, *OR*, Ser. 1, Vol. 50, Pt. 2, 458 (quotation).
22. Creel to Carleton, Chihuahua, Mexico, March 10, 1863, NA, RG 393, Pt. 3, DA, ULR 1862–70 (quotation).
23. Carleton to West, Santa Fe, NM, May 25, 1863, NA, RG 393, Pt. 3, DA, ULR 1862–70.
24. West to McFerran, Hart's Mill, Tex., May 2, 1863, NA, RG 393, Pt. 3, LS, DA, Sept. 1862–Aug. 1869; Smith to Cutler, April 17, 1863; Smith to Cutler, May 11, 1863; Smith to Cutler, May 15, 1863; Abreu to Henderson, June 11, 1863; Smith to Cutler, July 21, 1863 (quotation two); Abreu to Henderson, July 23, 1863 (quotations one, three, and four); Smith to Cutler, July 24, 1863; Latimer to Henderson, July 28, 1863, all in NA, RG 393, Pt. 5, Fort Stanton, NM, Entry 2, LS 1863–65. Major Smith reported that all of Marques's men stated the attacking Indians were Apaches: specifically, two-hundred warriors and their families. During the engagement, Marques lost all of his animals (sixteen horses and seventeen mules). Following the skirmish on the Hondo, Captains F. P. Abreu and Emil Fritz, with a detachment of men from the First New Mexico Volunteers and First Cavalry, California Volunteers, pursued the Apaches for forty-five miles and attacked them in camp on July 22, recovering two horses and six mules. The Indians managed to escape and when last seen were headed towards the Capitan Mountains.
25. Latimer to Henderson, July 28, 1863, NA, RG 393, Pt. 5, Fort Stanton, NM, Entry 2, LS 1863–65 (quotation one); Smith to Cutler, July 30, 1863, ibid. (quotation two).

26. Smith to Cutler, July 30, 1863, ibid. (quotation); Smith to Cutler, Cavalry Inspection Report, Oct. 31, 1863, ibid. (October scout on Pecos).

27. Hagelsieb to Creel, Presidio del Norte, Mexico, Oct. 2, 1863, RG 393, DNM Headquarters, ULR, M1120, R29; Dickinson to Turner, Nov. 23, 1863, in Andrew G. Dickinson Confederate Compiled Service Record, NA, RG 109, M331.

28. Dickinson to Turner, Nov. 23, 1863; Miller to Angerstein, Dec. 13, 1863 (quotations one and two); Angerstein to West, Dec. 15, 1863, all in NA, RG 94, AGO, LR, M619, R283; Cuniffe to Davis, Dec. 30, 1863, NA, RG 94, AGO, LR, Box N87, 1864; Creel to West, Chihuahua, Mexico, Sept. 1, 1863, RG 393, Pt. 3, DA, ULR 1862–70.

29. Ford to Pyron, Jan. 20, 1864, Rip Ford Papers, UDC Collection, Haley Memorial Library (hereafter cited as RFP), TCM94.1.0784; Ford to Turner, Jan. 22, 1864, *OR*, Ser. 1, Vol. 53, 952–53; Magruder to Ford, Jan. 24, 1864, NA, RG 109, TNMA, Ch. 2, Vol. 126, LS (quotation).

30. Magruder to Ford, Jan. 24, 1864, NA, RG 109, TNMA, Ch. 2, Vol. 126, LS. State cartographer A. R. Roessler produced a series of maps from Skillman's scout entitled *Best Route for the Movement of Troops from San Antonio to El Paso* [sic] *-Texas, Being the One Travelled by the State Geological Corps of Texas in 1860 and by Henry Skillman's Party in March 1864*. See Plats 1004 B and 1004 J, Map Collection, Texas State Library and Archives Commission (TSLAC). The accompanying narrative journal by Roessler is in Folder T1-10-1 at the same archives. Only two of three plat maps Roessler describes are in the state archives. Plat #2 (1004 B) ends at Fort Davis, Texas. It may be that Skillman never had time to complete his data for the last map to El Paso, hence only the two surviving West Texas plats in the state archives.

31. Magruder to Ford, Jan. 24, 1864, NA, RG 109, TNMA, LS, Ch. 2, Vol. 126 (quotation one); Magruder to Ford, Feb. 7, 1864, ibid. (quotation two). By March 1864 Albert H. French had been promoted to captain, First Cavalry, California Volunteers.

32. Magruder to Kirby Smith, Jan. 29, 1864, NA, RG 109, TNMA, LS, Ch. 2, Vol. 126; Kirby Smith to Chief of Texas Cotton Bureau, Jan. 29, 1864, ibid. (quotation); Merritt to Ford, Feb. 11, 1864, and Ford to Duff, Feb. 9, 1864, both in RFP, TCM94.1.0443 (outfitting Skillman).

33. Skillman spy company prisoners Jarvis Hubbell, Peter Allen, John Dowling, and Winfield Scott Garner statements, in Carleton to Hoffman, June 27, 1864, NA, RG 249, Office of the Commissary General of Prisoners, LR, 1864, C729 (hereafter cited as CGP); French Report; French to Carleton, May 5, 1864, NA, RG 393, DNM, LR, M1120, R23 (hereafter FC). Garner appears in various documents from 1854 to 1864 as William "Clown" Garner, George "Clown" Garner, and Winfield Scott Garner. Garner drove stagecoaches before the war and was also a participant in James Wiley Magoffin's San Andreas salt war in 1854 with local Hispanics. See Ely, *The Texas Frontier*, 319.

34. Magruder to Ford, Jan. 29, 1864, NA, RG 109, TNMA, LS, Ch. 2, Vol. 126 (quotation); Ford to Alexander, Jan. 24, 1864, RFP, TCM94.1.0001; Ford to Riordan, Jan. 24, 1864, RFP, TCM94.1.0196; Hutchison to Ford, Jan. 25, 1864, RFP, TCM94.1.0124; Ford to Turner, Feb. 8, 1864, RFP, TCM94.1.0919a&b; Ford to Turner, Feb. 15, 1864, *OR*, Ser. 1, Vol. 34, Pt. 2, 968; Edgar to Ford, Feb. 23, 1864, ibid., 993.

35. Riordan to Ford, Feb. 5, 1864, RFP, TCM94.1.0197 (quotation one); Wayne R. Austerman, *Sharps Rifles and Spanish Mules: The San Antonio–El Paso Mail, 1851–1881* (College Station: Texas A&M University Press, 1985), 188 (quotation two). When Union lieutenant (later captain) Albert H. French visited Forts Davis, Stockton, Lancaster, and Camp Hudson in September and December 1862 while transporting rebel prisoners of war, he found all of the outposts deserted. French noted that the first settlement he encountered east of the Pecos River was at Pedro Pinto, seven miles from Fort Clark (near present-day Brackettville, Texas). By 1864 even Fort Clark had been abandoned. Maj. Gen. Zenas R. Bliss, who served on the West Texas frontier 1854–61 and 1870–86, says that during the Civil War "all [the] settlers fell back to Uvalde, on the El Paso Road, and to Fredericksburg, north of San Antonio." Such accounts graphically illustrate the extent of the wartime depopulation occurring in this western section of the state. Because Confederate and Lone Star troops could not adequately safeguard Texas's western frontier during the Civil War, the line of settlement in many sections receded back to its position in 1849. French to West, San Elizario, Tex., Dec. 3, 1862, NA, RG 393, Pt. 3, DA, ULR; Ely, *Where the West Begins*, 44–45, 51–52, 57–58; Bliss, *Reminiscences*, 233 (endnote quotation). Bliss was in command of Fort Quitman in April 1861 when the rebels took over. He also served at Forts Clark, Stockton, Davis, and at Camp Hudson.
36. Carleton to Halleck, March 20, 1864, *OR*, Ser. 1, Vol. 34, Pt. 2, 671, 672 (quotations one and two), 673.
37. Ibid., 672–73. Carleton's expedition never got beyond the planning stages.
38. Ibid.; French Report; Carleton to Hoffman, June 27, 1864, CGP (quotation). In February 1864 plans to capture Skillman and his spy company were put into motion. General Carleton wrote to Col. George Washington Bowie, instructing him "to endeavor to capture" Skillman's party and authorizing Bowie to hire several spies to assist him in this effort. Carleton had recently received a confidential letter advising him that Skillman's group could be easily captured "if a sufficient large enough party would watch for them" on the trail to Presidio del Norte. See Wood to Bowie, Las Cruces, NM, Feb. 10, 1864, NA, RG 393, Pt. 3, DA, ULR 1862–70.
39. French Report (quotation).
40. Ibid. (quotation). The Puerto del Paisano Road, first scouted by Capt. William H. Emory in 1852, ran from Presidio del Norte, Mexico, to Leon Holes, Texas, and was part of the Chihuahua Trail to San Antonio and Indianola, Texas. *Pressler's 1867 Map of Texas* from the Texas General Land Office shows the intersection of the Leon Holes–Presidio and Fort Davis–Presidio Roads near San Esteban Waterhole. Regarding Alamo Spring, on May 4, 1875, Stanislaus Hernández filed a claim on this historic Presidio County site, eleven years after Skillman stopped there. See GLO, Bexar Preemption File 990, for more on Alamo Spring and Hernández.
41. FC (quotation one); Allen Statement, CGP (quotation two). Regarding Spencer's Ranch, Texas, over the years there has been some confusion as to the exact location of this site. John W. Spencer, born in 1822, was a farmer and rancher from Missouri. Spencer's Ranch was in J. W. Spencer Survey 5, the site of modern Presidio, Texas.

Spencer's home was in Old Town Presidio, south of O'Reilly Street, next to the Lovett Street intersection. A sliver of Spencer's Ranch was also in the adjacent Ralph Wright Survey 12, from which J. C. and Amelia Slade donated an acre of land for a Catholic church in 1877. The Catholic Church lot is on the north side of O'Reilly Street. See 1860 Federal Census, Presidio County, Tex., NA, M653, R1293, 73; GLO Map #7420, *Map of J. W. Spencer Survey*, No. 5, Presidio County Rolled Sketch WR; GLO Map #9804, Sketch of Town of Presidio, Presidio County Rolled Sketch T-2; Presidio County Deed Records, Sept. 17, 1877 (Slade); author field trip to Old Town Presidio, June 15, 2008, with Roland Ely, Carlos Armendariz, and Luis Armendariz. The Armendariz brothers are J. W. Spencer's great-grandsons. Gravediggers at the Catholic Church in Presidio allegedly found "an earlier burial: a huge skeleton . . . with blond hair and a long blond beard." Locals believe these were Skillman's remains. The story is plausible, as the church property is part of Spencer's Ranch, and primary records show that the April 15, 1864, firefight occurred at Spencer's Ranch, a quarter of a mile from the Presidio del Norte crossing on the Rio Grande. The Texas Historical Commission originally placed a marker for Skillman at the Catholic Church. The marker was later moved a few blocks to a park. See Roy L. Swift and Leavitt Corning Jr., *Three Roads to Chihuahua* (Austin: Eakin Press, 1988), 356n60, (endnote quotation).

42. Special Orders No. 25, May 8, 1864, NA, RG 393, Pt. 5, Fort Bliss, Tex., #18, Gen. Orders 1863–64, Box 9; Statements of Allen, Garner, Dowling, and Hubbell (quotation), CGP; Baird to Turner, April 30, 1863, *OR*, Ser. 1, Vol. 15, 1064; Hubell to Baird, April 28, 1863, ibid.; Burgess to Scurry, March 17, 1863, ibid., 1065; Baird to Turner, May 5, 1863, ibid., 1075; 1860 Federal Census, Presidio County, Tex., NA, RG 29, M653, R1293, 108 (Ford). Dowling said he farmed at Fort Stockton before the war. Army guide John Dowland of Connecticut appears in the 1860 Fort Stockton census; see ibid., 87. Rebel exile Ben Dowell of El Paso County, Texas, was at John Burgess's house when William Ford arrived on the morning of April 15. Dowell and Ford later rode on together to El Paso del Norte, Mexico. See Nancy Hamilton, *Ben Dowell: El Paso's First Mayor* (El Paso: Texas Western Press, 1976), 35. William Ford served as El Paso County's first sheriff starting in 1852. After the war Tom Rife worked as a policeman in San Antonio and as custodian of the Alamo. See El Paso County Sheriff's Office, s.v. "History," https://www.epcounty.com/sheriff/comm_history.htm (accessed Aug. 6, 2020); Ely, *Texas Frontier*, 310–11, 313, 318–19, 404n16.

43. Prisoner statements, CGP; French Report; Merino to A. H. French, April 15, 1864, in Bowie to Cutler, April 29, 1864, NA RG 393, DNM, LR, M1120, R22; Capt. A. H. French to José Merino, Spencer's Ranch, April 15, 1864, RG 393, Pt. 3, DA, ULR, 1862–70; Juan Cordona Lake File, GLO, Crane County Abstract No. 1, Bexar 1454. Interestingly, in October 1864 seven former members of Captain French's company started an enterprise called the Salinas Salt Mining Company with a number of Mexicans "of very good character." The company's directors had taken possession of the salt lakes on the west side of the Guadalupe Mountains and proposed mining salt and selling it to wagon trains and caravans for a nominal fee. Carleton's subordinate Colonel Bowie blocked the company from commencing operations as legal title to the acreage was unclear.

These same salt lakes would feature prominently in El Paso County history thirteen years later during the 1877 Salt War. See Salinas Salt Mining Company to Carleton, San Elizario, Tex., Oct. 28, 1864, RG 393, Pt. 3, DA, ULR 1862–70 (endnote quotation).

44. French Report; Merino to French, April 15, 1864, in Bowie to Cutler, April 29, 1864, NA RG 393, DNM, LR, M1120, R22. Rufina Vigil was Henry Skillman's common-law wife. See El Paso County Deed Records, Sept. 26, 1866, and March 5, 1867 (Rufina's sale to French and French's later sale of same property); 1860 Federal Census, El Paso County, Tex., NA, RG 29, M653, R1293, 3 (Rufina Vigil and Henry Skillman). The four captured spies remained in prison for several months. On July 7, 1864, Allen took the oath of allegiance and was released on parole. See NA, RG 393, Pt. 1, NM, #3214, Provost Marshall, Vol. 121/298 NMEX. Carleton released Hubbell in June 1864, let him move to El Paso del Norte, Mexico, in October, and ignored his subsequent requests for a travel permit to the United States. Hubbell led a star-crossed life. He died in January 1869 during an Indian attack on his stagecoach in Bass Canyon, Hudspeth County, Texas. See Ely, *The Texas Frontier*, 307; NA, RG 393, Pt. 4, Fort Marcy, NM, #798, Guard Reports, June 21, 1864, Vol. 103–5 NMEX; ibid., Aug. 23, 1864. Garner and Dowling were still in prison on August 23, after which they disappear from the guard rolls.

45. James Wiley Magoffin, prominent El Paso County pioneer and secessionist, abandoned his home in the summer of 1862 and accompanied Sibley's men back to San Antonio. In February 1863 Magoffin offered to serve as a supply contractor for a Confederate invasion of the Southwest. In February 1864 he submitted his services as a spy in the Trans-Pecos and Mexico. In his letter of support recommending Magoffin for the position, Major A. G. Dickinson said that despite his age, he was worth twenty men. Dickinson boasted, "I'll warrant that he can know the movements and intentions of the enemy from the time he reaches El Paso." See J. W. Magoffin Confederate Citizens File, NA, RG 109, M346 (endnote quotation).

46. Connelly to Carleton, June 22, 1864, NA, RG 393, Pt. 5, Fort Bascom, NM, Entry 3, LR 1863–65 (quotation two); Carleton to Bergmann, June 4, 1864, ibid.; Carleton to Evans, June 26, 1864, NA, RG 94, AGO, LR, M619, R285 (quotation one); Leo E. Oliva, *Fort Union and the Frontier Army in the Southwest: A Historic Resource Study, Fort Union National Monument, Fort Union, New Mexico* (Santa Fe: National Park Service, 1993), 773–74; Pittman, *Rebels in the Rockies*, 175–76. Both Cedar Springs (Cedar Creek on some maps) and Cold Spring Creek empty into the Cimarron River and are located in the Oklahoma Panhandle, a short distance east of the New Mexico line. Manuel Antonio Otero was one of six boys born to Vicente and Gertrudes Otero of Valencia County, New Mexico. One of Manuel's brothers, Antonio, served on the New Mexico Supreme Court, while a second, Miguel, served as New Mexico Territory attorney general and in the U.S. House of Representatives. In the 1860 census Manuel Antonio Otero listed his net worth at $164,550, and in 1870 at $174,500. Manuel had a business partnership with Felipe Chávez, "maintained close economic ties with Chihuahua," Mexico, and later "became involved in banking ventures." Manuel had a sizeable estate south of Albuquerque named La Constancia. See Boyle, *Los Capitalistas*, 84, 90

(endnote quotations), 92; George B. Anderson, *History of New Mexico: Its Resources and People* (Los Angeles: Pacific States Publishing, 1907), 2:536–37. In January 1871 José Ygnacio Esquibel was serving as justice of the peace in San Miguel County, New Mexico. See January 27, 1871, Valdez and Abreu Indian depredation claim affidavit notarized by Esquibel in *Abreu and Valdez v. The United States and the Apache Indians*, Case No. 3362, IDC.

47. Connelly to Carleton, June 22, 1864, NA, RG 393, Pt. 5, Fort Bascom, NM, Entry 3, LR 1863–65 (quotation two); Carleton to Bergmann, June 4, 1864, ibid.; Carleton to Evans, June 26, 1864, NA, RG 94, AGO, LR, M619, R285 (quotation one); *HTO*, s.v. "Adobe Walls, Texas," by H. Allen Anderson, http://www.tshaonline.org/handbook/online/articles/hra1o (accessed Nov. 13, 2020); Lt. E. H. Ruffner, *1877 Map of the Department of the Missouri*, Sheet 2, NACP. Palo Duro Creek (also called Skull Creek on historic maps), flows west of present-day Spearman, Texas. Two tributaries, North and South Palo Duro Creeks, merge into South Palo Duro Creek near Morse, Texas, before finally joining with Hannas Draw north of Morse and becoming Palo Duro Creek. Palo Duro Creek eventually empties into the North Fork of the Canadian River in the Oklahoma Panhandle. Ruffner's 1877 Department of the Missouri map of the region shows an established trail running from Dodge City, Kansas, to Adobe Walls on the Canadian River, crossing Palo Duro Creek en route. A number of Department of New Mexico reports from June to October 1864 specifically refer to a camp at Palo Duro frequented by Comanches and Kiowas. The camp at Palo Duro and Palo Duro Creek are not to be confused with another Palo Duro Creek and Palo Duro Canyon, near Canyon, Texas. General Carleton said that both of these May 1864 wagon train attacks occurred on the Cimarron branch of the Santa Fe Trail, but Governor Connelly clearly states that the May 20 raid was at Palo Duro. Regarding Comanchero Félix García, see Commissioner of Indian Affairs George Washington Manypenny to New Mexico governor and Indian superintendent David Meriwether, March 11, 1856, RG 75, RNMSIA, LR 1849–80, T21, R2; Probst and Kirchner agreement with Félix García and Z. Staab and Bros., Oct. 15, 1869, NA, RG 393, LR, DNM, 1865–90, M1088, R10.

48. Connelly to Carleton, June 22, 1864, NA, RG 393, Pt. 5, Fort Bascom, NM, Entry 3, LR, 1863–65 (quotation).

49. *Mining Journal* (Black Hawk, Colo.), Aug. 31, 1864; Shoup to Maynard, District of Colorado, Pueblo, Aug. 13, 1864, *OR*, Ser. 1, Vol. 41, Pt. 2, 753 (quotation); Pittman, *Rebels in the Rockies*, 175–77.

50. *Mining Journal*, Aug. 31, 1864 (quotations).

51. There is some confusion as to exactly when the original band of twenty-two men split up. Reynolds gang member Thomas Holliman claimed that after the May 21 Otero wagon train raid, "some of the leaders quarreled . . . and 13 turned and went back [to Texas] and we saw no more of them. The other nine of us came on [to Colorado to continue raiding]." See *Mining Journal*, Aug. 31, 1864 (endnote quotation). One of the nine men kept a muster roll of the group's members and an incomplete journal of their exploits in a small memorandum book. This book, some of which was published in a newspaper, indicates that all twenty-two men in the original party went back to Texas

in early June. A short time later, on June 23, 1864, nine men (including the Reynolds brothers and Thomas Holliman) left Fort Belknap, Texas, en route to Colorado for another round of raiding. The other thirteen did not accompany them. See *Rocky Mountain News* (Denver), Aug. 13, 1864; Shoup to Maynard, District of Colorado, Pueblo, Aug. 13, 1864, *OR*, Ser. 1, Vol. 41, Pt. 2, 753; Pittman, *Rebels in the Rockies*, 175–77.

52. Chivington to Curtis, Denver, Aug. 23, 1864, *OR*, Ser. 1, Vol. 41, Pt. 2, 828; Curtis to Chivington, Fort Leavenworth, Aug. 24, 1864, *OR*, Ser. 1, Vol. 41, Pt. 2, 843; Browne to Curtis, Denver, Oct. 3, 1864, *OR*, Ser. 1, Vol. 41, Pt. 2, 596 (quotation one), 596–97 (quotation two); Testimony of Second Lt. Joseph A. Cramer, "Sand Creek Massacre," *Report of the Secretary of War*, 39th Cong., 2nd Sess., Sen. Exec. Doc. No. 26 (Washington, D.C.: Government Printing Office, 1867), 52 (quotation three). On March 11, 1865, the army sent the Reynolds Gang files to Chivington, at his request, "for correction of some informality." Chivington never returned them. See Wright to Bock, Feb. 26, 1875, James Reynolds, Civilian, Case No. 3481, NA, RG 153, Army Court-Martial Case Files, Records of the Office of the Judge Advocate General (endnote quotation).

53. Abreu to Cutler, Oct. 18, 1864 (Palo Duro), Carleton to Steck, Oct. 29, 1864, and Davis to Carleton, Oct. 30, 1864, all in NA, RG 94, AGO, LR, N584 1864.

54. Carleton to Steck, Oct. 29, 1864 (quotation two), and Davis to Carleton, Oct. 30, 1864 (quotation one), NA, RG 94, AGO, LR, N584 1864.

55. Abreu to Cutler, Oct. 10, 1864, *OR*, Ser. 1, Vol. 41, Pt. 3, 771; Gorham to Bristol, Oct. 13, 1864, Abreu to Cutler, Oct. 18, 1864, Carleton to Carson, Oct. 23, 1864, and General Orders No. 32, Oct. 22, 1864, all in NA, RG 94, AGO, LR, N584 1864; C. B. McClure, ed., "The Battle of Adobe Walls," *Panhandle-Plains Historical Review* 21 (1948), 30, 36, 42.

56. General Order No. 4, "Synopsis of Indian Scouts and their results for the year 1864," NA, RG 94, AGO, LR, M619, R389, 10, 13; Carson to Cutler, Dec. 4, 1864, *OR*, Ser. 1, Vol. 41, Pt. I, 939–42; McClure, "Battle of Adobe Walls," 41–42, 44, 56–57, 64–65; Blackshear, *Fort Bascom*, 112–13. On June 27, 1874, another clash, the Second Battle of Adobe Walls, took place near the old adobe fort, this time between buffalo hunters and Native Americans. An excellent map detailing the Canadian River region in Texas and the Adobe Walls site is the September 1875 *Map of Wegeforth County*, GLO Map #16784. This map includes "Bents Fort," "Bents Creek," "Adobe Creek," and "Paladora Creek" (all spellings as they appear on map).

57. Creel to Carleton, May 25, 1864, NA, RG 94, AGO, LR, M619, R286 (quotation).

58. Creel to Carleton, June 27, 1864, NA, RG 94, AGO, LR, N334 1864 (quotations one through three).

59. Ibid. (quotations one and two); Contreras to Tejada, Jan. 31, 1865 (quotation three), included in Carleton to AGO, Feb. 22, 1865, NA, RG 94, AGO, LR, M619, R389. Edward Hall, "chief of . . . these villains" at Fort Leaton, was a "bad rebel," a "desperado," and had an unsavory reputation in the Big Bend and West Texas. See Fergusson to West, Feb. 13, 1863, *OR*, Ser. 1, Vol. 15, 685 (endnote quotations); and Morgenthaler, *The River Has Never Divided Us*, 115.

60. Creel to Carleton, June 27, 1864, NA, RG 94, AGO, LR, N334 1864; Creel to Carleton, Sept. 18, 1864, ibid., M619, R287 (quotations one and two). In a November 1864 letter, Creel said that Burgess "bribed the local authorities" at Presidio del Norte. Creel to Carleton, Nov. 10, 1864, NA, RG 393, NM, LR, M1120, R23 (endnote quotation).

61. Contreras to Tejada, Jan. 22, 1865 (quotations one and two), and Tejada to Carleton, Jan. 31, 1865, included in Carleton to AGO, Feb. 22, 1865, NA, RG 94, AGO, LR, M619, R389; Kennedy to Pyron, Feb. 20, 1865, *OR*, Vol. 53, Supplement, 1044–46.

62. Magruder to Boggs, June 6, 1864, *OR*, Ser. 1, Vol. 34, Pt. 4, 651 (Hunter expedition); Magruder to Hunter, July 29, 1864, NA, RG 109, TNMA, LS, Ch. 2, Vol. 124 (quotations one and two); Kennedy to Pyron, Feb. 20, 1865, *OR*, Vol. 53, Supplement, 1044–46; Confederate Return for Western Sub-District of Texas, August 1864, *OR*, Vol. 41, Pt. 2, 1098. (Sherod Hunter's Pecos expedition likely took place in July 1864.) L. Boyd Finch, *Confederate Pathway to the Pacific: Major Sherod Hunter and Arizona Territory, C.S.A.* (Tucson: Arizona Historical Society, 1996), 215–16, 279; Mamie Yeary, comp. *Reminiscences of the Boys in Gray, 1861–1865* (Dallas: Smith and Lamar, 1912), 449 (for J. P. Hale's account of Sherod Hunter expedition and Fort Lancaster Indian fight). Hale says 70 men were in the expedition, while Confederate returns cite 150. Another firsthand report of this Lancaster fight, R. H. Williams's *With the Border Ruffians: Memories of the Far West, 1852–1868* (New York: E. P. Dutton, 1907), 363–72, is badly garbled and should be used with great caution.

63. Arzata to Tejada, Jan. 27, 1865 (quotation), Contreras to Tejada, Jan. 22, 1865, and Tejada to Carleton, Jan. 31, 1865, included in Carleton to AGO, Feb. 22, 1865, NA, RG 94, AGO, LR, M619, R389.

64. Ibid.

65. Ibid.

66. Ibid.

67. Kennedy to Pyron, Feb. 20, 1865, *OR*, Vol. 53, Supplement, 1044, 1045 (quotations one and two), 1046.

68. Kennedy to Pyron, Feb. 20, 1865, *OR*, Vol. 53, Supplement, 1044–46; Arzata to Tejada, Jan. 27, 1865, Contreras to Tejada, Jan. 22, 1865, and Tejada to Carleton, Jan. 31, 1865, included in Carleton to AGO, Feb. 22, 1865, NA, RG 94, AGO, LR, M619, R389; Walker to Murrah, March 15, 1865, NA, RG 109, TNMA, LS, Ch. 2, Vol. 123, (quotation).

69. Contreras to Tejada, Jan. 22, 1865, NA, RG 94, AGO, LR, M619, R389 (block quotation); Adams to McCulloch, Oct. 21, 1861, *OR*, Ser. 2, Vol. 2, 1526–30 (A. F. Wulff case).

70. Carleton to Tejada, Feb. 22, 1865, *OR*, Ser. 1, Vol. 48, Pt. 1, 951, 952 (quotations).

71. Finch, *Confederate Pathway*, 208–11, 217–21; Owings to Walker, Feb. 27, 1865, *OR*, Vol. 53, Supplement, 1046–47; Beaumont to Darden, Oct. 22, 1864, and Beaumont to Seddon, Oct. 21, 1864, *OR*, Ser. 1, Vol. 41, Pt. 4, 1009–10, 1011 (quotation); Baylor to Seddon, Dec. 21, 1864, and Seddon commentary on Baylor plan, Dec. 30, 1864, *OR*, Ser. 4, Pt. 3, 960–62. In January 1865 Sherod Hunter received Richmond's blessing for a second invasion expedition, but the plan never matured.

72. Baylor to Magruder, Jan. 29, 1863, *OR*, Ser. 1, Vol. 50, Pt. 2, 298; Magruder to Cooper, June 8, 1863, NA, RG 109, TNMA, LS, Ch. 2, Vol. 132; Magruder to Boggs, June 6,

1864, *OR*, Ser. 1, Vol. 34, Pt. 4, 650–51; Magruder to Baird, April 13, 1864, NA, RG 109, TNMA, LS, Ch. 2, Vol. 124.

73. Statement of William J. Davis, Carleton to AGO, May 9, 1865, NA, RG 94, AGO, M619, R390 (quotations one and two).

74. Walker to McCulloch, Dec. 21, 1864, NA, RG 109, TNMA, LS, Ch. 2, Vol. 123 (quotations one and two); Magruder to Boggs, April 8, 1865 (quotation three), and Jack to Magruder, April 15, 1865, ibid., Telegrams Sent, Ch. 2, Vol. 137.

Chapter 3

1. Felipe Delgado was also a politician, having served as a territorial delegate; see Boyle, *Los Capitalistas*, 49. William J. Parish calls the relationship and economy that existed between urban merchants and Hispanos farmers "mercantile capitalism"; see Parish, *Charles Ilfeld Company*, 35.

2. Keithley came to New Mexico in the 1830s and did business with Santa Fe traders like Louis Robidoux and Antonio Martínez. He was a citizen of Mexico when the Treaty of Guadalupe Hidalgo was signed. In 1853 he sold a trading post and grist mill to fellow traders Henry Connelly and Edward F. Mitchell. He became the agent for the Cimarron agency in 1862; see Doyle Daves, "Levi Keithley, Ineffective Government Man in Territorial New Mexico," *Wagon Tracks*, no. 3 (May 2018), 17–20; Marcus Gottschalk, "Pioneer Merchants of the Las Vegas Plaza: The Booming Trail Days," *Wagon Tracks*, no. 2 (Feb. 2002), 10; Ralph Emerson Twitchell, *Leading Facts of New Mexican History* (Cedar Rapids, Iowa: Torch Press, 1912), 2:17, 18.

3. Burton L. Reese and William Moore purchased land from Keithley and William Shepard, August 31, 1860, Deed Record Book 2, p. 36, San Miguel County Court House, Records Building, County Clerk's Office, Las Vegas, NM (hereafter SMCA); 1860 Federal Census, San Miguel County, El Chaperito, NM, NA, RG 29; 1870 Federal Census, San Miguel County, Ranch of Gallinas Crossing, ibid.

4. Alexander Hatch purchased land from Connelly in 1854. See SMCA, Deed Record Book 1, p. 108. On Cayeto and José Piedad Tafoya's transactions with Hatch, see ibid., 223–25. Tafoya purchased approximately 160 acres from Hatch. A part of the payment for this land was contingent on delivering a fall corn crop. See SMCA, Deed of Mortgage, Deed Record Book 2, June 22, 1859, pp. 223–25.

5. Sandoval also served as auditor and as adjutant general for the legislative assembly. He was also president of the senate. For details, see W. G. Ritch, comp., *The Legislative Blue Book of the Territory of New Mexico: With the Rules of Order, Fundamental Law, . . . Etc.*, (Santa Fe: Charles W. Greene, Public Printer, 1882), 120, 121. Pascual Baca called him a "peddler and freighter." Pascual Baca deposition, *Anastacio Sandoval v. The United States*, Case No. 6131, IDC.

6. Carleton to Wood, Fort Union, Dec. 21, 1863, "Condition of the Indian Tribes," *Report of the Joint Special Committee, 1867: An Appendix*, Report 156, 39th Cong. 2nd Sess. (Washington, D.C.: Government Printing Office, 1867), 150 (hereafter cited as "Condition of the Tribes, 1867").

7. Mary J. Straw Cook, *Doña Tules: Santa Fe Courtesan and Gambler* (Albuquerque: University of New Mexico Press, 2007), 66, 67. D. Bernard Koch put up the thousand-dollar bond for Fernando Lucero on Oct. 2, 1865; for Edward Martinas on Sept. 30, 1865; and for both James Giddings and Florencio Aragón on Oct. 30, 1865. For all of the licenses associated with Koch's bonds, see RNMSIA, LR 1865–65, R6, and the appendix to this work. For Giddings's license, see Oct. 30, 1865, ibid. For Gervais Nolan's license and the bond that Beck and Conklin put up, see Dec. 1853, RNMSIA, LR 1854–56, R2. It is interesting to note that Giddings and Beck were in a partnership in 1853 when Beck backed Nolan's trading expeditions. For information on Nolan, see David J. Weber, *The Taos Trappers: The Fur Trade in the Far Southwest, 1540–1846* (Norman: University of Oklahoma Press, 1980), 181. Pablo Aragón was employed by both Giddings and José Piedad Tafoya. Long after he had served as justice of the peace and constable of Puerto de Luna, Aragón recalled his time on Giddings's ranch. He noted that his boss owned a lot of wagons to haul freight. When asked where Giddings got his cattle, Aragón replied, "from the states." Pablo Aragón's deposition, *William B. Giddings, administrator of the estate of James M. Giddings, deceased, surviving partner of the firm of Giddings and Company, consisting of James M. Giddings and Preston Beck Jr. vs. The United States and the Navajo Indians*, Case No. 2647, IDC.

8. See Brooks, *Captives and Cousins*, 365–68; and Kavanagh, *The Comanches*, 406–10.

9. "Report of Pedro Urioste to Lt. H. B. Bristol," Aug. 1861, LS and LR, R2, Records of the U.S. Army Commands, RG 98, Meketa Microfilm Collection, Center for Southwest Research, University of New Mexico (hereafter cited as "Report of Urioste to Bristol, August 1861").

10. Manuel Urioste, Application for Pass, Feb. 27, 1865, RNMSIA, LR 1864–65, R6.

11. Ibid.

12. Blackshear, *Fort Bascom*, 109–14.

13. Kenner, *Comanchero Frontier*, 146–47. In an 1867 report to Commissioner Taylor, newly appointed superintendent Norton said that both the previous superintendent, Felipe Delgado, and Carleton were guilty of giving out too many passes. See A. B. Norton, Superintendent of Indian Affairs (SIA), NM, to N. G. Taylor, Commissioner of Indian Affairs (CIA), *Report of the Secretary of the Interior, pt. 2, 1867*, "Message of the President of the United States and Accompanying Documents," Ex. Doc. 1, 40th Cong. 2nd Sess. (Washington, D.C.: Government Printing Office, 1867), 194, 195 (hereafter cited as Norton to Taylor, *Report of the Secretary of the Interior*, 1867).

14. José Felipe Madrid was employed by Pedro Antonio Márquez on Aug. 23, 1865, RNMSIA, LR from the CIA 1864–65, R6; and Lorenzo Valdez, Oct. 14, 1865, ibid. Juan de Dios Tapia went to Texas for Anastacio Sandoval on July 8, 1865, ibid.

15. I used Gottlieb Fischer to Andrew Johnson, Dec. 26, 1865, NA, OIA, LR 1824–81; Reg. of LR 1824–80, NM Superintendency, 1849–80, Kiowa Agency 1864–80, M234, R375; G. W. Todd to D. N. Cooley, CIA, Dec. 24, 1865, NA, OIA, LR, Kiowa Agency 1864–80, M234, R375; Andrew J. Hamilton, Gov. of Texas, to CIA, Dec. 18, 1865, ibid. Rudolph Fischer remained with the Comanches until 1877, when his father purchased him for $100. By then he was an adult who had little interest in once again adapting to a new

culture. While he became a farmer, it was on the Comanche reservation. These Indians remained his neighbors. See Scott Zesche, *Captured: A True Story of Abduction by Indians on the Texas Frontier* (New York: St. Martin's Press, 2004), 226, 250.

16. Kavanagh, *The Comanches*, 407, 411; Zesche, *Captured*, 124, 127.

17. Kavanagh, *The Comanches*, 405; Goldbaum to Carleton, June 7, 1866, NA, OIA, LR, Kiowa Agency 1864–80, M234, R375. Reference to government beef contract comes from, *Sara Goldbaum, Administratix of the estate of Marcus Goldbaum, deceased v. The United States and the Comanche Indians*, Case No. 6908, IDC. As chapter 5 notes, this butcher also supplied beef to other posts.

18. Goldbaum to Carleton, June 7, 1866, NA, OIA, LR, Kiowa Agency 1864–80, M234, R375. David S. Koffman notes that Goldbaum later negotiated for the release of Adolph Korn. While Korn was eventually returned to his family, he was never really happy; see Koffman, *The Jews Indian: Colonialism, Pluralism, and Belonging in American* (New Brunswick, N.J.: Rutgers University Press, 2019), 153. Pahruacahiba was probably Bear's Back, or Paruaqhahip. See, Kavanagh, *The Comanches*, 405.

19. Bergmann to Headquarters, Santa Fe, Aug. 11, 1866, NA, LS, DNM, RG 393, in Arrott Collection, Special Collections, Donnelly Library, New Mexico Highlands University, Las Vegas (hereafter cited as Arrott Collection), Vol. 49, 70–73; Blackshear, *Fort Bascom*, 120. Bergmann purchased these cattle in late 1863. He was still trying to get his $200.24 back in 1868. See Bergmann to Charles E. Mix, Acting CIA, April 30, 1868, NA, OIA, LR, NM, 1868, M234, R555.

20. *Edward H. Bergmann v. William V. B. Wardwell*, Records of the U.S. Territorial and New Mexico District Courts for Socorro County, Civil Case #00168, Folder 168, New Mexico State Records Center and Archives, Santa Fe (hereafter NMRCA). José P. Tafoya deposition, *Charles Goodnight and John Sheek vs. The United States and Comanche Tribe of Indians*, Case No. 9133, IDC.

21. John Watts's involvement in this trade is detailed on the application and the approved pass, issued to the son, also John Watts, Oct. 28, 1865, RNMSIA, LR 1864–65, R6.

22. Bergmann to Headquarters, Santa Fe, Aug. 11, 1866, NA, LS, DNM, RG 393, in Arrott Collection, Vol. 49, 70–73; Blackshear, *Fort Bascom*, 120; Kavanagh, *The Comanches*, 407.

23. Bergmann to Headquarters, Santa Fe, 11 Aug, 11, 1866, NA, LS, DNM, RG 393, in Arrott Collection, Vol. 49, 72–73.

24. Superintendent Norton to Labadie, May 1, 1867, RNMSIA, LR 1866–67, R7.

25. Ralph Emerson Twitchell, *The Spanish Archives of New Mexico*, vol. 2 (Iowa: Torch Press, 1912); Simmons, *Little Lion of the Southwest*, 113; Cook, *Doña Tules*, 83, 84.

26. Simmons, *Little Lion of the Southwest*, 111.

27. Ibid., 113.

28. Ibid., 125.

29. There is no date associated with Pedro Leon's pass, but it is was filed within the letters received for the years 1854–56, when Labadie was the agent at Abiquiú. The thousand-dollar bond was held by Rio Arriba residents Antonio Vigil and Juan Quintana. Pedro Leon's bond was for three months and was signed by Labadie. See Leon's pass, RNMSIA,

LR 1854–56, R2. See Bernardo Sánchez pass, bondholders Juan Neposena Valdez and José Tomás Montaño, agent approving, Lorenzo Labadie, Sept. 15, 1855, RNMSIA, LR 1854–56, R2.

30. The quote from Carleton on Giddings's "fortification" comes from J. R. Doolittle, "Condition of the Indian Tribes," *Report of the Joint Special Committee, 1876* (Washington, D.C.: Government Printing Office, 1876), 186; Simmons, *Little Lion of the Southwest*, 113. On the marriage between George and Benigna, see Find a Grave Online, s.v. "Benigna Labadie Giddings," https://www.findagrave.com/memorial/152658551/benigna-giddings (accessed June 18, 2019); Cook, *Doña Tules*, 66, 67.

31. Lehman Spiegelberg deposition, *Lorenzo Labadi, as surviving partner of the firm of Chaves and Labadi vs. The United States and the Navajo Indians*, Case No. 3252, IDC. (Most historical references spell it "Labadie," but sometimes you will see the above spelling "Labadi.")

32. Pass for Juaquín Larriva, Sept. 13, 1865, for two months. The bondholders were Miguel E. Pino and Anastacio Sandoval. For Larriva, see RNMSIA, LR 1864–65, R6. The records note that Felipe Delgado awarded four passes in 1865 to Sandoval to trade in Texas. Two of those passes were approved on consecutive days. Sandoval held additional bonds (i.e., vouched for other traders) eight different times during this period.

33. Thompson, *Civil War History of the New Mexico Volunteers*, 4.

34. On Labadie becoming a sheriff, see Larry Ball, *Desert Lawmen: The High Sheriffs of New Mexico and Arizona, 1846–1912* (Albuquerque: University of New Mexico Press, 1992), 370. See also "History of the Santa Fe County Sheriff's Office," at https://www .santafecountysheriff.com (accessed June 17, 2019). The "Indian trader" quote comes from Thompson, *Civil War History of the New Mexico Volunteers*, 101. On Labadie working at the "agency at Anton Chico" in August 1862, see *Chavez and Labadi v. The United States*, Case No. 3252, IDC. Also found in Thompson, *Civil War History of the New Mexico Volunteers,* 81; and in Father Stanley Crocchiola, *The Apaches of New Mexico 1540—1940* (Pampa, Tex.: Pampa Print Shop, 1962), 302.

35. Bailey, *Bosque Redondo*, 128.

36. Labadie continued to represent the Mescaleros as an off-site agent until these Indians eventually escaped the reservation; see Frank D. Reeve, "The Federal Indian Policy in New Mexico, 1858–1880," *New Mexico Historical Review*, no. 3 (July 1938), 195; Bailey, *Bosque Redondo*, 128. On Morton's and Labadie's issues, see Wood to McCleave, Fort Sumner, Oct 19, 1864, Conditions of the Indian Tribes, 1867," 294; Superintendent A. B. Norton to Labadie, May 1, 1867, RNMSIA, LR 1866–67, R7. Regarding this incident, Gerald Thompson noted that Brig. Gen. Marcellus Crocker always had a "queasy" feeling about Calloway; see Thompson, *Army and the Navajo*, 75, 76.

37. Steck talked about Labadie's replacement in Steck to Labadie, Jan. 19, 1865, RNMSIA, LR 1864–65, R6.

38. Carleton, DNM, to Adj. Gen. of the Army, Washington, D.C., March 22, 1865, NA, RG 393, LS, DNM, in Arrott Collection, Vol. 16, 156; Carleton to Commanding Officer, Fort Sumner, April 7, 1865, ibid., 189; Carleton, Tecolote, to Maj. Herbert Enos, Fort Union, April 11, 1865, ibid., 194. This "oufit" also included Jules L. Barbey, another

former California Column veteran who later commanded Fort Canby. Carleton later fired him for, among other things, drinking on the job. Carleton ordered that he too be brought to Santa Fe for questioning. On Barbey's history in New Mexico, see Thompson, *Civil War History of the New Mexico Volunteers*, 310–11. On Kitchens, see Carleton, Hatch's Ranch, to Maj. Herbert Enos, Fort Union, April 20, 1865, NA, RG 393, LS, DNM, in Arrott Collection, Vol. 16, 206; Thompson, *Army and the Navajo*, 75, 76.

39. Cooley to Delgado, March 3, 1866, RNMSIA, LR 1864–65, R6; three-month pass for Fernando Lucero, Oct. 2, 1865, ibid.

40. Two-month pass for Pablo Lucero, Sept. 13, 1865, ibid.

41. Donald Lucero, *The Adobe Kingdom: New Mexico, 1598–1958* (Santa Fe: Sunstone Press, 2009), 250; Chris Emmet, *Fort Union and the Winning of the Southwest* (Norman: University of Oklahoma Press, 1965), 194–95; Kenner, *Comanchero Frontier*, 190.

42. David Delgado, "Founders of Santa Rosa: Don Celso Baca's Family Tree," *Santa Rosa News* (New Mexico), June 28, 1990. David Lucero notes that Labadie and Baca were close. Lorenzo and Rayitos Labadie sponsored Baca's daughter María Ana Celestina Baca. The Baca ranch later became known as "Eden"; Lucero, *Adobe Kingdom*, 326n8.

43. Steck to Labadie, April 25, 1865, RNMSIA, LR 1864–65, R66; A.B. Norton to Labadie, May 1, 1867, ibid., LR 1866–67, R7.

44. Norton to Labadie, May 1, 1867, RNMSIA, LR 1866–67, R7; Labadie to Norton, July 19, 1867, and Aug. 27, 1867, ibid.

45. Labadie to Norton, July 19, 1867, and Aug. 27, 1867, ibid.; Kavanagh, *The Comanches*, 406–10.

46. Labadie to Norton, Aug. 27, 1867, RNMSIA, LR 1866–67, R7. The additional description of Quitaque comes from Labadie to Norton, Dec. 1, 1867, RNMSIA, OIA, LR 1868, M234, R555.

47. Labadie to Norton, Dec. 1, 1867, RNMSIA, OIA, LR 1868, M234, R555.

48. Labadie to Norton, Aug. 27, 1867, RNMSIA, OIA, LR 1866–67, R7.

49. Ibid.

50. Capt. Edmunds B. Holloway, Eighth Infantry, to Capt. Dabeny H. Maury, AAG, NA, DNM, Santa Fe, Oct. 5, 1860, M619, R42.

51. Ball, *Desert Lawmen,* 370; "History of the Santa Fe County Sheriff's Office," https://www.santafecountysheriff.com (accessed June 17, 2019); Labadie to Norton, Dec. 1, 1867, RNMSIA, OIA, LR 1868, M234, R555.

52. Labadie, Agua Negra, to Norton, Sept. 10, 1867, RNMSIA, LR 1866–67, R7.

53. Ibid.; Labadie to Norton, Dec. 1, 1867, RNMSIA, OIA, LR 1868, M234, R555.

54. Labadie to Norton, Dec. 1, 1867, RNMSIA, OIA, LR 1868, M234, R555.

55. These additional chiefs included "Tecoví, Ulloni, Nocay, and Efielle," ibid.

56. Ibid.

57. Ibid.

58. Ibid.

59. Labadie issued a license to Pedro Leon to trade with the Utes in 1854, RNMSIA, LR 1854–56, R2; Labadie and Julio García put up the bond for José Piedad Tafoya on Oct. 9,

1865, RNMSIA, LR 1864–65, R6; and along with Jesús María Baca y Salazar, he put up a similar bond for José Costillo on Oct. 10, 1865, RNMSIA, LR 1864–65, R6.

60. Blackshear, *Fort Bascom*, 106, 114, 218; Kenner, *Comanchero Frontier*, 148–49; Morris, *El Llano Estacado*, 192. Additional examples include merchant D. Bernard Koch, bondholder for James Giddings's license, Oct. 19, 1865, RNMSIA, LR 1864–65, R6; Anastacio Sandoval, July 8, 1865, ibid.; Edward Hamburger, bondholder for Fernando Lucero, Oct. 2, 1865, ibid.; John S. Watts, bondholder for John Watts and ex-Indian agent John L. Collins, Oct. 28, 1865. ibid.

61. W. H. Henrie came west as a French scout, working for both John C. Frémont and Brigham Young. By the 1860s he was a successful Albuquerque businessman who partnered on city projects with W. T. Strachan and Salvador Armijo. For a brief biography, see Anderson, *History of New Mexico*, 2:1039. Henrie put up the bond for fellow businessman and trader W. T. Strachan on Oct. 5, 1865, RNMSIA, LR 1864–65, R6, but was not above sending out his own goods to trade for cattle. In 1870 he asked Maj. William Clinton if he (Henrie) could "send out a party on a trading expedition to the Comanche Indians." While the request was declined, this correspondence, printed in the *Republican Review*, when coupled with the bond for Strachan, proves that two of Albuquerque's leading citizens were involved in the trade. See Henrie to Clinton, July 5, 1870, *Republican Review*, July 9, 1870. Francisco Baca y Ortíz acted as the bondholder for trader Anastacio Sandoval on Feb. 28, 1865, RNMSIA, LR 1864–65, R6; land baron and politician Miguel E. Pino acted as a bondholder with Sandoval on trader Juaquín Larriva's pass, Sept. 13, 1865, ibid.; Indian agent Jesús M. Baca y Salazar was the bondholder for trader Pedro Antonio Marques, Aug. 23, 1865, and José Costillo, Oct. 8, both ibid. Before he became the agent for the Pueblo Indians, John Ward acted as one of the bondholders for trader Juan Chama, Nov. 19, 1865, ibid.

62. Patrick Healy, Late Capt. First New Mexico Inf. to CIA, Washington, D.C., Oct. 15, 1866, NA, OIA, LR, NM, 1868, M234, R375.

63. Ibid.

64. Ibid. As to Leavenworth's recommendation, see RNMSIA, Kiowa Agency 1865–80. In *The Comanchero Frontier* (158, 159) Kenner covered the same material, but this history requires a retelling with a fresh look at the primary sources.

65. Healy's letter to Carleton was dated Jan. 22, 1867. Carleton replied three days later. This information and his correspondence are in Carleton to SIA, March 2, 1867, RNMSIA, LR 1867–68, R8. José Piedad Tafoya deposition, *Goodnight and Sheek vs. The United States et al.*, Case No. 9133, IDC.

66. While still serving in the army, Jennings replaced Calloway as the farm superintendent at the Bosque Redondo Indian reservation. See Returns from Military Posts, Fort Sumner, NA, RG 94, Sept. 1864, M617A, R81; Jewett to De Forrest, May 14, 1870, NA, RG 393, LS, DNM, in Arrott Collection, Vol. 49, 151, 152.

67. Carleton to superintendent of Indian Affairs, March 2, 1867, RNMSIA, LR, Misc. Papers 1867–69, R8; Blackshear, *Fort Bascom*, 133.

68. Richard Flint and Shirley Cushing Flint, *The Coronado Expedition: From the Distance of 460 Years* (Albuquerque: University of New Mexico Press, 2012), 140, 146.

69. On Pino, see Blackshear, *Fort Bascom*, 28–31.

70. Archives of New Mexico, Series I, Surveyor General Records, Reel 12, Preston Beck Grant, 12, 26, located in Special Collections, Donnelly Library, New Mexico Highlands University, Las Vegas.

71. Jewett to De Forrest, May 14, 1870, NA, RG 393, LS, DNM, in Arrott Collection, Vol. 49, 151, 152; "List of Traders," Office of SIA, Sept. 10, 1867, RNMSIA, LR 1866–67, R7.

72. Norton to Taylor, CIA, *Report of the Secretary of the Interior 1867*.

73. Tafoya deposition, *Goodnight and Sheek vs. The United States et al.*, Case No. 9133, IDC.

74. Labadie had put up previous bonds of a thousand dollars each for both José Costillo and José Piedad Tafoya in 1865. See Costillo's pass, dated Oct. 8. 1865, and Tafoya's pass, dated the next day, Oct. 9, 1865, RNMSIA, LR 1864–65, R6. Labadie's complaints and Norton's observations are found in A. B. Norton to N. G. Taylor, CIA, Sept. 10, 1867, RNMSIA, LR 1866–67, R7.

75. Records for Brown and Abreu's 1864 licenses are in "Internal Revenue Assessment Lists for the Territory of New Mexico 1862–1870, 1872–1874," Treasury Department, NA, RG 58, M782, R1, online at Ancestry.com, http://search.ancestry.com/search/dbextra .aspx?dbid=1264 (accessed August 8, 2014) (hereafter cited as "Assessment Lists for the Territory of New Mexico 1862–1870, 1872–1874"). Discussions regarding Brown becoming the sutler and an Indian trader are found in Cooley to Norton, Sept. 18, 1866, and Cooley to Norton, Sept. 28, 1866, RNMSIA, LR 1866–67, R7; Brown to Norton, Oct. 3, 1866, ibid.; and John Y. Simon, ed., *The Papers of Ulysses S. Grant*, 16:182, 183, 184.

76. SMCA, County Clerk Records, Warranty Deed Book #5, 167–68, July 20, 1869. Brown bought the land from Vose for $250.

77. Pass for José Valdez, Jan. 9, 1867, RNMSIA, LR 1866–67, R7. Pueblo Indians had been trading with Plains Indians for decades if not centuries. It seems what Henderson was up to was the norm, for Pueblo Indian agent Silas Kendrick was issuing passes to these Indians to trade in Texas in 1861. See Lt. Col. B. D. Roberts to Maury, Hatch's Ranch, New Mexico, Feb. 27, 1861, AAG, NA, DNM, Santa Fe, M619, R42.

78. Taylor to Norton, April 13, 1867, RNMSIA, LR 1866–67, R7.

79. Capt. George W. Letterman, Ft. Bascom, to Second Lt. Edward S. Merritt, for AAAG Cyrus De Forrest, HQ, Sept. 2, 1867, RNMSIA, LR 1866–67, R7; A. B. Norton to N. G. Taylor, CIA, Sept. 10, 1867, ibid.

80. Frederick Nolan, *The Lincoln County War: A Documentary History* (Norman: University of Oklahoma Press, 1991), 40; Hana Samek, "No Bed of Roses: The Careers of Four Mescarelo Indian Agents, 1871–1878," *New Mexico Historical Review* 57, no. 2 (1982): 140–44. Murphy's quote is from Peter Thompson, "The Fight for Life: New Mexico Indians, Health Care, and the Reservation Period," *New Mexico Historical Review* 69, no. 2 (April 1994): 157. More on Murphy's and Fritz's illegal activities can be found in David T. Kirkpatrick, "The Archaeology of Billy the Kid," in *Presenting Archaeology to the Public: Digging for Truths*, ed. James H. Jameson (Walnut Creek, Calif.: Altamira Press, 1997), 246.

81. Harwood P. Hinton, "John Simpson Chisum," *New Mexico Historical Review* 31, no. 3 (July 1956): 191, 192. By this time Thomas B. Catron held the mortgage on Murphy and Dolan's enterprise and was particularly interested in the cattle. He sent his brother-in-law to Lincoln to oversee his interest there; see Hinton, "John Simpson Chisum," 193.

82. Nolan, *Lincoln County War*, 36–47. William Calloway's private business on the Pecos River is found in "Internal Revenue Assessment Lists for the Territory of New Mexico" and "Record of Personal Taxes Assessed in New Mexico, 1868, Division 3, W. P. Calloway, Los Esteros," in "Internal Revenue Assessment Lists for the Territory of New Mexico 1862–1870, 1872–1874;" *Santa Fe Weekly New Mexican*, Dec. 1, 1868.

Chapter 4

1. See *Charles Probst and August Kirchner v. The United States*, Case No. 2248, IDC.
2. August's wife Nestora applied for a military pension based on her deceased husband's service in 1902. Certificate no. 5977 notes that he served in the "Indian Wars," in the Third U.S. Infantry with a rank of "band." See Veterans Administration, Reel 4, 328, Personal Index File, from "United States Index to Indian Wars Pension Files, 1892–1926," NARA microfilm publication T318. August Kirchner's fourteen-year-old niece Augusta married Charles Probst. The same month that Nestora applied for a military pension, Augusta did as well. Charles Probst's military pension certificate no. 3818 also notes that he served in the "Indian Wars," in the Third Infantry with the rank of "band."
3. Santa Fe County census records for 1860 show Probst and Kirchner were living in the same house in Santa Fe: 1860 Federal Census, RG 29, Records of the Bureau of the Census, NMT, Santa Fe County, p. 35, reel no. M653-714. The 1870 census notes that they were still living in the same house, as was another Prussian, Henry Mauler. Mauler's profession was also butcher. 1870 Federal Census, RG 29, Records of the Bureau of the Census, NMT, Santa Fe County, M593-896, p. 42.
4. Kirchner deposition, *Probst and Kirchner v. The United States*, Case No. 2248, IDC. Kie Oldham represented many Southern Plains Indians in depredation cases. Oldham later represented Arkansas in the U.S. Senate.
5. Catron commented on Kirchner's health and mental state in Thomas B. Catron deposition, *Charles Probst and August Kirchner v. The United States*, Case No. 1646, IDC, Thomas Catron, MSS 29, B.C. Series 803, Box 1, Center for Southwest Research, UNM Albuquerque (hereafter Catron Papers, CSR).
6. Kirchner deposition, *Probst and Kirchner*, Case No. 2248, IDC.
7. Ibid.
8. Ibid.
9. David L. Caffey, *Chasing the Santa Fe Ring: Power and Privilege in Territorial New Mexico* (Albuquerque: University of New Mexico Press, 2014), 250. Rosenthal and Stockton bid to supply beef to Fort Defiance; see *Santa Fe Weekly Post*, Dec. 30, 1871. Information on the location of these merchants' establishments can be found

in R. L. Polk and Co. and A. C. Danser, *The Colorado, New Mexico, Utah, Nevada, Wyoming and Arizona Gazetteer Business Directory* (Chicago: 1884–85), 352–54.

10. Kirchner deposition, *Probst and Kirchner*, Case No. 2248, IDC; Kirchner deposition, *Charles Probst and August Kirchner v. The United States and the Ute and Jicarilla Apaches Indians*, Case No. 2109, IDC (hereafter *Probst and Kirchner*, Case No. 2109, IDC).

11. Nolan, *Lincoln County War*, 47.

12. Ibid.; Tobias, *History of the Jews in New Mexico*, 71–75.

13. Charles Probst deposition, *Probst and Kirchner*, Case No. 2109, IDC.

14. After leaving his job as superintendent of Indian Affairs, Felipe Delgado got back into the family business. The vermillion listing can be found within an invoice for $626.25 for purchases from the Staab brothers on May 29, 1868. See Felipe Delgado Papers, Folder 10, NMRCA.

15. Probst deposition, *Probst and Kirchner*, Case No. 2109, IDC.

16. Lawyer Robeson response, ibid.

17. Anastacio Carillo deposition and Felipe Vigil deposition, ibid.

18. As to the street the butcher shop was on, see *Santa Fe Daily New Mexican*, July 31, 1872, NMRCA. In an 1880 article describing Santa Fe, the caption beneath a drawing of the "Sister's Chapel," at the "head of San Francisco Street" shows the notation, "from Rio Chiquito"; see Henry Mills Alden, ed., "A Villa de Santa Fe," *Harper's New Monthly* 60 (Dec. 1879–May 1880), 673. Author Richard Leviton notes that it later became Water Street in *Santa Fe Light: Touring the Visionary Geography of Santa Fe* (Bloomington: Indiana University Press, 2009), 56. Anastacio Carillo testified that Kirchner's butcher business was "in front of the soldiers' quarters, near Felipe Delgado's house" (*Probst and Kirchner*, Case 2109, IDC). While Fort Marcy was constructed several hundred yards to the northeast of the plaza, most soldiers used the old Mexican barracks that were located next to the Governor's Place, which fits in with other descriptions as to where the butcher shop was located.

19. For location of this ranch, see Charles Dominick deposition, April 1, 1912, *Probst and Kirchner*, Case No. 1646, Catron Papers, MSS 29, Series 803, loose documents, Folder 18, CSR. In 1912 Augusta Probst recalled that foreman Charles Dominick and Jesús Mestas made frequent cattle drives from La Porte Chiquito to Santa Fe. She remembered these trips vividly because these men always stayed at their house when they were in town; see Augusta Probst deposition, ibid. Another employee, Patricio Montoya, called this ranch "Rincón de Tierra Amarilla." Montoya noted that Kirchner also ran an ad hoc butcher shop on the banks of the Rio Chiquito. Patricio Montoya deposition, April 18, 1902, *Charles Probst and August Kirchner v. The United States and the Navajo Indians*, Case No. 3476, IDC (hereafter *Probst and Kirchner*, Case No. 3476, IDC).

20. 1860 Federal Census, 8th Precinct, Rio Arriba County, NM, NA, RG 29; 1870 Federal Census, Santa Fe County, NM, ibid.; Parish, *Charles Ilfeld Company*, 16. Ilfeld also offered that Marcus Goldbaum occasionally carried their money to Elsberg and Amberg (ibid.). Refugia Baca y Kirchner's deposit information can be found in Deposit Journal: Second National Bank, Santa Fe, AC 84, Box 32-5, pp. 22, 30, 32, New Mexico State History Museum, Santa Fe.

21. This partnership came to light in 1876 when Kirchner sued Elsberg for eight hundred dollars. William Breeden, the butcher's lawyer, detailed the 1862 contract in the lawsuit he filed on June 3, 1876. See *Santa Fe New Mexican*, June 24, 1876. Albert was Jacob Amberg's brother.

22. Blackshear, *Fort Bascom*, 87, 24, 129. Camp Plummer later became Fort Lowell, which was in operation until 1869. Reference to Labadie working in Anton Chico as the Mescalero agent can be found in William A. Keleher, *Turmoil in New Mexico, 1846–1868* (Albuquerque: University of New Mexico Press, 1982), 281, 287.

23. Bergmann to De Forrest, April 6, 1867, Catron Papers, MSS 29, loose documents, Box 1, Folder 26, CSR; Bergmann to Getty, DNM, May 17, 1867, ibid., Folder 23; Labadie to Norton, Dec. 1 1867, NA, OIA, LR, NM, 1868, M234, R555.

24. De Forrest to Elkins, U.S. District Attorney, Santa Fe, NM, July 4, 1867, Catron Papers, MSS 29, loose documents, Box 1, Folder 24, CSR.

25. E. A. Rollins, Treasury Department, Office of Internal Revenue, to Stephen B. Elkins, U.S. District Attorney, Santa Fe, NM, July 16, 1867, Catron Papers, MSS 29, loose documents, Box 1, Folder 15, CSR.

26. Willison deposition, July 20, 1898, *Probst and Kirchner*, Case No. 2109, IDC.

27. Captain Eagan's characterization of Kirchner's control over the commissary department comes from Darlis Miller, *Soldiers and Settlers: Military Supplies in the Southwest, 1861–1885* (Albuquerque: University of New Mexico Press, 1989), 191. Willison deposition, July 20, 1898, *Probst and Kirchner*, Case No. 2109, IDC. It is significant that Willison noted that both James L. Johnson and James Patterson had butcher shops in Santa Fe. In 1865 D. Bernard Koch supplied the bonds for legal Comanchero expeditions led by the likes of James Giddings and Fernando Lucero. See D. Bernard Koch as bondholder for trader Giddings, Oct. 30, 1865, and for trader Lucero, Oct. 2, 1865, RNMSIA, LR 1864–65, R6.

28. Bryan W. Turo, "An Empire of Dust: Thomas Benton Catron and the Age of Capital in the Hispanic Borderland, 1840–1921" (PhD diss., University of New Mexico, 2015), 90, 100.

29. On Willison, see *Mariono F. Sena v. The United States*, Cases and Points of the Supreme Court of the United States, Transcript of Record, Oct. Term, 1902, No. 40 (Washington, D.C.: Judd and DeTweiler, Printers, 1902). Robert Willison deposition, July 20, 1898, *Probst and Kirchner*, Claim 2109, IDC.

30. Nolan, *Lincoln County War*, 442, 443.

31. John Taylor deposition, August 6, 1878, *Report and Testimony in the Matter of the Charges against Samuel B. Axtell, Governor of New Mexico*, Oct. 3, 1878, NA, RG 48, Special Collections, Donnelly Library, New Mexico Highlands University, Las Vegas.

32. Taylor's tax record for a license is from 1868; see "Internal Revenue Assessment Lists for the Territory of New Mexico, 1862–1870, 1872–1874"; "1870 Village of Apache Springs—NM AHGP," Apache Springs 1870 Federal Census, RG 29, Records of the Bureau of the Census, San Miguel County, NMT, p. 1, NA, nmahgp.geneologyvillage .com/Grace%20Censuses/sm1870apachesprings.html (accessed Jan. 2, 2021).

33. Adolph Seligman deposition, July 21, 1898, *Probst and Kirchner*, Case No. 2109, IDC.
34. Ibid.
35. Thomas B. Catron deposition, *Probst and Kirchner*, Case No. 1646, Catron Papers, MSS 29, B.C. Series 803, Box 1, CSR.
36. Catron deposition, ibid. Harry Peyton to Catron and Catron, Oct. 17, 1910, Catron and Catron to Peyton, Oct. 21, 1910, Peyton to Catron and Catron, June 25, 1911, Peyton to Catron and Catron, Jan. 26, 1912, Peyton to Catron and Catron, April 5, 1912, all in Catron Papers, MSS 29, Series 803, Box 1, Catron and Catron Cases, CSR.
37. Catron deposition, *Probst and Kirchner*, Case No. 1646, IDC.
38. Ibid.
39. Ibid.
40. Ibid.; José Piedad Tafoya deposition, *Goodnight and Sheek v. The United States et al.*, Case No. 9133, IDC; Manuel Gonzales deposition, ibid.
41. *HTO*, s.v. "Goodnight, Charles," by H. Allen Anderson, https://www.tshaonline.org/handbook/entries/goodnight-charles (accessed Nov. 13, 2020).
42. Goodnight deposition, *Goodnight and Sheek v. The United States et al.*, Case No. 9133, IDC.
43. District of New Mexico commander Col. George W. Getty revoked Healy's license in September 1867 on the basis that he had sublet it to "scoundrels." See Getty to Dubois, Sept. 12, 1867, NA, RG 393, LS, in Arrott Collection, Vol. 21, 115. Healy ended up in Albuquerque where he opened a meat market on Main Street. A theme begins to develop regarding butchers, cattle brokers, and Comancheros. Somewhat ironically, in May 1871 Healy was killed by Comanches while on his way to Texas to accept a job with Edmund J. Davis's new state police. On the meat market and his death see, the *Republican Review*, May 18, 1871; Goodnight deposition, *Goodnight and Sheek v. The United States et al.*, Case No. 9133, IDC.
44. Tafoya deposition, *Goodnight and Sheek v. The United States et al.*, Case No. 9133, IDC. Tafoya recalled that U.S. soldiers took about nine hundred of these cattle once he crossed into New Mexico. He was not clear regarding exactly how this happened. It is probable that different herds came through at different times. While he specifically noted that these nine hundred cattle were taken from him in the spring of 1867, he does not detail how many were not taken. Patrols from Fort Bascom were probably involved in this action. In the same deposition he named several people who participated with him in the Comanchero trade, including José Feliz Ulibarri, Teodosio Valdez, Fernando Gallegos, Román Martínez, Francisco Gallegos, Gertrudis Medina, José García, Bento Mestas, José María Madril, Melquiendes Flores, José Armijo, Manuel Armijo, José Castillo, Teodosia Salas, and 'Cresecncus' (probably Crescenciano Gallegos, from Guadalupe County). Crescenciano was Antonio José Gallegos's son and was a lawyer and cattle rancher.
45. Tafoya deposition, *Goodnight and Sheek v. The United States et al.*, Case No. 9133, IDC.
46. Goodnight deposition, ibid.
47. Richard Greenwood, "Natural Historic Landmark Nomination Form: Theme #6, Western Expansion 1763–1898: Western Trails and Travelers," FHR-8-250

(October 1978), item 17, p. 3, https://npgallery.nps.gov/GetAsset/794b3983-7f44-47ea
-bddb-398c6eb67482 (accessed June 17, 2019).

48. Ibid.; Blackshear, *Fort Bascom*, 126–58; Hämäläinen, *Comanche Empire*, 315; Charles
Irving Jones, "William Kroenig: First New Mexican Pioneer," *New Mexico Historical
Review* 19, no. 3 (1944): 309. Kroenig also partnered with merchant William Moore,
who sold merchandise in Tecolote and was the Fort Union sutler for a time. See voucher
signed by Carleton to Bell, Chief Commissary of Subsistence, U.S. Army, Feb. 10, 1866,
NA, RG 393, LS, Fort Union, USAC.

49. Goodnight deposition, *Goodnight and Sheek v. The United States et al.*, Case No. 9133,
IDC.

50. Greenwood, National Historic Landmark nomination form, 77; Goodnight deposition,
Goodnight and Sheek v. The United States et al., Case No. 9133, IDC.

51. Manuel Gonzales deposition, *Goodnight and Sheek v. The United States et al.*, Case
No. 9133, IDC. Gonzales lived in La Cuesta and Chaperito. He also vouched for a claim
made by Teodosio Salas, as did Juan Gallegos, both of whom Tafoya identified as San
Miguel County Comancheros; see Teodosio Salas deposition, ibid.

52. Manuel Gonzales deposition, ibid.

53. José Getrude Medina deposition, ibid.

54. Blackshear, *Fort Bascom* 140–41, On the Abreu licenses, "Internal Revenue Assessment
Lists for the Territory of New Mexico"; Lorenzo López license to trade, Oct. 19, 1865,
RNMSIA, 1864–65, R6.

55. William B. Stapp deposition, *Goodnight and Sheek v. The United States et al.*, Case
No. 9133, IDC.

56. Vernon Maddux, *John Hittson: Cattle King on the Texas and Colorado Frontier* (Boulder:
University of Colorado Press, 1994), 158; Eugenio Romero deposition, *Goodnight and
Sheek v. The United States et al.*, Case No. 9133, IDC; José Piedad Tafoya deposition,
ibid.; Sept. 10, 1867, RNMSIA, LR 1866–67, R7; NA, RG 393, LS, DNM, in Arrott Collection, Vol. 49, 151; Oct. 15, 1866, NA, OIA, LR, NM, 1868, M234, R375.

57. Eugenio Romero deposition, *Goodnight and Sheek v. The United States et al.*, Case
No. 9133, IDC; Tafoya deposition, ibid.

58. R. J. Hamilton, "Atrocious Murder," Hatch's Ranch, NM, Dec. 12, 1868, *Santa Fe Daily
New Mexican*, Dec. 17, 1868; *Santa Fe Daily New Mexican*, Jan. 5, 1869. On Hamil-
ton's failed attempt to get a license of his own, see Robert J. Hamilton, Aug. 30, 1865,
RNMSIA, LR 1864–65, R6.

59. Most of this account comes from the *Santa Fe Daily New Mexican*, Jan. 5, 1869. I also
used *Nuevo Mejicano Diario*, dispatched from Puerto de Luna, Dec. 26, 1868, in *Santa
Fe Daily New Mexican*, Jan. 5, 1869. The denunciation, entitled "Proclamation," is found
in *Santa Fe Daily New Mexican*, March 16, 1869.

60. *Nuevo Mejicano Diario*, Dec. 26, 1868, in *Santa Fe Daily New Mexican*, Jan. 5, 1869.

61. *Nuevo Mejicano Diario*, Dec. 26 and 30, 1868, in *Santa Fe Daily New Mexican*, Jan. 5
and 16, 1869. Sam Gholson deserves his own book. He lived his last days in Tucumcari.
On Gholson, see Robert W. Stephen, Texas Ranger War Pensions, Ind: Sur. #8870. On
Elkins, see John M. Elkins, *Life on the Texas Frontier* (Beaumont, Tex.: Green Print,

1908), 89. On Labadie's run-in with Texas Confederates in Las Cruces, see Thompson, *Civil War History of the New Mexico Volunteers*, 4. On Labadie serving with Manuel Chaves at the Battle of Glorieta Pass, see Lorenzo Labadie deposition, in *Chavez and Labadi v. The United States*, Case No. 3252, IDC.

62. Haley, *Charles Goodnight*, 218, 219. Another account of Calloway's involvement can be found in Frank D. Reeve, *The History of New Mexico*, vol. 2 (New York: Lewis Historic Publication Co., 1961), 310.

63. *Nuevo Mejicano Diario*, Dec. 26 and 30, 1869. The 1870 Federal Census for San Miguel County shows that R. James Hamilton was living at Hatch's Ranch, owning land valued at $5,000 and personal property of $1,000. Sixty-six other people lived in what the census noted as being the village of Hatch's Ranch; see 1870 Federal Census, San Miguel County, NM, NA, RG 29, p. 57a.

64. *Santa Fe Daily New Mexican*, March 16, 1869.

Chapter 5

1. Stephen G. Hyslop, *Bound for Santa Fe: The Road to New Mexico and the American Conquest, 1806–1848* (Norman: University of Oklahoma Press, 2002), 75.

2. Kenner, *Comanchero Frontier*, 186–91; Hämäläinen, *Comanche Empire*, 320.

3. Hämäläinen, *Comanche Empire*, 320.

4. *Santa Fe Daily New Mexican*, July 20, 1868; Lee Scott Theison, "Frank Warner Angel's Notes on New Mexico Territory," *Arizona and the West*, no. 4 (Winter 1976), 350.

5. F. M. Willburn [*sic*] and T. L. Stockton of Red River Station, Articles of Agreement, Oct. 8, 1869, RMNSIA, LR from the Headquarters DNM (U.S. Army) 1869, R10. Eaton's experience can be found in Miller, *Soldiers and Settlers*, 191.

6. See Probst and Kirchner's agreement with Félix García and Z. Staab and Bros., Oct. 15, 1869, RMNSIA, LR from the Headquarters DNM (U.S. Army) 1869, R10. Joseph Larue had been post sutler for Fort Sumner and an Indian trader. When he signed this document he was a cattle broker. Wilburn and Stockton show up in the same household in 1870 Federal Census, Precinct 3, Cimarron, Colfax County, NMT, 3.

7. Probst and Kirchner's (hereafter P&K) bond contract with Wilburn and Stockton, Oct. 11, 1869, RMNSIA, LR, DNM 1849–80, R10; P&K agreement with Félix García and Z. Staab and Bros., same date, ibid. Félix García and J. Rivera were awarded a pass to trade with the Pueblo Indians in 1854; see Manypenny to Meriwether, Letter from the Indian Office to the Governor of New Mexico, ibid., R2. Abraham and Zadok Staab had the largest wholesale merchandise operation in New Mexico in 1858. The Staab brothers were involved in all facets of the New Mexico economy during the period in question. See Parish, *Charles Ilfeld Company*, 7, 8, 67.

8. P&K bond contract with Wilburn and Stockton for Cimarron agency, Oct. 11, 1869, RNMSIA, LR, DNM 1849–80, R10.

9. Robert C. Carriker, *Fort Supply, Indian Territory: Frontier Outpost on the Plains* (Norman: University of Oklahoma Press, 1990), 42, 60, 75, 81, 86.

10. See Report: Superintendent of Indian Affairs, H.E.D. Meriwether, Sept. 1, 1854, RNMSIA, LR 1854–56, R2.

11. William T. Hagan, "Kiowas, Comanches, and Cattlemen, 1867–1906: A Case Study of the Failure of the U.S. Reservation Policy," *Pacific Historical Review* 40, no. 3 (Aug. 1971), 334.

12. Boone Report, Medicine Bluff, Indian Territory, Feb. 12, 1869, Kiowa Agency, 1869–70, NA, OIA, LR 1824–81, M234, R376; Stan Hoig, *Cowtown Wichita and the Wild, Wicked West* (Albuquerque:University of New Mexico Press, 2007), 67, 68.

13. *Santa Fe Daily New Mexican*, July 18, 1870.

14. Ibid., Sept. 1, 1870; William A. Pile, "Proclamation," ibid., Aug. 13, 1872.

15. Maddux, *John Hittson*, 140.

16. Ibid., 137, 138; Frederick J. Rathjen, *The Texas Panhandle Frontier* (Austin: University of Texas Press, 1973), 196, 197.

17. *Santa Fe Daily New Mexican*, May 24, 1871, June 6, 1871, and June 12, 1871. That July this paper published the bid abstract of contractors seeking to sell beef to the territory's military posts. These bids came from "Wilburn and Stockton," Emil Fritz, George Huth, and P&K also submitted bids; see *Daily New Mexican*, July 1, 1871. The Isleta Indians reference comes from the same paper, July 8, 1871. "Mexicans and the Indian squaw," quote from *Daily New Mexican*, July 25, 1871. The cattle in question never left their possession; see Kenner, *Comanchero Frontier*, 188.

18. Gregg to Clendenin, Feb. 25, 1871, NA, LS, DNM, RG 393, in Arrott Collection, Vol. 25, p. 48.

19. Kenner, *Comanchero Frontier*, 191, 192. Glen Sample Ely saved me from embarrassment by pointing out that sometimes the Comancheros were not to be believed. Ortíz lied to the officers who caught him, telling them he was from Chama. As noted, he was from La Cuesta but also lived in Puerto de Luna. See RG 29, 1900 Federal Census, DNM, Puerto de Luna, Precinct 10, taken by Lorenzo Labadi. Ortíz's statement can be found in NA, RG 393, LS to AAG, April 15, 1872, Fort Concho, Tex.

20. Kenner, *Comanchero Frontier*, 191, 192; Ortíz statement, NA, RG 393, LS to AAG, April 15, 1872, Fort Concho, Tex.

21. Kenner, *Comanchero Frontier*, 191, 192.

22. Haley, *Charles Goodnight*, 205; Maddux, *John Hittson*, 145, 146. As Frederick Nolan attests, after Sheriff William Brady was shot down in Lincoln County, a Jim Patterson was a part of the posse that formed to go after his killers. One of their targets was Billy the Kid; see Nolan, *Lincoln County War*, 279n14.

23. Maddux, *John Hittson*, 145, 146; *Daily Rocky Mountain News*, April 29, 1873.

24. Written in Las Vegas on October 5, 1872, the article on these bands was published in the appropriately named *Republican Review*, Oct. 26, 1872.

25. See "Bill of Indictment," *Territory of New Mexico v. Charles Probst and August Kirchner*, July 30, 1867, Case 157A, C. Probst and A. Kirchner, Folder 67, NMRCA; and "Public Nuisance," Folder A. Kirchner 366A, July 30, 1870, and Jan. 10, 1872, NMRCA. As to the location of Rio Chiquito, a caption for an illustration of the Sister's Chapel in Santa

Fe, which ran in *Harper's*, reads "from Rio Chiquito"; see Henry Mills Alden, "La Villa Real de Santa Fe," *Harper's New Monthly* 60 (Dec. 1879–May 1880), 673.

26. William A. Keleher, *The Fabulous Frontier, 1846–1912* (Alburquerque: University of New Mexico Press, 1962), 120, 122.

27. Turo, "Empire of Dust," 90, 100.

28. Ibid., 98, 99.

29. Ibid. The quote from Dolan comes from Caffey, *Chasing the Santa Fe Ring*, 250.

30. Turo, "Empire of Dust," 90, 100.

31. Support for Kirchner can be found in "Good Workers," *Santa Fe New Mexican*, Sept. 5, 1873. Kirchner's San Francisco Street meat market was situated close to the businesses of many of his supporters: Zadok and Abraham Staab had a general store on the northwest corner of the central plaza on San Francisco Street; Felipe Delgado had a general merchandising business on San Francisco Street opposite the plaza, as did Willie Spiegelberg; see Polk and Danser, *Colorado, New Mexico . . . Business Directory*, 352–54. In addition to doing business with the government, the Spiegelbergs were in the wholesale and retail business and participated in a variety of ventures with numerous Santa Feans, including Anastacio Sandoval. As outlined in the introduction, Sandoval was a merchant and part-time Comanchero who both funded and participated in expeditions to Texas. See Floyd S. Fierman, *Guts, and Ruts: The Jewish Pioneer on the Trail in the American Southwest* (Brooklyn, N.Y.: Ktav Publishing, 1984), 10. David Catanack applied for a pass to trade with the Comanches in 1869; see letter dated May 20, 1869, RNMSIA, R10.

32. On Ring affiliations, see Caffey, *Chasing the Santa Fe Ring*, 14–24.

33. See, "Bill of Indictment," *Territory of New Mexico v. Charles Probst and August Kirchner*, July 30, 1867, Case 157A, C. Probst and A. Kirchner, Folder 67, NMRCA; and "Public Nuisance," Folder A, Kirchner 366A, July 30, 1870, and Jan. 10, 1872, NMRCA.

34. The bargain struck between Elkins and Kirchner is found in Robert B. Willison deposition, *Probst and Kirchner v. The United States et al.*, Case No. 2109, IDC.

35. "From La Junta," *Santa Fe New Mexican*, Jan. 30, 1872; *Santa Fe Weekly New Mexican*, Feb. 6, 1872.

36. "Row in Trinidad," *Santa Fe New Mexican*, Feb. 13, 1872.

37. "From Rio Abajo: Los Lunas, N.Mex., April 15, 1871," *Santa Fe Daily New Mexican* April 20, 1871.

38. Maddux, *John Hittson*, 137; Blackshear, *Fort Bascom*, 163. On the *Santa Fe Daily New Mexican's* loyalty to the Republican Party, see Theison, "Frank Warner Angel's Notes," 350. The Hughes and Church reference comes from Kenner, *Comanchero Frontier*, 192.

39. Catron deposition, *Probst and Kirchner v. The United States et al.*, Case No. 1646, IDC, in Catron Papers, MSS 29, B.C. Series 803, Box 1, CSR. Reference to Marcus Goldbaum opening a meat market on "Main Steet" is in *Santa Fe Weekly Gazette*, Aug. 5, 1865; Marcus Goldbaum to Carleton, June 7, 1866, RNMSIA, LR, Kiowa Agency 1864–80, R375. Catron's loan to Goldbaum can be found in Victor Westphall, *Thomas Benton Catron and His Era* (Tuscon: University of Arizona Press, 1973), 33.

40. *Santa Fe Weekly New Mexican*, July 2, 1872.
41. While no name is provided, the *New Mexican's* prior disdain for Probst and Kirchner can be found in an article about Angel's investigation into Governor Axtell's business ties with Santa Fe Ring operators. One column commented on who approved of Angel's work, such as "a sleeve button lawyer in Santa Fe" (probably Kirchner and Probst's lawyer, William Breeden), as well as "two butchers" and "four pimps" who had "unduly convinced him" to make a negative report about Axtell. When Probst spoke to Angel about Axtell, he also made several negative comments about Elkins. See *Santa Fe Weekly New Mexican*, Aug. 17, 1878, in Theisen, "Frank Warner Angel's Notes," 336. Details concerning Santa Fe merchants who were Democratic Party leaders and stood in opposition to the Ring can be found in Bryan Turo's recent dissertation on Catron. Turo also details how Kirchner and the merchants he often partnered with began to support Republican candidates, particularly Elkins. However, Turo failed to make the connection between Hittson, Kirchner, the merchants, and the Comancheros. See Turo, "Empire of Dust," 100–102; *Santa Fe Daily New Mexican*, July 31, 1872. The Rosenbaums, Zechendorfs, and Ilfelds, who made a lot of money selling beef and dry goods to the government, were some of these Democrats; see Tobias, *History of Jews in New Mexico*, 70–77. Aside from Republican stalwart Romero, Las Vegas merchant Charles Ilfeld certainly sold a lot of goods to the reservations and had a close relationship with Kirchner and Goldbaum. While still working with Adolph Letcher in Taos, Ilfeld used "trusted friend" Kirchner to deliver cash to their supplier in Santa Fe, Elsberg and Amberg; see Parish, *Charles Ilfeld Company*, 16; *Santa Fe Daily New Mexican*, Aug. 8, 1872. W. H. Henrie of Albuquerque also put up bonds for a legal expeditions to "Comanche country" in 1865 and sought to carry out his own trade with the Comanches in 1870; see W. H. Henrie, bondholder, Bureau of Indian Affairs, Nov. 17, 1865, RNMSIA, LR 1864–65, R6.
42. On Friedman, see 1870 Federal Census, Taos County, NM, Red Willow Indian Reservation, NA, RG 29, Reel No. M593-846, p. 23. As a part of Guttman, Friedman and Co., along with Zadok Staab and the Spiegelbergs, he was a staunch Democrat who defended the butcher against Catron when the lawyer sued him. See Tobias, *History of the Jews in New Mexico*, 85. Guttman and his partners were competitors of Wilburn and Stockton; see *Santa Fe Daily New Mexican*, July 1, 1871.
43. On Wilson, see Haley, *Charles Goodnight*, 205, and Maddux, *John Hittson*, 146. On Allison and Colbert, see Frank Clifford, *Deep Trails in the Old West: A Frontier Memoir* (Norman: University of Oklahoma Press, 2011), 15, 31, 258n6. Robert K. DeArment argues that Stockton recruited these gunfighters for the raids; see DeArment, *Bravo of the Brazos: John Larn of Fort Griffin, Texas* (Norman: University of Oklahoma Press, 2002), 29, 30. On Clifton House, see Marc Simmons, *Following the Santa Fe Trail: A Guide for Modern Travelers*, rev. ed. (Norman: University of Oklahoma Press, 1986), 136, 137. On Wilburn's involvement in Zack Crumpton's death, see Nolan, *Lincoln County War*, 53, 500.
44. Maddux, *John Hittson*, 158.
45. Kenner, *Comanchero Frontier*, 194; Maddux, *John Hittson*, 146.

46. Dalton and Hittson visited this meat market on July 30, 1872; see Maddux, *John Hittson*, 156. John Dalton, Application for Pass, March 25, 1866, RNMSIA, 1866–67, R7; item on Patterson going to the Pecos in *Santa Fe Weekly New Mexican*, Aug. 6, 1872; "Los Tejanos," *Revista Republicana*, Aug. 10, 1872.

47. *Territory v. John Hittson, Thomas Stockton, and Joseph [Martin] Childers*, Case No. 397, "stealing four cows," NMRCA, San Miguel County District Court (hereafter SMDC), 1868–76 (Aug. term, 1872), 133.

48. *John Hittson v. Desidero Romero*, Case No. 406, "replevin," and *Alexander Grzelachowski v. John Hittson et al.*, Case No. 408, "trespassing," both NMRCA, SMDC (March term, 1873), 143. Information on Desiderio Romero is from "Baptisms: Romero Surnames, Santa Fe County, NM," US GenWeb Archives, https://www.usgwarchives.net/nm /santafe; "Los Tejanos," *Revista Republicana*, Aug. 10, 1872.

49. Francis C. Kajencki, "Alexander Grzelachowski, Pioneer Merchant of Puerto de Luna, New Mexico," *Journal of the Southwest* 26, no. 3 (Autumn 1984), 250.

50. *Manuel Romero v. James Patterson*, Case No. 440, "replevin," NMRCA, SMDC (March term, 1873), 151, "outsized file" no. 014, "Judges-Civil Docket, 1868–76," Serial #14752; Gonzales, *Política*, 980nn92–94; *Jose Maria Montoya v. Martin Childers*, Case No. 451, "trespass," NMRCA, SMDC (Aug. term, 1873), 163; *Louis Sulzbacher v. John Hittson*, Case No. 489, "assumpsit," NMRCA, SMDC (Aug. term, 1874), 188; *May Hays v. John Hittson*, Case No. 492, "assumpsit," NMRCA, SMDC (Aug. term, 1874), 189. Of Probst and Kirchner's case, on Oct. 22, 1872 the *Santa Fe Weekly New Mexican* sarcastically commented, "We learn that messr. Probst and Kirchner's cattle taken by the Texans was replevied until a final determination can be made[. T]he cattle are 'browsing quietly in the county of Rio Arriba.'" The charges filed in San Miguel County are recorded in the August 1872 term, which was before the Loma Parda raids and illustrates that this was more than an isolated incident. These cases were refiled in March 1873 before being moved to Colfax County that same month. Noting each of these charges helps to show that there was a legal response to these raids, but other than Childers's arrest, they did not get anywhere. Case No. 390, *Territory v. John Hittson, Thomas Stockton and Joseph Childers et al.* "stealing 4 cattle" NMRCA, SMDC (Aug. term, 1872), outsized file 005, 1871–76, serial no. 14743 [hereafter case no., crime, last names only of those charged (and no term listed unless it has changed)]; No. 391, "stealing a cow," Hittson, Stockton, Childers, et al.; No. 392, "stealing cattle," Hittson, Stockton, Childers, et al.; No. 395, "stealing cattle," Hittson, Stockton, Childers, et al.; No. 396, "stealing cattle," Hittson, Stockton, Childers, et al.; No. 397, "assault in a menacing manner," Hittson; No. 398, "assault in a menacing manner," Childers; No. 399, "assault and wounding," Frank Chapman, with a handwritten note that Chapman pleaded guilty. (The case is not clear here, but Chapman was a major rancher and merchant near Hatch's Ranch and is not listed in any other source regarding the raids. Since he is listed chronologically within these cases, I include him. Chapman has ties to several other Las Vegas merchants.) No. 401, "carrying arms," Patterson; No. 402, "carrying arms," Childers; No. 403, "carrying arms," Stockton; No. 404, "carrying arms," Hittson; No. 405, "stealing cattle," Hittson, Stockton, James Patterson [first inclusion], Childers; No. 406, "stealing a

cow," Martin Childers; No. 418, "riot," Thomas Stockton et al. These cases were reprinted in the March 1873 court docket that was moved to Colfax County. This helps to explain why no one ever served any time. Stockton lived in Colfax County. Another interesting case that made the docket that March concerned a Hugh M. Childress, Case No. 427, NMRCA, SMDC (March term, 1873), who was found not guilty of stealing four horses. Kenner argues that it was this Childress, and not Childers, who led the raid on Loma Parda. While this case puts Childress in New Mexico and associates him with stealing horses (Julián Baca's horses?), the bulk of the evidence identifies Childers as the Texan with the more significant role. See Kenner, *Comanchero Frontier*, 195n63.

51. Simmons, *Following the Santa Fe Trail*, 164, 166. For one of William Tipton's proposals to supply beef to Fort Union, see abstract of bids, posted in *Santa Fe Weekly New Mexican*, May 13, 1872.

52. Raber quoted in George A. Root, "Reminiscenses of William Darnell," *Collection of the Kansas State Historical Society, 1923–1925*, vol. 16 (Topeka: Kansas State Printing Plant, 1925), 321–22; Ely, *Texas Frontier and Butterfield Overland Mail*, 102–4.

53. *Goodnight and Sheek v. The United States et al.*, Case No. 9133, IDC.

54. 1870 Federal Census, Loma Parda, Mora County, NM, NA, RG 29.

55. That the McMartins were cattle brokers can be found in "Colfax County, New Mexico Biographies," Geneology Trails, http://genealogytrails.com/newmex/colfax/biographies .htm (accessed July 15, 2019); Henry C. Meyers, "The Founding of Loma Parda," *Wagon Tracks* 7 (August 1993): 11–12; David P. Keener, "A Town Maligned: Loma Parda, New Mexico" (MA thesis, Northern Arizona University, 1988), 85. On the McMartins' wagon-taxi, see Jan Mackall Collins, *Good Time Girls of Arizona and New Mexico: A Real Red-Light History of the American Southwest* (Guilford, Conn.: Two Dot Press, 2019), 90.

56. The 1870 Federal Census notes that Charles Duetschmann had three employees living with him, two of whom were from Prussia: 1870 census, Loma Parda, Mora County, NM, NA, RG 29; Oliva, *Fort Union and the Frontier Army*, 127.

57. Keener notes that Matías Baca, not Julián, was the "principal" who signed this bond in conjunction with the others. In the 1880 Federal Census Julián Baca's designation is "huckster." Other references are from Keener, "Town Maligned," 82

58. See Frank Clark, 1870 Federal Census, Loma Parda, Precinct 13, Mora County, NM, NA, RG 29; Frank Clark, Case No. 265, Catron Papers, 1866–68, MSS 29, B.C. Series 803, Box 1, Folder 10, CSR; *United States v. Samuel L. Simmons, Loma Parda*, "retail liquor dealer," ibid.

59. C. Blanchard, *Revista Republicana*, Aug. 17, 1872. Four more Loma Pardans may have died during this same period, which would have brought the death count to nine before the major cattle raid. Larry Ball noted that four Loma Parda "stock thieves" where lynched in July or August 1872. This could also be referencing the same victims that Blanchard wrote about; see appendix C in Ball, *Desert Lawmen*, 379.

60. See note 50 above on the discrepancy in the record regarding "Childers" versus "Childress." While I will use several contemporaneous newspaper accounts to reconstruct

what happened in Loma Parda, the first account, written only five days after the major raid of September 10, 1872, from Watrous (La Junta) probably gives the most accurate details. They are all cited in "The Murder of Garcia and Seaman," *Santa Fe Daily New Mexican*, Sept. 18, 1872, written from La Junta. Charles L. Kenner's reconstructions (in *Comanchero Frontier*) are also used.

61. "Murder of Garcia and Seaman," *Santa Fe Daily New Mexican*, Sept. 18, 1872.
62. Ibid.
63. Ibid.
64. Ibid.
65. Ibid.
66. *Daily New Mexican* September 18, 1872. This same paper offered its own take on what happened, charging that it was only after Seaman stuck a gun in Childers's face that another Texan was forced to shoot the sheriff in the back of the head; see *Santa Fe Daily New Mexican*, Sept. 26, 1872. Writing from Stockton's ranch, Patterson claimed that "reliable men" had told him that the Texans had given receipts for the cattle taken. He began this rebuttal by addressing the reading audience as "Gents." His account did not mention that the Texans had visited Loma Parda two days previous to the cataclysmic event. See James Patterson, "The Loma Parda Tragedy," *Santa Fe Daily New Mexican*, Oct. 1, 1872. In that same edition Patterson identifies M. Childers as the leader of the raid. (This would have been Martin or, more accurately, Joseph Martin.) This confusion over Childers's name began with a recounting by Joseph C. McCoy in *Historic Sketches of the Cattle Trade of the West and Southwest*, vol. 8, ed. Ralph Bieber (Glendale, Calif.: 1931–32), 132; Kenner repeated it in *Comanchero Frontier*.
67. Patterson, "The Loma Parda Tragedy," *Santa Fe Daily New Mexican*, Oct. 1, 1872.
68. The meeting with the superintendent comes from Maddux, *John Hittson*, 166n4; *Santa Fe Daily New Mexican*, Sept. 14, 1872. The chronology is as follows: the final raid was on September 10; the first account was written on September 14; this account was not published until September 18. The possibility that a Paul F. *Herlow* and not Paul T. Herlon met with this same superintendent is related to information found in Frederick Nolan, *The West of Billy the Kid* (Norman: University of Oklahoma Press, 1999), 37.
69. *Santa Fe New Mexican*, Oct. 22, 1872.
70. Ibid.
71. William A. Keleher, *The Maxwell Land Grant: A New Mexican Item* (Albuquerque: University of New Mexico Press, 1964), 37.
72. Ibid. William F. Switzer noted that the Elkins Ranch was on the Pecos in *A History of Boone County, Missouri: Written and Compiled from Most Authentic Official and Private Sources* (St. Louis: Western Historical Co., 1882), 857. A map entitled "Territory of New Mexico, USDI-General Land Office 1876," identifies the Elkins Ranch a mile or so to the northeast of present-day Santa Rosa on what was called Tanos Creek, which fed into the Pecos River. Pablo Aragón testified that Giddings employed him as a cattle and sheep herder at Agua Negra. Found in Aragón deposition, *James M. Giddings v. The*

United States and the Navajo Indian, Case No. 2647, IDC. Tafoya lists Pablo Aragón as
one of his employees in José Piedad Tafoya pass, Oct. 9, 1865, RNMSIA, R6; Granger's
reference is found in Kenner, *Comanchero Frontier*, 197. On Calloway being a horse
thief, see Frances Levine and Tom Merlan interview with Pablín Ulibarrí, Colonias,
New Mexico, July 26, 1977, in Frances Levine, "A Unified Anthropological Approach
to Historial Archaelogy: A Study from Los Esteros Lake, Guadalupe County, New
Mexico" (PhD diss., Southern Methodist University, Dallas, 1980), 100.

73. Samuel Elkins to Stephen "Dear Brother" Elkins, Oct. 18, 1869, NMARC, Miscellaneous
Letters and Diaries, File 20, 15817.

74. María E. Montoya, *Translating Property: The Maxwell Land Grant and the Conflict
over Land in the American West, 1840–1900* (Lawrence: University of Kansas Press,
2002), 115–17. Much of the violence in Colfax County that has been associated with the
Maxwell Land Grant occurred before Elkins and Marmon did their survey. Clay Allison
(a possible participant in Stockton's raid on Loma Parda) was one of the cattlemen
who followed John S. Chisum and Charles Goodnight out of Texas. He took part in
these events, shooting Cruz Vega for the murder of Rev. Franklin J. Tolby. While there
are several books that cover the so-called Colfax County wars, Montoya's is probably
the best. She covers this incident quite succinctly on pages 112–13. On John T. Elkins's
resurveying the Anton Chico grant, see Father Stanley Crocchiola, *The Anton Chico
Story* (Pampa, Tex.: Pampa Print Shop, 1969). Although a bit far-fetched, the Elkinses
might have been interested in acquiring land in this region because of a proposed U.S.
mail route, to be a part of the infamous "star route" that would run north of Esteros
Creek, a tributary of the Pecos River, and thus pretty close to the Elkins Ranch. This
portion of that line was to run from Fort Bascom past Conchas and Cabra Springs
and then connect with Gallinas Springs before turning north to Chaperito. Any such
government-instituted route meant more traffic in the area, so anyone who owned
land along or near such routes stood to gain. This same route was under serious con-
sideration for a rail line: so much so that several maps show railroad tracks following
the same path. Although never implicated in the star route scandal, which involved
government kickbacks, Elkins did play a subtle role in the approval process. (Even its
main instigator, Stephen W. Dorsey, was absolved of any crime.) A well-traveled road
already connected Gallinas Springs to Beck's property and later the Elkins Ranch. For
more on the star route scandal, see Myers, *History of the Great American Fortunes*,
3:335, 336. A Rand McNally map from 1879 notes a proposed rail line for the Atlantic
Pacific Railroad Company running across the Gallinas River just south of Gallinas
Springs, and the corresponding stage road that ran in a southeasterly direction from
"Whittemore's" ranch across Esteros [Hurrah] Creek, just north of José Leandro Perea's
Rancho de los Esteros and Elkins's property; this indexed map of New Mexico reveals
state lines, counties, lake, and rivers. Retrieved from the Library of Congress, www
.loc.gov/item/98688517/ (accessed March 17, 2018). For information on Rancho de los
Esteros, see "Treaty of Guadalupe Hidalgo: Definition and List of Community Land
Grants in New Mexico: Exposure Draft" (Washington, D.C.: General Accounting
Office, 2001), 25.

75. 1870 Federal Census, Mora County, NMT, NA, RG 29, p. 306b. The census notes that Samuel Elkins, born in Missouri, was twenty-three in 1870. This correlates to the Jackson County, Missouri, 1860 Federal Census, which finds all four Elkins brothers there: eighteen-year-old Stephen, sixteen-year-old John T., and fourteen-year-old Samuel. They had a younger brother as well, James Elkins; see 1860 census, Jackson County, Mo., NA, RG 29, M635, R625.

76. *Santa Fe New Mexican*, Feb. 13, 1872. On Childers's arrest, see *Santa Fe Daily New Mexican*, Dec. 12, 1872.

77. Ilfeld Papers, Book 9, "John T. Elkins and Co.," Sept. 1871, p. 325, CSR. On Comanchero and Comanche charms, see Alvin R. Lynn, *Kit Carson and the First Battle of Adobe Walls: A Tale of Two Journeys* (Lubbock: Texas Tech University Press, 2014), 141, 146, 147.

78. *Santa Fe Daily New Mexican*, Dec. 27 and 29, 1872. In addition to surveying and ranching, the Elkins brothers were also involved in the mining business. See Miller, *Soldiers and Settlers*, 152; William Baxter, *Gold and the Ortiz Mine Grant: A New Mexico History and Reference Guide* (Santa Fe: Lone Butte Press, 2014). 113.

79. Charles L. Kenner, "The Great New Mexico Cattle Raid, 1872," *New Mexico Historical Review* 37, no. 4 (Oct. 1962), 256, 257; *Santa Fe Weekly Post*, June 17, 1871.

80. Kenner, "Great New Mexico Cattle Raid," 256; *Denver Rocky Mountain News*, April 29, 1873; *Pueblo Colorado Chieftain*, Jan. 5, 1873.

81. *Colorado Chieftain*, Jan. 5, 1873.

82. John Hittson to Honorable William Veale, Chairman of the Committee on Indian Affairs, Palo Pinto, Tex., Feb. 10, 1873, as it appeared in the *Daily Statesman* (Austin, Tex.), March 21, 1873.

83. Catron deposition, *Probst and Kirchner v. The United States et al.*, Case No. 1646, in Catron Papers, CSR. An additional account that verifies Kirchner's cattle were replevied comes from the *Santa Fe Weekly New Mexican*, which reported they were found, "browsing quietly in the county of Rio Arriba," Oct. 22, 1872.

84. Paul L. Tsompanos, *Juan Patrón: A Fallen Star in the Days of Billy the Kid* (N.P.: Brandylane Press, 2012), 159; Nolan, *Lincoln County War*, 502.

85. Tsompanos, *Juan Patrón*, 159; Nolan, *Lincoln County War*, 502.

86. Nolan, *Lincoln County War*, 278, 279, 474; David Johnson, *The Horrell Wars: Feuding and Fighting in Texas and New Mexico* (Denton: University of North Texas Press, 2014), 59.

87. Nolan, *Lincoln County War*, 508; James Bailey Blackshear, *Honor and Defiance: The History of the Las Vegas Land Grant in New Mexico* (Santa Fe: Sunstone Press, 2013), 91, 97.

88. Tsompanos, *Juan Patrón*, 126, 146.

89. Ibid.

90. *Santa Fe New Mexico Union*, March 20, 1873; *Santa Fe New Mexican*, Oct .16, 1873.

91. Paul Weideman, "Historic Breweries Were All Gone by 1900," *Santa Fe New Mexican*, July 1, 2000. Information on Kirchner's connection to the Shonnard House can be found at Historic Santa Fe Foundation, s.v. "Eugene Shonnard House," historicsantafe

.org/eugene-shonnard-house (accessed Feb. 20, 2020). It must have been quite hard for Kirchner to go legit. Evidence that he occasionally strayed is found in an 1885 newspaper report regarding the theft of eight of Francisco Perea's cattle. Doing his own investigation, Perea discovered that noted thief Perfilio Casaus had sold his cattle to Kirchner. See *Santa Fe New Mexican*, July 27, 1885.

92. Historic Santa Fe Foundation, s.v. "Agua Fría as a State of Mind," by William Mee, historicsantafe.org/agua-fria village (accessed March 7, 2020).

93. John Taylor deposition, Aug. 6, 1878, *Report and Testimony in the Matter of the Charges against Samuel B. Axtell, Governor of New Mexico*, Oct. 3, 1878, NA, RG 48, Special Collections, Donnelly Library, New Mexico Highlands University, Las Vegas.

94. The *Rocky Mountain Sentinel* interviews were reprinted on Aug. 24, 1878, in *Las Vegas* (NM) *Gazette*. The editor of the short lived *Sentinel* was A. M. Williams. He was probably the reporter who interviewed Angel and Elkins, but there was no byline. After his investigation Angel prepared a notebook for new territorial governor Lew Wallace that contained notes on several individuals the new governor might encounter. Of Probst, he wrote, "Honest, reliable—but shallow." He called Stephen Elkins "silver tongued, further comments unnecessary." Of John Elkins, he noted that he was honest, a strong Ring member, and dependent on his old brother. See Theisen, "Frank Warner Angel's Notes," 351.

95. The *Sentinel* interviews, reprinted in *Las Vegas Gazette*, Aug. 24, 1878.

96. Ibid.

97. Caffey, *Chasing the Santa Fe Ring*, 242.

98. *Sentinel* interviews, reprinted in *Las Vegas Gazette*, Aug. 24, 1878.

99. Ibid.

100. Ibid.

101. Ibid.; Catron deposition, *Probst and Kirchner v. The United States et al.*, Case No. 1646, IDC, in Catron Papers, CSR.

102. Elkins's attempt to go around Angel is found in Joel Jacobsen, *Such Men as Billy the Kid: The Lincoln County War Reconsidered* (Lincoln: University of Nebraska Press, 1997) 195, 197.

103. Nolan, *Lincoln County War*, 513, 518.

104. Jacobsen, *Such Men as Billy the Kid*, 195, 197.

105. Catron deposition, *Probst and Kirchner v. The United States et al.*, Case No. 1646, IDC, in Catron Papers, CSR. For the listings of commercial property and landowner rankings, see Linda T. Tigges, "Santa Fe Land Ownership in the 1880s," *New Mexico Historical Review*, no. 2 (April 1993), 172. Other commercial property owners on the list include Thomas B. Catron and the Delgado and Yrissari families. Kirchner was related to the Yrissaris through marriage. The top two landowners in Santa Fe were merchants Abraham Staab and Lehman Speigelberg. Tigges notes that in 1882, Probst's land was subdivided into "part of the Capitol addition," 172.

106. *HTO*, s.v. "Goodnight, Charles," by H. Allen Anderson, https://www.tshaonline.org /handbook/entries/goodnight-charles (accessed Nov. 13, 2020).

Chapter 6

1. Ford to Runnels, Camp Runnels, Tex., June 2, 1858, Box 301-27, Hardin Richard Runnels Papers, TSLAC (quotation); Blain to Houston, WIA, I.T., April 5, 1860, Box 301-32, Sam Houston Papers, TSLAC; Neighbors to Mix, San Antonio, Tex., Jan. 17, 1858, NA, LR, AGO, RG 94, M567, R591. For more on the organized gang of white rustlers known as the Old Law Mob who terrorized the Texas frontier during this time, see Ely, *The Texas Frontier*, 102–15, 371–74.

2. Twiggs to Thomas, San Antonio, Tex., Jan. 30, 1858, NA, AGO, RG 94, M567, R591; Van Dorn to Withers, Camp Colorado, Tex., Nov. 1 and Nov. 10, 1857, NA, AGO, RG 94, M567, R572; Burleson to Ford, Camp Runnels, Tex., March 30, 1858, in Winfrey and Day, *Indian Papers of Texas*, 3:279; Capt. T. J. Johnson to Col. M. T. Johnson, Fort Belknap, Tex., May 14, 1860, Box 301-32, Sam Houston Papers, TSLAC; Col. M. T. Johnson to Gov. Sam Houston, Fort Belknap, Tex., May 30, 1860, ibid. (quotation).

3. Leeper to Greenwood, Fort Cobb, I.T., May 2, 1860, NA, WIA, RG 75, M234, R928 (quotation). Captains Macintosh, Cabell, Huston, and Sturgis, along with Lieutenants Burnet, Williams, and Lomax, from the First Cavalry and the First Infantry stationed at Fort Cobb, all endorsed Leeper's letter. Bent's New Fort at Big Timbers on the Arkansas River was thirty-eight miles downstream from Bent's Old Fort (near present-day La Junta, Colorado). Originally built in 1833 by brothers Charles and William Bent and business partner Ceran St. Vrain, Bent's Old Fort was abandoned in 1849. The National Park Service reconstructed the old trading post in 1975. For more on Bent's Old Fort and Bent's New Fort, see State Historical Society of Colorado, *Bent's Old Fort* (Denver: State Historical Society of Colorado, 1979); David Lavender, *Bent's Fort* (Lincoln: University of Nebraska Press, 1954); Douglas C. Comer, *Ritual Ground: Bent's Old Fort, World Formation, and the Annexation of the Southwest* (Berkeley: University of California Press, 1996). A good map detailing Bent's Fort, Big Timbers, and Kansas Territory is *A New Map of Nebraska, Kansas, New Mexico, and Indian Territories, by Charles Desilver, Philadelphia, 1859*, David Rumsey Historical Map Collection, www .davidrumsey.com.

4. Lee to Thomas, San Antonio, Tex., March 6, 1860, NA, AGO, RG 94, M567, R615; Lowe to Thomas, Camp Cooper, Tex., Feb. 21, 1860 (quotation one); Houston to Thompson, Austin, Tex., Feb. 17, 1860, Box 301-31, Sam Houston Papers, TSLAC (quotations two and three).

5. Sam Houston to Turner, Austin, Tex., May 31, 1860, Sam Houston Executive Order Letterpress Copybook, Microfilm R5, TSLAC.

6. Turner to Houston, Camp Cobb, I.T., July 10, 1860, Turner to Houston, Camp Radzminski, I.T., July 18, 1860, and Turner to Houston, Old Camp Colorado, Tex., July 29, 1860, all in Box 301-32, Sam Houston Papers, TSLAC; Houston to Turner, Austin, Tex., Aug. 6, 1860, Sam Houston Executive Order Letterpress Copybook, Microfilm R5, TSLAC.

7. Comer, *Ritual Ground*, 155; Nolie Mumey, *Old Forts and Trading Posts of the West*, vol. 1, *Bent's Old Fort and Bent's New Fort on the Arkansas River* (Denver: Artcraft Press,

1956), 145–46; Miller to Haverty, Leavenworth City, Kan., Oct. 14, 1857, in *Report of the Commissioner of Indian Affairs, 1857*, 35th Cong., 1st Sess., House Exec. Doc. No. 2, 436 (quotation).

8. Miller to Haverty, *Report of the Commissioner of Indian Affairs, 1857*, 436 (quotations); Mumey, *Old Forts*, 145–46.

9. Mumey, *Old Forts*, 153; Marion Sloan Russell, *Land of Enchantment: Memoirs of Marion Sloan Russell along the Santa Fe Trail*, ed. Garnet M. Brayer (Albuquerque: University of New Mexico Press, 1981), 81 (quotation).

10. Lavender, *Bent's Fort*, 186–89; Mumey, *Old Forts*, 130–31; Kavanagh, *The Comanches*, 384–85, 386 (quotations).

11. Lavender, *Bent's Fort*, 186–89; Mumey, *Old Forts*, 130–31.

12. Greenwood to Bent, Washington, D.C., March 17, 1860, and Bent to Greenwood, Washington, D.C., March 17, 1860, NA, AGO, RG 94, M567, R625; Miller to Robinson, Bent's Fort, Kansas Territory, Aug. 17, 1858, in *Report of the Commissioner of Indian Affairs for 1858* (Washington, D.C.: Wm. A. Harris, 1858), 98.

13. Bent to Greenwood, Washington, D.C., March 17, 1860, NA, AGO, RG 94, M567, R625.

14. Greenwood to Thompson, Washington, D.C., March 20, 1860, and U.S. Army Adjutant General Samuel Cooper, March 27, 1860, endorsement on March 23, 1860, Interior Department message, NA, AGO, RG 94, M567, R625 (quotation).

15. Mumey, *Old Forts*, 173–84, 214 (endnote quotation); Lavender, *Bent's Fort*, 186–89. In 1923 George Grinnell described William Bent's home as a stockade situated on the west bank of the Purgatory River, one hundred yards south of the Arkansas. Until his death on May 19, 1869, Bent continued his business dealings with the Indians at his new location and "also went to trade in the camps and sent out parties of men to trade for him." Bent is buried in the Las Animas, Colorado, cemetery, near the historic community of Boggsville. He left behind an estate estimated at between $150,000 and $200,000 ($4.8 million to $6.4 million today).

16. Leeper to Greenwood, Washington, D.C., Jan. 19, 1861, NA, WIA, RG 75, M234, R928; Jody Lynn Dickson Schilz and Thomas F. Schilz, *Buffalo Hump and the Penateka Comanches* (El Paso: Texas Western Press, 1989), 47.

17. Loving to Lubbock, Palo Pinto County, Tex., 1862, in Dorman H. Winfrey and James M. Day, eds., *The Indian Papers of Texas and the Southwest, 1825–1916*, vol. 4 (Austin: Texas State Historical Association, 1995), 67 (quotation).

18. S. B. Watrous to San Antonio, Tex., *Daily Ledger and Texan*, Fort Union, NM, Dec. 18, 1859, part of WIA files, NA, RG 75, M234, R928.

19. Ibid. (quotations).

20. Sublett to Dalrymple, Elm Creek Station, Tex., April 7, 1861, Texas Ranger records, Texas State Troops records, Texas Adjutant General's Department Civil War records, Box 401-830, Folder 3, TSLAC. Prairie Dog Town Fork is the main tributary of the Red River. It heads in Randall County, Texas, four miles northeast of Canyon, Texas, and flows 160 miles southwest through Palo Duro Canyon and Armstrong, Briscoe, Hall, and Childress Counties, before merging with the North Fork of the Red River, twelve miles northeast of Vernon, Texas. See *HTO*, s.v. "Prairie Dog Town Fork of the

Red River," https://tshaonline.org/handbook/online/articles/rnp04 (accessed Feb. 18, 2020).

21. Hudson to Dashiell, Gainesville, Tex., Feb. 22, 1863, and Hudson to Dashiell, Gainesville, Tex., March 8, 1863, 21st Brigade Correspondence, Box 401-826, Folder 12, TSLAC.

22. Diamond to Steele, Gainesville, Tex., March 3, 1863, *OR*, Ser. 1, Vol. 22, Pt. 2, p. 800 (quotation); Bourland to McCulloch, Gainesville, Tex., Dec. 24, 1863, *OR*, Ser. 1, Vol. 26, Pt. 2, p. 531.

23. Isbell to Throckmorton, Decatur, Tex., Oct.19, 1864, Texas Ranger Correspondence 1864–65, Box 401-830, Folder 6, TSLAC; Carson to Bourland, Fort Belknap, Tex., Oct. 16, 1864, *OR*, Ser. 1, Vol. 34, Pt. 4, pp. 885–86; Zachariah B. Adams deposition, *Coggin and Parks v. The United States et al.*, Case No. 5007, IDC; Mildred P. Mayhall, *The Indian Wars of Texas* (Waco: Texian Press, 1965), 124 (quotation), 125–45; James K. Geer, ed., *Buck Barry: Texas Ranger and Frontiersman* (Lincoln: University of Nebraska Press, 1978), 175–81; Joseph Carroll McConnell, *The West Texas Frontier* (Palo Pinto: Texas Legal Bank & Book Co., 1939) 2:118–26; Ty Cashion, *A Texas Frontier: The Clear Fork Country and Fort Griffin, 1849–1887* (Norman: University of Oklahoma Press, 1996), 66–68.

24. Barry quoted in J. W. Wilbarger, *Indian Depredations in Texas* (Austin: Hutchings Printing House, 1889), 452; Cliff D. Cates, *Pioneer History of Wise County* (Decatur, Tex.: Wise County Historical Society, 1971), 127; W. Henry Miller, *Pioneering North Texas* (San Antonio: Naylor Co., 1953), 70; *HTO*, s.v. "Clay County," by Clark Wheeler, https://www.tshaonline.org/handbook/entries/clay-county (accessed Nov. 13, 2020); Young County Commissioners Court Minutes, April 10, 1865; *HTO*, s.v. "Young County," by John Leffler, https://www.tshaonline.org/handbook/entries/young-county (accessed Nov. 13, 2020); McConnell, *West Texas Frontier*, 2:124, 148; Orrick to Quayle, Jacksboro, Tex., Sept. 27, 1864, Adjutant General's Correspondence, Box 401-387, TSLAC. Peter Allen, part of Henry Skillman's rebel spy party traveling from San Antonio to the Trans-Pecos in March 1864, observed, "There are very few people on the frontiers of Texas." See Peter E. Allen statement in Carleton to Hoffman, June 27, 1864, NA, RG 249, CGP, LR 1864, C729 (endnote quotation). In gauging the exact extent of this depopulation, the researcher must be careful not to compare 1870 Federal Census figures to those for 1860. One needs to remember that in late 1866 and throughout 1867, the U.S. Army regarrisoned much of West Texas. The presence of federal troops, therefore, encouraged many settlers to move back to the frontier prior to the 1870 census. For federal regarrisoning dates in Texas, see Frazer, *Forts of the West*, 139–64.

25. John Salmon Ford, *Rip Ford's Texas*, ed. Stephen B. Oates (Austin: University of Texas Press, 1963), 349 (quotation). For more on Texas's inadequate frontier defense and the receding line of settlement, see Ely, *Where the West Begins*, 35–74, and Ely, "Gone from Texas," 161–84; McCord to Magruder, Camp Verde, Tex., May 2, 1864, *OR*, Ser. 1, Vol. 34, Pt. 3, p. 803.

26. Steck to Carleton, Santa Fe, NM, Oct. 26, 1864, NA, AGO, LR, N584, 1864 (quotations). In November 1863 Capt. Peter William Livingston Plympton, Seventh Infantry, reported from Fort Bascom, New Mexico, that he had seized wagons, oxen, and property

(including whiskey and gunpowder) belonging to several Comancheros. The owners of the wagon train admitted to Plympton that they "were on their way to trade with the Comanches" in Texas. General Carleton commented that "it is doubtless from ignorance . . . that these men were taking powder and whiskey to trade with Indians." Carleton ordered Plympton to confiscate the contraband and issue the traders a warning. See Plympton to AAG, DNM, Nov. 20, 1863, NA, RG 393, Pt. 5, Fort Bascom, NM, Entry 3, LR, Box 1 (endnote quotations).

27. José Piedad Tafoya deposition, *Goodnight and Sheek v. The United States et al.*, Case No. 9133, IDC. Prominent natural features in the Quitaque vicinity include the Quitaque Peaks (2,800 to 3000 feet high), Quitaque Creek, Los Lingos Creek, and Valle de las Lágrimas (valley of tears).

28. Letter to P. Murrah, Bonham, Tex., March 18, 1864, Governor Pendleton Murrah Papers, Box 301-45, Folder 22, TSLAC; Walker to Boggs, Oct. 10, 1864, NA, RG 109, TNMA, LS, Ch. 2, Vol. 123. For more on Texans' Civil War beef trade with the enemy, see Ely, *Where the West Begins*, 35–74, and Ely, "Gone from Texas," 161–84. John S. Chisum was born in Tennessee in 1824. In June 1860 his net worth was almost $60,000 (about $1.92 million in today's value). Chisum died in December 1884. See 1860 census, Denton County, Tex., NA, RG 29, M653, R1292, 404. From 1996 to 2011 Glen Ely held numerous discussions with leading Chisum authority Harwood Perry Hinton Jr. regarding the cattleman's ranching operations in Denton, Coleman, and Concho Counties, discussions that have greatly aided in shaping this narrative.

29. Magruder to Anderson, Jan. 31, 1863, NA, RG 109, TNMA, LS, Ch. 2, Vol. 133.

30. T. U. Taylor, "Life Sketch of John Simpson Chisum," *Frontier Times* 13, no. 8 (May 1936), 397, 399; T. U. Taylor, "Trailing John Chisum to New Mexico," *Frontier Times* 13, no. 9 (June 1936), 422–23, 424; GLO, Concho County Abstract 746 File Notes. At Theodor Sterzing's request, the District of Bexar surveyed his land in August 1847. In 1854 Sterzing, a Comal County resident, sold Survey 1859 (Abstract 746) and Survey 1857, totaling 640 acres, to G. H. Sherwood for $80.00. In May 1936, W. G. Currie of Paint Rock, Texas, owned Survey 1859 and the old Chisum ranch site. A small cemetery, also on the property, contains the graves of two Chisum cowboys who were killed by Indians. Survey 1859 is now underwater, part of O. H. Ivie Reservoir.

31. Sidney W. Smith, *From the Cow Camp to the Pulpit: Being Twenty-Five Years Experience of a Texas Evangelist* (Cincinnati: Christian Leader Corporation, 1927), 89 (quotation), 95, 98. Fitzgerald worked for Chisum for many years. In June 1860 the forty-year-old Tennessean was living at Chisum's Denton County ranch. After the war Fitzgerald continued to run cattle at the Concho-Colorado confluence. See 1860 Federal Census, Denton County, Tex., NA, RG 29, M653, R1292, 404. See also Beatrice Grady Gay, *Into the Setting Sun: A History of Coleman County* (Santa Anna, Tex.: self-published, 1936), 24 (ten thousand cattle according to Dick Fiveash). Historic regional map showing location of Chisum, Coffey, Coggin, Fitzgerald, and Tankersley ranches in *Richard F. Tankersley v. The United States et al.*, Case No. 6501, IDC; see also *C. C. Fitzgerald v. The United States and Comanche Indians*, Case No. 5118, IDC; Leaday, Tex., USGS 1:24,000 scale topographic map and 1:12,000 scale color aerial photograph, Terrain

Navigator Pro v. 8.71 software (TNP); Amy C. Earls and Patrick O'Neill, et al., *Cultural Resource Investigations in the O. H. Ivie Reservoir, Concho, Coleman, and Runnels Counties, Texas*, vol. 5 (Austin: Historical Resources, Mariah Associates, Inc., Technical Report 346-V, Dec. 1993), 73–90, 122–35 (detailing archeological excavations done at the Chisum #41CC131 & Coffey #41CN253 ranch sites). Photographs of ruins at the Chisum ranch site in Concho County can be viewed at the Texas Archeological Research Laboratory, University of Texas at Austin (TARL). See Chisum Ranch Site #41CC131, Photos C425-26, C434, C438, and C447, TARL.

32. Richard Coffey, a farmer and stock raiser, was born in Georgia in 1823 and moved to Texas in 1851. He died on February 7, 1897. See depositions of Richard Coffey, Richard "Fog" Coffey Jr., and William A. Coffey in *Richard Coffey v. The United States and Comanche Tribe of Indians*, Case No. 5003, IDC; depositions of Richard Coffey and John W. Coffey, *Richard Coffey v. The United States and Comanche and Kiowa Tribes of Indians*, Case No. 7807, IDC. Tankersley says that he brought 1,500 head of cattle, including 500 calves, with him to the Concho-Colorado junction in 1864, all of which he subsequently moved to his South Concho spread in November 1864. See depositions of R. F. Tankersley, James Dofflemyer, and John Hart, *Tankersley v. The United States et al.*, Case No. 6501, IDC; Smith, *From the Cow Camp*, 114; Fayette Tankersley "Reminiscences" typescript, and Clara Wheelberger to Hal Noelke, McAllen, Tex., Nov. 28, 1960, Tankersley File, Fort Concho National Historic Landmark Archives; Norma King, "Mary Tankersley Lewis," *Junior Historian* 4, no. 5 (March 1944), 10.

33. Thomas Robert Havins, *Camp Colorado: A Decade of Frontier Defense* (Brownwood, Tex.: Brown Press, 1964), 61–63; Ely, *Where the West Begins*, 54, 149n48.

34. Deposition of Samuel R. Coggin in *Coggin and Parks v. The United States et al.*, Case No. 5007, IDC (Coggin operations in 1861); James Cox, *Historical and Biographical Record of the Cattle Industry and the Cattlemen of Texas and Adjacent Territory* (New York: Antiquarian Press, 1959), 364 (Coggin), 470 (Tankersley); Martha Doty Freeman and Joe C. Freeman, *A Cultural Resource Inventory and Assessment of the Proposed Stacy Reservoir, Concho, Coleman and Runnels Counties, Texas*, vol. 2, Historic Cultural Resources (Austin: Espey, Huston & Associates, Inc., 1981), 3:5–7 (Coffey background); "Some Early Coleman County History," *Frontier Times* 2, no. 2 (Nov. 1924), 8–9; Gay, *Into the Setting Sun*, 15–18. William C. Franks was born in Marion County, Alabama, in September 1836. See 1900 Federal Census, Santa Rita, NM, NA, RG 29, MT623, R1000, p. 12B. Emory Peter said that he sold Chisum's store at Trickham and its stock of goods to Shell Wilson in the fall of 1873. Wilson lived twelve to fourteen miles south of Trickham on the Colorado River. See E. B. Peter deposition, *Chisum v. The United States et al.*, Case No. 5388, IDC; *Texas Road Atlas*, 90. The November 1924 *Frontier Times* article states that L. L. Shield, not Shell Wilson, bought the log cabin store from Chisum in the early 1870s (May 1871) and that Shield subsequently built a rock building on the site to replace the cabin. Ruins of the old Shield store can still be seen in Trickham today, located near the junction of FM 1176 and CR 216 in southeast Coleman County, Texas. Mukewater Creek flows into Home Creek south of Speck Mountain, a short distance above Home Creek's junction with the Colorado River.

35. "Some Early Coleman County History," 9 (quotation one); Gay, *Into the Setting Sun*, 15–16 (quotation two); Taylor, "Life Sketch of John Simpson Chisum," 397, 399; Taylor, "Trailing Chisum to New Mexico," 422–24. The Fiveash family was among the first to settle in the Mukewater Creek–Trickham area.
36. Regarding the geographical area of the free-ranging cattle, see the depositions of Messrs. Connell, Winn, Arch, Coggin, Peter, and Kemp in *Emory B. Peter, as survivor of the firm of E. B. Peter and John Chisum, v. The United States and the Comanche Tribe of Indians*, Case No. 6801, IDC, and its companion case, *Fitzgerald v. The United States et al.*, Case No. 5118, IDC; argument of U.S. Assistant Attorney General John G. Thompson in *Samuel R. Coggin, Moses J. Coggin, and William C. Parks, partners, v. The United States and Comanche Indians*, Case Nos. 5007, 5008, 5009 (all three cases were later consolidated into one claim), IDC (quotation one); deposition of James Dofflemyer in *Tankersley v. The United States et al.*, Case No. 6501, IDC (quotations two through four).
37. Deposition of M. M. Callan, *Coggin and Parks v. The United States et al.*, Case No. 5007, IDC; deposition of James Dofflemyer, *Tankersley v. The United States et al.*, Case No. 6501, IDC (quotation).
38. Deposition of J. M. Halcomb, *Coffey v. The United States et al.*, Case No. 7807, IDC; deposition of Jesse J. Hittson, *Mary M. Mann, Administratix of Clay M. Mann, v. The United States and Comanche Indians*, Case Nos. 3091, 3092, 3093, 4689, 4692, 4693, 4696, IDC; defendant's brief, *Peter v. The United States et al.*, Case No. 6801, IDC, 4–7 (quotation and 1864–66 roundup figures).
39. Defendant's brief, *Peter v. The United States et al.*, Case No. 6801, IDC, 5 (Chisum pens); Gay, *Into the Setting Sun*, 16; Smith, *From the Cow Camp*, 102; deposition of Thomas Murray, *Patterson and Franks v. The United States et al.*, IDC.
40. Taylor, "Trailing Chisum to New Mexico," 422; Gay, *Into the Setting Sun*, 81–82, 168–69, 172. Waide and Chisum Roads (named after the Waide and Chisum families) are located north/northwest of Bolivar in Denton County, Texas. See *Texas Road Atlas*, 66.
41. Emory Peter deposition, *Peter v. The United States et al.*, Case No. 6801, IDC.
42. McCulloch to Murrah, Bonham, Tex., March 20, 1864, Pendelton Murrah Papers, Box 2014/022-2, Folder 49, TSLAC (quotation).
43. Erath to Culberson, Oct. 4, 1864, Adjutant General Departmental Correspondence, Box 401-387, Folder 5, TSLAC; General Orders No. 9, Brig. Gen. John David McAdoo, Headquarters Second and Third Frontier Districts, Texas State Troops, Fredericksburg, Tex., Dec. 15, 1864, Box 401-830, Folder 17, TSLAC.
44. Erath to Murrah, Waco, Tex., March 20, 1864, Pendelton Murrah Papers, Box 2014/022-2, Folder 49, TSLAC; William C. Doss to P. Murrah, Gillespie County, Tex., May 2, 1864, ibid., Box 2014/022-3, Folder 65; J. W. Throckmorton to Murrah, McKinney, Tex., December 9, 1864, ibid., Box 2014/022-4, Folder 97; March 26, 1864, Proclamation No. 55 by P. Murrah, in Winfrey and Day, *Indian Papers of Texas*, 4:80–81; Texas Legislature's May 24, 1864, joint resolution/ratification of Murrah's Proclamation

No. 55, in *General Laws of the Tenth Legislature* (Houston: Galveston News, 1864), 15 (quotation), 16.

45. T. U. Taylor, "W. A. Peril Makes Five World Records," *Frontier Times* 13, no. 12 (September 1936), 600; T. U. Taylor, "Aunt Ollie Peril, a True Pioneer Mother," *Frontier Times* 17, no. 2 (November 1939), 49; W. A. Peril, "From Texas to the Oregon Line," in *The Trail Drivers of Texas*, ed. J. Marvin Hunter (Austin: University of Texas Press, 2003), 411–13; Hunter to Murrah, March 20, 1865, Pendelton Murrah Papers, Box 301-45, TSLAC; Walker to Murrah, March 15, 1865, ibid.; Aldrich to Murrah, Oct. 11, 1864, ibid.; Mitchell to Murrah, Dec. 12, 1864, ibid.; Murrah to Walker, March 20, 1865, ibid., Box 301-47; Walker to Murrah, March 15, 1865, NA, RG 109, TNMA, LS, Ch. 2, Vol. 123; Special Orders No. 13, Dec. 19, 1864, NA, RG 109, Ch. 8, Vol. 277, Misc. Special Orders, Adjutant General of Texas, 1862–65, 478; Special Orders No. 21, Jan. 19, 1865, ibid., 483. The evidence suggests that Burgess lied about Hunter and that the major sold his entire herd at Presidio del Norte; see Creel to Carleton, Nov. 10, 1864, NA, RG 393, LR, DNM, M1120, R23.

46. Deposition of William C. Franks, *Patterson and Franks v. The United States, et al.*, Case Nos. 10323 and 5622, IDC. (The Patterson and Franks partnership formed summer 1864.) July 20, 1864, entry, NA, RG 393, Pt. 1, NM, Entry 3214, Provost Marshal, Vol. 121/298 NMEX (Franks's Santa Fe arrival).

47. Endorsement #1436 on June 1, 1865, letter to Carleton from Patterson and Roberts, Franklin, Tex., NA, RG 393, Pt. 1, NM, Entry 3151, Endorsements Sent 1861–67, Vols. 1–7, Nos. 28–33, NMEX; Carleton to McCleave, July 11, 1865, and Carleton to Shoemaker, Sept. 2, 1865, LS, DNM, M1072, R3 (keeping Carleton informed of Texas trade and Carleton providing escort for Roberts's Texas herds). For more information on Patterson and Franks's operations, see their Indian depredations claims, Case Nos. 494, 5622, 5623, 6214, and 10323, IDC. Capt. Thomas L. Roberts enlisted in Company E, First California Infantry, on Aug. 26, 1861, and mustered out on Sept. 13, 1864; see Orton, *Records of California Men*, 354.

48. Conwell to Carleton, Dec. 3, 1864, NA, RG 393, LR, DNM, M1120, R24; Special Orders No. 37, June 21, 1864, NA, RG 393, Pt. 5, Fort Bliss, Tex., Entry 18, General Orders, Box 9. First Sgt. James Conwell, Company B, Fifth Regt. of Infantry, California Volunteers, received a promotion to second lieutenant in April 1863 but mustered out of service as a first sergeant on December 12, 1864, in Franklin, Texas. After his trip to Texas, Conwell reenlisted at Franklin on March 11, 1865, as a corporal in Company E, First Battalion of Veteran Infantry; see Orton, *Records of California Men*, 404, 681.

49. Conwell to Carleton, Dec. 3, 1864, NA, RG 393, LR, DNM, M1120, R24 (quotation).

50. Barry to Adjutant Inspector General, Jan. 20, 1865, Box 401-387, TSLAC (quotations one through three).

51. Barry to Adjutant Inspector General, Jan. 20, 1865, Box 401-387, TSLAC; Conwell to Carleton, Dec. 3, 1864, NA, RG 393, LR, DNM, M1120, R24; John F. Hart, J. L. Lawson, and James Dofflemyer depositions, *Tankersley v. The United States et al.*, Case No. 6501, IDC; Marion M. Callan deposition and L. P. Baugh affidavit, *Coggin and*

Parks v. The United States et al., Case No. 5007, IDC. J. L. Lawson said that the white rustlers struck either in 1864 or 1865. John F. Hart said the raid occurred "about the close of the war." James Dofflemyer, whose brother was in the posse that confronted the Anglo outlaws on the west side of the Pecos River, stated that the raid was during the summer of 1865. Texas surrendered on June 2, 1865. Rancher R. F. Tankersley was also part of the posse. L. P. Baugh said that the gang of rustlers was comprised of two white men and some Mexicans who had been recruited in Mexico. Out of five depositions concerning this 1865 raid, Baugh's is the only one to mention Mexicans being part of the group.

52. Smith, *From the Cow Camp*, 98, 102; Havins, *Camp Colorado*, 153–54; Emory Peter deposition, *Peter v. The United States et al.*, Case No. 6801, IDC (quotation).

53. Smith, *From the Cow Camp*, 102–4. Two families desiring to leave Civil War Texas accompanied the cattle drive westward. Smith tells an amusing story of hunting buffalo with James Patterson's rifle during a layover at "Scentrailier [sic] Station," also known as Llano Estacado Station, an old Butterfield Overland Mail stage stop in Centralia Draw, Reagan County, Texas. In November 1871 mail contractor F. C. Taylor built a new stage stop a few miles to the east of Llano Estacado Station, calling it Centralia Station. See Ely, *The Texas Frontier*, 192–96, 212–13, 386n24.

54. Smith, *From the Cow Camp*, 104. For more information on Fort Davis, see Ely, *The Texas Frontier*, 284–85, 297–300, 401–2nn44–46.

55. Smith, *From the Cow Camp*, 104 (quotations). For more information on El Muerto, Van Horn's Wells, Eagle Spring, and Quitman Canyon, See Ely, *The Texas Frontier*, 286–311, 402–4.

56. Endorsement #1436 on June 1, 1865, letter to Carleton from Patterson and Roberts, Franklin, Tex., NA, RG 393, Pt. 1, NM, Entry 3151, Endorsements Sent 1861–67, Vols. 1–7, Nos. 28–33 NMEX. Confederate general Edmund Kirby Smith, commanding the Trans-Mississippi Department (including Texas), surrendered to Union general Edward R. S. Canby on June 2, 1865. See *HTO*, *s.v.* "Smith, Edmund Kirby," by Thomas W. Cutrer, https://www.tshaonline.org/handbook/entries/smith-edmund-kirby (accessed Nov. 13, 2020).

57. Smith, *From the Cow Camp*, 104–5. Smith's name appears on a June 1865 deserter/refugee list from Franklin, Texas. See June 10, 1865, Descriptive List of Texas Refugees, NA, RG 393, LR, NM, M1120, R26. Also on this same list are six Texas Rangers (five privates and one bugler) who deserted from Camp Colorado in Coleman County in the spring of 1865, before Texas surrendered.

58. Smith, *From the Cow Camp*, 105 (quotations); Cox, *Historical and Biographical Record of the Cattle Industry*, 330. Wylie had a cattle ranch at Horsehead Crossing in the late 1870s and early 1880s. He sold out in 1882 and this acreage later became the TX Ranch. See also deposition of Emory Peter, *Peter v. The United States et al.*, Case No. 6801, IDC. Emory Peter described Patterson and Franks's herd as "a little bunch." He likely was referring to the size of their first drive to El Paso County, Texas, in the spring of 1865, not to their second drive of 1,500 cattle during the summer of 1865.

59. Smith, *From the Cow Camp*, 106 (quotations one through four). For more on Wild China Ponds, see Ely, *The Texas Frontier*, 196–98, 214, 387n39.

60. Smith, *From the Cow Camp*, 106. For more on Castle Gap, see Ely, *The Texas Frontier*, 198–200, 214–16, 387–88. For more on Horsehead Crossing on the Pecos River, see ibid., 185, 200–205, 216–18, 388n64.

61. Smith, *From the Cow Camp*, 106, 107 (quotations); Juan Cordona Lake File, GLO, Crane County Abstract No. 1, Bexar 1454. Native Americans, Mexicans, and Texans all harvested salt from Juan Cordona Lake throughout the nineteenth century. Several West Texas ranchers made numerous trips to these rich salt deposits, namely Richard Coffey, John Chisum's neighbor at the confluence of the Concho and Colorado, and R. F. Tankersley, who ranched on the South Concho River. For more on Juan Cordona Lake, see Ely, *The Texas Frontier*, 225, 247–48, 389nn17–18; *Tankersley v. The United States et al.*, Case No. 6501, IDC; E. H. Swain, "Rich Coffee [sic]," *Edwards Plateau Historian* 5 (1969–73), 67.

62. Smith, *From the Cow Camp*, 108 (quotations one and two).

63. Deposition of William C. Franks, deposition of Pitser Chisum, and argument by U.S. Attorney George T. Stormont, *Patterson and Franks v. The United States et al.*, Case Nos. 10323 and 5622, IDC; Hinton, "John Simpson Chisum," 186–89.

64. Smith, *From the Cow Camp*, 102–13.

65. Carleton to McCleave, July 11, 1865 (quotation), NA, RG 393, LS, DNM, M1072, R3.

66. Abreu to De Forrest, Aug. 1, 1865, NA, RG 393, LR, DNM, M1120, R6; Hubbell to DeHague, Aug. 25, 1865, NA, RG 393, DNM, Part 5, Fort Bascom, NM, Entry #3, LR, 1863–65; Carleton to Shoemaker, Sept. 2, 1865 (quotations), NA, RG 393, LS, DNM, M1072, R3.

67. Deposition of William C. Franks, *Patterson and Franks v. The United States et al.*, Case Nos. 10323 and 5622, IDC; deposition of Emory Peter, *Peter v. The United States et al.*, Case No. 6801, IDC.

68. Deposition of Emory Peter, *Peter v. The United States et al.*, Case No. 6801, IDC; deposition of John S. Chisum, *Chisum v. The United States et al.*, Case No. 5388, IDC.

69. Haley, *Charles Goodnight*, 127 (quotation).

70. Haley, *Charles Goodnight*, 127 (quotation), 138. Upon Goodnight and Loving's arrival at Fort Sumner in July 1866, they sold their first herd to army beef contractor Thomas L. Roberts (the business partner of Patterson and Franks) for eight cents a pound. Roberts bought 1,300 of Goodnight and Loving's cattle, while the remaining 700 went unsold. Regarding Chisum, in 1906 Emory Peter's attorney, S. S. Burdett, wrote, "John Chisum was the owner of more cattle than any man in north-west Texas. In [1867] . . . he drove out the first considerable herd of cattle ever taken to the government markets in New Mexico and made what has for many years known as the 'Chisum trail.'" Argument by S. S. Burdett, *Peter v. The United States et al.*, Case No. 6801, IDC (endnote quotation).

Chapter 7

1. John S. Chisum, E. B. Peter, and B. F. Chisum depositions, *Chisum v. The United States et al.,* Case No. 5388, IDC; Emory Peter deposition, *Peter v. The United States et al.,* Case No. 6801, IDC (quotation).

2. Charles Goodnight deposition, *Goodnight and Sheek v. The United States et al.,* Case No. 9133; Haley, *Charles Goodnight,* 233–34.

3. Charles Goodnight, Martin Scoggins, and José Piedad Tafoya depositions, *Goodnight and Sheek v. The United States et al.,* Case No. 9133, IDC.

4. Emory Peter deposition and Robert Kelsey Wylie deposition, *Peter v. The United States et al.,* Case No. 6801, IDC.

5. Charles Goodnight deposition (quotation), *Goodnight and Sheek v. The United States et al.,* Case No. 9133, IDC. For more on Ben Krebs and his Butterfield Overland mail station, see Glen Sample Ely, *Murder in Montague: Frontier Justice and Retribution* (Norman: University of Oklahoma Press, 2020), 20–21.

6. William B. Stapp deposition, *Goodnight and Sheek v. The United States et al.,* Case No. 9133, IDC.

7. José Piedad Tafoya deposition and Julián Baca deposition (quotation), *Goodnight and Sheek v. The United States et al.,* Case No. 9133, IDC.

8. William J. Wilson deposition, ibid.; depositions of John S. Chisum, R. K. Wylie, James Patterson, and James Reynolds, *Chisum v. The United States et al.,* Case No. 5388, IDC.

9. Dennis J. Murphy deposition, *Dennis J. Murphy v. The United States and the Comanche Tribe of Indians,* Case Nos. 10367, 10368, and 8626, IDC (quotations). Before the Civil War Murphy's family operated a stage stop for the Butterfield Overland Mail in Young County. Murphy's brother Patrick and brother-in-law Edward Cornett were prominent members of the Old Law Mob that terrorized the North Texas frontier before the Civil War. See Ely, *The Texas Frontier,* 83–115.

10. William Beddo deposition, *William Beddo v. The United States and Comanche and Kiowa Indian Tribes,* Case No. 2, IDC; William J. Wilson deposition (quotation), *Goodnight and Sheek v. The United States et al.,* Case No. 9133, IDC; Winfrey and Day, *Indian Papers of Texas,* 4:373. In 1905 Richard Coffey's estate received $5,641.00 for livestock losses during the June 1871 raid. See *Richard Coffey v. The United States and the Comanche and Kiowa Indians,* Case No. 7807, IDC.

11. William Beddo deposition, *Beddo v. The United States et al.,* Case No. 2, IDC.

12. Depositions of R. F. Tankersley, William N. Adams, and Benjamin F. Jenkins and Claimant's Argument (quotation), *Coggin and Parks v. The United States et al.,* Case No. 5007, IDC; R. F. Tankersley deposition, *Tankersley v. The United States et al.,* Case No. 6501, IDC; Dennis J. Murphy deposition, *Murphy v. The United States et al.,* Case Nos. 10367, 10368, and 8626, IDC.

13. Jones to Roberts, Austin, Tex., Jan. 12, 1880, in Winfrey and Day, *Indian Papers of Texas,* 4:438 (quotation).

14. DeLacy to Vernou, Fort Chadbourne, Tex., Oct. 7, 1867, Fort Concho, Tex. Quartermaster, Ordnance, and Commissary Letters, Group B, Microfilm R9, Fort Concho

[Tex.] National Historic Landmark Archives; Heitman, *Historical Register*, 1:286, 325, 347, 960, 986. For more on Head of Concho Station, situated at the headwaters of the Middle Concho River, see Ely, *The Texas Frontier*, 189–91, 208, 385–86nn14–15.

15. Bliss to AAG, Dept. of Texas, Fort Stockton, Tex., July 11, 1872, Fort Stockton, Texas, Letters and Telegrams Sent, NA, RG 393, M1189, R1 (quotation). For more on Johnson's mail station and Centralia mail station, see Ely, *The Texas Frontier*, 187–88, 206–7, 385–86. For more on the Great Falls of the Pecos River, see ibid., 227–28, 249, 390nn26–31.

16. Bliss to AAG, July 11, 1872; Heitman, *Historical Register*, 1:225, 376; Hatch to AAG, Dept. of Texas, Fort Concho, Tex., June 16, 1872, in Ernest Wallace, ed., *Ranald S. Mackenzie's Official Correspondence Relating to Texas, 1871–1873* (Lubbock: West Texas Museum Association, 1967), 83. The 1872 attack took place at Dagger Bend of the Pecos, downstream from the Great Falls of the Pecos. From the fall of 1858 to May 1859, the Butterfield Overland Mail had a stage stop at Dagger Bend named after the station manager, Mr. Langston. Doctor Bartlett is also spelled as Bartley in the official reports; see Ely, *The Texas Frontier*, 225–26, 249, 389–390nn20–21.

17. Shoemaker to Post Adjutant, Fort Concho, Tex., Nov. 2, 1872, Frank Temple Microfilm R1, Records of the War Department, U.S. Army, Reports of Scouts, Fort Concho, Tex., 1872–81, and Fort Stockton, Tex., Reports and Maps of Explorations and Scouts, 1873–79, Fort Davis National Historic Site Archives (hereafter cited as FT); Heitman, *Historical Register*, 1:884. For more on Mustang Waterholes, see Ely, *The Texas Frontier*, 193–95, 210, 386–87n27.

18. Dodge to AAG, Dept. of Texas, May 13, 1873, Fort Stockton, Tex., Letters and Telegrams Sent, NA, RG 393, M1189, R2; Heitman, *Historical Register*, 1:376.

19. Dodge to AAG, May 13, 1873 (quotations); Perry to Jones, Camp Elm, Menard County, Nov. 21, 1874, Adjutant General's Department, Correspondence Box 401-392, Folder 15, TSLAC.

20. Cusack to Post Adjutant, Fort Concho, Tex., Aug. 10, 1873, FT; Heitman, *Historical Register*, 1:347.

21. *HTO*, s.v. "Red River War," by James L. Haley, https://www.tshaonline.org/handbook /entries/red-river-war (accessed Nov. 13, 2020); Hagan, "Kiowas, Comanches, and Cattlemen," 334.

22. Hagan, "Kiowas, Comanches, and Cattlemen," 334 (quotations).

23. Hatch to AAG, Dept. of Texas, Fort Concho, Tex., March 30, 1872, FT; Smith, *Old Army in Texas*, 154; *Record of Engagements with Hostile Indians 1868 to 1882* (Bellevue Neb.: Old Army Press, 1969), 32; Adjutant General's Office, *Chronological List of Actions*, 50; Charles M. Neal Jr., *Valor across the Lone Star: The Congressional Medal of Honor in Frontier Texas* (Austin: Texas State Historical Association, 2002), 105–9; 1870 Federal Census, San Miguel County, NM, NA, RG 29, M593, R895, 16. Apolonio Ortíz, a resident of La Cuesta, was born in New Mexico in 1843. In 1870 he was married to Tereza Ortíz and the couple had a two-year-old daughter named Juana. Around 1890 La Cuesta was renamed Villanueva. The town is on the Pecos River along New Mexico Highway 3, between San Miguel and Anton Chico. See *DeLorme Atlas of New Mexico*, 24–25.

24. Hatch to AAG, Dept. of Texas, Fort Concho, March 30, 1872; Wallace, *Mackenzie's Official Correspondence*, 65–69; Ernest Wallace, *Ranald S. Mackenzie on the Texas Frontier* (College Station: Texas A&M University Press, 1993), 66–74; Rupert Norval Richardson, *The Comanche Barrier to South Plains Settlement*, ed. Kenneth R. Jacobs (Abilene, Tex.: Hardin Simmons University, 1991), 197–201.

25. C. L. Sonnichsen, *The Mescalero Apaches* (Norman: University of Oklahoma Press, 1958), 139–42.

26. Ibid., 140–48; W. S. Nye, *Carbine and Lance: The Story of Old Fort Sill* (Norman: University of Oklahoma Press, 1974), 243, 247; Hämäläinen, *Comanche Empire*, 328–29.

27. *Chisum v. The United States et al.*, Case No. 5388, IDC. For more on Emigrant Station, see Ely, *The Texas Frontier*, 229–31, 251–52, 391.

28. John Chisum to E. P. Smith, CIA, Aug. 5, 1874 (quotation), and W. D. Crothers deposition, *Chisum v. The United States et al.*, Case No. 5388, IDC.

29. John Reynolds deposition, *Chisum v. The United States et al.*, Case No. 5388, IDC (quotation). The section of the Comanchero Trail described in these reports went from Little Tule Lake and Tule Lake (located six miles southwest of Melrose, NM) southeast to Tierra Blanca Lake (four miles southeast of Floyd, NM) and on to Los Portales (Portales Spring, six miles southeast of Portales, NM). See *DeLorme Atlas of New Mexico*, 34–35, 43; Map #575, *1864 Map of the Military Department of New Mexico, Drawn under the Direction of Brig. Gen. James H. Carleton by Capt. Allen Anderson*, NACP, RG 77, W83-2; Map #580, *1875 District of New Mexico Military Map by Lt. C.C. Morrison*, NACP, RG 77, W197-1; *1876 Map of the Country Scouted by Colonels McKenzie and Shafter, Capt. R. P. Wilson and Others in the Years 1874 & 1875 by Alex. L. Lucas*, NACP, RG 77, Southwest Collection, Texas Tech University; Map #1480a, *1878 Rand McNally Map of Texas*, TSLAC; *1879 Rand McNally Map of New Mexico* and *1879 U.S. Department of the Interior General Land Office Map of the Territory of New Mexico*, both in David Rumsey Historical Map Collection, www.davidrumsey.com; My Topo Terrain Navigator Pro Software, Version 10.3, topographic maps and aerial photographs, Muleshoe, Tex.; Clovis, NM; and Santa Rosa, NM.

30. Report of Second Lt. John William Wilkinson, Eighth Cavalry, July 27, 1874, *Chisum v. The United States et al.*, Case No. 5388, IDC; Heitman, *Historical Register*, 1:1037. A prosperous merchant and rancher, Lucien Bonaparte Maxwell was born in Illinois in 1818 and died at Fort Sumner, New Mexico, in 1875. Maxwell gave name to the famous 2,680-square-mile (1.7 million acres) Maxwell Land Grant in New Mexico and Colorado. See Keleher, *Maxwell Land Grant*, 25–38; Find a Grave Online, s.v. "Lucien Bonaparte Maxwell," https://www.findagrave.com/memorial/9925464/lucien-bonaparte-maxwell (accessed March 28, 2020).

31. James F. Randlett deposition, and Randlett to Post Adjutant, Fort Stanton, NM, Dec. 23, 1874 (quotation), in *Chisum v. The United States et al.*, Case No. 5388, IDC; Heitman, *Historical Register*, 1:815.

32. Davis to Smith, Austin, Tex., Dec. 9, 1873, Governor Edmund Jackson Davis Papers, Box 2014-110-28, Folder 331, TSLAC (quotations).

33. Keyes to Post Adjutant, Fort Concho, Tex., June 8, 1878, FT (quotations); Heitman, *Historical Register*, 1:595; Ely, *The Texas Frontier*, 226–28, 249, 390n29. On the north side of the Pecos River, overlooking the Great Falls site, one can still see the ruins of this old adobe town, likely a failed farming community dating from the 1870s. See also GLO, Map #63110, *August 1902 Map of Ward County, Texas*; GLO, Ward County Abstract 129; Ward County Field Notes Book 1, Block 34, Surveys 18–19, and Block 33, Survey 1. All three of these 1888 Ward County surveys specifically mention the adobe town. At the townsite numerous period artifacts—including square nails, colored glass, crockery, and lead-lined cans—litter the ground. The artifacts date the site from the late 1870s to the early 1880s. The survey for Block 33, Survey 5 from August 1888 mentions an irrigation ditch, so likely this was an irrigated farming community at that time.

34. Petition from Clarendon, Donley County, Tex., to AG John B. Jones, Dec. 30, 1878, in Winfrey and Day, *Indian Papers of Texas*, 4:406 (quotation); Patch to Post Adjutant, Fort Elliott, Tex., Jan. 22, 1879, Adjutant General's Department, Departmental Correspondence, Box 401-398, Folder 2, TSLAC.

35. Patch to Post Adjutant, Fort Elliott, Tex., Jan. 22, 1879, Adjutant General's Department, Departmental Correspondence, Box 401-398, Folder 2, TSLAC.

36. Haley, *Charles Goodnight*, 306, 307 (quotations).

37. Ibid., 308 (quotations).

38. Ibid., 310–311; Heitman, *Historical Register*, 1:511; Hatch to Jones, Fort Sill, I.T., Feb. 10, 1880, Adjutant General's Department, Departmental Correspondence, Box 401-399, Folder 2, TSLAC; and Arrington to Jones, Camp Roberts, Tex., March 10, 1880, ibid., Folder 4.

39. Lincoln to AAG, Dept. of Texas, Fort Griffin, Tex., Feb. 17, 1879, Adjutant General's Department, Departmental Correspondence, Box 401-398, Folder 5, TSLAC; Heitman, *Historical Register*, 1:633. George Washington Arrington (originally John C. Orrick Jr.) was born in Alabama in 1844. He served as a Confederate spy during the Civil War as part of John Mosby's guerillas. After killing an African American businessman in 1867, he moved to Texas and changed his name to Arrington. He joined the Frontier Battalion in 1875 and resigned in 1882. Arrington died in 1923, in Canadian, Texas. See *HTO*, s.v. "Arrington, George Washington," by H. Allen Anderson, https://tshaonline .org/handbook/online/articles/far20 (accessed April 5, 2020).

40. Arrington to Jones, Camp Loma Vista, Throckmorton County, Tex., Jan. 20, 1879, in Winfrey and Day, *Indian Papers of Texas*, 4:409–10; James Mooney, "Calendar History of the Kiowa Indians," *Seventeenth Annual Report of the Bureau of American Ethnology* (Washington, D.C.: Government Printing Office, 1898), 343 (quotation), 344.

41. Wheeler County Commissioners to Roberts, Fort Elliott, Tex., July 14, 1879 (quotations one and two); and Arrington to Jones, Sweetwater, Tex., June 21, 1879 (quotations three through five), Adjutant General's Department, Departmental Correspondence, Box 401-398, Folder 9, TSLAC.

42. Arrington to Davidson, Sweetwater, Tex., June 18, 1879; and Arrington to Jones, Sweetwater, June 18, 1879 (printed in the *Galveston Daily News*) (quotation); Heitman, *Historical Register*, 1:355.

43. Hatch to Jones, Fort Sill, I.T., Feb. 25, 1880, Adjutant General's Department, Departmental Correspondence, Box 401-399, Folder 3, TSLAC (quotation); Heitman, *Historical Register*, 1:511.

44. Hatch to Jones, Fort Sill, I.T., Feb. 10, 1880, Adjutant General's Department, Departmental Correspondence, Box 401-399, Folder 2, TSLAC (quotation), and Arrington to Jones, Camp Roberts, Tex., March 10, 1880, ibid., Folder 4; Robert Goldthwaite Carter, *Tragedies of Cañon Blanco: A Story of the Texas Panhandle* (Washington, D.C.: Gibson Brothers Printers, 1919), 6; Mike Cox, *Texas Ranger Tales II* (Plano: Republic of Texas Press, 1999), 102–4; George Washington Arrington, 1921 affidavit, Palo Pinto County, Tex., in "Captain Arrington's Expedition," *Frontier Times* 6, no. 3 (Dec. 1928), 97–102; Arrington to Jones, Sweetwater, Tex., June 18, 1879 (printed in the *Galveston Daily News*), Adjutant General's Department, Departmental Correspondence, Box 401-398, Folder 9, TSLAC; *Dodge City Times*, July 5, 1879. Crawfish Creek joins the White River in Blanco Canyon near the Mount Blanco Community in Crosby County, Texas. See *Texas Road Atlas*, 50.

45. Arrington to Jones, Camp Roberts, Tex., Feb. 9, 1880, Adjutant General's Department, Departmental Correspondence, Box 401-399, Folder 2, TSLAC (quotations); Arrington, 1921 affidavit, in "Captain Arrington's Expedition," 97–102. Arrington was mistaken as to the exact locations of Ranger Lake and Four Lakes (Lost Lake). Due west of Texas's Cochran-Yoakum county line, near Tatum, Lea County, New Mexico, is Ranger Lake. Due west of Ranger Lake is Four Lakes, at present-day Four Lakes Ranch. See *DeLorme Atlas of New Mexico*, 43.

46. Hatch to Jones, Fort Sill, I.T., Feb. 10, 1880, Adjutant General's Department, Departmental Correspondence, Box 401-399, Folder 2, TSLAC, and Hatch to Jones, Fort Sill, Feb. 25, 1880, ibid., Folder 3 (quotations).

47. "Captain Arrington's Expedition," 102 (quotations).

48. Arrington to Jones, Sweetwater, Tex., June 18, 1879 (printed in the *Galveston Daily News*), Adjutant General's Department, Departmental Correspondence, Box 401-398, Folder 9, TSLAC; *Dodge City Times*, July 5, 1879 (quotations).

49. Mooney, "Calendar History," 347; Kenner, *Comanchero Frontier*, 210–11.

50. Pat Floyd Garrett, *The Authentic Life of Billy the Kid* (Santa Fe: New Mexican Printing and Publishing Co., 1882), 85, 91, 92 (quotation), 110–13. Garrett killed the Kid on July 14, 1881, at Fort Sumner, where the Kid was subsequently buried.

51. Arrington to Jones, Camp Roberts, Tex., April 30, 1881, Adjutant General's Department, Departmental Correspondence, Box 401-400, Folder 16, TSLAC, and Nevill to Jones, Camp Musquiz Canyon, Tex., June 27, 1881, ibid., Folder 19.

BIBLIOGRAPHY

Archives

Center for Southwest Research, Zimmerman Library, University of New Mexico, Albuquerque
  Thomas B. Catron Papers
  Charles Ilfeld Papers
  Meketa Microfilm Collection
  Felipe Delgado Papers
David Rumsey Map Collection, https://www.davidrumsey.com
El Paso County Archives, El Paso, Texas
  Deed Records
  District Court Records
  Sheriff's Office
  Surveyor Field Notes
Fort Concho National Historic Landmark Archives, San Angelo, Texas
  Tankersley File
Fort Davis National Historic Site Archives, Fort Davis, Texas
  Records of the War Department, U.S. Army
    Reports of Scouts, Fort Concho, 1872–81
    Reports of Scouts, Fort Stockton, 1873–79
Haley Memorial Library, Midland, Texas
  Rip Ford Papers, United Daughters of the Confederacy Collection, Texas Division
Mora County Archives, Mora, New Mexico
  County Deed Records
  County Probate Records
National Archives and Records Administration, Washington, D.C., and College Park, Maryland
  Records of the New Mexico Superintendency of Indian Affairs, 1849–80
    Kiowa Agency 1865–80
    Letters Received from the Abiquiú and Cimarron Agencies, 1869
    Letters Received from the Cimarron Agency, 1870
    Letters Received from the Commissioner of Indian Affairs
    Letters Received from the Headquarters District of New Mexico, 1869, 1870–71

Letters Received from the Office of Indian Affairs, 1824–81
Miscellaneous Papers 1867–69
New Mexico Superintendency, 1849–80, 1849–53
Record Group 29: Records of the Bureau of the Census
Federal Census Records, 1850–90
Record Group 58: Records of the Internal Revenue Service
Record Group 75: Wichita Indian Agency
Record Group 77: Military Maps
Record Group 94: Records of the Adjutant General's Office, 1780s–1917
Applications for Former Confederates for Presidential Pardons, 1865–67
Letters Received
Returns from Military Posts
Fort Sumner
Record Group 109: Records of the Confederate War Department
Adjutant General of Texas, 1862–65
Confederate Citizens Files
Confederate Compiled Service Records
Confederate General William Steele's Command, March 1862–May 1863
Department of Texas
Department of the Trans-Mississippi
District of Texas, New Mexico, and Arizona
Miscellaneous Special Orders, Adjutant General of Texas
Record Group 123: Records of U.S. Court of Claims, Indian Depredation Cases
Anastacio Sandoval v. The United States and the Navajo Indians, Case No. 6131
C. C. Fitzgerald v. The United States and Comanche Indians, Case No. 5118
Charles Goodnight and John W. Sheek v. The United States and the Comanche Tribe of Indians, Case No. 9133
Charles Probst and August Kirchner v. The United States and the Mescalero Apaches, Case No. 2248
Charles Probst and August Kirchner v. The United States and the Navajo Indians, Case No. 3476
Charles Probst and August Kirchner v. The United States and the Navajo Indians, Case No. 1646
Charles Probst and August Kirchner v. The United States and the Ute and Jicarilla Apaches Indians, Case No. 2109
Dennis J. Murphy v. The United States and the Comanche Tribe of Indians, Case Nos. 10367, 10368, and 8626
Emory B. Peter, as survivor of the firm of E. B. Peter and John Chisum, v. The United States and the Comanche Tribe of Indians, Case No. 6801
John Chisum v. The United States and the Comanche and Mescalero Indians, Case No. 5388
Lorenzo Labadi, surviving partner of the firm of Chaves and Labadi, v. The United States and the Navajo Indians, Case No. 3252

*Mary M. Mann, Administratix of Clay M. Mann, v. The United States and Coman-
che Indians*, Case Nos. 3091, 3092, 3093, 4689, 4692, 4693, 4696

*Patricio Ortega and Juan Marquez, administrators of Francisco P. Abreu, deceased,
of the firm of Valdez and Abreu v. The United States and the Apache Indians*, Case No. 3362

Richard Coffey v. The United States and Comanche and Kiowa Tribes of Indians,
Case No. 7807

Richard Coffey v. The United States and Comanche Tribe of Indians, Case No. 5003

Richard F. Tankersley v. The United States and the Kiowa and Comanche Indians,
Case No. 6501

*Samuel R. Coggin, Moses J. Coggin, and William C. Parks, partners, v. The United
States and the Comanche Tribe of Indians*, Case Nos. 5007, 5008, 5009

*Sara Goldbaum, Administratix of the estate of Marcus Goldbaum, deceased, v.
The United States and the Comanche Indians*, Case No. 6908

*W. C. Franks, Jr., Administrator of W. C. Franks, deceased, surviving partner of
Patterson & Franks, v. The United States and the Navajo, Apache, and Mescalero Apache Indians*, Case Nos. 5622 and 10323 (consolidated)

*William B. Giddings, administrator of the estate of James M. Giddings, deceased,
surviving partner of the firm Giddings and Company, consisting of Preston
Beck Jr., v. The United States and the Navajo Indians*, Case No. 2647

William Beddo v. The United States and Comanche and Kiowa Indian Tribes, Case
No. 2

Record Group 153: Army Court-Martial Case Files, Records of the Office of the
Judge Advocate General

Record Group 249: Office of the Commissary General of Prisoners

Record Group 393: Records of the U.S. Army Continental Commands, 1821–1920
Department of New Mexico
Capt. Albert H. French Report on Scout and Skillman Attack, April 24, 1864
Endorsements Sent
Provost Marshal
District of Arizona
Fort Bascom, New Mexico
Fort Bliss and Franklin, Texas
Fort Concho, Texas
Fort Marcy, New Mexico
Fort Stanton, New Mexico
Fort Union, New Mexico
Southern Department of New Mexico
Unregistered Letters Received, June–Sept. 1862

New Mexico State Records Center and Archives, Santa Fe
Felipe Delgado Papers
Charles Probst and August Kirchner Files
Records of the U.S. Territorial and New Mexico District Courts

Samuel Elkins: Miscellaneous Letters and Diaries
San Miguel County Archives, Las Vegas, New Mexico
    County Deed Records
    County Probate Records
Southwest Collection, Map Collection, Texas Tech University, Lubbock
Special Collections, Donnelly Library, New Mexico Highlands University, Las Vegas
    James W. Arrott Collection
    Spanish Archives of New Mexico, Series I, Land Grant Documents
    Spanish Archives of New Mexico, Series II, Land Grant Documents
    Taylor, John. Deposition. *Report and Testimony in the Matter of the Charges against Samuel B. Axtell, Governor of New Mexico*, October 3, 1878. Originally in Record Group 48, National Archives and Records Administration. Washington, D.C.
Supreme Court of the United States. Transcript of Record. Supreme Court Case of U.S. Oct. Term, 1902, no. 40. *Mariano F. Sena v. The United States*. Washington, D.C.: Judd and DeTweiler, Printers, 1902.
Texas Archeological Research Laboratory, University of Texas at Austin
    John Chisum Concho County Ranch Site File
Texas General Land Office Archives, Austin
    Charles W. Pressler's 1867 Traveller's Map of the State of Texas
Texas State Library and Archives Commission, Austin
    Adjutant General's Correspondence
    Adjutant General Departmental Correspondence
    Edmund Jackson Davis Papers
    Hardin Richard Runnels Papers
    Map Collection
    Pendleton Murrah Papers
    Peter Hansbrough Bell Papers
    Ranger Records, Texas State Troops Records, Texas Adjutant General's Department Civil War Records
    Sam Houston Papers
    Sam Houston Executive Order Letterpress Copybook
U.S. House of Representatives. *Contracts Made by the Quartermaster's Department*. 38th Cong., 2nd Sess., 1865. House Exec. Doc. No. 84, Vol. 14, Serial 1230.

Books and Articles

Adjutant General's Office. *Chronological List of Actions, &c., With Indians, From January 1, 1866, to January 1891*. Washington, D.C.: Adjutant General's Office, 1906.
Alden, Henry Mills. "La Villa Real de Santa Fe." *Harper's New Monthly* 60 (Dec. 1879– May 1880): 670–83.
Anderson, George B. *History of New Mexico: Its Resources and People*. Vol. 2. Los Angeles: Pacific States Publication, 1907.

Austerman, Wayne R. *Sharps Rifles and Spanish Mules: The San Antonio–El Paso Mail, 1851–1881*. College Station: Texas A&M University Press, 1985.

Bailey, Lynn Robison. *Bosque Redondo: The Navajo Internment at Fort Sumner, New Mexico, 1863–1868*. Tucson, Ariz.: Westernlore Press, 1998.

Ball, Larry D. *Desert Lawmen: The High Sheriffs of New Mexico and Arizona, 1846–1912*. Albuquerque: University of New Mexico Press, 1992.

Baxter, William. *Gold and the Ortiz Mine Grant: A New Mexico History and Reference Guide*. Santa Fe: Lone Butte Press, 2014.

Bieber, Ralph P., ed. *Exploring Southwestern Trails, 1846–1854*. Glendale: Arthur H. Clark, 1938.

Blackshear, James Bailey. "Boots on the Ground: A History of Fort Bascom in the Canadian River Valley." *New Mexico Historical Review* 87, no. 3 (Summer 2012): 329–58.

———. *Fort Bascom: Soldiers, Comancheros, and Indians in the Canadian River Valley*. Norman: University of Oklahoma Press, 2016.

———. *Honor and Defiance: A History of the Las Vegas Land Grant in New Mexico*. Santa Fe: Sunstone Press, 2013.

———. "This Bean Bellied Army: A Study of Everyday Life at Fort Bascom in New Mexico Territory." *Military History of the West* 44 (2015): 1–27.

Bliss, Zenas. *The Reminiscences of Major General Zenas R. Bliss, 1854–1876: From the Texas Frontier to the Civil War and Back Again*. Edited by Thomas T. Smith, Jerry D. Thompson, Robert Wooster, and Ben Pingenot. Austin: Texas State Historical Association, 2007.

Boyle, Susan Calafate. *Los Capitalistas: Hispano Merchants and the Santa Fe Trade*. Albuquerque: University of New Mexico Press, 2000.

Brooks, James F. *Captives and Cousins: Slavery, Kinship, and Community in the Southwest Borderland*. Chapel Hill: University of North Carolina Press, 2002.

Burr, Baldwin G. *Historic Ranches of Northeastern New Mexico*. Arcadia Publishing, 2016.

Caffey, David L. *Chasing the Santa Fe Ring: Power and Privilege in Territorial New Mexico*. Albuquerque: University of New Mexico Press, 2014.

Campbell, Randolph B. *Gone to Texas: A History of the Lone Star State*. New York: Oxford University Press, 2003.

"Captain Arrington's Expedition." *Frontier Times* 6, no. 3 (Dec. 1928): 97–102.

Carriker, Robert C. *Fort Supply, Indian Territory: Frontier Outpost on the Plains*. Norman: University of Oklahoma Press, 1990.

Carter, Robert Goldthwaite. *Tragedies of Cañon Blanco: A Story of the Texas Panhandle*. Washington, D.C.: Gibson Brothers Printers, 1919.

Cashion, Ty. *A Texas Frontier: The Clear Fork Country and Fort Griffin, 1849–1887*. Norman: University of Oklahoma Press, 1996.

Cates, Cliff D. *Pioneer History of Wise County*. Decatur, Tex.: Wise County Historical Society, 1971.

Clifford, Frank. *Deep Trails in the Old West: A Frontier Memoir*. Edited by Frederick Nolan. Norman: University of Oklahoma Press, 2011.

Collins, Jan Mackell. *Good Time Girls of Arizona and New Mexico: A Real Red-Light History of the American Southwest*. Guilford, Conn: Two Dot Press, 2019.

Comer, Douglas C. *Ritual Ground: Bent's Old Fort, World Formation, and the Annexation of the Southwest*. Berkeley: University of California Press, 1996.

"Conditions of the Indian Tribes." *Report of the Joint Special Committee, 1867: An Appendix*. 39th Cong., 2nd Sess., Report 156. Washington, D.C.: Government Printing Office 1867.

"Condition of the Indian Tribes." *Report of the Joint Special Committee, 1876*. Washington, D.C.: Government Printing Office, 1876.

Connor, Seymour V. *Texas: A History*. Arlington Heights, Ill: AHM Publishing, 1971.

Cook, Mary J. Straw. *Doña Tules: Santa Fe Courtesan and Gambler*. Albuquerque: University of New Mexico Press, 2007.

Cox, James. *Historical and Biographical Record of the Cattle Industry and the Cattlemen of Texas and Adjacent Territory*. New York: Antiquarian Press, 1959.

Cox, Mike. *Texas Ranger Tales II*. Plano, Tex.: Republic of Texas Press, 1999.

Crocchiola, Stanley, Father. *The Anton Chico Story*. Pampa, Tex.: Pampa Print Shop, 1969.

———. *The Apaches of New Mexico 1540–1940*. Pampa, Tex.: Pampa Print Shop, 1962.

Daves, Doyle. "Levi Keithley, Ineffective Government Man in Territorial New Mexico." *Wagon Tracks*, no. 3 (May 2018): 17–20.

DeArment, Robert K. *Bravo of the Brazos: John Larn of Fort Griffin, Texas*. Norman: University of Oklahoma Press, 2002.

DeLay, Brian. *War of a Thousand Deserts: Indian Raids and the U.S.–Mexican War*. New Haven, Conn.: Yale University Press, 2008.

Delgado, David. "Founders of Santa Rosa: Don Celso Baca's Family Tree." *Santa Rosa News*, June 28, 1990.

DeLorme Atlas and Gazetteer of New Mexico. Yarmouth, Maine: Delorme, 2016.

Dupree, Stephen A. *Planting the Union Flag in Texas: The Campaigns of Major General Nathanial P. Banks in the West*. College Station: Texas A&M University Press, 2008.

Earls, Amy C., and Patrick O'Neill, et al. *Cultural Resource Investigations in the O.H. Ivie Reservoir, Concho, Coleman, and Runnels Counties, Texas*. Technical Report 346-V, Vol. 5. Austin: Historical Resources, Mariah Associates, Inc., 1993.

Emmet, Chris. *Fort Union and the Winning of the Southwest*. Norman: University of Oklahoma Press, 1965.

Elkins, John M. *Life on the Texas Frontier*. Beaumont, Tex.: Green Print, 1908.

Ely, Glen Sample. "Gone from Texas and Trading with the Enemy: New Perspectives on Civil War West Texas." In *Lone Star Blue and Gray: Essays on Texas and the Civil War*, 2nd ed., edited by Ralph A. Wooster and Robert Wooster, 161–84. Denton: Texas State Historical Association, 2015.

———. *Murder in Montague: Frontier Justice and Retribution*. Norman: University of Oklahoma Press, 2020.

———. "Skullduggery at Spencer's Ranch: Civil War Intrigue in West Texas." *Journal of Big Bend Studies* 21 (2009): 9–29.

———. *The Texas Frontier and the Butterfield Overland Mail, 1858–1861*. Norman: University of Oklahoma Press, 2016.

———. "What to Do About Texas? Texas and the Department of New Mexico in the Civil War." *New Mexico Historical Review* 85, no. 4 (Fall 2010): 375–408.

———. *Where the West Begins: Debating Texas Identity*. Lubbock: Texas Tech University Press, 2011.

Emory, William H. *Report on the United States and Mexican Boundary Survey*. Vol. 1. Washington, D.C.: Cornelius Wendell, 1857.

Fierman, Floyd S. *Guts and Ruts: The Jewish Pioneer on the Trail in the American Southwest*. Brooklyn, N.Y.: Ktav Publishing, 1984.

Finch, L. Boyd. *Confederate Pathway to the Pacific: Major Sherod Hunter and Arizona Territory, C.S.A.* Tucson: Arizona Historical Society, 1996.

Flint, Richard, and Shirley Cushing Flint. *The Coronado Expedition: From the Distance of 460 Years*. Albuquerque: University of New Mexico Press, 2012.

Ford, John Salmon. *Rip Ford's Texas*. Edited by Stephen B. Oates. Austin: University of Texas Press, 1963.

Frazer, Robert W. *Forts of the West*. Norman: University of Oklahoma Press, 1988.

Freeman, Martha Doty, and Joe C. Freeman. *A Cultural Resource Inventory and Assessment of the Proposed Stacy Reservoir, Concho, Coleman and Runnels Counties, Texas*. Vol. 2. Historic Cultural Resources. Austin: Espey, Huston & Associates, Inc., 1981.

Garrett, Pat Floyd. *The Authentic Life of Billy the Kid*. Santa Fe: New Mexican Printing and Publishing Co., 1882.

Gay, Beatrice Grady. *Into the Setting Sun: A History of Coleman County*. Santa Anna, Tex.: Self-published, 1936.

Greer, James K., ed. *Buck Barry: Texas Ranger and Frontiersman*. Lincoln: University of Nebraska Press, 1978.

General Laws of the Tenth Legislature. Houston: Galveston News, 1864.

Gonzalez, Phillip B. *Política: Nuevomexicanos and American Political Incorporation, 1821–1910*. Lincoln: University of Nebraska Press, 2016.

Gottschalk, Marcus. "Pioneer Merchants of the Las Vegas Plaza: The Booming Trail Days." *Wagon Tracks*, no. 2 (Feb. 2002): 8–18.

Gregg, Josiah. *Commerce of the Prairies*. 1844. Edited by Maurice Garland Fulton. Norman: University of Oklahoma Press, 1941.

Guffee, Eddie J. "The Merrell-Taylor Village: An Archeological Investigation of Pre-Anglo, Spanish-Mexican Occupation on the Quitaque Creek in Floyd County, Texas Site." Plainview, Tex.: Archeological Research Laboratory, Llano Estacado Museum, Wayland Baptist College, 1976.

Gwyther, George. "The Three Pueblo Spies, A Reminiscence of the Late Civil War." *Overland Monthly* 13, no. 4 (July 1874): 337–41.

Hagan, William T. "Kiowas, Comanches, and Cattlemen, 1867–1906: A Case Study of the Failure of the U.S. Reservation Policy." *Pacific Historical Review* 40, no. 3 (Aug. 1971): 330–40.

Haley, J. Evetts. *Charles Goodnight: Cowman and Plainsman*. Norman: University of Oklahoma Press, 1989.

————. "The Comanchero Trade." *Southwestern Historical Quarterly* 38, no. 3 (Jan. 1935): 157–76.

Hämäläinen, Pekka. *The Comanche Empire*. New Haven, Conn.: Yale University Press, 2008.

Hamilton, Nancy. *Ben Dowell: El Paso's First Mayor*. El Paso: Texas Western Press, 1976.

Havins, Thomas Robert. *Camp Colorado: A Decade of Frontier Defense*. Brownwood, Tex.: Brown Press, 1964.

Heitman, Francis B. *Historical Register and Dictionary of the United States Army, from Its Organization, September 29, 1789, to March 2, 1903*. 2 vols. Washington, D.C.: Government Printing Office, 1903.

Hinton, Harwood P. "John Simpson Chisum, 1877–1884." *New Mexico Historical Review* 31, no. 3 (July 1956): 177–88.

Hoig, Stan. *Cowtown Wichita and the Wild, Wicked West*. Albuquerque: University of New Mexico Press, 2007.

Hunt, Aurora. *Major James Henry Carleton, 1814–1873: Western Frontier Dragoon*. Glendale, Calif.: Arthur H. Clark, 1958.

Hyslop, Stephen G. *Bound for Santa Fe: The Road to New Mexico and the American Conquest, 1806–1848*. Norman: University of Oklahoma Press, 2002.

Jacobsen, Joel. *Such Men as Billy the Kid: The Lincoln County War Reconsidered*. Lincoln: University of Nebraska Press, 1997.

Johnson, David. *The Horrell Wars: Feuding and Fighting in Texas and New Mexico*. Denton: University of North Texas Press, 2014.

Jones, Charles Irving. "William Kroenig: First New Mexican Pioneer." *New Mexico Historical Review* 19, no. 3 (1944): 290–303.

Kajencki, Francis C. "Alexander Grzelachowski, Pioneer Merchant of Puerto de Luna, New Mexico." *Journal of the Southwest* 26, no. 3 (Autumn 1984): 243–60.

Kavanagh, Thomas W. *The Comanches: A History, 1706–1875*. Lincoln: University of Nebraska Press, 1999.

Keleher, William A. *The Fabulous Frontier, 1846–1912*. Albuquerque: University of New Mexico Press, 1962.

————. *The Maxwell Land Grant: A New Mexican Item*. Albuquerque: University of New Mexico Press, 1964.

————. *Turmoil in New Mexico, 1846–1868*. Albuquerque: University of New Mexico Press, 1982.

Kenner, Charles L. *The Comanchero Frontier: A History of New Mexican–Plains Indian Relations*. Norman: University of Oklahoma Press, 1994.

————. "The Great New Mexico Cattle Raid, 1872." *New Mexico Historical Review* 37, no. 4 (Oct. 1962): 243–59.

King, Norma. "Mary Tankersley Lewis." *Junior Historian* 4, no. 5 (March 1944).

Kirkpatrick, David T. "The Archaeology of Billy the Kid." In *Presenting Archaeology to the Public: Digging for Truths*. Edited by James H. Jameson. Walnut Creek, Calif.: Altamira Press, 1997.

Koffman, David S. *The Jews Indian: Colonialism, Pluralism, and Belonging in America*. New Brunswick, N.J.: Rutgers University Press, 2019.

Lavender, David. *Bent's Fort*. Lincoln: University of Nebraska Press, 1954.

Leviton, Richard. *Santa Fe Light: Touring the Visionary Geography of Santa Fe*. Bloomington: University of Indiana Press, 2009.

Lucero, Donald. *The Adobe Kingdom: New Mexico, 1598–1958*. Santa Fe: Sunstone Press, 2009.

Lynn, Alvin R. *Kit Carson and the First Battle of Adobe Walls: A Tale of Two Journeys*. Lubbock: Texas Tech University Press, 2014.

MacLachlan, Colin M., and William H. Beezley. *El Gran Pueblo: A History of Greater Mexico. Vol. 1, 1821–1911*. Englewood Cliffs, N.J.: Prentice-Hall, Inc., 1994.

Maddux, Vernon. *John Hittson: Cattle King on the Texas and Colorado Frontier*. Boulder: University of Colorado Press, 1994.

Mayhall, Mildred P. *The Indian Wars of Texas*. Waco: Texian Press, 1965.

McClure, C. B., ed. "The Battle of Adobe Walls." *Panhandle-Plains Historical Review* 21 (1948): 18–65.

McConnell, Joseph Carroll. *The West Texas Frontier*. Vol. 2. Palo Pinto, Tex.: Texas Legal Bank & Book Co., 1939.

McCoy, Joseph C. *Historic Sketches of the Cattle Trade of the West and Southwest*. 1874. Edited by Ralph Bieber. Glendale, Calif.: Arthur H. Clark, 1931–32.

Meyer, Michael C., and William L. Sherman. *The Course of Mexican History*. New York: Oxford University Press, 1991.

Meyers, Henry C. "The Founding of Loma Parda." *Wagon Tracks* 7 (August 1993): 10–12.

Miller, Darlis. *Soldiers and Settlers: Military Supplies in the Southwest, 1861–1885*. Albuquerque: University of New Mexico Press, 1989.

Miller, W. Henry. *Pioneering North Texas*. San Antonio, Tex.: Naylor Co., 1953.

Mills, Anson. *My Story*. Washington, D.C.: Byron Adams, 1918.

Mills, W. W. *Forty Years at El Paso: 1858–1898*. Edited by Rex Strickland. El Paso, Tex.: Carl Hertzog, 1962.

Montoya, María E. *Translating Property: The Maxwell Land Grant and the Conflict over Land in the American West, 1840–1900*. Lawrence: University of Kansas Press, 2002.

Mooney, James. "Calendar History of the Kiowa Indians." In *Seventeenth Annual Report of the Bureau of American Ethnology*. Washington, D.C.: Government Printing Office, 1898.

Morgenthaler, Jefferson. *The River Has Never Divided Us: A Border History of La Junta de los Rios*. Austin: University of Texas Press, 2004.

Morris, John Miller. *El Llano Estacado: Exploration and Imagination on the High Plains of Texas and New Mexico, 1536–1860*. Austin: Texas State Historical Association, 1997.

Mumey, Nolie. *Old Forts and Trading Posts of the West*. Vol. 1, *Bent's Old Fort and Bent's New Fort on the Arkansas River*. Denver: Artcraft Press, 1956.

Myers, Gustavus. *History of the Great American Fortunes*. 3 vols. Chicago: Charles H. Kerr, 1910.

Nathans, Benjamin. *Beyond the Pale: The Jewish Encounter with Late Imperial Russia*. Berkeley: University of California Press, 2002.

Neal, Charles M. *Valor Across the Lone Star: The Congressional Medal of Honor in Frontier Texas*. Austin: Texas State Historical Association, 2002.

Nolan, Frederick. *The Lincoln County War: A Documentary History*. Norman: University of Oklahoma Press, 1991.

———. *The West of Billy the Kid*. Norman: University of Oklahoma Press, 1999.

Norstrand, Richard L. *The Hispano Homeland*. Norman: University of Oklahoma Press, 1992.

Nye, W. S. *Carbine and Lance: The Story of Old Fort Sill*. Norman: University of Oklahoma Press, 1974.

Oliva, Leo E. *Fort Union and the Frontier Army in the Southwest: A Historic Resource Study*. Santa Fe: National Park Service, 1993.

Orton, Richard H. *Records of the California Men in the War of the Rebellion, 1861 to 1867*. Sacramento, Calif.: J. D. Young, 1890.

Parish, William J. *The Charles Ilfeld Company: A Study of the Rise and Decline of Mercantile Capitalism in New Mexico*. Cambridge, Mass.: Harvard University Press, 1961.

Peril, W. A. "From Texas to the Oregon Line." In *The Trail Drivers of Texas*. Edited by J. Marvin Hunter. Austin: University of Texas Press, 2003.

Pittman, Walter Earl. *Rebels in the Rockies: Confederate Irregulars in the Western Territories*. Jefferson, N.C.: McFarland, 2014.

Polk, R. L. and Co., and A. C. Danser. *The Colorado, New Mexico, Utah, Nevada, Wyoming and Arizona Gazetteer Business Directory*. Chicago: 1884–85.

Porter, Eugene O., ed. "Letters Home: W. W. Mills Writes to His Family." Part 3. *Password* 17, no. 3 (Fall 1972): 116–132.

———. "Letters Home: W. W. Mills Writes to His Family." Part 4. *Password* 17, no. 4 (Winter 1972): 179–190.

Rathjen, Frederick J. *The Texas Panhandle Frontier*. Austin: University of Texas Press, 1973.

Record of Engagements with Hostile Indians 1868 to 1882. Bellevue, Neb.: Old Army Press, 1969.

Reeve, Frank D. "The Federal Indian Policy in New Mexico, 1858–1880." *New Mexico Historical Review*, no. 3 (July 1938): 146–91.

———. *The History of New Mexico*. Vol. 2. New York: Lewis Historic Publication Co., 1961.

Report of the Commissioner of Indian Affairs, 1857, 35th Cong., 1st Sess., House Exec. Doc. No. 2.

Report of the Commissioner of Indian Affairs for 1858. Washington, D.C.: Wm. A. Harris, 1858.

Resendéz, Andrés. *A Texas Patriot on Trial in Mexico: José Antonio Navarro and the Texan Santa Fe Expedition*. Dallas: William P. Clements Center for Southwest Studies, 2005.

Richardson, Rupert Norval. *The Comanche Barrier to South Plains Settlement*. Edited by Kenneth R. Jacobs. Abilene, Tex.: Hardin Simmons University, 1991.

———. *Texas, The Lone Star State*. New York: Prentice-Hall, 1943. Reprinted, 8th ed., Upper Saddle River, N.J.: Prentice-Hall, 2001.

Ritch, W. G., comp. *The Legislative Blue Book of the Territory of New Mexico: With the Rules of Order, Fundamental Law, Official Register and Record, Historical Data, Compendium of Facts, Etc., Etc*. Santa Fe: Charles W. Greene, Public Printer, 1882.

Romero, Matías. *A Mexican View of America in the 1860s: A Foreign Diplomat Describes the Civil War and Reconstruction*. Translated and edited by Thomas Schoonover. Cranbury, N.J.: Associated University Presses, 1991.

Root George A. "Reminiscences of William Darnell." *Collection of the Kansas State Historical Society, 1923–1925*. Vol. 16: 321–32. Topeka: Kansas State Printing Plant, 1925.

Russell, Marion Sloan. *Land of Enchantment: Memoirs of Marion Sloan Russell along the Santa Fe Trail*. Edited by Garnet M. Brayer. Albuquerque: University of New Mexico Press, 1981.

Samek, Hana. "No Bed of Roses: The Careers of Four Mescalero Indian Agents, 1871–1878." *New Mexico Historical Review* 57, no. 2 (1982): 140–44.

Sánchez, Joseph P., Jerry L. Gurulé, Larry V. Larrichío, and Larry D. Miller. *Fort Union National Monument: Ethnographic Overview and Assessment*. Washington, D.C.: National Park Service, 2006.

"Sand Creek Massacre." *Report of the Secretary of War*. Sen. Exec. Doc. No. 26, 39th Cong., 2nd Sess. Washington, D.C.: Government Printing Office, 1867.

Schilz, Jody Lynn Dickson, and Thomas F. Schilz. *Buffalo Hump and the Penateka Comanches*. El Paso: Texas Western Press, 1989.

Schoonover, Thomas David. *Dollars over Dominion: The Triumph of Liberalism in Mexican–United States Relations, 1861–1867*. Baton Rouge: Louisiana State University Press, 1978.

Simmons, Marc. *Following the Santa Fe Trail: A Guide for Modern Travelers*. Rev. ed. Santa Fe, N.Mex.: Ancient City Press, 1986.

———. *The Little Lion of the Southwest: The Life of Manuel Antonio Chaves*. Chicago: Swallow Press, 1973.

———. *Spanish Government in New Mexico*. Albuquerque: University of New Mexico Press, 1968.

Simon, John Y., ed. *The Papers of Ulysses S. Grant. Vol. 16: 1866*. Carbondale: Southern Illinois University Press, 1991.

Smith, Sidney W. *From the Cow Camp to the Pulpit: Being Twenty-Five Years Experience of a Texas Evangelist*. Cincinnati: Christian Leader Corporation, 1927.

Smith, Thomas T. *The Old Army in Texas: A Research Guide to the U.S. Army in Nineteenth-Century Texas*. 2nd ed. Austin: Texas State Historical Association, 2020.

"Some Early Coleman County History." *Frontier Times* 2, no. 2 (Nov. 1924): 8–9.

Sonnichsen, C. L. *The Mescalero Apaches*. Norman: University of Oklahoma Press, 1958.

State Historical Society of Colorado. *Bent's Old Fort*. Denver: State Historical Society of Colorado, 1979.

Swain, E. H. "Rich Coffee [sic]." *Edwards Plateau Historian* 5 (1969–73).

Swift, Roy L., and Leavitt Corning Jr. *Three Roads to Chihuahua*. Austin: Eakin Press, 1988.

Switzer, William F. *A History of Boone County, Missouri: Written and Compiled from Most Authentic Official and Private Sources*. St. Louis: Western Historical Co., 1882.

Taylor, T. U. "Aunt Ollie Peril, a True Pioneer Mother." *Frontier Times* 17, no. 2 (Nov. 1939): 47–51.

———. "Life Sketch of John Simpson Chisum." *Frontier Times* 13, no. 8 (May 1936): 391–401.

———. "Trailing John Chisum to New Mexico." *Frontier Times* 13, no. 9 (June 1936): 422–28.

———. "W. A. Peril Makes Five World Records." *Frontier Times* 13, no. 12 (Sept. 1936): 600–602.

Texas Road and Recreation Atlas. Santa Barbara, Calif.: Benchmark Maps, 2019.

Theison, Lee Scott. "Frank Warner Angel's Notes on New Mexico Territory." *Arizona and the West*, no. 4 (Winter 1976): 333–70.

The War of the Rebellion: A Compilation of the Official Records of the Union and Confederate Armies. 70 vols. Washington, D.C.: Government Printing Office, 1880–1901.

Thompson, Gerald. *The Army and the Navajo: The Bosque Redondo Reservation Experiment, 1863–1868*. Tucson: University of Arizona Press, 1975.

Thompson, Jerry D. *A Civil War History of New Mexico Volunteers and Militia*. Albuquerque: University of New Mexico Press, 2017.

———. *New Mexico Territory during the Civil War: Wallen and Evans Inspection Reports, 1862–1863*. Albuquerque: University of New Mexico Press, 2008.

Thompson, Peter. "The Fight for Life: New Mexico Indians, Health Care, and the Reservation Period." *New Mexico Historical Review* 69, no. 2 (April 1994): 145–61.

Thrapp, Dan L. *Encyclopedia of Frontier Biography*. 3 vols. Lincoln: University of Nebraska Press, 1991.

Tigges, Linda T. "Santa Fe Land Ownership in the 1880s." *New Mexico Historical Review*, no. 2 (April 1993): 153–80.

Tobias, Henry J. *A History of the Jews in New Mexico*. Albuquerque: University of New Mexico Press, 1990.

Townsend, Stephen A. *The Yankee Invasion of Texas*. College Station: Texas A&M University Press, 2006.

Tsompanos, Paul L. *Juan Patrón: A Fallen Star in the Days of Billy the Kid*. [Richmond, Va.]: Brandylane Press, 2012.

Twitchell, Ralph Emerson. *Leading Facts of New Mexican History*. Vol. 2. Cedar Rapids, Iowa: Torch Press, 1912.

Wallace, Ernest, ed. *Ranald S. Mackenzie's Official Correspondence Relating to Texas, 1871–1873*. Lubbock: West Texas Museum Association, 1967.

———. *Ranald S. Mackenzie on the Texas Frontier*. College Station: Texas A&M University Press, 1993.

Wasserman, Mark. *Capitalists, Caciques, and Revolution: The Native Elite and Foreign Enterprise in Chihuahua, Mexico, 1854–1911*. Chapel Hill: University of North Carolina Press, 1984.

Weber, David J. *The Mexican Frontier, 1821–1846: The American Southwest under Mexico*. Albuquerque: University of New Mexico Press, 1982.

———. *The Taos Trappers: The Fur Trade in the Far Southwest, 1540–1846*. Norman: University of Oklahoma Press, 1980.

Weideman, Paul. "Historic Breweries Were All Gone by 1900." *Santa Fe New Mexican*, July 1, 2000.

Westphall, Victor. *Thomas Benton Catron and His Era*. Tucson: University of Arizona Press, 1973.

Wilbarger, J. W. *Indian Depredations in Texas.* Austin, Tex.: Hutchings Printing House 1889.

Williams, R. H. *With the Border Ruffians: Memories of the Far West, 1852–1868.* New York: E. P. Dutton, 1907.

Wilson, John P. *When the Texans Came: Missing Records from the Civil War in the Southwest, 1861–1862.* Albuquerque: University of New Mexico Press, 2001.

Winfrey, Dorman H., and James M. Day, eds. *The Indian Papers of Texas and the Southwest, 1825–1916.* 5 vols. Austin: Texas State Historical Association, 1995.

Yeary, Mamie, comp. *Reminiscences of the Boys in Gray, 1861–1865.* Dallas: Smith and Lamar, 1912.

Zesche, Scott. *Captured: A True Story of Abduction by Indians on the Texas Frontier.* New York: St. Martin's Press, 2004.

Dissertations, Presentations, and Special Publications

Allison, Austin. "From Wagon Trails to Flight Paths: Drone Technology in Surveying Sites along the Yellow House Draw." West Texas Historical Association Conference, Lubbock, 2017.

"Baptisms: Romero Surnames, Santa Fe County, New Mexico." US Genweb Archives Special Projects. www.usgwarchives.net/nm/santafe (accessed May 20, 2020).

"Colfax County and New Mexico Biographies." Genealogy Trails Online. genealogytrails.com/newmex/Colfax/ (accessed July 15, 2019).

Comar, Scott C. "The Tigua Indians of Ysleta Del Sur: A Borderlands Community." PhD diss., University of Texas at El Paso, 2015.

Greenwood, Richard. "National Historic Landmark Nomination Form: Theme #6, Western Expansion 1763–1898: Western Trails and Travelers." National Historic Register, December 18, 1984. FHR-8-250 (Oct. 1978, item 17, p. 3). npgallery.nps.gov/GetAsset /794b3983-7f44-47ea-bddb-398c6eb67482 (accessed June 17, 2019).

Humphries, Holle. "Yellow House Draw: Geographic Corridor." West Texas Historical Association Conference, Lubbock, 2017.

"Internal Revenue Assessment Lists for the Territory of New Mexico 1862–1870, 1872–1874." Treasury Department. National Archives. RG 58, M782, R1. Ancestry Online. http://search.ancestry.com/search/dbextra.aspx?dbid=1264 (accessed August 8, 2014)

Keener, David P. "A Town Maligned: Loma Parda, New Mexico." MA thesis, Northern Arizona University, Flagstaff, 1988.

Levine, Frances. "A Unified Anthropological Approach to Historical Archaeology: A Study from Los Esteros Lake, Guadalupe County, New Mexico." PhD diss., Southern Methodist University, Dallas, 1980.

Mosser, Dolores. "Ancient Portal for Ancient People: The Portales River Valley Passageway to the South Plains." West Texas Historical Association Conference, Lubbock, 2017.

Turo, Bryan W. "An Empire of Dust: Thomas Benton Catron and the Age of Capital in the Hispanic Borderland, 1840–1921." PhD diss., University of New Mexico, Albuquerque, 2015.

"Treaty of Guadalupe Hidalgo: Definition and List of Community Land Grants in New Mexico: Exposure Draft." Washington, D.C.: General Accounting Office, 2001.

"United States Veterans Administration Pension Payment Cards, 1907–1933." Database with images. Citing NARA microfilm publication M850. Washington D.C.: National Archives and Records Administration, n.d. Familysearch.org. https://www.familysearch .org/search/collection/1832324 (accessed Dec. 6, 2020).

Newspapers

Mining Journal (Black Hawk, Colo.)
Colorado Chieftain (Pueblo)
Austin Daily Statesman
Daily Ledger and Texan (San Antonio)
Dodge City Times (Kansas)
Houston Tri-Weekly Telegraph
Las Vegas Gazette (N.Mex.)
Las Vegas Optic (N.Mex.)
New Mexico Union (Santa Fe)
Nuevo Mejicano Diario (by *Santa Fe New Mexican)*
Revista Republicana (Albuquerque, N.Mex.)
Republican Review (Albuquerque, N.Mex.)
Rocky Mountain News (Denver, Colo.)
Rocky Mountain Sentinel (Santa Fe)
San Antonio Semi-Weekly News
Santa Fe New Mexican
Santa Fe Weekly Post
Santa Fe Daily New Mexican
Santa Fe Weekly New Mexican
Santa Fe Weekly Gazette

INDEX

Page numbers in *italic* type indicate illustrative matter.